FIRELIGHT OF
A DIFFERENT
COLOUR

Firelight of a Different Colour:
The Life and Times of Leslie Cheung Kwok-wing

By Nigel Collett
Published by Signal 8 Press
An imprint of Typhoon Media Ltd
Copyright 2014 Nigel Collett
ISBN: 978-988-15542-6-0

Typhoon Media Ltd:
Signal 8 Press | BookCyclone | Lightning Originals
Hong Kong
www.typhoon-media.com

All rights reserved. No part of this book may be reproduced in any form or by any means, except for brief citation or review, without written permission from Typhoon Media Ltd.

Cover design: Justin Kowalczuk

Cover photo credit: Amanda Lee and Jamie Law

Dedicated to the memory of
Leslie Cheung Kwok-wing and to the
many who keep it alive

Contents

Acknowledgements 9
Introduction 11
Note 17

EARLY DAYS

Chapter 1: The Kid 21
Chapter 2: Days of Being Wild 29

TIME OF STRUGGLE

Chapter 3: Dreamin' of The Future 45
Chapter 4: Castles of Sand 61
Chapter 5: Fresh Wind, New Waves 75

STAR

Chapter 6: Standing Up 99
Chapter 7: A Better Today 115
Chapter 8: A Career in Concert 137
Chapter 9: Sunset in Hong Kong 151

CANADA

Chapter 10: Days of Being Away 173
Chapter 11: Palme D'or 191
Chapter 12: He's the Man 211

ON TOP OF THE WORLD

Chapter 13: Yin and Yang 225
Chapter 14: Happy Together 247
Chapter 15: Time to Remember 265
Chapter 16: Passion 281

DECLINE AND FALL

Chapter 17: Inner Turmoil 303
Chapter 18: Ashes of Time 327

Bibliography 339

ACKNOWLEDGEMENTS

This biography grew from a discussion with Ms Annabella Choi, my business adviser and friend, and I thank her warmly for encouraging me to write it. She also introduced me to two people without whose help I could never have begun: JoJo and Julie of Leslie Cheung Cyberworld, two of the key figures in the continued commemoration of Leslie in Hong Kong and two focal points of the worldwide web of Leslie's admirers. Jojo and Julie introduced me to the fans who live in or visit Hong Kong, invited me to the commemorative events they help to organise, and helped me find much of the published material that made this book possible. This was in many languages and came from many volunteers in different countries. Jojo and Julie contacted these and sought information from them. They were tireless in giving help and advice. I am indebted immeasurably to them and thank them and their colleagues and friends across the world most warmly. I would particularly like to thank Amanda Lee, one of the principal among Leslie's fans, for her very kind help and information about them.

The web site of Leslie Cheung Cyberworld is at: http://www.lesliecheung.cc/.

I would also like to thank Father Francisco de las Heras, Supervisor and Principal of Rosaryhill School, for allowing me to visit the school and for talking to me about Leslie's time there. I thank the principal of Buddhist Wong Fung Ling College for allowing me the privilege of visiting and Ms Anna Sum for showing me the college. I thank Ms Alice Leung of the Education and Manpower Bureau of the Government of the Hong Kong S.A.R. for information on Wellington College. I warmly thank Mr Sean Symington, proprietor of New Eccles Hall School, Norfolk, for allowing me to visit the school and for providing documentation and information about Leslie's time there.

Many people have helped me with information about Leslie's life who wish to remain anonymous, particularly those who provided information about his part in Hong Kong's gay scene, and I thank them all here.

I would like to thank who researched and corrected many of the details of the book and whose advice was invaluable.

Finally, I wish to thank warmly my publisher, Marshall Moore, for taking on this work and guiding me through to its completion.

Any mistakes, and the opinions expressed in this book, are, of course, the author's own.

Nigel Collett
Hong Kong
2013

INTRODUCTION

On the 1st of April, 2003, Hong Kong was stunned by the news that superstar Leslie Cheung Kwok-wing had died at the age of 46. Despite the date, this was no April Fool. The news sent Hong Kong into shock. Crowds gathered and stayed outside the Mandarin Oriental Hotel in Central, adding flowers to the growing mound on the spot where his body had been found. The media, already immersed in the gloom of the SARS epidemic, then at its height in the territory, hastily abandoned other stories and focussed on his death. Beyond Hong Kong's borders, across the whole Chinese world and throughout eastern Asia, the shock waves rippled outwards, spreading dismay, sorrow, incomprehension, and grief.

The next day, the Cheung family released a notice of Leslie's death, as customary listing those closest to him, but, uniquely for Hong Kong, heading the list with the name of a man, Daffy Tong Hok-tak, who was shown as his closest love.[1]

Already depressed by SARS and the economic crisis, which were both then ravaging the city, Hong Kong went into mourning as if for royalty. Radio shows played memorial music throughout the day and their lines were clogged with people calling in, many in tears. The websites of his innumerable fans opened memorial books, only to become inaccessible for days due to the enormous number of hits they received. Five days after his death, while Leslie's body lay at rest in a funeral parlour, over 500 fans braved the fear of SARS (which had closed cinemas, restaurants and even church services) to gather outside the Mandarin for an evening ceremony.[2] They displayed posters of his face, sang his songs, and chanted prayers. Most spent the entire ceremony in tears.

The family arranged for Leslie's casket (but not his body, which was not shown at any ceremony) to be available for view at the funeral home on 7 April.[3] The press had first view from 5 to 5.30 pm and the two hours from 6 to 8 pm were allotted to his fans. This proved totally inadequate, as huge numbers gathered outside, some of them having flown in from around the world. They had begun to line up at seven o'clock that morning and by evening there were some 10,000 queuing around the funeral home, humming and singing Leslie's songs, wearing white ribbons, and folding paper swans, a symbol of blessing. Everyone had been asked to wear a surgical mask and to stand apart from each other to prevent the contagion of SARS, but this was wildly impractical advice in the crush that developed and was ignored. Flowers filled the funeral home and burst out all around it. Doors were opened early, at 5.20, to ease the strain, and fifty at a time were allowed in for one minute each. Most took off their masks inside and wept openly. When the doors were scheduled to close, those still outside refused to go home, and mourners continued to troop past the coffin until 11 pm.

Celebrities attended the viewing in large numbers, including stars Anita Mui Yim-fong, Cherie Chung Chor-hung, Anita Yuen Wing-yi, Chow Yun-fat, and comedienne Lydia Shum Din-ha, popularly known as Fei-Fei. Cherie Chung broke down in the funeral lobby and had to be supported out. Singer/actor Jacky Cheung Hok-yau's actress wife, May Law Mei-mei, shook so badly that she had to be helped away. Many of the stars were in tears. Anita Yuen collapsed when she saw Leslie's photographs, which had been placed around the room, and had to be helped to her feet. Anita Mui, his closest friend, stayed for two hours and broke down completely.[4]

The funeral service followed by cremation took place the next day. In the notice placed in the press, again uniquely, Leslie's family listed Daffy's name in the place reserved for the surviving spouse.[5] Fans flocked to the funeral home from early in the morning, once more braving SARS and the drizzle that was falling. Many carried Leslie's photograph. Two hundred invited guests attended the ceremony, most of them showbiz celebrities; there had not been such a big gathering of the stars since the death of Bruce Lee in 1973.[6] Many gave speeches; some broke down in tears.[7] TV clips of Leslie's shows were screened during the ceremony and at the end a series of slides of Leslie and Daffy were shown. By then, Daffy could barely stand.

With Daffy bringing up the rear, Leslie's casket was borne out by eight celebrities, a galaxy of Hong Kong's glitterati, including representatives of its showbiz industry and men who had known Leslie through his career, gently lifting, then solemnly bearing the coffin enclosing the body of their dead friend, now on his last, sad journey.[8] As the hearse drove out, with Leslie's niece in front next to the driver, the fans called out "Leslie" and his nickname "Gor Gor"; two of them fainted on the spot. Through streets blocked off by the police, the cortege made its way to Cape Collinson crematorium, where it arrived at 12.45 to find many more fans assembled. Celebrities crowded into the crematorium; there were more cries of Leslie's name; the coffin was carried inside, where Daffy, in desperate agony and weeping incessantly, pressed the button to consign it to the furnace.

Eighteen tables of guests gathered at Hong Kong's Conrad Hotel for the wake.[9] Anita Mui cried so hard she had to leave after forty-five minutes, but Daffy stayed to the last at 4.20 pm. That evening, fans continued to lay flowers and chant Buddhist prayers outside the house that Leslie and Daffy had shared, and the flowers they left grew into an ever-widening sea of colour there and outside the Mandarin Hotel for days to come.[10] For over a month, the airwaves remained full of Leslie's songs, and his death continued to dominate the headlines. Across the border in mainland China, the melody of Leslie's song "The Wind Blows On" was heard on a multitude of radio channels throughout the month of April. CCTV News, the state channel, reported that there had never been an artist whose death had caused so many people to shed tears.

This enormous outpouring of grief made it plain to the world just how special Leslie Cheung was to the Chinese and to a wider Asia. Few Westerners knew this then or comprehend it today. When he died, his face, still in middle age perhaps the most beautiful male face on the Chinese screen, was iconic in all the lands where Chinese had settled and amongst many of the Asian countries of the Pacific Rim. Leslie was, and remains to this day, the idol of millions across the world, and they still commemorate him annually in hugely attended ceremonies in Hong Kong to mark the days of his birth and of his death.

What he represented to Hong Kong was much more than his stardom, his place in its culture as a performer with an unrivalled name. The reason he was treated as royalty in Hong Kong was that he had come to encapsulate the place itself. For his career had matched, as it developed year by year, the growth and development of the personality of the city. For nearly three decades, as the city had matured and risen to the world status it now possesses, as its language and culture had crystallized on cinema and TV screen, Leslie had been at the forefront of its art and its music, forging simultaneously his own artistic identity while he wove the potent and magical blend of East and West which became Hong Kong's soul. No single Western star has ever had both the talent and the timing to find himself in such a position.

Leslie had achieved this pre-eminence despite the fearsome handicap, as it still is in the Chinese world, of possessing a different sexual orientation. He was openly gay and in this he was also unique. Even now, as the years pass by after his death, Hong Kong's entertainment industry, the media, and the public still conspire to deter their stars from being honest about their sexuality. Leslie was, at least for the last decade of his life, open about his sexual orientation. Alone in the world of Hong Kong stardom, he had prised open the closet door. For almost half his private life, he had starred in his own love story with just one other actor: his partner, Daffy Tong. That was the meaning of the family declarations at the funeral. For the most part, Hong Kong and the world that knew him admired him for doing what no other man in his position had ever done before.

Few in the West know much, if anything at all, of Leslie Cheung. I was included in this ignorance until the time of the handover of Hong Kong to China in 1997, when I first watched a DVD of his film *Farewell My Concubine*. I was staggered by his acting. I fell in love with his face. I began to watch everything I could find of the work he had done. I had still, though, failed ever to even see him live, let alone meet him, before the thunderbolt of his death struck in 2003. I was in Hong Kong at the time, scurrying with everyone else to hide away indoors from what was more than a 50% chance of death if afflicted by the SARS virus. I drove past the Mandarin the night after he died and saw the crowds. I saw people's faces all over the city. Their grief and shock were palpable. With Hong Kong, I was appalled and saddened. I could not understand why this gilded man—one who, it seemed had everything—had died.

This book, the brief and provisional story of his life, is my attempt to understand Leslie's achievement and the cause of his death. It is not an authorized biography. At the time of its writing, his family did not want such written, and it is perhaps too soon, the pain still too raw, for a full biography. So this book can only be a first step in bringing Leslie to the notice of the English-speaking world. It is the sincere hope of its author that it will not be long before it is properly superseded.

Note

Chinese words are written as they are generally transliterated in Hong Kong, so there is no attempt here at academic consistency. Most Chinese names have three parts: the first is the family name, the second two the personal name. The second two may be linked by a hyphen, as in Cheung Kwok-wing. English names are usually added before the Chinese family name, as in Leslie Cheung Kwok-wing.

EARLY DAYS

CHAPTER 1

THE KID

1956 – 1968

Leslie Cheung was born in Hong Kong on 12 September 1956 in his father's flat on the second floor of 76 Des Voeux Road Central, in the heart of the city.[11] His parents named him Cheung Fat-chung, Cheung being the family name, a common one in the southern Chinese province of Guangdong, from which Hong Kong sticks out to sea like a rocky appendix.[12]

Leslie's father, Cheung Wut-hoi (whose name was often anglicized as Wood-hoi) had emigrated from China to Hong Kong sometime before the Second World War, though Leslie's grandfather had chosen to stay. Leslie's father remitted money back home, making Leslie's grandfather a relatively wealthy man and enabling him to buy land and lend money, all matters of extreme suspicion in the Communist new order that was established after the Nationalist government fell in 1949. The family had good reason to mistrust the People's Republic, which now encircled the small patch of British territory where they, along with millions who had fled the Communists, had taken refuge. It would take Leslie many years to overcome his inherited fear of what was across the border.[13]

Like many immigrants settling their families in Hong Kong,

Leslie's father took what work he could find to earning his living and became a tailor. He did well, surviving the austerity of the years of the brutal Japanese occupation by making clothing for the Japanese, and building up a successful business as Hong Kong recovered after the War. By the time of the birth of Leslie, his tenth and last child, he had acquired the nickname of "the tailor king," a craftsman to whom the rich and famous came for their suits. He boasted of the patronage he won from Hollywood figures like Alfred Hitchcock, Cary Grant, and Marlon Brando. In 1960, when William Holden was in Hong Kong to star in *The World of Suzie Wong*, he had his clothes made by the tailor king.[14] The business provided enough money to keep three establishments on Hong Kong Island: the tailor shop at 81 Wan Chai Road, where he and his wife lived on the 3rd floor; another flat in Wan Chai, where the younger offspring, including Leslie, were housed; and the flat in Central where Leslie was born. Wan Chai in 1956 was a noisy, congested district just east of central Hong Kong, where row upon row of untidy buildings huddled in concrete chaos above teeming streets lined with outdoor markets and bars. There, too, were the brothels in which the British garrison's servicemen sought out the sisters of Suzie Wong.[15]

Cheung Wut-hoi was a bad father, a philanderer and a man who beat his wife regularly. He took a concubine, as was often the custom among Hong Kong's affluent classes, and entertained mistresses in rooms he rented in the highly expensive Peninsula Hotel across the harbour in Kowloon.[16] With the wealth he retained in Hong Kong, Cheung provided his family with a comfortable home life though not a happy one. His first wife, Poon Yuk-yiu, was a Hong Kong-born girl whose family, like many, had moved from Guangdong. She married her husband when very young and went to work for his business as his secretary and administrative assistant.[17] She never reconciled herself to her husband's womanising, nor to his concubine, though she was forced to live with her for a time. The family home was often rent by quarrels, and her complaints led to more beatings by her husband. The concubine and her adopted daughter had moved out of this unhappy household before Leslie was born, but from her new establishment the woman continued to treat the children of her rival spitefully when they crossed her path. Leslie recalled later that she had once poured urine over him.[18]

Leslie's father had a short temper and little time for his children. He would go to see them only rarely, either at festivals or on family occasions, and when he did so he was often drunk. Leslie remembered him staying with them only once for as long as five days, at the Spring Festival, though his father was drunk for three of them.[19] Leslie had a nurse—in local terms, an *amah*—named Luk Che, who had come to work for the family when Leslie was two. She was a *mui tsai* (little sister), the traditional type of domestic servant who foreswore marriage and was indentured to the family that employed her. Luk Che filled the place in his Leslie's heart which should have been belonged to his father and mother, and she alone looked after him in his very early years. Luk Che would take him to visit his father at the tailor's shop; once, while still very young, Leslie embarrassed everyone by saying loudly that his father was a stranger to him. Everyone knew it was true.[20]

Leslie's mother had herself suffered a very hard childhood and had been unwanted by her own family. Perhaps because of this, perhaps because of her bad relations with her husband, and perhaps because of a lack of warmth in her own personality, Leslie's mother proved little better than his father at providing him affection. She lived apart from her children and visited them only on Saturday nights, refusing to sleep in their flat in Wan Chai and leaving their upbringing to her aged mother and her servants.[21] In Leslie's early childhood, his maternal grandmother was so old and infirm that she spent most her life in a large rattan chair in the room in which he slept. She was unable to move unless assisted by the servants. She died in 1962 when he was six.[22] So Leslie was left to Luk Che, the one person in his life he came to believe loved him unconditionally. There was much sorrow, of course, for a little boy who felt yet could not understand the absence of his parents' love. In return, he found unsurprisingly as he grew older that he could not love them. Instead, he suffered from guilt that he did not love his parents as he should.[23]

Leslie was a very lonely little boy. His parents had strict ideas about their status and forbade him to play with the children of neighbours, whom they considered beneath them. He was given very few toys and was often left alone by himself, playing in a corner with a Barbie doll or G.I. Joe. His brothers and sisters were much older (he was eight years younger than his closest brother), and they had little to do with him.[24] Of his original nine siblings, only four sisters and two brothers were still alive by the sixties. The two eldest were Ophelia (whose Chinese name was Cheung Luk-ping) and Louisa, both in their late teens by Leslie's birth and both widely considered beauties. As Ophelia was so much older, and because of her quick intelligence, common sense, and strong personality, she tended to manage the household affairs that were neglected by her mother. The servants turned to her for instructions and treated her with respect.

The Cheung's third child, a boy, and the fourth, a daughter, had both died young. The remaining siblings formed two pairs, each close in age; the fifth and six children were sisters named Serena and Aileen; and the seventh and eighth were brothers, Eddie (in Chinese, Cheung Fat-wing) and Didi (Cheung Dai-wing). Leslie didn't like his seventh brother, who bullied him, but eighth brother Didi would defend him and so forged a bond that was to endure. The ninth child, a boy, had died of meningitis before Leslie's birth. Leslie was born on the dead child's birthday and so was regarded in the family as his reincarnation.[25]

So Leslie was left for most of the time with Luk Che, who

would occasionally take him out for a treat, such as to the Cantonese opera to listen to famous stars of the day like Pak Suet-sin and Yam Kim-fai. Leslie was to get to know and love the first of these two women later in life. They were a unique couple, both for their massive fame and for the fact that they lived together in a partnership that lasted most of their lives and about which everyone was too discreet to comment. Leslie loved their music. Such happy interludes, though, were few. For the most part, though he was a beautiful little boy with a sweet nature who charmed all around him, Leslie endured an empty, friendless childhood. When he spoke of it in later years, he would do so with bitterness.

***

There was nothing in Leslie's family that foretold either a rich or an artistic future for him, though they lived a comparatively privileged life in the Hong Kong of the times. The Second World War had ended only eleven years before his birth and had left Hong Kong a desolate city largely ruined by its Japanese occupiers. By 1956, rebuilding had long been underway, and prosperity was steadily increasing. Insecurity remained, though, for across the border with China loomed the Communist regime, still very hostile to Hong Kong's British government, with which it had been at war in Korea three years before Leslie was born.[26]

The poor were still everywhere in Hong Kong in those difficult years. The two million refugees who had crossed into Hong Kong since 1949 mostly lived in squalor in cardboard and corrugated iron tenements climbing the hillsides of the colony, where the cramped, impoverished conditions made for tension and strife. In October of the year of Leslie's birth, rioting killed fifty-nine people before the army and police could restore order. Over the border, in 1958, Mao Tse Tung launched the Great Leap Forward, which caused many millions to die of starvation and sent a wave of refugees seeking safety in Hong Kong.

In 1960, at the age of four, Leslie joined a local kindergarten.[27] Two years later, in 1962, he started primary education at St Luke's, a school (now demolished) where his eldest sister, Ophelia, and her first husband, Ackbar Abbas, were teaching, a factor which was to make life difficult for Leslie. Ophelia was a highly capable woman, one who was to go on to much greater things. Her highly successful career was all her own work, and none of her family's, for when she told her father that she wished to go to university (still unusual for a girl at that time), he refused to pay her fees. So she took a job as a teacher and paid her own way through till graduation from the University of Hong Kong. She joined the Hong Kong Administrative Service in 1969 and rose rapidly to become a District Officer in the important Central District. In 1974, she would become the first Executive Director of Hong Kong's Consumer Council.[28] She was an attractive, tough, and very determined woman.

Leslie was neither a bad student nor an especially diligent one, just an ordinary boy in fact, but Hong Kong's education system was hugely competitive and all pupils were under great pressure to succeed. Leslie fell at the first hurdle by failing to pass out of his first class, Primary 1, and was required to undergo the year again. This must have been shameful for Ophelia, and she, helped by her sister Serena, determined to improve Leslie's performance by tutoring him at home.[29] Leslie resented this, and it is perhaps not a coincidence that now began what was to become a permanent aversion to education.

Nevertheless, the plan succeeded and Leslie started to do better at primary school, on a couple of occasions attaining second or third place in his Chinese class, and for now his education went reasonably well. School enabled him to make friends for the first time.

One of them was a boy named Daffy Tong Hok-tak, the son of one of his mother's friends. Strangely, in the light of what the two boys would later mean to each other, Leslie's mother felt fate drawing her to Daffy and made him her godson.[30] Daffy had been born on 18 February 1959, so Leslie was the older and still the bigger and stronger of the two; when they tussled, he usually got the upper hand. Their relative sizes would be somewhat different when they met again two decades later.[31]

In 1964, Leslie's father changed his son's Chinese personal name, Fat-chung, to Kwok-wing; there is no record available to explain this.[32] Leslie was now in Primary 2 and making friends, one his first childhood girl friend, Kwong Mun-yin, with whom he remained friendly until she emigrated with her family to Canada some years later.[33]

As Leslie reached Primary 3, across the border in the Mainland, Mao Tse Tung launched the Great Proletarian Cultural Revolution, an upheaval that would destroy the lives of millions, among them that of Leslie's grandfather, who lost all his remaining property and died after the ill-treatment meted out to him by the Red Guards. Accused of being a money-lender and a landlord, he was forced to kneel on broken glass and was left in the open without food and water until he died. All the wealth he had accumulated from the sums that Leslie's father had sent back to China disappeared. At a stroke, Leslie's father lost both his own father and the fruits of much of his life's work.[34] All contact was lost with what remained of the family across the border, as the troubles convulsing the cities of China spilled over into Hong Kong. Riots broke out in the colony and had to be suppressed by firing. A series of bombings killed fifteen people, some of them children. Communications and trade were disrupted by strikes, and the supply of basic commodities ran short. Huge queues formed as people were reduced to taking water from standpipes in the street. Gradually calm returned, but the

Cultural Revolution was to ebb and flow in China for another four years. Leslie was old enough now to understand something of what had happened to his grandfather. The family's fears of the dangers of Communism had been all too well founded.

Increasingly now, Leslie was showing himself uninterested in study. He stayed at St. Luke's until 1968 when, now aged twelve, he left his Primary 6 class, seemingly before finishing it, perhaps to enable him to enter secondary schooling with the year band of his birth. He now joined Rosaryhill, a Roman Catholic school built in the hills behind Wan Chai.[35]

CHAPTER 2

DAYS OF BEING WILD

1968 - 1978

As Leslie moved schools in 1968, he took his first English name, Billy, a name given him, perhaps, in his new class. Although he was later to joke that Rosaryhill was a school for bad boys, it was in fact a fee-paying school with high academic standards. Many of its pupils were driven to school by their father's chauffeurs, though Leslie caught the school bus. Roman Catholicism was evident everywhere in the school's ethos and its decorations and statuary, but pupils were not pressured to adopt the faith, and Leslie was one who did not. There is no evidence then or later that he ever had any interest in any form of organised religion.

Leslie entered the school some way down the pecking order in Form 1F (1A being the top class) and did not settle in well, failing to pass into the second grade in the summer. Once again held back a year, he was forced to spend the year 1969 to 1970 in Form 1A. His school photograph that year shows him a conventional, quiet-looking boy matching everyone else in his class with his short-back-and-sides haircut. He later ruefully recalled the effect his "army haircut" had on the first girl he tried unsuccessfully to date.

Rosaryhill was strong on extramural activities and Leslie won prizes in elocution.[36] His badminton (a sport he was to play well throughout his life) was already good enough for him to be chosen to play with the principal, Father Lionel Xavier Brown, a teacher and mentor with whom Leslie was to stay in touch throughout his life.[37] It was at Rosaryhill that Leslie showed his first interest in music, singing in the school's music festival, though he did not yet have the confidence in his singing to participate in its talent contests.[38] At the time, many boys entered these with acts mimicking the popular female Mandarin singer Yiu So-yung, of whom Leslie was a fan, having watched her in concert with Luk Che and having learned her songs from his collection of records. Out of school, Leslie started to develop a taste for Western rock and pop, his first favourites in this field being the bands Creedence Clearwater Revival and Deep Purple. He often went to the cinema to watch the Mandarin Chinese films that were popular in Hong Kong at the time and found that he had a taste for Western movies, among others Franco Zeffirelli's 1968 version of *Romeo and Juliet*. This contained a nude scene that caused something of a scandal at the time and so was barred to the underaged; Leslie must have sneaked into the cinema to see it.

At Rosaryhill, things continued to go wrong with Leslie's education. In 1970, he managed to move up to the next grade and entered form 2D, but at the end of the year he was held back for a third time and remained in class 2B for the following year. By now he had fallen two years behind his contemporaries and had left behind his sister's tutoring as Ophelia's own education and career took her away from her family. His father, increasingly worried about his son's underachieving, began to pay for a private tutor, but this did not prove to be the success the family had hoped. Leslie found mathematics particularly difficult, though he did better at English. Because of his good English speaking voice, he was asked occasionally to lead school prayers. He enjoyed English literature and later claimed to recall (somewhat surprisingly) reading

Shakespeare and D.H. Lawrence with pleasure. His overall record, though, gained him a reputation for academic failure that stuck to him at the school. Many years later in 1983, when he was on his way to stardom, he returned to Rosaryhill to give a benefit concert for the school's twentieth anniversary. Overhearing some of the pupils making snide remarks about his poor school results, he was so embarrassed that he fled to the toilet and had to be persuaded by the principal to come out and sing. He would always be sensitive about his academic failure in later life. Yet he was fond of the school, participated in another fundraiser for it held at the Baptist College in 1987, and came back to the school again for the celebration of its 30th anniversary in 1989.[39]

Leslie's school photographs show his personality developing between 1970 and 1972, his hair thickening and growing, just slightly, longer. Later in life he said that he had been very rebellious at school, goaded by the inferiority complex he blamed on the lack of love in his family.[40] He perhaps exaggerated here. Though he was suspended for a fortnight for cheeking his sports teacher, ironically someone who actually liked him, he was not thought of at the school as a bad boy. Suspension at home, though, would not have improved his relations with his parents.

At least part of Leslie's adolescent problems may have been due to his growing awareness of his sexual orientation, which, after puberty, he could already sense was different from that of most of his fellows. This must have been very difficult to come to terms with. Neither his conservative Chinese family nor his Roman Catholic school would have tolerated anything they would have seen as sexually abnormal. The social pressures of the day left only two choices: conform or suffer. Despite his evident liking for girls, with whom he claimed several friendships, Leslie, now in his mid teens, found no real girlfriend and confessed to his female badminton-playing friend Wong that whilst the other boys chased girls, he played tennis. Subsequently, he made slightly more positive claims about his relationships with female school friends. In an interview he gave the magazine *City Entertainment* in 1985, he related that for most of his time at school he was on the tennis court or chasing girls,[41] though in the same interview he would also describe all his early friendships with girls as "puppy love."[42]

Though he must have wanted to be as "normal" as the rest, it was not girls who were on his mind, but boys. Years later, he told his close friends of his relationship with a classmate at Rosaryhill. The two boys were very close. One day they sneaked into the school chapel, which they knew would be deserted at the time, and stood together before the altar. They held hands and kissed. Leslie later characterized this startlingly bold deed as a deliberate provocation, a challenge to the heavens to object if they could. Of course, no thunderbolt flashed from on high, but it was a remarkably brave and defiant thing to have done, and it would not be the last gauntlet Leslie would lay down before fate.[43]

***

By now it was all too clear that at Rosaryhill Leslie had proved a failure, so Leslie's father removed him in 1972 to give him a fresh start and sent him now to the Buddhist Wong Fung Ling College in Happy Valley.[44] This was a much smaller school whose principal, Mr Shuen Po-yuen, was renowned for achieving high pass rates in the Hong Kong Certificate of Education. It was closer to home, too, allowing Leslie to walk there and back. Now at the age of sixteen, to what must have been his keen sense of shame, Leslie started again for the third time in Form 2. He marked his fresh start by taking a new English name, Bobby, but the new name did not give him fresh impetus and his studies failed to improve. Leslie was to spend only one year at Wong Fung Ling. He never developed any feeling for the school, never spoke of it in subsequent years, and never went back there after he left in 1973. There is little trace of him at the school today. His examination report for the year 1972-73 shows that he was 32nd in a form of 40, that he achieved only 48.24% against the required pass mark of 50%, and that he was graded only B1 for conduct.[45] The attempt to rescue his education had again been a failure.

There must now have been a good deal of heated discussion in the Cheung household about what to do with their youngest son. He was sixteen going on seventeen and had nothing to show for all his years of education. Something drastic needed to be done if Leslie were to avoid ending up on life's scrap heap. He was only partially aware of this debate. He said later that he had thought it was his father's idea to send him abroad to study, but he later found out that his mother had suggested it. She for once took an active role and pleaded with his father to send him to England, where she thought Leslie might find things easier.[46]

His father, for once, accepted her view, and decided to send Leslie to Eccles Hall, a minor public school in the county of Norfolk. In the English system, "public" designates a private school, for which parents of pupils, like Leslie's father, have to find the fees. The Cheungs had friends, also named Cheung,[47] running a restaurant in Southend-on-Sea on the Essex coast a few hours' drive from the school, so perhaps they had helped to identify it.[48] On 15 July 1973, using the name Bobby Kwok-wing Cheung, Leslie wrote to apply for a place, his sister Ophelia helping him out with his typed letter of application and with the essay he had to write to accompany it.[49] He was honest in his letter, telling the principal, Mr Mortimer B. Simington, about his poor academic record and informing him that he was "a 16-year-old Chinese youth, studying Form 2." Once more, he signified his search for a fresh start by changing his name; in a separate handwritten letter dated 25 July,

Frankie Bobby K.W. Cheung wrote that he had heard of the school from one of its students, his "best friend" Tommy Chow. He applied to start in the fourth form, requesting that he be allowed to go on to take A-Levels, which he optimistically said he thought would take him another three years.[50]

Leslie was accepted and, on 7 September 1973, with his friend Tommy Chow, he took the Laker Air flight to England, his family coming to the airport at Kai Tak to see him off. Leslie was elated to be leaving Hong Kong. He had been given another chance to make something of his life. By the time he arrived in England, he had ditched the name Bobby, perhaps, he hoped, along with his past, and was now Frankie Cheung. It was the name in his first passport.[51]

***

Eccles Hall was about as far-removed as it was possible to be from the concrete, dirt, and hubbub of Hong Kong. It lay deep in the East Anglian countryside near the village of Quidenham, twenty or so miles south of Norwich. Served by a sporadic bus service and with an unmanned halt on a nearby minor railway line, it wasn't easy to get to. Its pupils must have felt it extremely remote. It was, though, an idyllic place to study. The main building was an old country house set in green parkland, woods, and fields. The school was known for providing an education to children of the local farming stock and had about 185 boys aged between eleven and eighteen, of whom about sixty, including Leslie, lodged in the house.[52] The principal was the founder and proprietor of the school, and he had established a custom, which survives to this day, of accepting foreign students, often several of whom at any one time came from Hong Kong. There were two Hong Kong boys there in Leslie's day.

The experience must initially have been a great shock to a youth who had never been out of Hong Kong. Everything was alien, and for someone used to the rich and varied Cantonese cuisine, the food was strange, bland, and unpalatable. Leslie remembered with any pleasure only the evening Ovaltine and biscuits. The damp, cold weather, especially in the dark of winter, would have been a trial to someone used to Hong Kong's subtropical climate. Leslie must have spent a lot of time trying to keep warm.[53] Another shock must have been the level of education he was expected to achieve; consonant with his desire to take A-Levels in three years, and more in keeping with his age, he had been placed in Form V, the O-Level class, not the Form IV he had requested.[54] This must have made life very hard for a boy unused to applying himself academically.

The school, though, was a sympathetic environment for a young man used to some independence. It had a liberal approach to rules and behaviour, in keeping with the trends of the times, for this was England in the early seventies and moulds were breaking. At Eccles Hall, hair could be worn longer; pupils could have motorbikes and even drive cars off-road in the woods. Whilst pupils could not go out of school in term time, Leslie was able to travel to Southend at half-terms and at Christmas to see the Cheungs. He worked for them as a bartender and, for the first time, began to sing in public, banging out versions of current pop songs for their restaurant guests.[55] He was at this stage a fan of David Bowie, then in his outrageous Ziggy Stardust phase. In the evenings, Leslie watched English films, including the movie *Jeremy*; the theme song of this, "Blue Balloon," became one of his favourites. He later recalled watching the 1939 classic *Gone with the Wind*, starring Clark Gable and Vivien Leigh, though it was Leslie Howard, the film's second male star, who took his fancy. As did his name, one Leslie was later (after he had left Eccles Hall and was back in Hong Kong) to adopt.[56] As he later recounted, he chose this name because he loved the film, because he liked Leslie Howard, and because he was intrigued by the fact that the name was sexually ambivalent and could be either a man's or a woman's.

Eccles Hall was a very lively school. Small animals and horses were kept in the grounds and Leslie joined field trips conducted by the geography master, of whom he became fond. One was to Leeds, where the party stayed at the YMCA. Leslie even took to sport and played football, chosen for his agility as a winger in a sport better suited to his size than the rugby preferred by many of the farmers' sons. He very swiftly picked up an attractive and educated English style of speech, which would ever after characterize him when he spoke that language. Despite saying later that he'd faced problems with discrimination at Eccles Hall, he made friends. He became particularly attracted to a boy in his class, a lad named Alan, who, as they all would have been, was younger than him.

Things at last seemed to be going well, but in the summer of 1974, after only one year at the school, Leslie left Eccles Hall, taking with him no qualifications whatsoever. When he left, his school report shows that though he had worked hard, he had not been able to catch up "enough to make a good pass at O-Level likely."[57] Once more, he had failed to make a success of his education. Given his earlier poor academic record, it had probably been too much to have expected him to catch up with his contemporaries whilst working in their foreign tongue.

This, though, was not the full story, for what had happened was something much more unfortunate, a personal disaster brought on by the foolish and over-zealous parent of another pupil at the school, Raymond Kelly, a boy over four years younger than Leslie. Mrs Kelly had found a letter sent by Leslie to her son, who was at home for the Easter holidays. What Mrs Kelly stupidly failed to see was that Leslie's letter was a gentle brush-off in reply to a letter sent him by her son, who was clearly infatuated with him. Leslie wrote:

Kelly, I like you a lot if a dont met Alan first, I think I will probably like you more than him. You are really a nice boy, keep on please. You can enjoy many real friendships later on, because you are such a sweet little guy that everyone would like to being turn on by you. However Kelly, I really cant move away Alan's image, the things that we've done, I can still clearly remember, he is part of my life, even he cheated me or not ... Will you please forgive and I really do like you a lot.[58]

Raymond Kelly, fourteen years old, had evidently written to Leslie making a pitch for his affection. His mother, either too irate or naïve to see that, sent the letter to the Chief Education Officer of the London Borough of Bexley, which paid Kelly's fees. He in turn forwarded it to Eccles Hall, though he did not ask for any action to be taken, perhaps having the percipience to understand it better than had Mrs Kelly.

The letter, though, put Mr Simington in a very difficult position, for he had already had occasion to warn Leslie about his friendships with junior boys, warnings which Leslie had ignored. Such friendships were of course just the norm in English boarding schools, and the situation would not have been beyond Mr Simington to handle. He opted to delay. However, matters took a further turn for the worse when he sought to discuss the letter with one of the Southend Cheungs, a Miss Eva Y.W. Cheung, who was acting as guardian to Leslie. For some reason she took it upon herself to betray her ward and unfortunately put the matter beyond easy resolution by telling Mr Simington that she had "had trouble with him," which she related consisted of "his dying his hair, using make up wearing ladies shoes etc."[59] Mr Simington felt he had no option now but to write to Leslie's father, but he did so after some days, indicating, perhaps, that he had given the matter a great deal of thought. Quite clearly rather sadly, he asked Leslie's father to make immediate arrangements to take his son from the school.[60]

The letter took some days to arrive in Hong Kong and caused consternation when it did. Leslie's father sent a telegram on 2 May announcing the arrival of "your shocking letter" and asking for time for arrangements to be made. He followed this with a typewritten letter to the school on 11 May apologising for the trouble his son had caused and saying that "My wife, and I and the rest of the family are very shocked and sad about the matter." He told the headmaster that he had asked a relative who was in London to come to the school, and requested that Leslie be allowed to stay at Eccles Hall till the school year ended, when he would have the chance to sit for his examinations and so not waste the year's education. Ominously, he added:

> *From the information I have gathered so far, it would appear most likely that Frankie would need medical attention or psychiatric treatment or both, in which case it would be desirable to keep him in U.K. I have discussed the matter with several educationalists and physicians in Hong Kong, and they have all advised that that would be the best course of action to take.* [61]

This option was not, at least immediately, taken, for Leslie seems to have arrived back in Hong Kong at the end of June. Mr Simington had taken pity on him and allowed him to complete the year.[62]

That Leslie found this period acutely painful and embarrassing in later life is evident from the various accounts which he would give of it. He spoke often of his English schooling and of his return to Hong Kong, but tended to be vague or misleading about his age, the dates, and the subjects he had studied in England, going so far as to claim that he had gone on from Eccles Hall to study textile management at Leeds University. Muddying the waters even further, on one occasion he added that he had won a scholarship to Leeds from a school in Chelmsford, a town in Essex not far from Southend and somewhere he had never studied. He would also tell the world that he had been recalled from Leeds before completing his degree when his father suffered a stroke and demanded him by his side to run the business.[63]

The truth was rather different, though quite how different still remains unclear. Leslie never sat for his A-Levels, there is no record of his studying in Chelmsford[64] and none that he studied at Leeds.[65] Instead, as we have seen, he returned to Hong Kong.

When he arrived there in 1974, his reception at home is likely to have been dramatic and very unpleasant. We do not know what happened to him when he reached there. Whether his father acted on the remarks he had made to Mr Simington about medical or psychiatric treatment is unknown. At the time, various kinds of psychiatric treatment, some that would now be regarded as of a barbarous nature including emetics and electric shock, were widely used to "cure" homosexuality. Coincidentally, one of the centres of such treatment in the United Kingdom was at Leeds. If Leslie was forced to undergo some such regime, it might help explain some of the bitterness with which he spoke of his parents for many years to come. It goes without saying that, if he were subjected to any such treatment, it failed to change his orientation.

By 1975, back in Hong Kong, everything must have looked to Leslie depressingly bleak. What could he do now? He was nearly nineteen and had not a qualification to his name. He could not have been at all popular at home; living with parents and siblings who now knew his sexual orientation must have been highly unpleasant. He had failed in two Hong Kong secondary schools, wasted a lot of private tuition, and cost his father a year at an English private school, all with nothing to show for it. Once again he was living at home in Wan Chai. He and his parents must have despaired of his ever making his way in the world.

***

To save at least something from the wreck of his education was now the only sensible solution. Leslie was sent to Wellington College, a school situated in Kowloon, across the harbour from his home, which took pupils in all secondary grades up to A-Level.[66] The college has been demolished, and where it once stood is now the smart district of restaurants and bars that make up the night spot of Knutsford Terrace. No college records survive, but according to an account Leslie himself gave later, he entered Form 5 and studied English, Chinese, and Mathematics. We do not know when Leslie entered Wellington College and have no record of how long he was there.[67] It seems that he studied there again using the name Bobby, and that he'd abandoned the name Frankie he'd used in England. It probably had too many bad memories.

Life at Wellington College had its compensations. Leslie made friends with his fellow students, and there were parties and picnics in Hong Kong's countryside. He met up at least once with his old Rosaryhill girlfriend, Wong, taking her with him to Macau on the Christmas Eve of 1974 or 1975. He recounted this experience in his radio autobiography in 1985, saying that the girl was very important to him and that he believed she really was his first love.[68] He described the relationship a little more fully many years later to the Japanese journalist Chitose Shima, to whom he related that it was on the trip to Macau that he had had his first sexual experience, "at the age of 16."[69] He added that the two were very much in love and were very natural together, though they found they had many differences in thinking and values and eventually split up, Wong going on to marry another classmate and to have children. They had, he told Chitose Shima, met since then, though just to have a chat, and had remained friends.[70]

This story reappeared in 1989, on James Wong's TV programme *Off-Guard Tonight*, when Leslie hinted that he and Wong had gone to bed together in Macau and that he had lost his virginity there. He told the audience that he had really liked her and had pursued her by letter from England, though she had not replied. When he got back to Hong Kong and had managed to save a few hundred dollars, he took her to Macau on the 7.30 pm speedboat, scheduled to arrive at 9 pm. The boat broke down halfway to Macau and, by the time they finally arrived, at almost 10.30 pm, all they could find was a cheap hotel.[71]

If they did have sex on this occasion, it seems that they did not repeat the experience. Perhaps this was a real attempt on Leslie's part to lead a heterosexual life. He had every reason to prove himself to both himself and his family at the time, and this would not be the last time he made an effort to "go straight." It was clearly an important event to him then and later.

✻✻✻

Leslie's thoughts were turning now more to music than romance. He and some friends at the college formed a band called Onyx, with Leslie as its lead singer.[72] The band entered several competitions, though without making a mark. Leslie also started to enter TV talent competitions as an individual, but he didn't make much headway and in the process earned the nickname "Three Lights" from a show in which he was scored three lights out of five by the panel. He also unsuccessfully auditioned for TV parts.[73] It is clear that he had already resolved on a career as a performer. Where he acquired the confidence that he had enough talent to make a career in show business is something of a mystery. Apart from school performances and singing occasionally in his guardians' Southend restaurant, he had no stage experience at all and there was nothing to prove so far that he could either sing or act. It must have been clear to him, though, that were he to succeed, he could escape from the failures of his past and prove himself to his family and to the world. That was more of an amazing gamble than a plan, but even at this stage in his life it seems that Leslie's faith in his own abilities was absolute. All he needed now was the opportunity.

His time at the college ended in 1976. Leslie later claimed to have achieved an A grade at A-Level English, a pass in Chinese, and a fail at Mathematics, though it is hard to see how he could have reached further than O-Level at any of them. Whatever certificates he did achieve were not enough to set him on the path to a standard career.

Leslie's father was by now drinking heavily and slowly spoiling his business, though the family was still relatively well-off. Leslie said later that his father drank so much that it paralysed the lower half of his body.[74] It is doubtful that Leslie could have stomached working in the family business with a father he so disliked, or indeed that his father would have wanted him to. After he left Wellington College in 1976, his father got him an interview with a law firm that was looking for an errand boy, but Leslie refused to take the job. Such lowly drudgery was not the way he intended to spend his life. So he set out on his own and took work in shops, spending some time as a shoe salesman earning a meagre wage and then, when this didn't work out, selling Levi's jeans, a job that lasted only two weeks.[75]

When that ended, Leslie was broke, stuck at home, miserable, and with no tangible prospects. Things, though, were at last about to change in his favour.

TIME OF STRUGGLE

CHAPTER 3

DREAMIN' OF THE FUTURE

1977 – 1979

To Leslie, the answer to all his troubles seemed to be the dream world of show business, and the magic path to that, for a young man like him with no connections, training, recognised talent, or experience as a performer, could only lie in winning a talent competition. By now, these were a popular form of entertainment in Hong Kong, but the chances of winning, of course, were very small, as he'd already found while at Wellington College. Leslie, though, never lacked a strong belief in his own talent. He *knew* he could make it.

In May 1977, RTV announced that it was to host the local stage of a regional talent competition, the Asian Broadcasting Union's Asian Amateur Singing Contest '77. They promised a TV contract for the Hong Kong winner. Matt Monro was to star. The entry fee was set very low at only HK$5, but Leslie didn't have even this small amount; he'd been out of work for months. Luk Che did what she always did and rescued him by giving him HK$20 to cover the entrance fee and the bus fare to the studio.[76] Despite his lack of funds, Leslie managed to put together an eye-catching costume in a kind of American style, with a white open-necked shirt that had heavy red embroidery over the shoulders, matched with a long red scarf and red knee boots, an ensemble which suited his thick, dark, swinging locks. He entered the competition at RTV's studios on 16 May, describing himself to the press as "a fashion model."[77] There were sixteen finalists from eight Asian cities. When his turn came, Leslie walked out onto the stage with as complete a confidence as if he'd been strutting it for years, and sang Don McLean's 1971 hit "American Pie." His energetic rhythm, faultless English rendering and relaxed stage-presence impressed both the judges and the studio audience.[78]

The night was one of amazing promise and coincidences that no one could have appreciated at the time. Michael Lai Siu-tin, musician and TV celebrity and one of Leslie's judges that night, would later be the key to Leslie's career. In the audience was Florence Chan Suk-fun, the music manager with whose support Leslie would eventually reach the pinnacle of his fame; that night she saw immediately how good-looking he was and was sure that he would win the competition—though when the scores were announced, she was disappointed that he won only second place. His performance, though, was good enough to impress RTV's station manager, Steve Wong Sak-chiu, who, with his deputy Mrs Mok Ho Mun-yee (the mother of the future singer Karen Mok Man-wai, who many years later was to become a close friend of Leslie), went backstage to tell Leslie he'd make him a star.

Second place in Hong Kong put Leslie through to the next round, so with the Hong Kong competition winner, a Filipino singer named Ding Mercado, he flew to Hawaii to compete in the eight-nation finals. He managed only fifth place this time, something attributed to favouritism on the part of the Filipino judge, but the resulting complaints in the Hong Kong press that Leslie had been marked down unfairly did him no harm at home, and immediately on his return RTV honoured Steve Wong's promise. Director of Programming Chung King-fai (a famed Hong Kong personality known universally as "King Sir") signed Leslie for a three-year contract. King Sir would become Leslie's first professional mentor, watching over the first years of his showbiz career.

As he signed his five-year contract with RTV, Leslie also signed a three-year recording contract with Polydor Hong Kong. All seemed set fair. Leslie was starting off on the dual-tracked career of singing and acting that was the well-trodden path to stardom at the time.[79]

On the day that he joined RTV in 1977, Leslie walked out of his parents' home and never went back to live there.[80] The speed of his departure and the bitter way he later spoke in public about his family make it plain that he couldn't move out fast enough. With the HK$1,000 bonus he received on signing his first TV contract, he put down a HK$500 deposit on a flat near the RTV studio at Broadcast Drive in Kowloon, and with a few thousand dollars borrowed from King Sir, bought enough furniture to make it liveable.[81] The rent for the first flat he could ever call his own was a full HK$500 a month, but despite his feelings, and in traditional Chinese style, he dutifully gave his mother HK$200 every month from the remains of his salary. By eating in the RTV canteen he could economise on food, and by taking the free clothes which the studio arranged from the couturier supplying costumes for their programmes, he could set out to enjoy himself with the HK$300 he had left each month.

Though his self-confidence in his abilities was deep-rooted, he was not cocksure about his prospects. On the contrary, he realised the realities of show business life and gave himself only three years to succeed in the business or quit.[82] It seemed at first that things were going well; after only nine months with the studio he got a raise to something over HK$2,500 (rumoured to be to prevent his moving to rival station TVB) and was able to move to a bigger apartment in Lai Wan, further away from the studio on the west side of the Kowloon peninsula.[83] There the rent was $1,000 a month, double that of his first flat. Though he had to get to the studio at Broadcast Drive by bus, he had begun to go up in the world, and rapidly at that.

Strangely, though, having set his cap at becoming a singing star, and having got his entry into show business through a singing contest, Leslie found that the door that the competition had opened led not to singing stardom but to a career in television. This was not what he had wanted, nor was it at all where he saw his future, but, for the time being, he found he had to accept that TV was where he would first make his name. It was a name, incidentally, which he was about to change. He was still using the English name Bobby at this time, and people in the industry knew him by it for some time longer, but by the time his first album of songs appeared this year, he had adopted the name Leslie to which he'd become attracted back in England.

In starting a career in TV, Leslie was like many other Hong Kong performers of the time, for TV had become an important cultural force. Hong Kong culture was in the process of growing away from its mainland Mandarin roots. The colony's growing prosperity enabled a rapidly increasing number of people to afford entertainment in a leisure time they had never had before.[84] By 1977, about 80% of households owned a TV, and the studios were setting the cultural pace by showcasing music and drama with a particularly local flavour. The theme songs and music of TV soap operas were especially influential in helping create a Cantonese popular music (by now known as Cantopop) that was drowning out the old Mandarin songs. TV was bringing the faces of a new generation of Canto stars into everyone's living rooms. It may not have been what Leslie had wanted, but in reality he was lucky to have been picked up as a TV star. It was a good time to start a career on the small screen.[85]

The field was, at that stage, a large one, for in the seventies three TV studios were competing for dominance. TVB was the major studio, the first to open a free-to-air service in Hong Kong back in 1967, and it had the prime position it was to keep for twenty years. RTV, the company that had signed Leslie, had started out first in the field. Its full name was Rediffusion Television, and it had opened the first cable TV service in Hong Kong in 1957, but it had been slow to follow TVB into free-to-air and was losing ground when Leslie joined. It was forced to close its film unit the following year. The third channel, Commercial TV, or CTV, was largely Taiwanese managed but did not make money, and despite being founded only in 1975, was to go out of business in 1978.[86] In addition to these channels, the government-owned but independently-run Radio Television Hong Kong (RTHK) had started in 1970 to make TV programmes, mostly of an educational type. RTHK had no broadcasting network of its own and the commercial broadcasters were obliged to carry its product, which to the networks' detriment increasingly added entertainment to supplement the educational content.

At first, RTV tried Leslie out in a number of variety shows, mostly aired on Sundays on their Chinese channel.[87] He naturally got junior billing beneath the major stars of the day, one of whom was Michael Lai, his talent competition judge. This was a lucky meeting as it gave Lai a chance to see Leslie's talent again, close up. Leslie was, of course, as low on the studio pecking order as it was possible to be; he didn't enjoy this lowly status and the disdain with which the old hands treated newcomers.[88] Nor did his status improve with time, as audience reaction to his variety show performances was poor and the station gradually reduced his slots. By 1978, they dried up altogether.[89]

He did, though, find other work, and initially this was in the film industry. Mirroring the world of television, Hong Kong movies were entering an exciting time.[90] The stereotypical films of an earlier age were being replaced by films with a newer look. The martial arts films of Bruce Lee, who had died only four years before, in 1973, were developing into an ever more elaborate and visually stunning genre dominated by Jackie Chan, while at the same time the Mandarin dramas churned out by the Shaw studios were being replaced by Cantonese films with more local themes. However, it was not in one of these that Leslie would make his first appearance on the big screen.

Just after signing with RTV in 1977, Leslie was offerred the starring male role in the film *Erotic Dream of Red Chamber*.[91] The film's producer, Ng See-yuen, who was a reasonably well-known Hong Kong filmmaker, lured Leslie into taking the part by telling him that a famous RTV actress would star with him. Leslie accepted, only to find that the film was low-budget soft porn, a hasty filming of the classic 18th century Chinese novel *The Dream of the Red Chamber*. He found to his chagrin that his part of Jia Bao Yu (Precious Jade)—the spoiled, childish, and prettily effeminate scion of a rich house—was a vehicle to exploit his own youth and beauty to make a quick buck. Leslie was too intimidated to withdraw: he feared that there was perhaps triad involvement in the film, something all too common in Hong Kong's movie industry, and thought that if this was so, as a first-time film actor he could not afford to offend any less-than-savoury investors. He was perhaps persuaded, too, by the money he was offered—he was certainly in need of cash at the time—though it wasn't very much, just HK$6,500. Many years later he was to give his own view of the film to the critic Frederic Dannen; it was, he said, "a disaster, a low-budget movie, very indecent."

Despite all this, Leslie did a good job in the role. Many years later, he was beautifully described in this performance by the writer

Too Kit as having a complexion as delicate as powder, lips elegant as a shower of rouge, cheerful speech and loving glance, in his eyes a world of desire and a sea of yearning![92]

The censor was not beguiled by any of this and banned the film after it had taken just over a million dollars at the box office during the seven days it ran in January 1978. Leslie found the whole experience rather shocking and vowed at the time that he'd keep away from the movie industry in future. He proved unable to keep this vow and was to break it almost immediately.

Singing was what Leslie wanted to do but his record company gave him little chance to fulfil his hopes. The music they first chose for him and the styles that they insisted he adopt were both unsuited to his talents. Leslie needed tuition, training, and guidance as a singer and these he did not get. At this early stage Leslie's singing voice was incapable of attracting an audience, and he had not even begun to develop any strong personal style that could mark him out from the herd.

Perhaps persuaded by Leslie's good English and the success he had made of singing "American Pie," Polydor tried him out in his first release with an English compilation of easy-listening songs, which included Billy Joel's "Just the Way You Are" and Barry Manilow's "Even Now." These were lazily gathered into an unexciting album entitled *Daydreamin'*.[93] This was a strange decision. Cantopop was already sweeping away both the English music and the old Mandarin Taiwanese pop ballads that had dominated Hong Kong's music scene in the early seventies. Leslie's main attraction at this time was his youth, but the record company picked him songs suited to a middle-aged audience. As a result, in his debut at the age of twenty-one, he came across as oddly old-fashioned. Young record buyers lambasted his "chicken voice," particularly in the song specially arranged for him, "I Like Dreamin'." Whilst his English was sharp and clear, his phrasing was dull, his tone was thin, and his voice lacked power. Only occasionally does his singing here hint at the abilities he would later develop.

Audiences threw the record's dreamin' image back in his face when he was billed in a live "Pop Folk" show along with the Wynners, a successful group whose soon-to-be stars, Alan Tam Wing-lun and Chung Chun-to, popularly known as Kenny Bee, sang in Cantonese. Also on stage was Cantopop's leading star of the day, the vastly popular singer-songwriter Sam Hui Koon-kit. Leslie sang from his new English song collection and was booed from the beginning till the end of his performance.[94] The crowd of a few thousand amused themselves and mortified Leslie by chanting "Go back home and sleep."

Leslie's audiences made it plain that they did not appreciate his performing style. Unlike his successful contemporaries, he didn't stand still to sing in front of the mike but moved around the stage, rocking with the music. His flamboyant costumes, which would have raised no eyebrows in the United Kingdom or the States, were very different from the conservative dress worn by most of the major singers of the day and, coupled with his boyish looks, gave rise to accusations of effeminacy. Despite all this, Leslie did manage to win that year's award of Most Promising Newcomer in the local newspaper *Wah Kiu Daily News*. Someone must have liked him, though Polydor certainly didn't. Disappointed by the reaction to *Daydreamin'*, they made no more recordings with him for over a year. The only songs he recorded in 1978 were the Cantonese title themes of two RTV soaps, *Chasing Dynasties* and *The Roving Swordsman*.[95]

It was an uncomfortable time in other ways. He had not long been under contract when he underwent an operation to remove two lumps in his left wrist.[96] The lumps proved benign, but the operation shortened and weakened his hand, and he needed a long period of physiotherapy to bring full use back to it. He was pretty much alone during this difficult time, for though he still sent money home to his mother, he had largely cut himself off from his family. He kept in touch, though, with his sister, Ophelia, who had married for a second time. She was now wife to an English civil servant named Ian Macpherson. Ironically, in light of Leslie's earlier educational failure, she asked him to tutor her twin girls by her first marriage, Alisha and Ayesha, in English. Leslie was good in the language and took this on, travelling weekly to the Macphersons' home on Hong Kong Island by bus.[97]

Compensation for his troubles came from TV. Whatever his first audiences had thought, Leslie's work had attracted the attention of producer-director Johnny Mak Don-hung, who was at that time powerful in the company's drama department and was in the middle of a run of successful soaps. Johnny Mak asked Leslie to join his soap opera *Crocodile Tears* in the small semi-autobiographical role of Johnny, a young singer going through tough times. Though Leslie had no acting training, he had already shown in his first movie that he was a natural on the big screen, and his first TV soap proved to be a success. Leslie's career as an actor had begun.[98]

The success of *Crocodile Tears* led immediately to parts in other soaps, the first of any importance being *Love Stories*, a twenty-episode series made by RTV in 1977 that screened till the next year.[99] In this show he worked with the new actress Teresa Mo Sun-kwan, here in her first role. They took to each other, so much so that they were to be lifelong friends, and it seemed that this time, perhaps, Leslie had found a girl he could be happy with. He took her to meet some of his siblings, who liked her and were sure from the passionate way the couple behaved that they were in love. It was not to be, though. Many years later, Leslie let slip in a Cable TV show that he had proposed marriage to Teresa in 1978, adding that he'd scared her away by acting so precipitously.[100] She turned him down as a husband, perhaps surprised by his rapid courtship, but kept him close as a friend. Their relationship, of course, was noted in the media, as was their "break-up."

Leslie also appeared during 1978 in *Under the Same Roof: Teenagers*, a ground-breaking serial made by RTHK about a bunch of Hong Kong kids living together in a house deep in the country of Hong Kong's New Territories.[101] Leslie landed a principal role, though not the starring one, that of a schoolboy going through the usual complications of friendships and puppy love. He worked here for the first time with Annie Ngai Sze-pui, with whom his name would later be romantically linked in the media. The show brought Leslie to audience attention and encouraged the studio to give him more work, so he began to pick up parts in the martial-arts shows that were as popular on Hong Kong's TV screens as they were at the movies.

This was yet another area of which Leslie had no knowledge, but he didn't allow this to deter him and practised painfully till he got the moves right, the beginning of a life-long habit of going over and over a part till he had convinced himself it was perfect. Luckily, he was a swift learner and moved well enough in the fight scenes to be offered a leading part in the martial-arts drama *The Spirit of the Sword*, which reached TV screens between 1978 and 1979.[102] The character he played was a fighter brought up from childhood to protect Chinese martial arts, and the plot called for childhood scenes in which his character was played by a child star named Jimmy Wong Shu-kei. Despite his own youth (he was still only 22), Leslie took care of the boy both on set and outside the studio, cooking him noodles at his own flat after shooting. This time, too, Leslie was brought together again with Michael Lai, who starred in the show and again wrote a soundtrack for it that included a song performed by Leslie, the third he sang for a TV series.

RTV brought Leslie into contact with celebrities who could help him in his career. One of these was Roman Tam Pak-Sin, whose stage name was Lo Man, a flamboyant performer and singer who was widely considered to be the "godfather" of the emerging Cantopop world and whose high-camp image of glittering costumes, shiny shoes, and sultry, erotic body movements seems to have had an influence at the time on Leslie.[103] Tam had just returned to Hong Kong from Japan and was beginning to make it very big indeed. He acted as a mentor to Leslie and introduced him to his first agent.

Roman Tam and the younger pair he also mentored, Danny Chan Pak-keung and Paul Chung Bo-law, would become Leslie's closest friends.[104] Their playground was Hong Kong's underground of gay-friendly bars and saunas.[105] Leslie met Danny Chan, the member of this group with whom he would become closest, by chance. He recounted the meeting to Commercial Radio a few years later, telling the audience that he and friends were at the Bang Bang restaurant in Kowloon when a boy suddenly came over and announced that some people said they looked alike. On asking who he was, Leslie was stunned to find he was Danny Chan.*[106]*

Danny was about two years younger than Leslie, was from a richer background, had been educated in America, and was making his name as a pop composer and singer. He had won third place in the Hong Kong Pop Song Composition Competition in the year Leslie had won his singing contest. Danny was fast becoming seen as the composer and singer for those who aspired to a more refined type of music, more of a class act than Leslie had even approached at this point. He was now making his acting debut with RTV's rival station, TVB, in their drama *Sweet Babe*. He was on a roll that year, winning first prize at Yamaha's Hong Kong Festival and going on to hold his first concert. Leslie could not help but be impressed. He thought Danny must be very wealthy because he had so many expensive things, including a Louis Vuitton trunk and many Cartier rings and necklaces.[107] However, if Leslie felt himself at a disadvantage in terms of career and family background, Danny was not without insecurities of his own to balance the relationship, some stemming from his birth. His mother was the concubine of his father, not his wife. Leslie and Danny became firm friends and began to spend most of their spare time together.

Neither Roman Tam nor Danny Chan was ever to marry, and it is clear that from his early days in showbiz Leslie moved primarily in a milieu that was markedly gay, albeit one that was limited at that time: a few gay saunas in obscure sites and a bar or two in the larger hotels, known for their male clientele. The Ambassador Hotel in Tsim Sha Tsui was a well-known gay watering hole, and other places frequented by gay men were the President Sauna in the basement of the Harbour Hotel in Gloucester Road, Wan Chai, and Dateline Bar & Restaurant, a highly popular venue in a basement in Wellington Street in Central. Every evening after seven, Dateline was by unwritten rule reserved for "members," or gay men. It had a dance floor and a small bar, and was a place where Eastern and Western boys would meet.

The scene was beginning to open up slowly. Around this time a flamboyant entrepreneur named Gordon Huthart opened Disco Disco in Lan Kwai Fong, the area of bars and restaurants just behind the financial district of Central. It was the first disco and bar of its type in Hong Kong and was almost exclusively for a gay clientele.[108] This was a bold step, for homosexuality was still illegal in Hong Kong and was to be so until 1991. For Huthart it was soon to prove one step too far, for he was prosecuted for buggery in 1979 and spent thirteen weeks in jail.[109] Disco Disco, though, survived and became Leslie's favourite night spot. Jimmy Ngai Siu-yun, one of Leslie's friends at the time, later called his group "the DD crowd."

It was not easy for a young man seeking company of his own sex to find friends with such a limited number of places to go and so few people brave enough to chance their exposure in them. Those who needed more discretion than would be afforded in a bar sought out the darker lighting and restricted access of the sauna, and there were several operating then in Hong Kong. Leslie used to visit the Yuk Tak Che sauna, a Shanghainese-style bathhouse with a palm court décor, at the junction of Lai Chi Kok and Nathan Roads in Mongkok, Kowloon. This was a favourite haunt of the gay scene, and Danny Chan was often there, in his case usually seeking Caucasian company, which he preferred. The masseurs there were famed for the "happy endings" they gave those who could pay for them. Leslie could not, though he was at the sauna three or four times a week. He was not one of those who stayed after midnight when the doors were closed and men could sleep over or have group sex in the sauna. He was known by the friends he made there for being careful and for not taking drugs, as many of the others there did. He soon became well-known by those who frequented the place but was careful whom he got to know and gained a reputation amongst some for being difficult to approach—connected, perhaps, with his lack of means, which also earned him a reputation amongst the staff of being stingy. He could only afford HK$20 tips. He made some friends there amongst the casual contacts and met up with at least one of them on occasions outside the sauna. The Yuk Tak Che was not the lonely place that might be imagined, and it catered to a real need.[110]

At the same time, and this of course in public, Leslie dated women. He may have done this because he still had in mind the possibility that he, like many he was meeting at the discos and sauna, could marry and settle down. He may also have been seeking to satisfy the hopes and demands of his family and his managers. In any case, Leslie always made female friends easily. He liked women and enjoyed their company. Now that he had some financial means, he started to take girls out on dates, treating those he liked most as girlfriends, something that he'd continue to do for over a decade. One of the first of these, in 1978, was the highly attractive daughter of tycoon Albert Yeung, Cindy Yeung Lok-si, who became a close friend and whom he would continue to see on and off for several years. This was noticed and their names were linked in the press.[111]

What with the ending of his RTV variety show performances and the lack of singing work from Polydor, Leslie found little to do musically in 1978 other than his theme songs and a short trip abroad to appear in a variety show on South Korean TV. Similarly, he appeared in a small part in only one movie, the oddly named *Dog Bites Dog Bone* (also known as *Cat and Dogs*; both names are approximate translations of the Chinese title), a film written and directed by his mentor Michael Lai.[112] Leslie appeared as a nameless guest at a party which turns into a brawl, wearing a costume remarkably similar to the one he wore for his South Korean TV appearance; the studio was making this one on the cheap and it was not a success. When it screened in July, it grossed only HK$800,000 and disappeared without a trace.

Though TV work did not come again soon in 1979 after *Spirit of the Sword* had completed its run, Leslie was now already a well-known face on the colony's TV screens, and this prompted his agent to engineer a slight recovery in his singing career. He was booked to sing other performers' Cantonese songs on TV and to perform in local gigs. He sang with a band for the Malaysian National Day Ball held in the Sheraton Hotel that year.[113] He was also booked for a mini concert at the Kung Hau theatre in Macau.[114] Naturally, he got billing beneath the better-known stars with whom he appeared, the singer Frances Yip Lai-yee, the popular-martial arts actor Kent Tong Chun-yip, and his best friend Danny Chan. Danny, who had just released his album *First Love*, had asked Leslie to listen to a tape of his new songs; Leslie particularly liked one which had a telephone tone in the background, a song named "Shedding My Tears for You," which was to be a big hit. As they arrived in Macau, it was being played on the hydrofoil's speakers.[115]

"Shedding My Tears for You" would help make Danny a star, and Leslie would have had to be a saint not to have found this galling. The disparities in their fortunes and careers would from now on increasingly engage the two men in a rivalry that was deliberately encouraged by the industry and by the crowd they both hung around with. The rivalry would eventually ruin their friendship, but in 1979 Leslie and Danny were very close. When Leslie was performing Cantonese songs on RTV, Danny sang English songs on TVB's variety programme, *Enjoy Yourselves Tonight*, and would come round to the studio to wait for Leslie to go out on the town. Towards the end of 1979, they started work together on a film called *Encore*, a better film than anything Leslie had appeared in so far and one that would set them both up as figures in the cinema. This was fun and they enjoyed each other's company.

In the Macau concert, Leslie experienced none of the negative reactions he had faced in his first live performance in the "Pop Folk" concert of 1977, and, perhaps encouraged by this, Polydor decided to give him another chance with an album of Cantonese songs entitled *Lover's Arrow*.[116] Despite the switch of language, this was not a success. Seven of the twelve tracks were songs from RTV soaps, and Leslie was roundly criticised, even by his friends, for making such a bad rehash of other singers' work. Clearly, the record company still hadn't worked out what sort of singer he was. His cover image was still the one he'd started out with, his thick, dark hair still hanging in curling locks that reached down to the collar of his dark brown shirt, which sparkled with massive embroidery across the shoulders. The songs Polydor chose for the album were unexciting: some rip-offs of Western tunes; others slow, easy-listening local ballads. None of them allowed Leslie the chance to show his exuberance or express any real feeling. His voice had got noticeably stronger and his enunciation had improved, but he still lacked depth of tone, and the "chicken" thinness that had been criticised by his first audiences had not been entirely banished. The album flopped. Polydor tried again in 1979 with two singles issued separately, "Do You Wanna Make Love" and "Cupid's Arrow," but both proved damp squibs and destroyed their belief that Leslie could make them money.[117]

That this was much their own fault did not prevent their giving up on him, though he did not realise that they had done so quite yet.

CHAPTER 4

CASTLES OF SAND

1980 - 1981

Leslie's TV work did more than keep his career afloat in 1980, it made him a TV star. First, he took a minor role in *No Big Deal*, a drama made by Selina Chow Shuk-yee, the powerful station director and an important figure in Hong Kong's entertainment world.[118] This was followed by a part in a sequel to a historical drama titled *Dynasty II* and another in *Bandits from Canton*, during the filming of which he fell sick for a time.[119] He won what was his first real starring role in the seventy-six part series *Gone with the Wind*, a nostalgic tale of the precarious Hong Kong of 1949.[120] He took another lead in the very popular teenage soap *Pairing* that ran till 1981, a show pretty much the Hong Kong equivalent, for its time, of the much later American comedy soap *Friends*[121]. *Pairing* was deliberately designed to build on his earlier success, *Under the Same Roof*. Its storyline featured four boys sharing the lower floor of a house in the New Territories, where they lived below four girls who shared the floor above. One of the female stars was Annie Ngai, with whom Leslie had already worked and would work again.[122]

When the making of *Pairing* ended, the formula was too good to abandon, and Leslie was soon cast by RTHK in a follow up to

Under the Same Roof, this time called *Under the Same Roof: Dead Knot*.[123] Leslie still played a teenager, though one now already out of school. By now, his appearance had begun to mature and the studio was grooming his hair to make it shorter and less bushy, more apt for the role of the teenage boy next door, which even at the age of twenty-four he could easily play without stretching the credulity of his audiences.

Leslie was developing into an actor who was capable of taking on more powerful roles than the rather cardboard characters he'd been allowed to play so far. One of the highlights of Hong Kong's TV screen in 1980 was the very popular RTHK show, *Heritage: The Young Concubine*, the show that was to spread Leslie's popularity for the first time among audiences of all ages.[124] *The Young Concubine* was taken from a story by Lilian Li Pik-wah (known in the West as Lilian Lee), and the show was the occasion when she first became aware of Leslie's talents, something that would bear fruit in later years. The show was a painstakingly made period drama set in the Guangdong province of the 1920s, somewhere, perhaps, just over the border from Hong Kong. Such careful efforts were made to incorporate many traditional Chinese customs that nowadays the film is a record of a way of life that had already long vanished when the series was made. Leslie plays a landlord's son who returns home from studying, imbued with progressive social ideas, only to fall in love with his father's younger concubine. Their affair is discovered and the unfortunate girl suffers the traditional penalty: she is bound in a bamboo cage and thrown into the sea. The show was the first in which Leslie was given the chance to demonstrate serious acting skills, and he rose to the challenge, showing a depth of feeling and naturalness of characterisation that gave a clear indication of what he would do in the future. The show garnered a Gold Prize at the Chicago International Film and Television Festival and a Silver Award at the 1st Commonwealth Film and Television Festival, the first in the series of awards that would gradually become such a feature of Leslie's life.

This success in TV was beginning to be matched by a series of opportunities that Leslie was offered by film studios, which were keen to capitalise on the growing recognition he was achieving. The making of the first of these, *Encore*, had begun the year before, in 1979. Leslie got junior billing behind Danny Chan in this film that was deliberately made in the mode of the TV series of the day. It became the first in a long line of teenage movies that gained great popularity with Hong Kong audiences;[125] Leslie was pioneering teenage movies as he had pioneered teenage soaps on the small screen. This time, though, the personality of the sweet "boy next door" that he had developed for TV was abandoned; for the first time, he took on the role of a rebel. *Encore*'s director, Clifford Choi Kai-kwong, had spotted something sultry and rebellious in Leslie that TV had missed, and the "bad boy" role that he gave Leslie was the first of a series that would establish a very different image indeed. From now on, largely as a result of this film, the public, especially the younger female public, became fixated on Leslie's "bad boy" persona and took to booing him in cinemas when he appeared on screen.

In *Encore*, Leslie played Gigo, a rough-edged teenage student who competes in a singing competition (another of those autobiographical touches loved by Hong Kong studios) against Paul, played here by his friend Paul Chung. Paul is the younger brother of conservative and sophisticated Ken, the film's lead, played by Danny Chan. Their rich parents live in a comfortable house with a swimming pool while Gigo's working-class family lives on a government estate. This screen relationship, of course, mirrored to some degree the real life relationship between Danny and Leslie. At a time when Leslie's singing career was going nowhere, he found it galling to work alongside Danny, whose singing was featured in *Encore* and whose song of that name became a big hit after the film was released.[126] That all this grated with Leslie was something, perhaps, that enabled him to dig deep into his own character to play Gigo, who, smouldering and sultry, explodes at times with frightening violence. Leslie told a reporter a few years later that he had felt oppressed by Danny; "I felt miserable," he said.[127] What romantic interest there was in the film was provided by the young actress Jean Yung Jing-Jing, who would appear again later with Leslie.[128]

Despite the irritations, Gigo was Leslie's first major role in a mainstream movie. When *Encore* proved a reasonable success at the box office, in the two weeks that it ran in October 1980, his promise both as an actor and as a box office draw was not missed by the studios. The public were at this stage unaware of any antagonism between Leslie and Danny Chan, and their names were by now linked in the popular mind with Paul Chung as "the Three Musketeers."[129]

In the summer of 1980, Leslie was cast in a small TV film that, like *The Young Concubine*, would show his increasing skills as a character actor. This was *Island Stories Series: Castle of Sand*, a short directed for RTHK by Alex Law.[130] Leslie played a young novice monk in a remote monastery on Lantau, a mountainous island off Hong Kong's coast. Leslie's character doesn't speak in the film, so his part depended on facial expressions and body movements, yet despite this handicap he managed to bring the boy to life as an innocent, slightly mysterious and unworldly acolyte, a survivor in ultra-modern Hong Kong from another, quieter era. He had to shave his head for the part (as he had done for the TV martial arts series the year before) and these shows effectively marked the end of the bouffant hairdo that had been his hallmark till then. Having shaved off the luscious locks of which he had been very fond for over four years made him highly self-conscious, and he forbade pictures being taken of him until his hair had grown back a little. *Island Stories* screened in 1981, when it received less notice than it deserved.

With all this work on the small and large screens coming his way, Leslie could have counted 1980 as a success, had it not been that the musical career on which he had set his heart had come to a disastrous close. When his contract expired with Polydor, they declined to give him another. Leslie spoke of this a few years later on the radio, saying that the Polydor executive responsible for his contract, Fung Tim-chi, told him that the response to his two records had not been what they'd hoped, so he was now free to choose his own recording company. This was, of course, merely a polite way of saying that any further contract would not be with Polydor.[131] Leslie was so mortified by this news that he hid it from his friends. When he finally summoned up the courage to tell them, he lied to them and told them that he had quit.

Leslie, Danny, Paul, and the rest of their set carried on burning the candle at both ends that year at all the usual places. Leslie carried on mixing this with dating girls, and one female romantic interest was noted in the press. This was a girl named Shirley Yim Suet Lee, who was introduced to Leslie by her sister, the actress Michelle Yim Wai-ling. Leslie was not happy about this press speculation and soon made plain in public that they were not in a relationship.[132] This was not surprising, for at the time Leslie was experimenting with what was to be his most intimate and longest lasting relationship with a woman. It was one that would cause deep turmoil in Leslie's life, though news of this did not surface for another four to five years until, in 1985, Commercial Radio broadcast his radio autobiography. In this broadcast, Leslie rather unwisely revealed that he had lived for some time with a girl whom he had first met in a disco, whom he introduced to his family, but who eventually "swindled" him in love.[133] He made the rather startling allegation that she had tried to cheat him out of a car and that in the ensuing quarrel he had felt so threatened by her gangster associates that he had fled his home and stayed for a while in a hotel. After the programme was broadcast, a girl named Kai Yee-lin made a statement to the media threatening legal action should Leslie identify her as the girl, declaring that she and Leslie had lived together for six months from January to July 1980. Leslie, she said, had given her a Chopard watch and Cartier earrings (which, if he did, was quite something at the time, as he was by then earning only HK$3,000 a month).[134] She also claimed to have herself put down the deposit of HK$10,000 for a car, money which had apparently gone missing. Despite the fact, she said, that she had not had sex with Leslie during the entire six months they cohabited, Leslie had proposed marriage to her. She further revealed that after they separated she had tried to commit suicide. Leslie would corroborate some of this fourteen years later when he stated that he had thought about marrying a girl but that she had a nervous breakdown.[135] At the time of the broadcast, in 1985, Leslie was forced to respond to the media. Though he was careful not to name the girl involved, he did not deny Kai Yee-lin's statements that they had cohabited and that they had not had sex. He did, however, deny much of the rest of her account, including her claim that he had proposed to her. They had separated, he said, because of an accumulation of incompatibilities. He added that she had hurt him deeply and that he still hated her.

How is one to consider these extraordinarily embarrassing revelations? It seems established that in the first half of 1980 Leslie was making a long-term effort to live with a woman, but if Kai Yee-lin is right, and Leslie did not deny this, the two had not had sex. If this is so, the most simple explanation is that Leslie seems to have been making a genuine attempt to conform to what was expected of him by society, his studio, his family, and maybe even himself—but that the attempt had failed.

One slight indication that his family's wishes may have played a part (for it was only now five years since the sad affair at Eccles Hall) is found in the statement Leslie gave the press, which mention his family's assistance in the handling of the scandal when it broke in 1985. They had helped him, he said, and in particular he credited his eldest sister Ophelia with managing the matter with discretion. Whatever the reasons for the affair, the outcome would be great public humiliation. At the time, his failure to make a success of this relationship can only have hurt Leslie badly.

This was Leslie's second proposal of marriage in two years. In retrospect, one might suggest that Leslie was perhaps interested more in the marital state than in the identity of his bride. It looks very much as though he was still hoping that he could live a heterosexual life, fulfil his family's hopes, and advance his career. If he thought this in 1978 and 1980, these experiences disillusioned him and he did not repeat them. By the age of twenty-four, Leslie ceased to seek a female partner.

***

While all this was happening, Leslie carried on enjoying himself in Hong Kong's bars, discos, and saunas. All through 1980 and into 1981, Danny Chan and his set remained the major influence in Leslie's life. Their friend Jimmy Ngai later described the pair as being very close when they were shooting the movies *Encore* and *On Trial*. They were, said Jimmy Ngai, doing pretty much the same things as other youngsters did in their leisure time: going to discos (and Ngai made it clear that he meant gay discos), playing mahjong, watching movies, eating, and drinking. They were both young and restless and were going out most of the time and sleeping very little. The strain of this double life must have been considerable. [136]

The growing rivalry between Danny and Leslie was at first kept to their work. They often played mahjong, sometimes with Leslie's old *amah*, Luk Che, who had by then retired from the Cheung family's service and was living in Quarry Bay.[137] Leslie was at this stage still renting a flat in Lai Wan, which at this time was still a quiet suburb completely unlike the concrete sprawl of Lai Chi Kok, which later subsumed it. From here, Leslie took the bus to visit Luk Che, travelling through the new tunnel that now linked Hong Kong Island to Kowloon. He always visited her if she was sick and sometimes took his friends along. Leslie and Danny's circle included Jimmy Ngai, who was a producer with Commercial Radio,[138] and Paul Chung and D.J. Suzie Wong, who hosted Ngai's shows.[139]

Without a record-company contract, Leslie made no recordings at all in 1981, and his agent managed only to secure him a slot in a variety show at a small venue inside the City Hall on 17 May.[140] Danny's career was now rocketing skywards, leaving Leslie far behind. Danny was with EMI, with whom he produced the successful album *No More Tears*, and in 1981 he signed with Warner Brothers. His first albums with them, *Encore* and *Sunflower*, brought him to the peak of his popularity. His relationship with Leslie could not survive this yawning gulf of fame. Their friendship waned, then hit the rocks.

As the pair drifted away from each other, the party spirits in Hong Kong's disco community were dampened as the Hong Kong Government unleashed an anti-gay witch-hunt in the colony. High-profile figures in the administration and the Royal Hong Kong Police were placed under investigation, prosecuted, and had their careers terminated or stalled. This calamity stemmed from arrests of homosexuals in 1979 and the death the following year of a twenty-nine-year-old Scottish police inspector, John MacLennan. Under threat of prosecution for alleged gross indecency with eight male Chinese prostitutes, MacLennan was found dead in his locked police quarter with five revolver bullet wounds to his body. The inquest refused to accept that the death was suicide and pronounced an open verdict. An inquiry ensued and the witch hunt following the case paralysed much of the gay community. This was not a time for being out about the town.

Despite their growing coolness, Leslie and Danny continued to appear together in the first half of 1981, combining in a fundraising concert for their friend Paul Chung, who had injured his leg while shooting a TV drama. Leslie performed first and Danny second, and the audience made it very plain that they preferred Danny.[141]

So Leslie's hopes of a musical career remained unfulfilled in 1981, and his career continued to be based on TV performances. As showings of *Pairing* drew to a close, his first new TV series of the year was yet another teenage drama, the mundane soap *Make a Wish*,[142] one of the growing number aimed at a teenage audience whose economic clout was growing with Hong Kong's increasing wealth. The martial-arts sequel, *Tai Chi Master II*, made in 1980, showed on TV; it, like *Pairing*, gave him little chance to demonstrate acting ability.[143] However, Leslie was becoming a TV symbol for this new generation, and his boyish looks made it easy for him still to take teenage parts. In *Agency 24* he was cast as Mike, a designer, who, in another story with echoes of Leslie's own career, leaves his job to become a singer, only to find himself exploited financially by his manager.[144] Leslie appeared here with his close friend, Paul Chung, and with Annie Ngai, his co-star in *Under the Same Roof*, who became one of the "romantic interests" with which the studio and the press credited Leslie that year. Leslie and Annie seem to have enjoyed each other's company and saw each other occasionally during the time they worked together in TV soaps. Leslie also took a small role in a TV show named *Hong Kong '81*, in which he sang several songs including the Carol King favourite "You've Got a Friend."

Leslie's shows got good ratings, but his TV station, RTV, was going through bad times. It was losing badly in the ratings war with TVB, was making less revenue, and as a result was making fewer shows. It was about to save itself by reorganisation and re-branding as ATV but this would not help its stars for a while.

The career in film that *Encore* had seemed to presage did not take off soon enough to improve Leslie's position. The one film in which he found a role in 1981 was a mediocre flop that was almost immediately forgotten, but it provoked the crisis that destroyed Leslie's friendship with Danny Chan.

It was typical of studio attempts to capitalise on what had already made money that an attempt was made immediately to repeat the success of 1980's *Encore*. Clarence Fok Yiu-leung (also known as Clarence Ford) directed a derivative project with the cast of *Encore*. This was *On Trial* (sometimes known as *Job Hunter*), which first screened on 26 August.[145] Once again, Danny Chan (typically and unimaginatively cast as Danny) and Paul Chung (similarly cast as Paul) played kids from a rich family whose schoolmate, played by Leslie, was from a poor one.[146] Unable to compete, Leslie's character turns to drugs, dying of an overdose, while Danny writes a winning song and makes it big. That this was such a gratuitous piece of art imitating life was made worse for Leslie by the perfect singing performance turned in by Danny. *On Trial* screened over a week during the late summer of 1981, grossed about HK$2.7 million and gained Danny Chan Best Supporting Actor at the 3rd Hong Kong Film Awards the next year, beating Leslie, who had also been nominated.

The collapse in Leslie and Danny's friendship came during the negotiations for the making of *On Trial*. Danny had refused to appear in the film if Leslie did, despite the fact that Leslie was again billed below him. Leslie recounted this incident in his radio autobiography, claiming that Danny knew his filmmaking skills were not as good as his. This was true, and director Clarence Fok insisted on casting Leslie. Danny might be a rising star in the world of music but he was not a successful enough actor to get away with this sort of prima donna behaviour and he eventually had to yield, though he worked with Leslie very unwillingly and made his discontent plain on the set.[147] This must have been the final straw for Leslie, who got his own back in public at the preview launching *On Trial*. He announced to the startled press that he would not in future collaborate with Danny in any way, either in a movie or in a musical performance.[148] It was something of a pyrrhic victory, for the end of their friendship left Leslie lonely and nursing a long-lasting bitterness. Jimmy Ngai later recalled that Leslie told him that he had done a lot for Danny, even at the lowest point of his own career, but that Danny never remembered it. But Leslie did.[149]

Leslie had for some time been burning the candle at both ends, working busily on TV soaps in the day, indulging in the evenings and nights in the pleasures of Hong Kong's gay scene with Danny whilst trying, at least on the surface, to lead a heterosexual life. By the middle of 1981, the pressures of this were proving too great. Leslie had failed in his live-in relationship and had been turned down twice for marriage. Now his friendship with Danny Chan was collapsing. His singing career seemed to be at an end. TV work was drying up. As Leslie's private life went steadily off the rails, the TV studio could but notice the effect upon his morale and offered Leslie less and less of the little work they still had.

There was a period of about three months this year when it seems that Leslie could not work. He had to take time out.

Leslie's agent, K.K. Tam, decided it was time to get Leslie away from the atmosphere that was paralysing him in Hong Kong, and he set out to do so by getting him some international exposure.[150]

He guessed, rightly as it proved, that foreign gigs would give Leslie the chance to practise before audiences less hypercritical than those of Hong Kong. They might very well give him back his confidence. Leslie had been unlucky, Tam told the *Hong Kong Standard*, but he had hopes that this would change. Leslie told the *Standard* that he thought so too and that he liked to sing. He'd keep cutting records when the opportunity appeared. He still felt, though this was not to last, that his agent Tam would get him a great chance. So, in September 1981 Leslie set off to tour Singapore and Thailand.[151] At the time, Hong Kong TV programmes were frequently shown all over Southeast Asia and the faces of stars of their soaps, including Leslie's, were well known, so there was a good prospect that people would be curious enough to come and see him in the flesh. And so it proved. The workload of the tour was heavy but the financial rewards were lucrative; at one point Leslie sang two performances a day for twenty-one days without a break. The concerts gained Leslie a following across the region, something he would build on later. Audiences in Thailand proved particularly enthusiastic, mostly due to the facts that they were keen on martial-arts dramas and that Thai TV had just shown *The Spirit of the Sword*. He later recounted to Commercial Radio that he used to get fan mail from Thailand, which made him realise that he had made a name for himself there.[152] So successful did these concerts prove that Leslie would return to Southeast Asia four times to perform in solo concerts over the next three years.

The tour gave Leslie sufficient money to put down a deposit on a house in Hong Kong's New Territories near the country town of Yuen Long, not far from the border with China.[153] This was in Fairview Park (Gam Sau Fa Yuen) a development built in 1976 in a location that at the time was remote and from which commuting to town could only be done by a long journey via bus and train. Daily travel to the studio would have been very tiring, so Leslie was not to live there permanently, but it was his first investment in property and started him off on what would become a profitable trail of real-estate purchases. His trips to Thailand also made him friends there, including the famous Chinese actress of the sixties, Ka Ling, who had married a Thai and settled there. Leslie would remain good friends with her for many years.[154]

Now refreshed and fully recovered from the problems of earlier in the year, Leslie was hired by Shaw Brothers to make a romantic movie called *Teenage Dreamers* (the film's Chinese name actually translates as *Lemon Cola*). This time, happily, the film did not feature Danny Chan and for the first time in film Leslie was given the lead,[155] reverting here to the "boy next door" image he had established on TV and playing, once more despite his age of twenty-five, a love-struck teenager. Leslie's boyish looks still allowed him to get away with playing teenage roles, though he himself wondered in an interview he gave the *Hong Kong Standard* at the time just how much longer that could last. When the film screened over two weeks from March to April in 1982, it became the best-grossing teenage film in Hong Kong to date, and won its director, Clifford Choi, Best Director at the Hong Kong Film Awards in 1983.

Leslie both wrote and sang songs for the soundtrack. He later claimed (perhaps with some tongue in cheek) to have felt rather jaundiced about this, believing the film company was merely trying to save money. He told his radio audience a few years later that he had asked the film company to get a songwriter, but they had been too cheap to do so and had just sent someone over from the marketing department to help with the lyrics.[156] It was good experience though, and the start, if not a totally enjoyable one, of what would be a long song-writing career. There were other aspects of the movie that Leslie did not much like. On location in Macau, he was asked to share a room with the lighting engineer. He wasn't prepared to accept this treatment and, though he was not well paid, he rented a room out of his own pocket.

Leslie had proved a success the first time he took a leading role on the big screen. From this point, he could with justice have claimed to be a second-tier movie star. Leslie was pleased with his performance and with the film. At last he had been given the opportunity to do something he liked, and he retained fond memories of *Teenage Dreamers*, which was the first teenage movie in Hong Kong to earn more than HK$5 million at the box office. He had at last done something that Danny Chan could not claim to have achieved.

1981 had been a time of trial, but Leslie had come through, and, though he could not have been sure about it then, he had begun to turn the corner.

CHAPTER 5

FRESH WIND, NEW WAVES

1982 – 1984

The year 1982 did not start well. Leslie's agent made no progress in getting him a recording contract, so Leslie cut no records, though he did start to record some new tracks. Even occasional gigs dried up until Leslie was booked for a single night's concert in August. Only one TV show came his way in the first part of that year, ATV's *The Cheap Detective*, a very distant Hong Kong echo of that year's *Columbo*, the detective spoof starring Peter Falk.[157] This so discouraged Leslie that in May 1982 he announced that he would quit TV and concentrate on making films and singing.[158]

In April, Leslie was interviewed about the film *Teenage Dreamers* by Evans Chan of the *Hong Kong Standard*.[159] He disclaimed any intention of leaving acting, adding that he thought it unlikely he would ever become a director. Chan described him as being soft, temperamental, and outspoken, even presumptuous at times. This was Leslie's first brush with the darker side of the media and it would, unfortunately, initiate a pattern that would dog his career and which would give him considerable unhappiness. Cattily, Chan wrote that on close inspection Leslie's face had slight wrinkles and that there were some white hairs amongst his well-styled locks. Leslie was all of twenty-five, and this must have been meant to irritate him, especially as Chan had quoted him acknowledging that he was quite vain and that he wouldn't mind being a sex symbol. The reporter made blatant hints at Leslie's sexual orientation, quoting him as saying that some directors apparently enjoyed watching him do sex scenes. Leslie's good looks, Chan thought, were rather androgynous, something Leslie was aware of, as he complained in the interview that people used to scoff at his "sissiness." All this was despite the fact that the film that was supposedly the focus of the interview was a very traditional boy-meets-girl story with no hint of effeminacy in the character Leslie played or in the way he played it. It is clear that some people, particularly those who didn't like him in the media, were intent on labelling Leslie gay from the very start of his career.[160]

Though his hope of success as a singer must have seemed much like wishful thinking at the time, he now had better reason to believe that his prospects were better in the cinema. Early in the year, Leslie starred with his friend Paul Chung in Chan Chuen's *Energetic 21*, yet another teenage film.[161] Leslie's role of Ben, the "Red Devil" of an illegal racing fraternity, was a reversion to the "bad boy" type he had last played in *On Trial*. It was ironic that "Red Devil" Leslie had only got his driving licence that summer. Hong Kong audiences were unimpressed and the film flopped when it showed over two weeks from September to October. The formula was already tired.

Change, however, was in the air.[162] Hong Kong's film industry was growing up and was searching for stories with new themes and local styles. Directors, actors, and technicians who had been trained in the TV world were moving out into the film industry, where they could make more money and win more artistic freedom. The result was the birth of Hong Kong's "New Wave," whose filmmakers adapted and expanded different styles into a mélange of Chinese and Japanese culture, Western *avant-garde,* and urban themes. Something peculiarly local was emerging.

This was aided by the fact that the amount of film made in Hong Kong was increasing exponentially, for the industry was very profitable and its sales were rapidly rising in both in Hong Kong and abroad. This attracted investors from Southeast Asia, Taiwan, South Korea, and Japan, and their new money encouraged innovation and greater artistic freedom. In the eighties, a number of new film companies rose to challenge the big studio monopolies, many of them so small that they had no studio of their own and filmed entirely on location, just as their crews had done in their TV days. Leslie recalled the buzz of this period in his radio autobiography, saying that after returning from his overseas singing tours he discovered that the movie industry was booming. Several production companies offered him parts.[163]

In the midst of this, director Patrick Tam Kar Ming's film *Nomad* at last gave Leslie the chance to star in a full length feature film of artistic significance.[164] *Nomad*'s reputation was made not so much from any box office takings (these were mediocre; it grossed HK$2.3 million in the single week that it ran in December), but from the fact that it was a critical success, so much so that it soon came to be seen as *the* film which captured Hong Kong's *zeitgeist*. It was a film about a society torn up from conservative roots and unsure of where it was going, whose young people were ensnared in materialism and had lost the spiritual compass by which the older generation had steered. Leslie played Louis: rich, hedonistic, and a member of the upper middle class that was the fruit of Hong Kong's economic success. His set has it all but wonders what good it has done them. Their confused response is summed up at one point by Louis in a line that reverberated in Hong Kong: "What society? We are society." The film attempts no answer to this quest for purpose and as its credits roll to the melancholy theme music (which was sung at both the end and beginning of the film by Leslie, here for once given a song in which he could invest his feelings), a ship sails to Arabia. Why, we are not sure; a symbol, perhaps, of a forlorn hope of escape to a never-never dream land somewhere else.

Leslie only later came to regard *Nomad* as his first real movie and was ambivalent about his role at the time.[165] Patrick Tam made clever use of his androgynous prettiness to get away from heroic stereotypes and customary certainties. In the process he made Leslie a symbol of what the New Wave saw was happening to Hong Kong, but it was an image with which Leslie may not have been entirely comfortable, for Louis is something of a sissy throughout the film. At their first meeting, taxi driver Pong accuses him of being a "sister" and kisses him fully on the lips to make sure the message gets across. This goads Louis to fight, which he does very badly, and pretty soon is reduced to running away from the fight. He acquits himself a little more bravely in the film's final scene, but even then he has to be rescued by his girlfriend. The film treats Leslie as hot but somehow unmanly, attractive yet vulnerable.[166] It was an image that would recur.

Around this time, Leslie sold his place in Fairview Park and moved to a much more conveniently located flat in Robinson Road on Hong Kong Island.[167] In August came his only singing slot in Hong Kong that year (though he toured again in Southeast Asia during it), a concert on 10 August in the Academy Hall of the Baptist College. He was interviewed before the show in front of the audience, jokingly suggesting that he wanted not to be a singer but to be a reporter. He was putting on a brave front for he knew that he really needed to make a good impression that night. He did not, alas, succeed. Leslie sang Rita Coolidge's "We're All Alone" (with its well-known refrain "Close the window, calm the light"). It was a song which, in its higher and more powerful moments, was still beyond his capabilities. He'd been working on his technique but as yet, at nearly twenty-six, he had yet to achieve the range and depth he needed to make a breakthrough.[168]

Things were definitely not helped by the fact that at this juncture Leslie and his agent K.K. Tam fell out over money. Suspicions led to accusations, and their relationship degenerated so badly that eventually the issue ended up in court, where Leslie lost the case. Apart from the fact that he now had no agent and little money, this dispute put Leslie's singing career even further on hold. The few songs that he had managed to record during the year were not released.

It was in 1982, though, that a series of events occurred which were to change the course of Leslie's life, and this came about through film.[169]

The Shaw Brothers director Richard Yeung Kuen was planning to make a film called *The Drummer*, in which he meant to include original songs which he wanted Leslie to sing. Yeung was frustrated by the difficulties of using Leslie's recordings, which had been frozen by the dispute with his agent, and when the court case was over, he suggested to Leslie that he join Capital Artists, the entertainment company and record label, one of whose leading executives was Michael Lai, whom of course Leslie knew very well. Lai had several times given him a leg up in his career and was now about to do so again, this time more substantially. Leslie told of all this later in his radio autobiography, relating how Yeung had introduced him to Florence Chan, then a manager at Capital Artists. She had asked him how much money he had in mind, but he told her that he didn't think money was an issue. All he wanted to do was to release the songs he had recorded. The result was a two-year contract for twenty-four cuts with Capital Artists. Leslie's singing career was back on the road.

Florence Chan, who managed the Capital Artists recording department, had been in the audience in 1977 when Leslie sang "American Pie."[170] There is little doubt that Michael Lai and she were taking a considerable risk in signing Leslie. They knew his singing career had hit a wall, and they must have been aware of the deterioration in Leslie's TV career that had set in only a few months before. Signing him was a commercial gamble, based though it was on an estimation of his potential, which Lai had been able to make at close range over the previous five years. It was also an act of considerable kindness on Lai's part, a deliberate attempt to give Leslie a helping hand, and Leslie was to hold Lai in grateful veneration for the rest of his life, making him his artistic "godfather." Leslie had good reason to be grateful.

Capital Artists had just begun to focus their attention exclusively on TVB, which was just initiating their annual series of singing contests, the New Talent Singing Awards. Leslie's own five-year contract with ATV was expiring that year, so he also now signed with their rivals, TVB, where, contrary to the announcement he'd made in May that he would abandon TV, his contract would bring him two more years of work in TV soaps.

Just before migrating between channels, Leslie performed in an ATV concert at Sha Tin, then still a small country town in the New Territories.[171] Due to the block on the release of his new songs, he had nothing new to offer, so for this concert he fell back on singing other people's numbers. This mistake was compounded by the costume he wore, a strange see-through plastic coat over a simple vest. He wore a hat to cover up his lack of hair (he had shaved it off once more for the earlier ATV martial arts serial, Tai Chi Master II). He was booed immediately when he walked on stage, and when he threw his hat into the audience in the middle of a song, he had the humiliation of having it thrown back at him, causing the audience to boo even more and clap to simulate the rebound of his hat. It was only with great difficulty that he kept his composure and finished his programme, and when he finally got off stage and met fellow singer Elisa Chan Kit-ling, he burst into tears. The pain didn't end in the theatre. When he got home after the performance, he found that someone in the audience had obtained his phone number and had left a message on his answering machine, telling him to go back to school and not to embarrass himself further. He was still pale and shaken that night when he met his friend Jimmy Ngai in Disco Disco and related what had happened.[172] The incident scarred him. He would never forget this audience rejection and in later interviews and even concerts would go back over it again and again.

The last TV show Leslie made before he left ATV aired only the following year, in 1983. This was a production for RTHK named *Crossroads: Woman at 33*.[173] Leslie, here playing a composer and singer in his early twenties who falls for his teacher, was given a line to speak in this unconventional story that would come to seem, in retrospect, to encapsulate exactly Leslie's own approach to life:

> I think that no one in this world can decide what's possible between us… You must decide if you're living for others not yourself.

The film's soundtrack included songs recorded by Leslie, which gave a foretaste to audiences of the style of the music he had been working on that year. Cheng Pei-pei, the older female lead, remarked while they were making the film how beautiful she thought him, but also how unhappy and depressed he seemed. He had not yet shaken off the clouds which had enveloped him over the preceding year.

After he joined TVB in the summer of 1982, Leslie's life began to improve and he kicked off his time in his new studio, preparing for the TV soaps which would start showing in later years. TVB was where he first met the girl who was to become the closest female friend of his life, Anita Mui Yim-fong. Anita was six years younger than him and at this point in her career on her way to becoming a star, both as a singer and as an actress.[174] She was a girl from a very deprived background, something of a Hong Kong version of Edith Piaf, who had been forced when very young to support her family by performing in fun fairs, road-side Cantonese operas, clubs, and even on the streets. She had got her big break into the world of showbiz when, with her rendering of Paula Tsui Siu-fung's song "The Windy Season," she'd beaten about 3,000 other contestants to win the first of Michael Lai's New Talent Singing Awards on TVB. Capital Artists had then signed her up.

Anita Mui was feisty and unconventional. Labelled the Madonna of Hong Kong, her tough exterior hid a vulnerability that showed through sometimes in her work. Leslie and she were drawn to each other by the hardships of their past, as well as by an immediate attraction. Despite her youth, Anita was like a big sister, someone who would help out her friends without reservation or restraint, and Leslie was to her a big brother. After they first met at TVB, their friendship was permanent.

The clouds which had still eddied around Leslie in the first half of the year were starting to dissipate, not only in his professional career but also in his private life. On 9 December 1982, Leslie was in the Regent Hotel in Tsim Sha Tsui, a spectacular hotel on the tip of Kowloon, a very popular watering hole in the Christmas season as its huge plate-glass windows fronted directly onto the sea and gave the best view of the Christmas lights decorating both sides of the harbour. Across the room was a young man he found strikingly attractive. Leslie asked friends who he was and was surprised to find out that it was his childhood friend, Daffy Tong. Daffy was, of course, no longer the boy Leslie remembered. He was stylish, tall, and slim, with a long, good-looking, slightly angular face. He was well dressed and elegant, much more prosperous-looking than

Leslie—unsurprisingly, as it turned out that he was a banker with one of Hong Kong's principal firms. Leslie went over to speak to him and they hit it off. Intrigued, they arranged to meet after the New Year, and on 2 January 1983 went out together on their first date.[175]

This was the start of a relationship that would last for the next twenty years. The fact that each was to be the love of the other's life was not, though, clear to either of them at the start; it took a while before they could be sure. Their different worlds made being together difficult, if not hazardous. Daffy was a very private man climbing successfully in a highly conservative profession. Leslie was a performing artist who still had a career to make, a minor celebrity with a reputation for flamboyance and already the butt of scurrilous talk about his effeminacy, a man whose movements attracted public attention and growing media coverage. At a time when homosexuality even in private was still illegal and gay relationships were anathema in Hong Kong's conservative society, it was necessary to be very discreet indeed. It was very hard to do this in Hong Kong, a small place where everyone knew everyone else and where it was almost impossible to move around without being seen. Daffy's banking employers were unlikely to look kindly on any same-sex relationship, and it was almost inevitable that he would have lost his job had any news of such become public. Subterfuge and planning were necessary if they were to conduct an affair out of the public eye. Despite all this, Leslie and Daffy were sufficiently attracted to each other to try to make a go of it. Tentatively at first, they embarked on an affair.

Their childhood roles were reversed now, and despite their two-year difference in age, Leslie, the older of the two, called Daffy "Gor Gor," the Cantonese for *older brother*, perhaps because Daffy was now the taller or maybe because it was Daffy, the calmer, steadier foil to Leslie's mercurial wit and quick temper, who provided the stability Leslie needed. Daffy had the business expertise required to rescue Leslie's finances, which were by then in a real mess. His sporadic earning had been unable to cover the expenses of his lifestyle, and the costs of the court case he had lost had put him in debt. It would not be long before Daffy found himself making Leslie a loan of many months' salary to get him back on his feet. Yet though Daffy also had the common sense to manage the complications of their new lives, and the discretion to conduct their affair out of the prurient and prying eyes of the press, it was still very hard for both of them to make the relationship work. They tried this for some months in 1983, but the cards all seemed stacked against them and they decided to separate amicably. They stayed apart for something like a year to eighteen months, but neither found anyone else in that time, and neither could forget the other.[176]

***

The times were unsettled ones for Hong Kong.[177] In June 1983, Margaret Thatcher won the British general election, and, as Prime Minister, was reluctantly brought to face the fact that the hundred-year lease the British held for Hong Kong's New Territories would run out in 1997. Business needed to know what would happen after that date. Negotiations with the Chinese were necessary to decide Hong Kong's fate. Talks began but soon encountered difficulties due to Thatcher's refusal to countenance handing to a Communist government the parts of the territory (Hong Kong and Kowloon) that were according to treaty British in perpetuity. The news of break in negotiations leaked and led to a financial crisis in Hong Kong as confidence evaporated. The Hong Kong dollar fell in value by 20%, and its slide could only be halted by pegging it to the US dollar. The British found that the ground had been cut from under their feet, and by November they had no choice but to commence serious negotiations for the return of the whole colony to the motherland.

While these momentous events were unfolding, TVB gave Leslie the starring role in what was to be the very popular TV show *Once upon an Ordinary Girl*, which screened the following year.[178] Here for the first time he established himself in the role he was to play often in future, that of a sophisticated, hedonistic playboy. *Once upon an Ordinary Girl* was set in the Hong Kong of the period just before the Japanese invasion of 1941. It had a lot of style: vast houses, fast sports cars, elegant clothes, and glittering parties, and was a perfect setting in which Leslie could show off his all boyish good looks and poise. Audiences loved the series and fell in love with him. Once again Leslie sang the show's theme song, this time a number by Michael Lai titled "I'm of Strong Sentiment." Theme songs were a way to get back into popular favour, and Leslie never ceased using them to build his singing career.

Leslie's next film, *The Drummer*, the making of which had brought him to Capital Artists the year before, finally saw the light of day in March 1983.[179] Leslie (who had been twenty-six when making the film) once more played a teenager, this time one whose dream was to become a drummer, a choice of career completely against the wishes of his father. Despite the attraction of its original musical score, which left a lasting legacy in Leslie's song "Swimming Up Slowly," the film bombed and closed after only five days. Leslie's next project, *First Time*, which screened for twelve days in May, was more successful, though only financially.[180] It was a drama totally unlike the American comedy of the same name that came out that year (the Hong Kong industry of the day made a practice of continually aping Hollywood films, stealing names, plots, and much else, though usually managing in the process to reduce the quality of the original ideas). Leslie got prime billing but the film was swiftly forgotten. The studio made some effort to manufacture a romantic interest between Leslie and his female lead, Jean Yung Jing-Jing, with whom he'd earlier starred in *Encore*, but that effort too sank without trace.

During this time, Michael Lai and Florence Chan got down to work at Capital Artists to develop a singing style and repertoire to suit Leslie's voice, along with an image for him in keeping with the times and his own personality.[181] In the five years he had known him, Michael Lai had noted Leslie's ability to sing over two octaves, which gave him a flexibility denied to many singers, as well as his talent for absorbing and expressing the emotion of a song. Given the right numbers and suitable promotion, Michael Lai thought, he could make Leslie a star.

The process of re-making Leslie's singing career had commenced back in 1982 and was not a swift one. It included a fact-finding reconnaissance to Japan.[182] By this time, Japanese music and fashion had won a huge influence in Hong Kong so Capital Artists had invested in the Japanese music industry, acquiring rights to some of its music. Lai took Leslie to the Tokyo Music Festival in 1983, ostensibly to watch a performance by a Capital Artist band, the Tiger Kids, but in reality to open Leslie's eyes to what was happening in Japan and to let him listen to live performances by Japanese stars. It was no coincidence that the two albums he was to issue over the next year would both contain songs which originated in Japan; they were the hits which established Leslie as a star.

Michael Lai also exposed Leslie to the talent that was then forging the new Cantopop world in Hong Kong. Now that he was with TVB, Leslie had the opportunity to get to know its stars. He began what was to become a habit over the next few years of attending the station's annual pop song awards.[183] His appearances bemused those who knew perfectly well that he would win nothing there. Few singers without the chance of an award would bother to turn up to the ceremonies, but Leslie was seen again and again in the front row. This got him noticed in the profession and in the media. It was also hard for Leslie to stomach, having to watch others winning and listen to their songs. It made it worse that through this time

Danny Chan's career was so enormously successful. One of Leslie's friends went with him to one of Danny's concerts and remembers:

> I sat next to Leslie at Danny Chan's concert in Hung Hom. Leslie was very, very sad throughout the concert and his clapping was perfunctory, mechanical.[184]

It was the title track of the album they were now working on, *The Wind Blows On*, which set Leslie on the path to stardom.[185] Produced personally by Michael Lai, this album, Leslie's first with the label, had twelve tracks of Cantonese songs and was, unsurprisingly, permeated by Japanese influences. For instance, the title track "The Wind Blows On" (which is often translated slightly differently, for instance as "The Wind Continues to Blow") was a version of "Last Song for You," a hit by the Japanese star Momoe Yamaguchi. The album was, though, no mere derivative recording and there was very little that wasn't new. Changed, too, was the Leslie of the earlier albums and performances. His voice was now softer, more romantic; here, at last, emerged the smooth, almost husky timbre of shot silk that would from now distinguish Leslie's performances. The melancholy of his tone matched perfectly the sadness and nostalgia of his songs. The "chicken" thinness which had marred his earlier singing had vanished.

The album cover indicated the new approach. It featured a close-up, full-face portrait of Leslie's face, staring provocatively with sultry eyes straight at the camera (and so, of course, at the record buyer). The cover fast established the iconic image of what fans came to believe was the most beautiful male face in Hong Kong.

Making a hit takes more than creating an outstanding album, and now Capital Artists' professionalism came into its own. Unsurprisingly, given that Leslie was not rated in Hong Kong as a singer, when the album was released there was little initial reaction.

Capital Artists pulled the stops out to get the record on air, but large numbers only began to be sold as people began to write in to radio shows demanding that it be played. Gradually, over the weeks that followed, the album became a hit, especially with young girls, who now formed the beginnings of Leslie's future fan base.[186] *The Wind Blows On* moved steadily up the charts and eventually sold so well that it won Leslie his first Golden Disc Award. The album established him as a singer; unsurprisingly, it was the one that always meant the most to him. When he opened a café many years later and placed his most important things on display there, it was the disc of this album that he displayed.[187]

Capital Artists increased Leslie's exposure by arranging gigs for him in big hotels across the city. Many of the stars of the time sang in hotel piano lounges, where programmes were short and the money was good.[188] Florence Chan, designated Leslie's manager, a reflection of the new success his album was achieving, planned to expand his reach into the Taiwanese market, and took both Leslie and Anita Mui to Taipei perform on TV.[189] This started a link that was to blossom into a relationship with a new Taiwanese recording Company, Rock Records, with which Leslie would work in future. The trip was also the first of many that Leslie made abroad with Anita, who was by now a firm friend.

Leslie's next overseas tour was, though, conducted on his own. Leaving Hong Kong in the early autumn, just after he released his album, he embarked on a testing and ambitious trip, first to the by-now-familiar Singapore and Bangkok, then on further to new pastures in the United States.[190] He opened his show in New York, after which he took the show to Atlantic City. Driving from place to place in a rented Thunderbird, Leslie was accompanied by an old school friend, Alex Law Kai-yui, the writer and director, who had known him first as Bobby Cheung and had made *Island Stories*,[191] and was studying at the time in the States. He skipped classes to accompany Leslie to Atlantic City, where Leslie sang in the casino, a daunting gig for a young Chinese singer so far unexposed to audiences in the West. Conditions were primitive for artists below top of the bill. The pair found when they arrived that there was no makeup, no hairdresser, and no costume support, and Leslie was forced to iron his own shirt. Leslie did so, but as he hadn't noticed that the iron wasn't plugged in, Alex Law ended up doing it for him while Leslie went out to have a look at the stage. The gig, though, went without a hitch, proved a great success and vindicated Michael Lai's faith in his protégé.

Capital Artists reinforced the success of Leslie's first album by issuing a second featuring Leslie later in 1983. Known by several English titles, usually as *Craziness*, sometimes as *A Bit of Craziness*, the twelve Cantonese tracks included several songs that became hits, including "Deep Affection for You" and the title track, "A Bit of Craziness."[192] The album confirmed Leslie's growing reputation as a star now much in public demand. His life started to take on that bit of craziness that pop-star status inevitably endows and which Leslie would never now live without. His commitments to music, film, and TV, with the photo shoots and publicity events surrounding them, became so heavy that he was reported now as managing to find time for only four hours' sleep a night.

Leslie moved home again during this year, this time to a newly built flat at Taikoo Shing on the north of Hong Kong Island, where he rapidly charmed his neighbours, carrying their shopping for them and signing autographs for their children.[193] After he and Daffy had parted, he had tried dating other men, but though he established some friendships this year, at least one of which was to last his lifetime, none of these led to a relationship. He found no one to compare with Daffy, and neither he nor Daffy could forget the other. Sometime around the end of the year, they decided to give things another go. Though, like any partners, they were destined to quarrel and even fight in years to come, and though the difficulties of a relationship in the spotlight would get worse, not better, as time passed, they would never break up again. For each, the other was the love of his life and they were to stay together now, whatever the pressures and difficulties, for the next twenty years. Leslie's days of going to saunas, bars, and discos looking for love were over.[194]

Just before Christmas 1983, Leslie's third film of the year, *Little Dragon Maiden*, opened in Hong Kong cinemas.[195] Shaw Brothers, attempting to jump onto an artistic bandwagon, wanted this film to be seen as a New Wave movie, but it was in fact a reversion to their older-fashioned *wu xia* or swordplay films. This one was very loosely based on Jin Yong's epic, *Return of the Condor Heroes*— so loosely, in fact, that it turned out to be a film unlike anything seen before in Hong Kong. It was a bizarre fairy tale set in a fabled "martial world" peopled by Taoist fighters, supernaturally powerful maiden kung-fu fighters, and a ten-foot-high monster bird, with a colourful screenplay matched by lavish and outlandishly fanciful costumes. Leslie took star billing as the destitute and rather disreputable youth Yang Guo, who for some reason is taken up by the much tougher Little Dragon Maiden of the title, played by Jean Yung Jing-Jing, here billed as Mary Jean Reimer. He spends the film being beaten, thrashed, and thrown from cliffs, the camera lingering on shots of a bound, bloodied, and bruised Leslie with his clothes ripped or whipped from his back. Throughout the film Yang Guo is bullied, insulted, and treated as a coward, and although he develops martial-arts skills as the film goes on, he is never up to fighting the villains, to whom he loses time after time. He is victimised by almost everyone in the plot.[196] The character recalled that of Louis in *Nomad*, and Leslie's handling of the part echoes his coy performance in *Erotic Dream of Red Chamber*. *Little Dragon Maiden* was the film where his comic flair came to the fore for the first time; he clearly had huge fun making it and at times showed that he could be very funny indeed. Leslie had never been called upon to make people laugh before; studios now saw that he could.

Yet despite the cult status it was to achieve, *Little Dragon Maiden* was not a success at the time; Hong Kong audiences were not sure what to make of it and the film closed after a week. It was just too zany.

***

Although it wasn't recognised then, the following year, 1984, turned out to be the high water mark of Leslie's career as a TV performer, for in this year he starred in a TVB serial that was to become a Hong Kong classic, a twenty-episode period drama (the only one of this type he made with TVB) titled *The Fallen Family*. It ran until 1985.[197] He co-starred here for the first time with Maggie Cheung Man-yuk, recent runner-up in the Miss Hong Kong pageant, now turned actress and following a path to success common among Hong Kong's female stars. They became lifelong friends and were to work together often in the future. Leslie once more sang the show's theme song, this one entitled "Living Like a Dream," and, with actress singer Susanna Kwan Kuk-ying (Michael Lai's wife), sang another of its songs, "Only You in the Heart." The show was highly popular, but it was the last soap in which Leslie was to take the leading role.

For from now on, following Michael Lai's advice, Leslie determined to concentrate both on his singing career, which was at last really taking off, and on film, where he had been gradually building up a solid reputation. His career had at last passed beyond the point at which it required the regular income and public exposure provided by television. He owed TV a great deal; it had laid the foundations for his professional success, but he was about to leave it behind.

With his next album, Leslie cemented his claim to Cantopop stardom. Simply entitled *Leslie Cheung Kwok-wing*, it was issued in July 1984. It was almost always to be known by the name of its principal track as *Monica* (or by the combination *Leslie–Monica*) and proved to be a huge and immediate success.[198] Produced again by Michael Lai under the Taiyo Music Hong Kong label for Capital Artists, it had twelve Cantonese tracks, among which were several hits, including the highly popular song "H2O," and the biggest hit of all, the song "Thanks, Monica."[199] This was a simple, highly rhythmic, very lively, even raucous number, miles away from the reflective music of his successes of the previous year, and its impossible-to-forget refrain "Thanks…, thanks…, thanks…, thanks, Monica" soon caught on throughout Hong Kong.

Leslie and Michael Lai had based this song on a number, also entitled "Monica," that they had heard in Tokyo the year before, sung by the young Japanese singer Koji Kikikawa. Koji was a dramatically handsome man with a clean-cut, boyish appearance, someone very much in Leslie's new style. The year before, at the Tokyo show, Leslie had told Michael Lai that he thought he could make the song a hit in Hong Kong, so Capital Artists bought the copyright.

Leslie was proved right: "Thanks, Monica" won him his first platinum disc, made number one in the charts for seven weeks, and was to win Leslie both TVB Jade's 7th Top Ten Chinese Solid Gold Songs Award and Commercial Radio's 5th Chinese Pop Songs Award. *Wah Kiu Daily News*, which had unsuccessfully tipped him for success way back in 1977, made him their Top Ten Popular Artist this year. Leslie would sing "Thanks, Monica" in all his future concerts and, despite the earlier success of "The Wind Blows On," it is this song that is often viewed as the real start of his star status. He was at last in demand everywhere. It was, he said later, "a moment of brilliance."[200]

It was also the moment at which Leslie the singer overtook Danny Chan. When "Thanks, Monica" became a hit, Leslie's friends in Disco Disco congratulated him on beating Danny. "Who? Danny Who?" he replied.[201] Their sad breach was now some three years old, and the two singers continued to refuse to appear on the same stage in shows where they were billed together.

Michael Lai sought to build swiftly on the popularity that Leslie had achieved with "Thanks, Monica," and planned a concert tour in Singapore and Malaysia, once again with Anita Mui.[202] Leslie had been going to Southeast Asia now for some years and was very popular there both as singer and as a TV star. In his radio autobiography, made the next year, he described his time there with Anita, recalling that he had gone down with bronchitis on that trip. Anita told him to go back to his room to rest, then spent the whole night practising all his songs (there were more than ten) so that she could stand in for him on stage.

In the summer of that year, Leslie began work on another Shaw Brothers film, *Behind the Yellow Line* (the Chinese title is better translated as *Destiny*).[203] One of his co-stars was Maggie Cheung, with whom he was currently appearing in the TV drama *The Fallen Family* and who was appearing here in her first movie. She played Monica, in good Hong Kong movie fashion a name carefully chosen to remind the audience of Leslie's recent smash hit. Also for the first time on screen was Leslie's other co-star, Anita Mui. The film was a slight, romantic comedy set in and around stations of the territory's Mass Transit Railway (locally known as the MTR), where loudspeakers entreat passengers to wait for trains "behind the yellow line." Leslie sang a duet—the song "Fate"—with Anita on the discordant and disjointed soundtrack. The low quality of this movie didn't stop it from being Leslie's best hit at the box office to date, and it grossed over HK$8.5 million in the two weeks it screened in October. Its success propelled Leslie to the slot of number 16 actor in Hong Kong, way behind Jackie Chan at number 1 but now in front of Chow Yun-fat, who was ranked twentieth.

Leslie was by now a bankable star and began to earn money in commercial endorsements. The first to take advantage of his fame was Café de Coral, a Hong Kong restaurant group. In his first TV commercial for them, Leslie danced on a stage erected inside a swimming pool. The advertisement was repeated in a different format the following year, on that occasion Leslie appearing in one of the firm's restaurants surrounded by dancing children.[204] He also had a hit with "There Always Will Be Luck," the theme song for the period drama, *The Duke of Mount Deer*, made for Taiwanese TV by China Television Company and released in Hong Kong by TVB and Capital Artists.[205]

The studios and the media continued to conspire to create some female interest in Leslie's life. More mention was made of his long-standing friendship with Cindy Yeung Lok-si, whom he had continued to see until she went to study in the States. At that point the press, in typically unpleasant fashion, reported that Leslie had ended the "affair" by phone. This was most unfair to both of them, as they remained the friends they always had been. Leslie told the press the next year that she was like a "younger sister" to him.

As Leslie's career began to gather speed, the foundations of the world in which he lived began to move in worrying ways. In September came the Sino-British Joint Declaration on the Future of Hong Kong, in which the British recognised publicly that they would leave Hong Kong in 1997 and in which China promised to keep things as they were in the capitalist enclave for fifty years after that. There was almost universal doubt of China's good faith amongst the population, and the trickle of overseas emigration— to Canada, Australia, and elsewhere, a phenomenon that had long been a feature of Hong Kong society—grew over the next decade into a flood, as those with the wealth and the means to escape made their homes and established their right to passports elsewhere.

The year ended with the screening of two films in which Leslie had minor roles. The first, *Double Decker*, which screened for a week in December, was an uninspiring film about a group of aimless Hong Kong losers who turn to crime in the absence of any better ideas for getting ahead in life and meet predictably unsuccessful outcomes.[206] The only noteworthy thing about the film, which made no impact at the time, was that the score was written by Chris Babida, a well-known Hong Kong musician and composer, with whom Leslie was to work often in the future.

Clifton Ko Chi-sum's *Merry Christmas* appeared in cinemas a week later. This was a much more successful film, a light-hearted comedy about the accidents of love, aimed to appeal to old and young alike.[207] It was timed for the holiday season and ran to packed houses till early January 1985, grossing the very large sum of HK$25.7 million. This was the first of what was to be a long series of comedies that Leslie made for holiday audiences, and he clearly enjoyed himself in it immensely. He was still way down in the billing and appeared for little of the action. The leading man was Karl Maka, who, apart from being one of the founders of the film company which produced this film, Cinema City, was in his own right a very popular Hong Kong comedian. This movie brought Leslie to Cinema City, and it led to a contract, his first with a film company that went beyond the making of individual films.

Also with a part in *Merry Christmas* was Danny Chan, starring ahead of Leslie as Karl Maka's son. Despite his bigger role, he made it known that he was very unhappy that they were appearing together again. He had good reason to be so, for the film made it very clear who was the better actor, and it was not Danny. Leslie was at ease and genuinely funny while Danny hammed it up as if he were playing a TV soap. Leslie, as he had proved in *Little Dragon Maiden*, was a natural comedian. The film ends with him draped drunkenly but seductively over a sofa while the credits role. There was an almost unnoticed female lead, Loretta Lee Lai-chan, and the studios tried to link Leslie's name with hers, but the talk was allowed to die away after the film closed.[208]

The year had ended well. Leslie was now undoubtedly a pop star; the dream upon which he'd gambled everything in 1977 had come true. He was also an up-and-coming movie star. All this had enabled him to turn his back on the world of TV soaps he had been forced to endure till then. Success in his public life was matched with happiness in his private; he and Daffy had been with each other for over a year. The times of struggle were indeed behind him at last.

STAR

CHAPTER 6

STANDING UP

1985 – 1986

Michael Lai and Leslie now set out to build on the previous year's hit, "Thanks, Monica"; music was going to be the central theme of 1985. Much was expected by the public and Hong Kong magazines were soon calling this "the year of Leslie." The first fruits of their work appeared in May, when Capital Artists, again under the Taiyo Music Hong Kong label, brought out the Cantonese song collection *For Your Love Only* (which at times is also confusingly translated as *Falling in Love with You, Love for You Only, Honestly Loving You,* or just *Loving You*).[209] The ten-track album was another smash hit and from it three songs—"Fickle Love," "Young Girl's Dream" (which is also known in English as "Young Girl's Concern") and "I Do"—shot up the charts. Anther track, "Restless Wind" (which is also translated variously as "Uninhibited Wind," "Cool Wind," "Unruly Wind," or "Wild Wind"), also proved tremendously popular. The title track "Falling in Love with You" was a song that had been written earlier for Andy Lau Tak-wah, a singer then managed by Capital Artists, but a contractual dispute had prevented his singing it, so Michael Lai had given it to Leslie. Lai not only produced the album this time but also made a personal appearance, playing synthesizer and electric piano for "Young Girl's Dream." The album quickly sold over 250,000 copies in Hong Kong and was to win Leslie the two major radio stations' principal awards the next year, RTHK's 8th Top Ten Chinese Gold Songs Award and TVB Jade's Solid Gold Best Ten Award. It also propelled him to the winning position in Commercial Radio's 6th Chinese Pop Songs Awards. He had made a clean sweep.[210]

Leslie was very proud of this disc, as he indicated in his radio autobiography that year, narrating that he was proud of the response to his recent records, especially the latest one *For Your Love Only*. He said that Florence Chan had helped him a lot in dealing with record production issues. When he had asked her to produce the cover of *For Your Love Only* in white plastic, she had straight away placed an order in Japan. He also said how grateful he had been to Michael Lai. He had another man to whom to be grateful, too. On the cover of the album, Leslie wore a Les Must de Cartier Trinity three-gold band ring, a unique combination of three colours of gold created in 1924, when it was popularised by the gay French artist and film-maker Jean Cocteau. The ring was a gift from Daffy.

The year had kicked off to a good start. Two films he had made before his new contract with Cinema City now reached cinema screens. Neither of them, though, was of a quality or popularity to match Leslie's musical progress. He was drawing ahead rapidly as a Cantopop star, yet he didn't seem able to escape the B-movie bracket. The first of these films was released over two weeks in June, inaptly titled *The Intellectual Trio*, for there is not (amazingly, given that it was written by Wong Kar-wai) an intellectual in sight in this oddball comedy which has four, not three, main characters.[211] The irrelevance of the film was summed up in its closing scenes, which included a seemingly pointless vision of Leslie emerging from a shower in a night dress and black wig. Leslie was by far the best thing in this mediocre film and ignoring its inadequacy managed to look so happy that he virtually shone. Capital Artists' commercial savvy was on display again here: the soundtrack included "H2O," Leslie's hit of the previous year, and a duet, "Miracle," which he sang with Cantopop star Connie Mak Kit-man. Mak was in dispute at the time with Capital Artists and, like Leslie had been in 1982, was unable to release any albums. She always remained grateful to Leslie for asking her to sing with him in this film.

At the start of August, the second film he'd made earlier was released, this with Leslie billed as a "special guest." *Crazy Romance* was a comedy of errors and love about a couple of criminals. One, Wing (his own name, of course), was played by Leslie, here back to being a pretty boy, philanderer, and smart-aleck, a stylishly dressed womaniser with three or four girls on the go at one time.[212] At one point, his fellow playboy, Hung, played by Nat Chan, interrupts Wing's attempted seduction of a whole group of girls by sashaying in and loudly impersonating Wing's supposed gay lover. They revert to this stereotypical badinage later in the film when they draw up at a traffic light alongside an obviously camp gay couple waiting on the pavement. They make mock of this pair and, as they drive off, Wing strikes one of them in the crotch. Leslie must have had misgivings about elements of this rather crude comedy, though he was too professional to let them show.

The lacklustre films of the summer were topped by Capital Artists' release of another well-selling disc, *Summer Best Collection – All Because of You*.[213] Florence Chan later described Leslie around this very busy and exciting time, telling a reporter how handsome and boyish he was, as well as how outspoken. She described some of the problems this had caused her with the press. His lack of tact, she said, caused unnecessary misunderstandings between him and the media, so she'd been forced to accompany him during interviews and press conferences. Sometimes this made her angry, but she had never managed to stay annoyed with him for long. Each time, knowing that he had to face the music, he'd embrace her and talk about something else in such a lovable way that she just had to swallow all her reproaches.[214]

The issue of this latest album was timed to capitalise on the next big step in Leslie's career, a summer concert. Michael Lai judged that it was now time for Leslie to step back onto the open stage in front of a huge Hong Kong audience and show that he had what it took to be a Canto superstar. So in the summer of 1985, at the age of nearly twenty-nine, Leslie was booked to give his first series of concerts. The show was called simply *Leslie Cheung in Concert '85* and was staged in the 12,000-seat Hong Kong Coliseum, the territory's major venue.[215] A concert series there was the mark by which success or failure in Hong Kong's music industry was measured. Leslie performed over ten consecutive nights between 2 and 11 August.

He could not have been anything but highly nervous about launching this concert series in Hong Kong. It had been only four years since his Sha Tin audience had thrown his hat back at him. The memory of the incident was still raw, and since then he had only appeared live in public in Hong Kong in hotels. He recounted the story of the Sha Tin disgrace to his audiences in the Coliseum (as he would often do later) and told them that he hoped they'd treat him better, which, of course, this time, they did. In fact, they loved him and screamed his name till they were hoarse, showering him with bouquets of flowers. On one night the audience got so wildly out of hand that it mobbed the stage, nearly overwhelming the security guards; they had to regroup to force the fans back. Interviewed during the concert series by the press, Leslie spoke of the care he'd taken with preparation for this concert and showed some of the anxiety it caused him. He had, he said, swum sixteen laps of the pool every morning and jogged every night. He admitted that he had been under no illusions that he had to grasp this opportunity of singing in the Coliseum for the first time. It was make or break.[216]

In the event he more than made it. Leslie performance wowed the crowds with a song list that included his major hits: "Thanks, Monica," "H2O," "Loving You," "First Time," and "The Wind Blows On," plus two songs redolent of his earlier difficult years, "American Pie," which had started it all, and "Swimming Up Slowly," the song from *The Drummer* and his personal comment on how long it had taken him to get where he now stood.

The show's musical director, Michael Lai, himself made an appearance playing as a piano solo the theme from the TV show, *Once upon an Ordinary Girl*.[217] Anita Mui was Leslie's special guest star. She was herself about to give a first series of concerts in Hong Kong, and Leslie wanted to give her a taste of what she would face. She sang her popular number "Love Is Over" and did a couple of duets with Leslie. The ecstatic reaction of the audiences to her performance amply repaid Leslie's invitation. She never forgot the favour he'd done her. Many years later, she related that Leslie had told her that it had been his idea, not that of Capital Artists, for her to be his special guest. He did this, he said, because she was his best friend and because she needed the chance to test an audience's response ahead of her own show. Leslie added that when he heard the cheers for her during his concert, he knew she would make it.[218]

On one night there was an unexpected reunion. Leslie spotted Danny Chan in the audience with their mutual friend Paul Chung, so he spoke to the fans about their past friendship and called Danny onto the stage. Danny was by no means dressed for an appearance and looked taken aback to be invited, but he leaped up and they hugged each other then walked around the stage holding hands, singing "Encourage," one of Danny's songs. Everyone could see the genuine feeling between the two.[219] Another touching moment, one doubtless more arranged, came when Luk Che brought Leslie bird's nest soup to drink at the Coliseum, reducing Leslie to tears.

Leslie's first Hong Kong concerts were a huge success, watched by a total of over 60,000 people.[220] They brought him an income so large that, with Daffy's careful management, he was likely never to have money worries again.

His screen career, though, was still not matching up to his musical success, largely due to the kind of work he found himself offered, and there wasn't enough of it yet to fulfil his resolution to abandon all TV appearances. He was still making the occasional appearances for TVB, partly as a vehicle for his music, partly to fulfil contractual obligations. In 1985, this took the form of an uninspiring musical drama called *Mystery Love*.[221] He also made a rare joint appearance with Danny Chan on the *100,000 Hours* show commemorating the broadcasting landmark achieved that year by TVB.

Leslie's first film with Cinema City, which he had worked on earlier in the year, was released to run for two weeks in September. This was *For Your Heart Only*, directed by Raymond Fung Sai-hung, not a particularly successful director who had written *Merry Christmas* the year before.[222] Co-starring this time with Leslie was Jimmy Wong Shu-kei, who had played the younger Leslie character in the 1980 TV drama *The Spirit of the Sword*. They hit it off again, and Wong found Leslie just as friendly and considerate as he had been five years before. Leslie resumed their relationship where they'd left off, once again giving Wong lifts in his car on the way home after shooting. The film was notable more for the fact that it featured Leslie's own music throughout than for much artistic merit; it was pretty much a marketing vehicle for his songs. It was suggested in Hong Kong that *For Your Heart Only* started a new trend in light musical comedy, but it was in reality no more than teenage froth. At the twenty-eight years he was when he made the film, even Leslie was beginning to look a little too mature for this type of role, and it was a disappointing start artistically to his time with Cinema City. He must have wondered if his contract with them would bring only more of the type of movies in which he'd starred in the past.

1985 was the year in which Leslie bared his soul in a radio autobiography broadcast on Commercial Radio.[223] Being asked to tell of his life was a sure mark of his new star status and he set out to be (and promised in his talk that he would be) as honest as possible in telling the story of his life. His resulting indiscretions were to cause him a good deal of woe, teaching him that it was just not possible for a star in the public eye to avoid dissembling at times. The biggest problem the talk caused him was the huge embarrassment of the scandal that arose after his remarks about his "love swindler." As we have seen, he could only deny some of the allegations that surfaced at the time. In his talk, he made use of the failure of his cohabitation of 1981 to explain why he did not ever want to marry, the first time he had directly addressed this issue in public. After that incident, he maintained, he had completely lost interest in women. The friends he'd largely made since, he added, were male (something, as we have seen, far from the truth, for his closest friend was Anita Mui and he had made a number of other female friends). Paul Chung of Commercial Radio was singled out as one of his male friends—a man, Leslie approvingly said, who had a lot of girlfriends but was serious about none of them. The failure of his relationship in 1981 had persuaded him, he said, that marriage could not bring happiness or contentment. Better, he thought, that a couple live together, even if they really loved one another very much.[224] The radio autobiography in which he had set out to be honest had, ironically through the revelation of his failure to live with a woman, become the beginning of his creation of the smokescreen with which he would for years be forced to hide his sexuality.

In the follow-up to the broadcast, he embroidered further, telling *City Magazine* that the failure of his parents' marriage had always worried him and had deterred him from marrying. He repeated to the magazine that he didn't think that marriage could make people happy. It would, he suggested, take more than ten years for a couple to even understand one another.[225] The rather knowing reporter from *City Magazine* quizzed him about his girlfriends, or the lack of them. Leslie obfuscated, claiming that he'd had several, perhaps more than three, though he claimed that he'd never counted. Pushed harder, he added that Teresa Mo and Annie Ngai had once been his girlfriends.[226] One can feel his discomfort. The public shame of the exposures must have been very hard to bear.

More positively, Leslie used the radio autobiography as an opportunity to make plain his priorities in life. He spoke lovingly of Luk Che, who by then was living with him again in his new home, a bigger flat in Federal Gardens on Conduit Road, halfway up the hill in the middle-class Mid-Levels district of Hong Kong Island.[227] He had brought her back to work for him now that he had the room to accommodate her, and he spoke of how bereft he had always felt when they were separated, even for the short times when she visited her family in China at Chinese festivals. He told his audience how much he feared her death. Their relationship, he made abundantly clear, had nothing to do with her cooking his food or washing his clothes; rather, she was both mother and grandmother to him. Though he would take his friends home to meet her, he confessed that he'd never introduce them to the rest of his family. In contrast, he spoke bitterly and coldly of his real mother, saying that she was strangely formal when she visited him and going so far as to add that their relationship was based solely on money, for which she apparently asked every month; she was by then separated from his father and living alone. Leslie made no reference at all to his father as anything but a figure from his past and made it absolutely clear that he had no love for him whatsoever.

It is obvious from the large amount of time he devoted to talking about her in his broadcast autobiography that he was by now extraordinarily close to Anita Mui, whose music he went out of his way to promote and whom he defended at length against the spiteful tittle-tattle being given column space in Hong Kong's Chinese press. At the time, the press was printing stories that Anita was a drug addict, that she had given birth to an illegitimate baby, even that she had tattooed her arms. He described the times they had shared on tour reading novels and coming home early, and her fear of the dark. Anita said much the same many years later, confirming that Leslie had always been there to comfort her when things were bad and had always encouraged her career, as, she said, she had done for him. She described to the vernacular newspaper *Ming Pao* how they would take the back row of the economy class when they flew together on tour and would take turns sleeping on the seats. They would take adjacent rooms in hotels so that Leslie could be close to her, something that on one occasion in New York allowed him to rescue her from an intruder who had entered her room. According to Anita, they would even share a bed, snuggled up together and talking till dawn.[228] She confessed that Leslie was the only person to whom she could show her vulnerability, which she usually took care to hide under her seemingly tough exterior. He was to her like a very loving brother. She told him everything and listened to his advice, even over her choice of partners.

Strangely, despite all this, when the press continued to try to conjure up some feminine romance in Leslie's life, they did not link him with Anita. *Ming Pao* printed the news that Leslie had gone to Japan in the summer of 1985 with Cindy Yeung Lok-si and her sisters Yeung Doi-si and Yeung Si-si.[229] In reality, Leslie was by now into the third year of his relationship with Daffy, and although he still went out occasionally to enjoy himself on the town, by 1985 his Disco Disco days were almost over, and his old friends, like Jimmy Ngai and Paul Chung hardly, if ever, saw him. Ngai told the press much later that at that time he had become like an ordinary fan, reading about Leslie in the news, asking for his autograph for his niece, watching him on TV, going to his concerts, sending flowers to his suite in the Regent Hotel when he stayed there during a concert.[230] The Regent was not far from the Coliseum, the site of Leslie's summer concert, something of a favourite for Leslie. He had met Daffy there. He no longer had much time, nor the need, to meet up with his old set.

His steadily increasing schedule did not give him much time for partying or clubbing. Leslie was back in Thailand again later in 1985 to give one of his regular concerts there, then on return played for two nights before a crowd of 4,000 at the Forum de Macau Stadium. It must have pleased Leslie that he now took top billing, no longer the also-ran he had been the last time he had been in Macau with Danny Chan. Now his fans went wild and distracted him by rushing towards the stage to give him bunches of flowers.[231] Elisa Chan, who'd appeared ahead of him on the billing in the past, and who three years before had been with him at the infamous concert in Sha Tin, was now his principal guest star, singing a duet with him from his *Summer Best Collection*, "Afraid We May Never Meet Again." The media were soon at their usual game, insinuating that the two had become a number; one of the TV reporters filmed the pair huddled together, happily chatting. This amused Jimmy Ngai, who couldn't help laughing when he saw Leslie and Elisa sweet-talking on the TV; he knew very well that what they had really been discussing was the previous night's mahjong game.[232]

By now, Leslie had well outpaced Danny Chan, but his new status brought him a fresh rivalry, this time with a star who had also eclipsed Danny. This was Alan Tam, who had been partnering Kenny Bee in the Wynners when Leslie had appeared with them in the disastrous Pop Folk concert of 1977.[233] Six years older than Leslie, Tam had won his first Hong Kong music awards in 1981 and from that year till 1988 he was to win at least one music award annually. So successful was he by 1985 that the popular press had nicknamed him "the Principal" and "the Most Favoured One." Tam had also acted in a string of films, many of them in Taiwan, where he won the Best Actor award at the Golden Horse Awards in 1981 for his role in *If I Were For Real*. Many thought him good-looking, though he had a more rugged style than Leslie's. He certainly could not be accused (as was Leslie) of being pretty, and he possessed none of Leslie's nuances of sexuality. Tam's romantic ballads had gained him a huge following in Hong Kong, and his fans guarded his reputation fiercely. They now took a fierce dislike to Leslie.

A feud fast developed between them and Leslie's supporters, and sometimes spilled out in violence onto the streets. They took every opportunity to barrack Leslie when he appeared on stage, mocking him as a "sissy" and questioning his manliness. So bad did this get at one point that Leslie later claimed it had almost made him quit the business. The atmosphere of sexual innuendo and downright insult became cruel, and the damage done was pretty much one way, as Leslie's fans didn't have similar ammunition to throw back at Tam. Neither singer encouraged this bad behaviour, but the factional rivalry made things cool enough between them that they wouldn't voluntarily appear together on stage. Yet there was nothing so personal in this rivalry as Leslie's older rivalry with Danny Chan. Leslie and Alan Tam had never been friends. Their rivalry was purely professional.

All this was just the price to be paid for being a Hong Kong star, and in reality Leslie was fortunate that he had begun to achieve success in the Cantopop world at a time when its star system was becoming fully established. Cultivated by the studios and assisted by TV, by music awards, and by the deliberately encouraged growth of fan clubs, a hugely profitable arena of merchandising had sprung up, which included the full gamut of accessories, posters, clothes, and toys. The teenage idolatry created by all this was whipped to fever pitch by the emergence of "super-concerting," in which stars performed long series of concerts, sometimes of over thirty or more consecutive shows. Multi-million dollar stardoms were thus created, mostly for male singers but also for a few iconic female stars like Anita Mui, who came herself to be dubbed the all-time "diva" of Hong Kong pop. In emerging now to stardom, Leslie had been lucky once more with his timing, as he was in the fact that in Michael Lai, Florence Chan, and Capital Artists, he had had found the means to make it all happen.

***

As the new year of 1986 opened, Leslie could be more than satisfied that he had fulfilled his dreams. "Thanks, Monica" and *For Your Love Only* had propelled him into stardom. This year would see him achieve the double, for it was to be the year he made the A-list on the screen.

It began, though, with more musical success and another hit, this time with a disc called *Stand Up*.[234] This had the usual ten Cantonese songs, two, including the title track, with English titles. "Stand Up" was a Cantonese version of Rick Springfield's song "Stand Up for Love," which had been released the year before, and it immediately became one of Leslie's best-known songs. It had been written for him by the Cantopop lyricist Richard Lam Chun-keung, who was widely esteemed in Hong Kong, and was something of a departure from what Leslie had done in 1985. Indeed, it was something of a reversion to an almost traditional rock-and-roll format, more in the style of his 1984 song "Thanks, Monica." Loud, brash, catchy, noisy, and vibrant, it was a song that once heard was impossible to forget. The album was once more produced by Michael Lai and contained a few other similarly lively, though not very notable, tunes diced with some slower, sweeter melodies. The cover photo, and those which were enclosed inside the album, neatly illustrated the dilemma in style this album represented. Leslie was snapped clutching a gaudy red guitar (an instrument he didn't play) and in animated rock-and-roll stances.[235] Yet, on closer inspection, he is styled with a modern, rather short haircut and is wearing sober, restrained clothes in black. Rock and roll refined for the Hong Kong masses, perhaps. But whatever the confusion in image, the masses liked this record and it added a further boost to his career.[236]

As always, Capital Artists worked hard on the PR and to expand Leslie's reach sent him out again on the road with Anita. At the start of the year, they toured in the States and Canada, Leslie's introduction to the latter country. There was a growing Chinese population in Canada, especially in Vancouver, where many of Hong Kong's richer families were now choosing to settle in the face of the return of Hong Kong to Chinese control in only eleven years' time.

Leslie was back in Hong Kong in time to perform once more in the Hong Kong Coliseum at the year's Top 10 Gold Song Awards.[237] He was also there to collect the principal award for the song "Restless Wind" from his album *For Your Love Only*, but the awards ceremony proved to be an occasion he was unable to enjoy. The rivalry between his and Alan Tam's fans erupted during the event. When Leslie went up to accept his award, Alan Tam's fans screamed out abuse including the words "faggot Wing," Wing being Leslie's Chinese name. Naturally, his own fans in the audience did not sit silent during all this and roared back insults and abuse at Alan Tam and his fans. Some on both sides scuffled with each other in the aisles. Leslie was too proud and shocked to reply to the abuse but Michael Lai came on stage and confronted the fans, asking them what they were shouting and repeatedly pretending he couldn't make out the words so as to shame them. Lai's presence of mind and commanding stage personality calmed the situation, and the ceremony continued at last. Leslie was always to remain grateful to his godfather for standing up for him, but he would never forget the abuse.

The build-up to the awards ceremony had itself proved uncomfortable for Leslie as he had featured on the February cover of *Ming Pao Weekly*'s Chinese New Year edition (in itself a mark of his growing fame). Their reporter went with him to a rehearsal at the Hong Kong Coliseum and quizzed Leslie about his love life. Still forced to play the usual games, he told the reporter that a fortune teller had predicted he would have two sons whose success would be greater than his. He was then forced to deny that Cindy Yeung Lok-si would be their mother. Their "affair," he said misleadingly, had finished.

April saw the screening of yet another of the films Leslie had made before signing with Cinema City, and it was yet another mediocre offering. This was *Last Song in Paris*, directed for Shaw Brothers by Chor Yuen.[238] The movie was a sugary and unlikely romance involving elements taken straight from the lives of Leslie and his fellow stars, Anita Mui and Joey Wong Cho-Yee. The film vanished without much notice after a single week at the cinemas. It was, though, another profitable airing of Leslie's music. It was all good promotional material, if not exactly art.

What with filmmaking, recording music, and public performances, Leslie was getting very busy now. He was not yet well established enough to turn down lucrative gigs like the ninety-minute performance he gave on 20 April in the Jade Ballroom of the Furama Hotel in Central, where he was backed by a band led by Michael Lai. Anita, as usual, appeared as his guest.[239] Several hundred fans in the audience wore yellow T-shirts printed with the words *Stand Up* and went crazy cheering and screaming his name.

In July, for a second time that year, Leslie travelled across the Pacific, this time to Vancouver, where, on the 18th, he represented Hong Kong at the '86 Expo, singing many of his recent hits including "Stand Up" and "Restless Wind."[240] The Canadian press flattered him with the title of "the Michael Jackson of Hong Kong," and this was the start of the warm relationship with Canada's West Coast he would develop over subsequent years. The Hong Kong press, though, covered the trip in their usual fashion. They linked Leslie with a girl named May Ng, who had been the first runner-up in that year's Miss Hong Kong pageant, for which Leslie had been one of three masters of ceremony. Just before they flew to Vancouver, Leslie and May had met again at the party thrown after the New Talent Awards on 13 July, spending much of the evening together. Both were reported to have drunk more than was good for them. Leslie ended up singing with May, and the paparazzi snapped a lot of photos. Their flight together to Vancouver caused a bubble of media speculation, which Florence Chan, in a remarkably forthright rebuttal of the story, proceeded to pop.[241] They were not having an affair, she said; really, they were not even good friends. Leslie later denied there was anything in their relationship, regretting that the rumours had caused May a good deal of trouble, not least from his fans, who resented her supposedly favoured place in his life.[242] It seemed that some of them, at least, now preferred their idol not to be romantically entangled with any woman. Leslie was already becoming something unique. In the hearts of his public, it was perhaps better that he stood alone. [243]

CHAPTER 7

A BETTER TODAY

1986 - 1987

Leslie had to wait till the second half of 1986 for the first major fruit of his new contract with Cinema City to come before the public. On 2 August, the company released the film that was to change his fortunes and propel him to the levels of stardom on screen that he had achieved in pop music. The film was John Woo's *A Better Tomorrow*, a movie that had the remarkable effect of making in one stroke the careers of its director and three of its stars (the others being its two principal leads, Chow Yun-fat and Ti Lung).[244] The film changed the face of Hong Kong cinema, establishing a new genre that became known as "the heroic bloodshed movie."[245] In its second film starring Leslie, Cinema City had, mostly by chance, hit upon a vehicle in which he could break out of the stereotypical roles he had been given before.

A Better Tomorrow was produced for Cinema City by Tsui Hark's own film production company, Film Workshop. Tsui Hark had up till now directed all his own films, but this time brought in his friend John Woo to direct. Woo was just back from Taiwan, where his career had been languishing. The pair sold the idea of the film to Karl Maka, the man who took the major decisions in Cinema City, on the backs of its two stars, Ti Lung and Leslie. Ti

Lung, whose real name was Tommy Tam Fu-Wing, was an actor of an older generation who had been a film star since the late sixties, having made a name in the Shaw Brothers' *wu xia* films. Since then, his career had declined, though he remained very well known in Hong Kong, and he and Leslie were sufficiently high-earning stars to make Woo's film seem financially attractive. The addition of Chow Yun-fat, who got third billing, did not help here as his acting career since he had left TV had not been a financial success.

John Woo wrote the script himself, basing it on a 1967 Hong Kong film, *Story of a Discharged Prisoner*, itself a movie that loosely followed Alain Delon's film *Once a Thief* of two years before that.[246] Whatever its antecedents, the way Woo approached the new movie was totally his own. He created a new blend of furious shoot-outs and fistfights choreographed in gory slow motion coupled with sassy, street-smart dialogue. The high-octane emotion, pushed often to the point of melodrama, meshed the masculine heroic ethics that drove the three principal characters and pointed to origins in the older martial-arts sword-fighting films. The Chinese title is much more indicative of this than is the English, being translated variously as *True Colours of Valour* or *The Essence of Heroes*.

At its core, the film is about the bonds of brotherhood, the ties of a man's kith and kin, both those he is born with and those to whom he is sworn. Ti Lung's character, the criminal counterfeiter Ho, and the rookie cop Kit, played by Leslie, are brothers, but Ho has ties of comradeship with Mark Gor ("Brother Mark," played by Chow Yun-fat). These prove more important and binding than life itself. Kit has different loyalties, to the ideals of the police force in which he serves. He is immaturely self-righteous, driven by fury at his elder brother Ho, whose criminal activities he blames for their father's death and for ruining his police career. He rejects his brother and swears to track him down.

The heroic themes and breathtaking action caught on like wildfire with youthful audiences in Hong Kong. The junior ranks of local triad gangs were said to have swollen with new recruits, and a fashion for the long coats sported throughout the film by Mark Gor became the rage for months in Hong Kong. The film spawned more than a decade of copies and derivatives exploiting the new "heroic bloodshed" genre, some of them to be made by John Woo himself. It screened for a solid two months and grossed HK$36.4 million. It made Leslie a major star, it launched John Woo as an internationally recognised director, it was the beginning of Chow Yun-fat's meteoric rise to stardom, and it re-launched Ti Lung's career.

This was the first big feature film in which Leslie starred. Never before had he been called upon to go beyond the teenage-sweetheart, bad-boy, and playboy roles he had filled so far. He rose to the challenge of this serious part. As the film starts, he is young, glowing, full of fun, and touchingly in love with his girlfriend. Despite his twenty-eight years, Leslie still manages to bounce across the screen like a teenager. In the early scenes before the breach with his brother, he is playful, boyish, the adoring younger brother, not yet the man his brother Ho or Mark Gor have long since become. It is his immaturity that turns him against his brother, and thereafter Kit exudes a consistent air of injured innocence, hardened, arrogant, and self-righteous. Yet he is torn still by love for Ho, and hates himself for what he is doing, smashing a mirror with his hand when he sees the hateful expression on his own face. He cannot, though, forget that he is a policeman, and he steels himself to his cold duty. When he realises his mistake, it is almost too late, for his rejection of his brother has led to the death of Mark Gor. Kit's is a tragic part, not one to which any audience could easily warm, and Leslie did not make the false step of trying to win them over; he was not afraid to portray Kit's immaturity and the flaws in his character. This won him recognition as a serious actor, not only in Hong Kong, but also in South Korea and Japan, where Leslie became second only to

Jackie Chan as the Hong Kong idol filmgoers wanted to see. The role, though, alienated many in his audiences at home.

The film's soundtrack included a new song by Leslie named "Past Love" (sometimes translated as "That Year's Love"), which had been written for the film and was subsequently released as a single. It was to do less well in the charts than another song from the movie, "Toiling Life in Wind and Rain," which was sung by his friend Roman Tam and which reached number one.

At the next year's Hong Kong Film Awards, *A Better Tomorrow* received eleven nominations and won best picture, Chow Yun-fat beating Ti Lung for best actor. Leslie was not on the list of nominees; perhaps the self-righteous character he played attracted the judges less than the good-natured and principled villainy of his co-stars. *A Better Tomorrow* became one of the most popular films of all time in Hong Kong. In 2005, the public voted it their "Most Unforgettable Film" in a competition held to mark 100 Years of Chinese Film History, and the Hong Kong Film Awards Association declared the film number two out of the top 100 Chinese films ever made.

To concentrate on making this film, and on his musical career, Leslie reduced his TV work to virtually nothing during 1986, only singing the theme song for TVB's costume drama *Turn around and Die*, which was released in October.[247] Much of the rest of that year was busy with music. In August, Leslie performed in a charity concert in Japan when *A Better Tomorrow* opened at the cinemas there, using part of the time to take a thousand or so photographs of himself for his forthcoming Christmas concert. He travelled with Anita Mui, who was famed for her shopping sprees, and spent a good deal of his spare time taking her around the Tokyo shops trying to prevent her spending all her money.[248]

When he got back to Hong Kong, a special meeting was arranged with his fans to celebrate his thirtieth birthday. He stunned them with the announcement that he had two children, adding (to their relief, when he had let that sink in for a bit) that these two children, one a two-year-old girl and the other a six-year-old boy, were both refugees from Vietnam. He had started to help them financially, giving each HK$6,000 a year.[249] In doing this, Leslie was sticking his neck out in Hong Kong for a cause he believed in, for the Vietnamese boat people arriving in the colony at this time were becoming highly unpopular with the population, resented by many for being fed and accommodated at the taxpayers' expense. As the number of boat people arriving in Hong Kong grew, and as no other country would take them, they piled up in unsanitary and horrifically cramped, prefabricated camps across the territory, penniless, the adults unable to work, their children unable to go to school. Leslie was later to sponsor four more children, not only from Vietnam, but also from Hong Kong and Africa.[250]

Leslie found these occasions with his fans difficult at first, and the stilted early meetings did not always produce results he was happy with. His skills at small talk took time to develop.[251] His fans were now gathered in several loose groups of supporters, all united by their adoration of their star. These had grown up in all the countries in which Leslie's name was now famous, Japan, South Korea, and Malaysia among them. The closest that existed to an official club in Hong Kong (and Leslie was never really happy with what he considered the exclusivity and falseness of official fan clubs) was run by a girl named Lettie Lee and helped answer the large amount of correspondence Leslie received.[252] He was already getting about 1,000 letters a day from all over the world. What drew many of the fans to Leslie, especially those he had met personally, was the kind and simple way in which he treated everyone with whom he came into contact.

One of the early figures in this world was a girl named Amanda Lee. She had first met Leslie in 1980, when, aged eight, she had been taken by her father for an audition for a child's role with RTV. She didn't get the part, and casting had made rude remarks that she was too fat for the role. She was crying disconsolately in the canteen when a young man approached her and said, "Little girl, don't cry" and gave her a carton of Green Spot orange juice to cheer her up. She called him *Gor Gor*, big or elder brother, the polite thing for a small girl to say to an adult in Cantonese and very common, but the first time we know of that anyone called him this, albeit in private this time; it remains the nickname by which he is known in Hong Kong today. Amanda's father told her that this was Bobby Cheung. She fell in love with him then, and when he became a star she was one of his principal fans. She became a fan club volunteer when she was about twelve after he moved to Capital Artists. Until his move to Canada, he used to meet his fan club volunteers occasionally for coffee. He never changed, she later recounted, and was always the kind-hearted, considerate man with everyone, no matter how rich and famous he became.[253] Many other fans recount similar stories. He was always more to them than a performer or a star. Everyone felt their relationship was personal. They still do.

***

Leslie and Anita were together again on tour during September 1986, for the first time in Australia.[254] With actress Bonnie Law Ming-chu, actor-singer David Lui Fong, and the newly arrived and at that stage not very popular boy band Grasshopper (who were, at that stage, protégés of Anita), they appeared together in what was billed as the Hong Kong Tri-star in Concert. It was a notable event, as they were the first Chinese stars to appear at the 8,000-seat Sydney Entertainment Centre. As usual, Michael Lai was along to make it all work. Back in Hong Kong, on 21 October,

Leslie performed with other Hong Kong stars before an audience including Queen Elizabeth II, who was spending several days in Hong Kong after a state visit to China.[255]

Speaking to the press around this time, perhaps more than a little tongue in cheek, Leslie claimed that he envied the quiet life of his rival Alan Tam, whose girlfriend was successful in keeping out of the limelight.[256] This, of course, was ironic, as his own partner, Daffy, was completely unknown to the fans and always managed to be extraordinarily discreet. Questioned again about his marital intentions, Leslie continued to hide behind the smokescreen that he didn't trust marriage, citing the fact that his parents' and three out of four of his siblings' marriages had by then broken up. Yet that he was put under some strain as a result of his work, his secret relationship with Daffy and the need to keep up appearances in public was shown by the fact that he was smoking a pack of cigarettes a day, something he himself admitted was due to tension.[257] Significantly, he made a completely unsolicited prediction in 1986 that he would probably quit showbiz in a couple of years and emigrate to Canada, the first sign that this idea was in his mind. At the time, no one thought to question what seemed just like a passing fancy.

Leslie and Michael Lai were still experimenting with Leslie's image, seemingly not quite sure yet which styles would best attract the public. The music of the year's first album had seemed light-years from the subtle and tuneful music of the year before, but had been, if anything, more popular still. His second album of 1986, released in October, was a different mix again. Leslie spoke at the time of Michael Lai's search for a more mature, "Julio Iglesias-like" style for him, though he made it plain that he was not impressed by this; he roundly told the press that he didn't agree with the idea.[258] This image would have suited him very badly and the idea was sensibly not taken further. Leslie was growing more confident now of working out his own musical destiny. He straightforwardly told the *Standard*'s reporter that it was his goal to be a superstar and that there was only one man (Alan Tam) left to beat to achieve this. He claimed, he said, half the credit for the songs chosen for his albums despite still not being able to read music, and indeed for his next album he was named as co-producer alongside Michael Lai. The disc was entitled *Cheung Kwok-wing (Allure Me)* (which is also known as *Fire of Love* or *The Past Love*).[259] The cover showed Leslie in a striking red jacket and tie, two images of him taken from different angles then superimposed. There were eleven tracks, from which "Who Can Be with Me" (which is also translated as "Who Will Echo with Me" or "Who Can Resonate with Me") and "Past Love" (the theme song of *A Better Tomorrow*) were to become very popular. "Past Love" was to win the RTHK 9th Top Ten Chinese Gold Songs Award the following year and, with "Who Can Be with Me," would be listed for the TVB Jade Solid Gold Best Ten Award, the latter song taking first slot. The album also had two songs in English, "Crazy Rock" and "Miracle." Leslie's musical achievements in 1986 earned him the 7th Commercial Radio Chinese Pop Songs Award and the position of RTHK's Top Ten Popular Artist in the next year's competition.

The success of the 1985 concert had given Leslie and Capital Artists the appetite to plan a bigger and more lucrative series of shows at the Coliseum at the end of 1986.[260] This initially caused friction with Danny Chan. Despite their brief reconciliation on stage the previous year and their joint appearance before the Queen, things between them again went sour. In the autumn, the press picked up rumours that both singers were planning Christmas concerts at the same time and place.[261] A spokeswoman for Capital Artists (which, strangely, represented them both—could the conflict have been a case of deliberate PR misinformation?) announced that Danny would sing at the Coliseum on 6 and 7 December, and that Leslie would hold ten days of concerts there later that month. She denied any rift between the two and claimed that they remained friends.

Leslie repeated this claim and told the press that he'd known since the spring that Danny was planning a Christmas concert, saying that he had gone ahead with his own as he had heard from Danny's manager that he had decided to delay. It now seemed that Danny had again changed his mind. Debbie Ng, appointed to produce Leslie's event, told the press that Leslie was easily able to cope with ten consecutive shows as he was a nice boy who took care of himself. After his shows, she said, it was his habit to go straight home to sleep. Stardom and Daffy had settled him down. Danny, though, was not leading such a quiet life. He had no long-term lover and never did settle down.

In the event, Leslie coped magnificently with not ten but twelve nights. His second personal concert at the Coliseum, *Leslie Cheung in Concert '86*, ran every day for two hours from 25 December to 5 January 1987.[262] He had different guest stars each night, including, of course, Anita Mui, his friend Elisa Chan and again the glamorous Connie Mak. Leslie's musical director was once more Michael Lai. The concert was sponsored by Konica, for whom Leslie had made a TV commercial that year[263] and it lit the Coliseum up as for Christmas (appropriately, as the concert began on Christmas Day). The fans waved thousands of electric candles throughout the performance and there was a stunning laser light show surrounding the stage.

Leslie's rapport with his ecstatic audiences was, if anything, even closer than it had been in his first concert series. What by now had become his permanent love affair with his fans was very much on show: "I love you," he told them all. "I don't often speak a lot. I just don't speak well, so I always sing instead," he added. He called Michael Lai "the fat Garfield" and in response Michael labelled him "a big monkey." The programme this time mixed his fans' favourite tunes with music made popular by others (such as Paula Tsui's "Affinity"). The show ended with a riotous rendering of

"Stand Up" sung as an encore followed by a medley of Leslie's own songs arranged by Michael Lai. Leslie ran around the stage shaking the hands of as many of his adoring fans as he could reach. They went crazy trying to embrace and kiss him, and he almost fell into the audience several times.

It was a triumphant ending to what had been a stellar year.

***

The success of Leslie's second Coliseum concert series was closely followed up in January 1987 with the release of his new album, *Love and Admiration* (also known as *Admire* or *Admirer*).[264] This time, Capital Artists teamed up in a joint production with the highly successful Taiwanese company, Rock Records, which Leslie had met when first with the company. This was a largely Mandarin album aimed at Taiwanese audiences; LP and cassette editions of the album had already come out in Taiwan on 26 November of the previous year. On the cover was another striking head shot of Leslie, pensive in half profile, half of his face obscured by the shadow which blended with the dark background and his high-collared jacket. The album had eight Mandarin tracks and only two Cantonese, these being "Let Me Disappear" and the title track "Love and Admiration," which was a hit in Hong Kong and won a place in that year's TVB Jade Solid Gold Best Ten Awards.

Love and Admiration was, though, the last record Michael Lai was to produce for Leslie, who now stunned the pop world by abandoning his musical godfather.[265] A professional rift had been growing between the two for some time, at its root Leslie's growing maturity as an artist and his steadily solidifying intention to take charge of his own destiny. When interviewed the previous year about his new rock-and-roll style, Leslie had bridled at the reporter's suggestion that he was anyone else's creation.[266] He was no longer sure that Michael Lai had a clear vision of what sort of singer he should be. Despite all their successful experimentation, Capital Artists had still not settled upon an image or a style which Leslie could feel was fully his own. The recent foray into rock-and-roll had begun to create a brash musical persona, someone not at all who Leslie felt he was. The gentler, more subtle style he and Michael had begun to work on two years before seemed to him now to both suit him better and to have more to offer in the long run. Leslie had also begun to establish his professional competence as a producer of his own music; being credited with the production of his own records alongside Michael Lai had given him a taste of independence. He had, over the last four years, grown up.

A strong impetus for this abrupt change was Florence Chan, who had become very close to Leslie since she had taken on the management of his musical career. She was now a great friend, but in November 1986 she had left Capital Artists, announcing to the press the following February that she was to manage Cinepoly Records, a newly founded subsidiary of Polygram Records and the film company Cinema City.[267] Much as Capital Artists and Michael Lai had linked with TVB, Cinepoly Records was now very neatly linked with Cinema City, the filmmaker to which Leslie was already contracted. Florence Chan's announcement started a frenzy of speculation in the press as to which stars she would poach from Michael Lai, and Leslie's name was immediately suggested. Two months later, at a joint press conference with the stars who were joining Florence Chan in her new venture, Leslie confirmed that he was among them.[268] He signed with Cinepoly and shortly thereafter signed again with Cinema City for a further two years.

All this was a bitter blow to Michael Lai, who was taken totally by surprise by the announcement. Leslie's defection had a personal sting. Lai had rescued Leslie from the depths of his failed singing career and by his personal guidance had made him a star. Now, Leslie had not even told him what he was going to do. After learning of the press conference, Lai tried to contact Leslie to dissuade him from leaving, but Leslie refused to speak to him and made it clear in public that the decision to move was a personal one. He said, rather woundingly, that he felt there was nothing new he could do with Capital Artists and that he needed to find new pastures. He was not, he claimed, fed up with doing things for Capital Artists, but did feel that he'd done a lot for them and that they didn't have much new to offer him. Perhaps more to the point, he added that the other side's offer had been much stronger.[269]

Ironically, Michael Lai's last production for Leslie, the song "Love and Admiration," moved almost immediately into TVB Jade's top ten. Lai made the best of things by releasing in July a compilation of the thirteen hit singles Leslie had made with Capital Artists in an album entitled *Love Songs Collection – Greatest Hits*. This included the songs "Admiration," "Past Love," "I Do," and a version of Elvis Presley's "Are You Lonesome Tonight" rewritten by screenwriter and producer, Edward Tang King-sung.[270] The cover of this compilation shows Leslie casually dressed (for the first time on an album cover) in a leather jacket and jeans. Lai followed this with another album simply entitled *Dance Remix 87*, Leslie this time shown on its cover in more formal attire in a dazzling white jacket.

Though Leslie later made it clear to the public that he held Michael Lai in great respect and affection, it would be some time before anything of the old relationship between them was restored. It was a sad end to the cooperation that had made Leslie a star.

Leslie and Florence Chan needed time to assemble his first album with Cinepoly, so to keep him in the public eye, she arranged a series of fifteen concerts at Hong Kong's Ocean Palace nightclub—entitled, unimaginatively, *Leslie Cheung Meets You at the*

Ocean Palace Restaurant Night Club.[271] The show ran from 29 May to 12 June, fifteen performances before audiences totalling around 10,000. Ocean Palace was a huge restaurant in Tsim Sha Tsui serving Cantonese food for up to 2,500 guests at a time, and this capacity made it a popular venue for the stars. Leslie in any case knew the founder, Cheung Yiu Wing, who managed many of Hong Kong's concerts, including Leslie's. For over an hour each night, he sang a medley of his own songs, starting with "Admiration" and including "H2O" and "Midnight Black." His rather risqué line in cabaret patter acquired something of a reputation. Seeing him sweating badly one night in the steamingly hot summer atmosphere of the less-than-well-ventilated restaurant, a fan handed him a tissue. He thanked her for the loan of her sanitary pad![272]

Leslie's public was by now an international one, so Florence Chan now reached out to reconnect with his fans overseas. After the Ocean Palace shows, he and Anita departed for Los Angeles to commence a concert tour of the States and Canada. Leslie then flew to Japan with Florence Chan to appear as a guest artist in the Tokyo Music Festival. He was the first foreigner to star in the Festival and used it to showcase his new song "Sleepless Night" (also translated as "I Don't Wanna Sleep" or "No Mood to Sleep"), which would feature on his forthcoming album and would be a huge hit. Appropriately, the song had a Japanese composer and was a version of the cover track from the CD *Jirettai* by the Japanese pop group Anzenchitai.[273] In Leslie's mind there must have been sad echoes here of his trip to Tokyo with Michael Lai when they had discovered "Thanks, Monica." Florence Chan had the tape of Leslie's live performance sent quickly back to Hong Kong and released on radio to give the fans a highly effective taster for the soon-to-be-released album.

Success had by now enabled Leslie to live not only comfortably but also with style. Making use of his growing wealth, he moved to an even bigger place, a 3,500-square-foot house on the beachfront at Repulse Bay, a scenic, much sought-after, and therefore highly expensive area on the undeveloped south of the island.[274] The beach in front of the house was a very popular one with Hong Kongers, but the walled properties overlooking it were secluded and private. In cramped and crowded Hong Kong, where real estate was increasingly expensive, living in a detached house with a garden was an unusual luxury. Leslie set about designing the interior, which he did in subtle shades of black and white, spending a huge sum—under a million, he said, which he modestly claimed that he could afford as he didn't go out much. He took great pains from then on to decorate the places he lived and became renowned for his interest in interior design.

That he was no longer out on the town so much was actually increasingly true, but not because of any need to save money. Leslie said at this time that he preferred to spend his time at home watching videos, though in reality he was spending what private time he had with Daffy, who wasn't living with him. They were still forced to maintain separate establishments. Their quietly arranged social life meant that Leslie had no more need to hunt for excitement.[275] Even Anita ruefully said that she felt he had forgotten her, something he was quick to deny and make up to her for when he heard what she'd said.

At Repulse Bay, Leslie no longer had Luk Che to look after him. She was now too old for full-time work, so he bought her a place for herself in eastern Hong Kong, where she lived half her time. From then on, she spent three months at home then three months in Repulse Bay with Leslie. In her place in his household, Leslie now had both an occasional driver and a young maid named Maggie, whom he had met during his last concert at the Coliseum, where she had acted as his assistant and errand girl. Like Luk Che before her, she made him bird's nest soup which he drank twice a week, as he believed it was good for his voice.

Cinema City now proved that they were indeed a studio with creative talent and marketing flair. In 1987, they followed *A Better Tomorrow* with two more successful films, the first *A Chinese Ghost Story*, a wild costume extravaganza of a ghost and martial-arts story made again by Cinema City's Tsui Hark.[276] The movie was directed by Tony Ching Siu-tung, a Peking opera-trained *wu xia* martial-arts actor, director, and film choreographer. Ching created a wildly unrealistic mix of ancient Chinese art, Japanese pop culture and modern ghost story encased in a classical frame, a mixture which had strong dramatic appeal for audiences not only in Hong Kong but worldwide.[277] Viewers found no difficulty in putting up with the movie's improbable plot twists and impossible action due to its fast pace and romance. Several directors had taken up the popular ghost story form to make films in Hong Kong in the eighties, but *A Chinese Ghost Story* broke new ground. All the ghosts and evil spirits of these past films were eclipsed by Ching's masterpiece, an evil bisexual tree monster with a mile-long tongue.

The screenplay fused costumes and sets to create a beautiful, eerie effect, with dark blue tones setting off long, billowing chiffon curtains and clothes. Gusts of wind parted clouds of mist, whipped up leaves and tangled creepers, crumbled ruined temples, and clanged the shutters of derelict inns. Dark waters swirled and ivy-clad tombstones loomed from the mist. This haunting, lyrical atmosphere was perfectly matched by the soundtrack for which Leslie sang the opening song; it became a favourite with his fans, and he was to feature it often in his later concerts.

The film stuck quite closely to a story taken from *Strange Stories from a Chinese Studio*, the collected fantasy stories of Master Liaozhai, Pu Songling (who lived between 1640 and 1715). A version had been filmed once before in 1960 by Li Hanxiang as *The Enchanting Shadow*. In the new film, Leslie played Ning, a naïve and bumbling scholar working as a travelling collector of bad debts. To get rid of him, the indebted townspeople send him to stay in a haunted temple to provide the next victim for dead siren spirit Sian, played by Joey Wong (with whom he had starred in *Last Song in Paris*). Sian is so taken by his gentle, bungling concern for her and by his genuine goodness that, rather than have him eaten alive, she rescues him and protects him from her dead sisters and the entity that controls them all, the tree demon. Ning and Sian fall in love, but at the end they are separated, and in the last scene Ning is left wondering whether he will ever find Sian again (a clear lead into a sequel, of course).

Leslie and Joey Wong struck sparks off each other. The first appearance of the beautiful Joey, her long strands of black hair rippled across her pale face by the breeze, became a classic Hong Kong screen image. As Ning, Leslie managed somehow to be the natural butt of all misfortune whilst remaining so pure of heart that his audiences had no difficulty in believing that the beautiful ghost could fall in love with him. Ning survives every misfortune by pure chance. Every spell or weapon he handles only works by luck or because he misuses it. He defeats his enemies often without even noticing they are there, falling through holes out of their reach and opening windows which let in the sun to turn them to dust. He is splattered with the blood of warriors who fight to the death around him while he's trying to eat his lunch, he's smothered in the sticky saliva oozing from the tongue of the tree demon, and he's besmirched with the mud and dust in which he inevitably sinks. He is a walking series of mishaps. Leslie in this part was very funny indeed, a natural comic actor who had clearly found a métier he enjoyed and could play to perfection. Yet his love scenes with Joey were poignant and sexy and in them the naturally romantic Leslie shone through the ineptness of the character he played. He was lovable in this part both when he was being very foolish and when he was in love. *A Chinese Ghost Story* allowed him to show a talent for a totally different kind of role from the Kit of *A Better Tomorrow*; it was proof of his newfound versatility.

Off the set, Joey Wong spoke respectfully and affectionately to Leslie, addressing him as *Gor Gor*, big or elder brother, the first recorded instance of the public use of the nickname for him (rather than of his use of it for Daffy). It was a nickname by which Leslie was to be increasingly recognised and which stuck to him throughout his career.

Leslie's relations with the media, however, were not enhanced by this film. In an erotic scene in the film, Sian saves Ning from her sisters by hiding him in her bath water. From the depths he sees her naked, and they end up kissing under water. The scene, which was re-shot so often that Leslie went down with a cold, quickly became known about outside the studio. A press reporter sneaked onto the set and managed to take photographs before he was seen by the crew, apprehended, and his camera confiscated. Leslie was criticised by the press for this, quite wrongly, for as it turned out he had not even noticed the incident.[278]

The film screened over nearly four weeks between July and August 1987, grossing HK$18.8 million and so becoming Leslie's second-best-earning film to date. *A Chinese Ghost Story* was to be highly influential in Hong Kong cinema as well as abroad, and it spawned many copycat movies. In Japan and South Korea, it added to the reputation Leslie had won in *A Better Tomorrow*, while further afield it was shown at the Berlin Film Festival and became the first of Leslie's films known in France, critics there labelling it the Hong Kong equivalent to their own *Nouvelle Vague*. In the following year's Hong Kong Film Awards, *A Chinese Ghost Story* took a series of prizes, but only minor ones and, unaccountably, Leslie missed out on any nomination. In truth, this was his film and he deserved better.

According to plan, Leslie made no TV appearances in 1987, though TVB said publicly that they still wanted him to perform for them occasionally. He was by now too important a star to be ignored, and his appearances at song contests and major shows were too popular for the stations to want to lose entirely. Leslie was increasingly sought after. That year, Pepsi signed him for the twelve-month series of radio and TV commercials for which they had recently signed Michael Jackson and Lionel Richie. It was the first time that Pepsi had signed a Hong Kong star.[279] For these, Leslie sang a number entitled "Rockin' the Pepsi Way" and his sixty-second slot alternated on TV with Jackson's *Bad*. Pepsi's agency in Hong Kong, BBDO, told the media that Pepsi had chosen Leslie as they believed he represented the new generation in Hong Kong, which in many ways he did. "We decided that Alan Tam was already over-exposed," they commented, which must have pleased Leslie greatly.[280]

Almost immediately after *A Chinese Ghost Story* closed, Cinepoly Records issued the first album Leslie had made with them, *Summer Romance '87*. Leslie was given credit as co-producer.[281] In its ten Cantonese tracks, five upbeat numbers, five slow, Leslie reached the fullness of his singing abilities. The music allowed his virtuosity full rein, and the depth and power of his voice came through now in a way that he had not achieved with any album made with Capital Artists. He had put the simple tunes and rhythms of his rock-and-roll days behind him. One track, "I Can't Control Myself," was a Cantonese version of Rod Stewart's "I Don't Want to Think about It". It had been written by the prominent lyricist Siu Mei, but it had also been given a more passionate form by Leslie himself, who wished to soften the original's bitter emotion. The last track was the opening song on the soundtrack of *A Chinese Ghost Story*. The CD cover matched the change. In place of the spirited rock-and-roller of Capital Artists' imaginings, Leslie was portrayed in a restrained, mature style, wearing a linen Chinese jacket over a yellow T-shirt and khaki slacks. Just as Tsui Hark's productions for Cinema City had lifted Leslie's film career to a new level, so now its sister company Cinepoly raised the level of his music.

Summer Romance quickly became the best-selling CD of the year, selling over 700,000 copies, breaking records and running out in the shops after the first three days. By October, after only one month on sale, the record had gone platinum no less than six times.[282] Leslie's fans went wild trying to get hold of the CD, and across Hong Kong they stole the advertising posters that had been put up in shops and on buses. The International Federation of the Phonographic Industry (IFPI) declared *Summer Romance* the best-selling album in Hong Kong. The disc won Leslie the RTHK 10th Top Ten Chinese Gold Songs Award and TVB Jade's Solid Gold Best Ten Award, both for "Sleepless Night," which became Jade's Gold Song of the Year. Commercial Radio's 8th Chinese Pop Songs Awards joined in, declaring *Summer Romance* the best album of the year. On the strength of all this, Leslie also won RTHK's Top Ten Popular Artist of the year.

So Leslie made a clean sweep of all he could have won that year. The edge was taken off this, sadly, by the continuing rivalry with Alan Tam. Perhaps recognising that he was being surpassed, Tam announced that he would no longer accept any awards for his singing, thus, in the eyes of Leslie's fans, evading what they saw was the fact that Leslie was now outdistancing this rival much as he had overtaken Danny Chan. This awards ceremony became very tense, and Leslie felt a need to defuse it by congratulating Alan Tam and having his photo taken with him. Nevertheless, it all left a nasty taste in the mouth—as did the fact that Leslie's new Japanese car was vandalized, rumour had it, by Alan Tam's fans when Leslie left it outside a charity concert they both attended.[283]

Fast on the success of *Summer Romance*, Leslie held a concert for his international fan club at Hong Kong's Ko Shan theatre on 2 September.[284] The theatre was a new venue in a park in Kowloon, the auditorium open in part to the elements, which on this humid and very hot summer afternoon left everyone in a puddle of sweat before the end of the three-hour gig. Leslie's guests for the show included Ti Lung, his fellow actor in *A Better Tomorrow*. Cinepoly Records' chief, Chan Siu-po, presented Leslie with the six platinum records his new album had earned, and Leslie mingled in relaxed form with his fans and had his photo taken with them. He was getting much better at this now. Ironically, Florence Chan later revealed that Leslie had not been in favour of the creation of an official fan club. Leslie felt, she said, that it was wrong to restrict his following to those who held membership of any club, and he preferred not to have to determine whether any group was or was not "official." She quoted Leslie as saying that as long as there were people who liked his songs and enjoyed his movies, that was enough for him.

In November 1987, Michele Trewick of the *Hong Kong Standard* assembled an article containing many of Leslie's quotations.[285] These included remarks about his characteristic cutting-edge approach to dress on the Hong Kong stage. Leslie had mused that perhaps he had just been too progressive at first, wearing singlets and jeans on stage when no one else did. Now that he could sometimes appear half-naked, he very much enjoyed it. He brought up again the idea of emigrating to Canada in two to three years' time and of retiring in about 1990. Toying as usual with the question of female companions, he professed himself scared he might never find the right woman to settle down with given the jealous reaction of his fans to May Ng.

Throughout the summer and autumn of 1987, Leslie carried on shooting films. The second to be released that year was the sequel *A Better Tomorrow II*, which was released in time for the Christmas holidays on 18 December and ran until 7 January the following year.[286] Though this was not as successful a film as the original, it still brought in a hefty HK$22.7 million. Cinema City's team from the first film was back: Tsui Hark produced; John Woo directed; Ti Lung, Leslie, and Chow Yun-fat starred.[287] This time, the film company's own director (and veteran actor) Dean Shek Tien joined the trio, and he received second billing in front of Leslie. Tsui Hark and John Woo fell out over the film and could not agree on the final cutting, which led to some messy compromises; as a result, the film did not hang together as well as the original. Nor did it have the earlier film's intense characterisations. Leslie sang the theme tune, a song entitled "Forward to the Days in the Future," a suitably vacuous title which reflected the fact that, apart from leading to another sequel (in which Leslie was not this time to star) this film was going nowhere new. It was Leslie's turn to die in this film, which he did to the strains of himself singing "Don't Ask Me about Today."

Leslie's two-year contract with Cinema City had done what he had hoped it would. After one false start, it had opened the door to bigger and more testing roles in major feature films. While the stereotypes of Leslie's earlier movies would occasionally surface in the future, he had now escaped their power to limit his career. He was truly in the A list now.

CHAPTER 8

A CAREER IN CONCERT

1988

About this time, Hong Kong saw the emergence of a highly talented group of directors who created its cinema's Second Wave.[288] The robust health of the industry had opened up a huge creative opportunity, for by the late '80s there were approximately thirty production companies churning out more than a hundred feature films a year. Golden Harvest, the leading company, made something like twenty local movies a year, and Cinema City another dozen or so. These studios were introducing Hong Kong film to a wider foreign audience, making, for instance, about twenty percent of their overall ticket sales in the Taiwan market, which in turn generated a flood of Taiwanese money for investment in the industry. Ominously, though, the seeds of future decline were being sown by this rapid expansion. The "get rich quick" mentality it spawned valued quantity over quality, and in the background loomed ever larger the trend of video piracy. By 1987, there were over 400,000 VCR owners in Hong Kong, and almost all were customers for the pirated tapes sold in the back streets. For now though, it was full steam ahead, and in 1988 Hong Kong cinemas achieved a never-to-be-exceeded peak of 66 million tickets sold in the year.

Leslie's second two-year contract with Cinema City allowed him to make films with other studios, and he took immediate advantage of this. To what must have been Cinema City's chagrin, the first film he had space to make with another company became a classic, amongst the best—some would say *the* best—that Leslie ever made.

This was director Stanley Kwan Kam-pang's masterpiece, *Rouge*.[289] Kwan was a Second Wave director who had, like so many of his fellows, started in TVB and had trained under the New Wave directors Ann Hui On-Wah and Patrick Tam. *Rouge*, his third feature film, was a typically nostalgic Second Wave story that rapidly became one of the most critically and financially successful Hong Kong films, both at home and abroad.[290]

Leslie had been lucky to land a part in it. When Golden Harvest first considered making a film based on the novel of the name by Lilian Lee, it had intended the leading man to be Adam Cheng Siu-chow, a TVB *wu xia* actor and husband of the ever-popular Hong Kong comedienne Lydia Shum. They had, however, already cast Anita Mui as the female lead, and she demanded that Leslie play opposite her. Despite the fact that he was more expensive to hire (he was by now Hong Kong's 7th-best-paid actor), she got her way, and the studio found itself having to extend the part beyond the existing script to accommodate Leslie.[291] They got a good return on this investment.

Rouge is a beautiful film, a meditation upon loss and change, both personal loss and the loss by Hong Kong of its older cultural roots. It is the story of Fleur, a courtesan in the Hong Kong of 1934, who catches the eye of Twelfth Master, Chen Chen-pang, played with languorous grace by Leslie. The film opens in the brothel where Fleur works, with an extraordinarily erotic encounter between the two. She sings to Twelfth Master in Nanying, classical Cantonese song, standing only inches from his confident, bemused, and increasingly bewitched face. They quickly become lovers and totally obsessed with each other. He gives her gifts, including an expensive jade locket for her rouge. Twelfth Master's family are rich merchants and already have his marriage planned elsewhere, but he wants neither wife nor businesses and dreams of becoming a Cantonese opera singer, going so far as to submit, but in secret, to its socially humiliating training. He finally fulfils his dream of appearing on stage, only to find his parents and fiancée in the audience on his first night. They storm backstage to demand that he return to conformity and abandon Fleur. Rather than separate, Twelfth Master and Fleur agree to commit suicide together. Fleur feeds them both raw opium and dies, but she had taken the precaution, as she thought, of preventing any second thoughts on the part of her lover by giving him sleeping pills as well, and these make him vomit and so save his life. Her doubt of his fidelity proves fatal to their tryst.

Fifty years later, Fleur is seen on a Hong Kong street looking for Twelfth Master on the anniversary of their suicide pact. Lost in a Hong Kong she doesn't comprehend, she is befriended by a journalist couple who don't realise who or what she is. They take her home where it becomes all too clear that she is a ghost. They overcome their horror and set out with her to find Twelfth Master, finally finding him eking out his last days as an aged film extra. His decay and the cowardice he showed in failing to follow her into death disgust Fleur. She hands him back the rouge locket and vanishes.

Stanley Kwan's film cuts back and forth over the fifty years, comparing the two Hong Kongs, usually to the disadvantage of the later period. The earlier scenes are vibrant whilst the modern are mostly shown in greys and sombre colours or in the darkness of night. Leslie as Twelfth Master encapsulates this. As a young man he is a carefree, stunningly handsome, totally masculine man who draws all female eyes (and the eyes of his cinema audience), but is feckless, hedonistic, unprincipled, and impractical. As an old man he is a muttering wreck of a human being. It is as the decadent Twelfth Master that Leslie comes into his own. No one in the Hong Kong cinema of the day could surpass his portrayal of abandoned sensuality. He created an unforgettable character in a film qualitatively superior to anything he had made before.

Rouge taught him much about serious acting. He said later that it was the first time he had realised that each scene in a film was an opportunity to charm an audience, so that a successful film actor needed to make each shot memorable.[292] He concentrated upon making this happen—driven, in part, by the shortness of his role (he is on screen for only about a quarter of the film). This was also the first movie in which he made great efforts to research his part, studying the Nanying singing Twelfth Master so admired and with which he was beguiled by Fleur.[293] Stanley Kwan told the media that he was proud of Leslie's performance. Leslie always regarded this as his finest piece of acting.[294]

Regrettably, film festival judges disagreed, feeling perhaps that Leslie's part was too short to qualify him for recognition, and though he was nominated for Best Actor in the next Hong Kong awards, he did not win. Anita took the honours, rightly, for she gave a fine performance, and won Best Actress, while Stanley Kwan took Best Director and the film won Best Film. Leslie was also unsuccessfully nominated for Best Actor in that year's Taiwan Golden Horse Awards, where Anita again won Best Actress. *Rouge* won a foreign critical acclaim new to Hong Kong cinema at the time. Commercially, too, the movie was a great success, grossing over HK$17 million over the six weeks it screened in Hong Kong between January and February 1988.

In the latter month, while *Rouge* was still running, Cinepoly Records released Leslie's new album, *Virgin Snow*.[295] Leslie chose the title himself and co-produced the ten Cantonese tracks. For a second time, he turned his hand to songwriting, composing the track "Thinking of You." The stylish winter landscape on the album's cover was designed by Alan Chen, a highly renowned Hong Kong graphic designer; it was clearly intended to be a classy affair. Its first track, "Killer of Love" (or "Love Murderer") and the second, "Hot, Hot, Hot" (or "Hot, Spicy, Spicy', a Cantonese version of *Voulez Vous Couchez Avec Moi*") were lively, rhythmic songs intended for the dance floor, but the third track featured his melancholy song from *A Better Tomorrow II*, "Forward to the Days in the Future." Many of the songs were arrangements by Japanese musicians, while two were arranged by Joseph Koo Ka-fai, an extraordinarily prolific and popular Hong Kong songwriter. Leslie re-arranged popular Cantopop singer Michael Kwan Ching-kit's gentle "Love in the Snow" for track number four; Kwan had retired that year, so this was something of a tribute.

Despite the obvious care and money that had been put into creating this album, it was not among his most outstanding releases, nor was it to be one of his most popular. It did not give Leslie the opportunity to show the sparkle and emotional depths of which he was capable. Only in the last track, "The Most Beloved," was he able to show what he could do with a song into which he could really invest his feelings. This number was a rearrangement by Joseph Koo of a song by the Taiwanese songwriter Jonathan Lee Tsung-chen. Very shortly afterwards, in March, Cinepoly issued a compilation record with a cover by Justin Chan showing art work including photos taken for *Virgin Snow*.

Leslie sang some of his new songs in *Concert 428*, a show held on 28 April at Hong Kong's Queen Elizabeth Stadium, the 3,600-seat concert hall in Wan Chai.[296] This was but the forerunner, though, of the big concert planned for this year, which was scheduled for the end of July at the much-larger venue of the Coliseum.

It was naturally sponsored by Pepsi, timed to coincide with their sixty-second TV advertisement entitled *Backstage*, which started screening in May and ran for much of the year.[297] This showed Leslie behind the scenes getting ready for a concert (in fact the concert for his fans of the year before) and failing at every attempt to get hold of a Pepsi. The soundtrack of the advertisement featured his song "Close to You."[298] Tickets for the concerts went on sale in April and were soon sold out. Leslie planned to beat his previous record of thirteen consecutive concerts in this show, and a figure of twenty or even forty was talked of. Leslie went abroad to Japan and Europe to shop for costumes.

In the summer, before the concert was staged, a Mandarin songs collection entitled *Cheung Kwok Wing* was issued, part of the successful exploitation of markets in Taiwan and China.[299] The second Cantonese album of the year, *Hot Summer*, followed this swiftly on 29 July, the day his concert series began. Once more co-produced by Leslie, this proved much more successful than his first album of the year.[300] Less trouble had been taken with the cover, for although it was again by Alan Chen, it included one of Leslie's least flattering photos backed by a strange collage including an astronaut and a dinosaur. The weirdness of the cover belied the high quality of the album, which had the standard ten Cantonese tracks and opened with the catchy title track "Hot Summer." The song "No Need for Too Much" was written by Albert Leung (better known in Hong Kong as Lam Jik), the highly successful Cantonese lyricist who was by then a Leslie fan; this was the start of what was to be a fruitful collaboration between the two. The track "Close to You" (or "Close to the Body") became a hit, as did "Silence Is Golden," a song composed by Leslie with lyrics by Sam Hui, which went on to become one of Leslie's signature tunes. He always experienced a calming effect when he sang it, he said; it was, he felt, a musical defence against the slings and arrows of the world. It very swiftly stormed the charts to reach number one. A vestigial Japanese feel was evident in at least one of the tracks and the last song, "Love Once More," was Leslie's take on Glenn Frey's "The One You Love." The album won Leslie pretty much a clean sweep of the next year's musical prizes, taking RTHK's 11th Top Ten Chinese Gold Songs Award as well as the year's IFPI Award for "Silence Is Golden" and "No Need for Too Much," as well as TVB Jade's Solid Gold Best Ten Award for "Close to You" and "Silence Is Golden." TVB was to vote him Most Popular Male Singer 1988, and Commercial Radio gave him their Ultimate Song Chart Male Gold Award 1988. The multiplicity of these awards is some indication, perhaps, of why stars like Alan Tam decided not to accept their awards in person, for appearance at the ceremonies usually involved a performance and was becoming a huge investment in time.

As *Hot Summer* hit the shops, Leslie's third concert series kicked off at the Coliseum. Entitled *Leslie Cheung in Concert '88*, it ran between 29 July and 20 August, twenty-three shows of three hours each, and took the record at that point as Hong Kong's longest male solo concert series.[301] Each show was staged before audiences of 12,500 cheering and adoring fans. They were of all ages, teenage girls accompanying their grannies. In place of Michael Lai as musical director, Cinepoly's Chris Babida started here what was to be a long musical relationship between himself and Leslie. Cinepoly had arranged that the eminent Hong Kong dancer Alvin Leung tutor Leslie and had invited the co-star of his forthcoming movie, *Fatal Love*, Ann Bridgewater, and singer Paula Tsui to be onstage with him for part of the show.

Leslie opened with hits from *Hot Summer*, after which Ann Bridgewater sang her song "A Rainy Day without an Umbrella." On the final night she appeared wearing a tight black skirt given her by Leslie to thank her for taking part.[302] Audiences, though, were unimpressed with her performance, and she failed to enhance her reputation on any of the nights; commercial linkages of figures from stage and screen did not always work out as PR departments intended. Other celebrities took seats in the audience on the last night and then came on stage: these included film star Jackie Chan, Anita Mui, Cantopop singer Sally Yeh (who had sung on the soundtrack of *A Chinese Ghost Story*), actor singer George Lam Chi Cheung, Leslie's old friend Connie Mak, and Jackie Chan's flamboyant manager, Willie Chan. Unrealistically pretending to be surprised that Sam Hui was in the audience, Leslie went on to sing "Silence Is Golden" as a duet with him. Staginess and ham acting have never been foreign to Hong Kong showbiz.

No expense had been spared in the costumes for the show. Leslie dressed himself at times very informally, stripping down to vest and shorts for his song "Don't Wanna Sleep," and at other times wearing costumes appropriate to the number, like those from his own films *A Chinese Ghost Story*, *Rouge*, and *A Better Tomorrow*. He sang old favourites like "Thanks, Monica," "Stand Up," "The Wind Blows On" (sung to a background of hundreds of light bulbs flickering through dry ice), and "Who Can Be with Me." He tried his hand at one English song, Victor Laszlo's "Stories," accompanied on the piano by Chris Babida, here carrying on a tradition established first by Michael Lai.[303] Lighting and sound had been imported from Japan and the lavish 18th-century costumes from Europe; Leslie dressed for that section as a highwayman.

The crowd on every night was totally Leslie's. His fans showed their appreciation by blowing the whistles they'd been given, and throughout the nights those close to the stage delivered bunches of flowers and fought to get a touch of their idol, who this time showed that he had learned his earlier lesson and kept a small distance from the edge of the stage to avoid being pulled into the crowd.

Yet the concerts were once again not an unalloyed triumph. Alan Tam's fans were again in evidence, and some of them left a coffin outside the Coliseum. It had been made for Leslie and contained a letter written in blood enclosing incense and paper money for the dead. By this stage, though, Leslie was professional enough not to allow it to be seen that this sort of thing affected him, and in any case it all added to the public relations for the event.

Cinepoly was hyperactive in marketing Leslie this year. The soundtrack of the concert was rushed out almost immediately. *Leslie in Concert 88* had twenty-three tracks on two discs and as before was co-produced by Leslie himself. The discs included many old chestnuts along with a few more recent songs, and featured "Close to You," "Hot Summer," "Hot Spicy Spicy," "Admiration," "H2O," "Stand Up," "A Chinese Ghost Story," "Rouge," and "The Wind Blows On."[304]

Leslie's name and face were now everywhere in Hong Kong as success in one medium reinforced success in the other. He was taking on the public persona of a megastar, semi-divine to most of his fans and inevitably more remote from the real world. He enjoyed the adulation but loathed the difficulty it all caused him in living a private life. In the small goldfish bowl of Hong Kong, it made his relationship with Daffy more and more difficult to keep out of the public eye.

On 11 August, as the concert series was still going on, the first film made earlier in the year for his new contract with Cinema City was released. It was a totally inadequate response to either the critical or the commercial success of *Rouge*, little more than a throwback, in fact, to Leslie's TV soaps and early movies. Entitled *Fatal Love*, it was directed by Leong Po-chih, who in later years was to move to Hollywood to direct Jude Law, Wesley Snipes, and Stephen Seagal. *Fatal Love* was far from being his finest hour. Leslie played an awkward and (for him) unattractive nerd named Chi Ken-wing (a lame pun on "Chicken Wing"). Co-starring were Cherie Chung, a star whose beauty had led her over her eight-year career to be labelled Hong Kong's Marilyn Monroe, and Ann Bridgewater, she of the not-to-be-repeated concert appearances. Taking a role in this Cinema City film was of course unavoidable due to the terms of his contract, but artistically it was the wrong choice. Typically, the soundtrack included a Leslie number, the rather insipid "Deep Love," which could not alone rescue the film.

Taking this role had closed off some better alternatives. Leslie probably regretted having to turn down a part in *Starry Is the Night*, a much more interesting drama directed by Ann Hui about the forthcoming handover of Hong Kong. There was talk in the press about now that Leslie would be asked to star in an Asian version of Andrew Lloyd Webber's *Cats*, which was being considered for Hong Kong's Cultural Centre, scheduled to open in Tsim Sha Tsui in 1989. Despite Leslie's remarks to reporters that like every artist, it was his dream to be offered such a role, this production never saw the light of day.[305] The pattern of a few rare opportunities for artistic creativity interspersed amongst a mountain of dross would plague Leslie's career till the end.

Domestically, things were also less than ideal. Living in Hong Kong in a relationship with Daffy, although they lived separately, called for careful arrangements and perpetual fear of exposure. Although Leslie had hoped his house in Repulse Bay would be a haven of peace, it did not contain Daffy. Luk Che was living with him for half the year and he now found himself accommodating his mother for the other half.[306] His parents had separated irrevocably and from now on lived apart. Leslie had on several occasions used their marital disharmony (and that of his siblings) as an excuse for his "fear of marriage," and in truth his parents' match had been an extremely unhappy one. His mother's presence must have been very constricting, but Leslie was now anxious to show her more love than she'd ever shown him and to prove himself a dutiful son. He found it very hard, in fact could never really find it himself to love her, but he did his duty by her. She was lucky indeed that he forgave her the past and looked after her now, for she had done little to deserve it. All of this lay behind Leslie's ideas of retiring and moving to Canada, which he again mentioned in the press in February and April. He had not, though, made any firm plans thus far.[307]

Leslie and Daffy had little choice but to get away from Hong Kong if they were to enjoy any freedom in each other's company, so they made 1988 a year of foreign travel. They took a holiday in Thailand after the summer concert, partly, Leslie said, to pray in front of a statue of the Buddha there to give thanks for the success providence had granted him.[308] He'd done the same, he revealed, after his concert series in 1986. He and Daffy later toured Europe, taking in Vienna and parts of Switzerland and France before reaching England, where they were joined by fellow star George Lam in September to spend time looking for property.[309] Back in 1986, on Daffy's advice, Leslie had purchased a house in London for £400,000. Two years on, it was worth £450,000, as he told a magazine that published a short extract from his diary this year. Another purchase, he said, would enable him to repeat that gain. The press was now beginning to refer to Leslie as a money-making machine. His earnings, unbeknownst to the media, were being safely managed by Daffy.

A book, *Stark Impressions*, was released in Hong Kong, Japan, Taiwan, and Singapore this year. Leslie had worked on this with the music video filmmaker Ma Yi Jung.[310] It was in part intended as part of the process of withdrawal from singing which Leslie intended for the following year, and was the publication of a collection of photographs taken of Leslie earlier.[311] This quickly sold out in the shops. The book would play a part in Leslie's series of farewells to his worldwide fans, as it was intended as much as a souvenir for them as to make any profit, though there is no sign its production made a loss.

During the year, Leslie gave several interviews to reporters and each time was questioned about girlfriends and marriage. He made sure that his replies were as various as they were misleading. When asked, yet again, about Cindy Yeung Lok-si, he made the remark that her father had leaked information about them to the press as he wanted Leslie for a son-in-law. On another occasion, Leslie said that he would date when he reached forty and maybe marry at fifty. He repeated his earlier comments that the unhappy marriages of his parents and some of his friends had taught him that marriage was not always for the best. For the first time, he revealed his relationship with Daffy in comments he made to the *Hong Kong Standard*, telling their reporter that his best friend was still Mr. Daffy Tong. They called each other at least once every day, he said, sometimes more, just to talk, and had been doing this for years, especially when Daffy was sent abroad by his company. It showed how caring and loving they were to each other, something Leslie characterised as a spiritual love—the most romantic, sincere, and perfect type of love, he thought, that could ever exist. This was a very remarkably brave revelation, which was allowed to pass without greater probing. It was the farthest Leslie would allow himself to go in speaking of Daffy for almost another decade.[312]

Apart from thanking the Buddha, Leslie showed his gratitude for his success by giving some of the money he earned to charitable causes. That year he gave HK$100,000 to the Hong Kong Association for Mentally Handicapped Children, in early October presenting his cheque to the Association's chairman in a ceremony at which he met some of the children his money would help. He told the press that he had a special feeling for helping children everywhere due to his own deprived childhood (he continued to talk of this in public despite his rapprochement with his mother).

He planned, he said, to donate part of the proceeds of the world concert tour he was scheduling for the next year to an international children's society.[313] Several other Hong Kong stars were in the limelight at the time giving money to charity, including Alan Tam, Anita Mui, and Jackie Chan, but it is clear that Leslie's philanthropy, which would continue throughout his life, was something he did not for PR reasons but from his heart.

Even at this stage, studios and the press could not break themselves of the habit of trying to forge romantic female links for him. There was fleeting talk in the press this year of a girl named Georgina, supposedly an old school friend, who was said to have gone to Canada with Leslie, but he denied there was anything here other than friendship and said that they had gone there to help Florence Chan look for a house.[314] In the real world, Leslie and Daffy had now been a couple for over five years. Leslie wasn't going out on the town much by this time; he was too famous now to expose himself enjoying Hong Kong's nightlife, but he still managed to get out occasionally. One of his friends, the film critic Betty Chiu Hung-ping, related later how in 1987, when she was chatting with Leslie on the set of *Rouge*, he was dragged off by his friends to a gay bar.[315]

It would have been unusual, of course, if he and Daffy had not had the occasional lover's tiff. They were, in this regard, as normal as all couples of whatever sexuality. A friend recalls that he was sitting in the back of their car one day when a quarrel erupted between the two. Whatever the argument was about is lost to time, but Leslie, who could exhibit a quick temper in reaction to others' remarks, thought that Daffy had threatened to leave him. He was driving, so put his foot down hard on the accelerator, speeding up and shouting that if Daffy was going to leave him, he didn't want to go on living any longer. They ended up going so fast and Leslie was by then driving so wildly that his two passengers were forced to apologise and plead for their lives. Leslie at last let the car slow down.[316]

One pleasanter event occurred in November of 1988, when Leslie and his erstwhile musical godfather, Michael Lai, were publicly reconciled. Lai offered an olive branch which Leslie gladly accepted, so they put behind them the resentments caused by Leslie's dramatic departure from Capital Artists. Lai managed this by inviting Leslie to join him in his concert *Michael Lai and Friends* at the Hong Kong Coliseum between the 11th and 15th of the month. Leslie had earlier announced his resolve to take a break from singing to rest his voice after the mammoth concert series of the summer, but this show was evidently important to him and for it he came back to the microphone. Lai had invited many of his friends, including Jackie Chan, Anita Mui, and actor-singer David Lui Fong. He asked Leslie to sing "Chasing," a song he had composed, which Leslie gladly did, following it with a performance of songs from *Rouge* and a duet with Anita. Leslie was very glad to be back in Michael Lai's good books, and they remained friends from then until the end.

The public was pleased that the show seemed to have mended the breach between the two, and in this case reality matched PR spin.

CHAPTER 9

SUNSET IN HONG KONG

1989

As the Chinese New Year was celebrated, and it came early that year, the comedy film *Aces Go Places V: The Terracotta Hit* opened across Hong Kong, running in the territory's cinemas from 18 January to 22 February. It was the second of Leslie's films made under his new contract with Cinema City and its poor quality reflected the tiredness of their ideas at the time. As its title indicated, this film was the fifth of the *Aces Go Places* series, until then the most popular comedies ever made in Hong Kong. The formula had so far been tremendously successful, the third of the series peaking at sales of HK$29 million. All the films starred Karl Maka and Sam Hui as "the Aces." Both men were directors of Cinema City, as well as forming a comedic duo which in each movie clumsily defeated a new set of criminal opponents and in the course of so doing made much mock of contemporary society and cinema. Each film had different guest stars and an appearance in Part V was a natural vehicle for Leslie. The series, however, was by now getting more than a little threadbare.[317]

The movie was only slightly amusing and was mostly a very silly romp, though it was clear from his performance that Leslie enjoyed making it. His role required little acting though a good deal of stunt work, enabling him to act cutely and with his usual aplomb whilst doing the minimum of work. The soundtrack included a song sung by him (as usual), this entitled "The New Partners." This was Cinema City's second artistic dud for Leslie but was nevertheless an immensely popular film and earned just over HK$20 million. It was, though, to be the last in the series, as the decline in revenues and quality was too obvious to ignore.

While the film was showing, Leslie and Daffy again escaped Hong Kong to take a ten-day holiday in America.[318] They spent the time in San Francisco, where Daffy had relatives, becoming almost marooned there when a snowstorm enveloped the city. This meant plenty of time for shopping, and Leslie spent US$20,000 on an oil painting, something which he said he valued as an investment rather than as a work of art. On their return to Hong Kong, the press noted cattily that he had put on a little weight. Leslie often fretted about this himself, but usually managed to take good care of his body, working out regularly, eating healthily, and going to bed early, so that changes in his size were scarcely ever noticeable. However, there was truth in the reporters' observations this time, for Leslie was now trying to cut down on the cigarettes he smoked and had halved his smoking from the thirty a day he had smoked previously. As a result he had indeed added a few pounds. He was very self-conscious about this and worked out hard until he had taken it all off again.[319]

As *Aces Go Places* closed, Leslie's next album, simply entitled *Leslie* (also known as *Leslie '89*), went on sale in the shops, Cinepoly once again successfully and seamlessly keeping his name before the public. The album is more often known as *Side Face* after its third track of that name and after the stylish black-and-white photo of Leslie's face, half in shadow, half turned to the observer, which adorns its cover. This time Leslie was billed as the album's executive producer, ranked above two other producers, one each for Hong Kong and Japan. The collection included a new song composed by him, "Starting from Zero" among the usual ten Cantonese tracks. There were numbers in the softer style he had earlier developed, mixed with livelier dance songs with markedly catchy beats. "Side Face," which had a particularly strong and simple rhythm as well as a highly memorable tune, became a firm favourite of the fans. Track six, "I Can't Break Away," another number with a strong dance rhythm, also became a hit, and tracks nine and ten of the album found places in Leslie's future concert repertoires. By now, Leslie's voice had reached a peak of maturity and in this album he sounds both strong and youthful in all the songs. He sang particularly sensitively in the ballads. No less than six tracks of this album, issued individually, won golden discs, and the album moved swiftly to take the bestselling position in the charts before going on to become IFPI's Best Album of the Year. "Start from Zero" won TVB Jade's Solid Gold Best Ten Award.

Side Face had just been released when Leslie was interviewed by Shirley Chan for the *Hong Kong Standard*'s "Buzz" column. He made remarks to her that would resonate in subsequent years though they were scarcely noticed at the time, for he repeated the intention he had first aired three years before of retiring from singing.[320] Yet still no one seemed to take any notice, even though on this occasion Leslie made it quite clear that the world tour he planned to start in May would be his last, and that he intended thereafter to concentrate on making films. Strangely, this time, given his earlier remarks that he had intended to settle in Vancouver, he was deliberately vague about where he had decided to live, and he muddied the waters by mentioning the apparently frivolous idea that he would like to open a coffee shop. The interview thus contained quite a collection of major and minor prophecies, none of which was appreciated at the time. Not only did he talk about ending his singing career, but for the first time he mentioned in public his desire to become a film director. The idea was clearly much in his mind this year as he mentioned it again in the summer. Interviewed on TV by James Wong, he made it plain that this was no new idea, saying that many people had been asking him when he was going to take this step. So far, he said, he had always replied that he would see next year.

As in his singing career he had moved on to produce his own albums, now in his screen career Leslie began to take greater responsibility for the production of shows in which he starred. One of the earliest in which he did this was the fulfilment of an earlier commitment he had made to star in a TV musical in France. It had been four years since he had made a TV special, but he now accepted a role in the *Leslie Cheung Special '89*, entitled *Sunset in Paris*, a seventy-minute feature directed by John Woo for TVB.[321] Though this film had some musical numbers embedded in it, it could hardly be called a musical. It harked back to *Last Song in Paris*, the "special" he'd made with Anita Mui and Joey Wong back in 1986. This time also there were two female stars, Cherie Chung (who'd just co-starred with him in *Fatal Love*) and Maggie Cheung (with whom he'd last worked in *Behind the Yellow Line* in 1984). He had personally invited both of these to take part. In addition to his involvement in the casting, it had been earlier suggested that he might write the script, though in this case he did not. Leslie was about the only attraction for his co-stars to join him in this TV film as it was made on a shoestring. Filming lasted only one week, starting in Paris on 22 March 1989, and the total cost of production amounted only to HK$200,000. The girls complained loudly about what they considered the poor conditions under which they were forced to live; Leslie, used in the past to the less lavish ways of TV, made no public complaint.[322]

The film was again a vehicle for Leslie's music and included five tracks from his latest album, including "Thinking of You," "Thorn of Love," and "Starting from Zero." It aired on TVB's Cantonese Jade channel on 23 April. The press reported the show as both "deadpan" and "slow"; critics were particularly unimpressed by the lack of chemistry between Leslie and Cherie Chung. The star casting, though, ensured high viewer ratings, and TVB could be content with the outcome.

Leslie was indulging in a good deal of TV exposure at the time. In early March, he had flown to Seoul to make a two-part commercial on South Korean TV for a company called To You Chocolates. Leslie wrote the jingle for this himself. The advertisement appeared as a story in two segments, very successfully hooking the audience's interest and ensuring that sales of the chocolates rocketed, fans clamouring for the showing of the advertisement's second part so that they could learn how its mini-story ended. Whilst in South Korea, Leslie appeared as a guest on a popular Korean TV show.[323] Back in Hong Kong, he was also to appear as a guest star and special juror in ATV's *Miss Asia Pageant 1989*, singing a slow version of "Are You Ready for Love" and, surprisingly, seductively touching his crotch, a move made famous elsewhere, of course, by his fellow Pepsi star, Michael Jackson.[324]

Leslie's management team had no compunction about making use of TV when it suited them. They arranged a rare TV interview for him that aired on 25 June, this on ATV's *Off-Guard Tonight* programme, hosted by James Wong Jim.[325] Wong, an old singer and actor himself, was by now a famed chat-show host known affectionately in Hong Kong as "Uncle Jim." His programme always included two of his friends as co-hosts, columnist and TV host Chua Lam and the writer Ni Kuan. The show featuring Leslie developed into a raucous evening with much laughter and banter among the four of them, more than a little aided by the quantities of wine drunk.

Leslie repeatedly called Uncle Jim "darling" and "a dirty old man," and Wong reciprocated by landing a kiss on Leslie's cheek, something Leslie accused him of trying to do every time he saw him. He christened Chua Lam and Ni Kuan "sugar" and "honey." This surprisingly and rather joyfully camp interview was popular enough to be issued later as a VCD.

Despite the fact that it must have been remarkably clear by this stage that Leslie was not going to find a girl and settle down, even now the media would not let the idea rest. During his TV interview with Uncle Jim, he recounted that he couldn't date showbiz girls; he'd tried it, he said, but found that it didn't work, mainly because girls in the business were only interested in material things.[326] Yet loose media talk continued to link Leslie's name with women, including Pansy Ho Chiu-king, the daughter of Macau casino mogul Stanley Ho Hung Sun. They were in fact friends, and were to remain so for the rest of Leslie's life, but this was enough for the press to embroider into a love match.

Cinepoly Records made hay while the sun shone (for they were beginning to accept during this time that Leslie's sun was not going to shine much longer for them) with the issue during the year of several remix compositions for the Hong Kong, Taiwanese, and Korean markets, all of which sold strongly. They issued another compilation with photography and artwork from *Virgin Snow* under a title again using Leslie's name alone.[327] This album had ten mixed Mandarin and Cantonese tracks from earlier albums such as *Summer Romance*. The studio sent Leslie and Ann Bridgewater together to Taiwan, still (rather vainly) promoting Ann by using Leslie's name. The pair stayed there for ten days with Florence Chan, and, whilst in Taiwan, Leslie recorded the song "Cruise Mood" as the theme for a motorcycle commercial.

There were shadows, though, gathering over this year. The first was the death of Leslie's father, though that does not seem to have hit Leslie hard: he did not refer to it publicly for another decade.[328] He had not seen his father for many years and could hardly have missed him now that he was dead; he was never to indicate any remorse for him. Worse was the shocking news that his and Danny Chan's old friend Paul Chung had killed himself by throwing himself from the window of his flat in Sha Tin, seemingly to escape the heavy debts that he had incurred. This was a great sadness to Leslie, perhaps the first loss he had suffered of someone who had been close to him.

Out of the blue, Hong Kong's skies turned very dark indeed. On 4 June 1989, Chinese tanks rolled into Tiananmen Square in front of Beijing's Forbidden City, firing upon the students who were camped there demanding reforms in China.[329] The soldiers killed many hundreds of people and injured thousands more. It is difficult to underestimate the effect that the Chinese government's crushing of the student democracy movement had upon Hong Kong. Growing wealth in the eighties, a boom time, had lured Hong Kong into a false sense of security. The June 4th Incident, as it came to be known, brutally put paid to this. A reaction of anger and protest within Hong Kong was immediate. People took to the streets in solidarity with the Beijing students. Candlelight vigils and political protests, phenomena new to Hong Kong, attracted thousands to the streets, and on one occasion a crowd estimated at a million people, or twenty percent of the population, marched in silence through the city.[330] The initial outrage gave way slowly to fear, depression then fatalistic despair as it became evident that the Chinese Communist Party was not about to loosen its hold on power across the border. The certainty that there would be Chinese troops on the streets of Hong Kong after 1997 terrified almost everyone. Emigration, already a feature of the earlier period, now sped up as more and more people decided to leave. Those who could not flee (the majority of the population, to whom the British refused to issue full passports) lost their faith in the future.[331]

This was perhaps the final straw for Leslie and Daffy. They began to turn their plan to escape Hong Kong and fly away to Vancouver into a reality. The couple had been formulating this scheme for a long time, and now everything they did was overshadowed by the looming abandonment of Leslie's singing career.

That year, too, Leslie again let slip to the media what was at the root of his thinking. He had, he said, thoughts of opening an interior design business "with my partner." He did not specify who that partner was and the hint was not picked up; Daffy was his only conceivable partner in this context.

When Cinepoly announced Leslie's *Final Encounter* concerts, it was at last impossible for his fans to deny that he really intended to retire. They had done their best to ignore this for a very long time. Leslie had started to make statements of his intentions as early as January 1986, when he'd first told the press about his thoughts of emigrating to Canada, though then he'd estimated it would be in five years' time (so this would have meant 1991).[332] He had repeated this in public in February 1988, and had even then given detail of his farewell concert plans.[333] Yet even when he was well into his concert tour in the summer of 1989, and was telling his fans in each of the overseas venues at which he played that this really was his last show, many disbelieved it or tried to persuade him to change his mind.[334] Back in Hong Kong, the amount of disbelief was enormous. Leslie was only thirty-two and was just reaching the peak of his singing career. Since surpassing Alan Tam to take the Gold music awards, he had been indisputably Hong Kong's premier pop star, and he had reinforced this in his output in 1989, work which was to win TVB Jade's Solid Gold Best Ten Award (for "Start from Zero") as well as their award for the Most Popular Male Singer of 1989. Commercial

Radio would award him their Ultimate Song Chart Male Gold Award 1989 as well as the very flattering number-one place in their list that year of Hong Kong Top Ten Most Beautiful People. His popularity was huge, both at home and abroad, and this was justly reflected in his inclusion in the Ten Most Outstanding Artists lists the next year. So how could he retire now? Even Florence Chan, after Daffy the person closest to Leslie, seems to have denied to herself that he would. At a music festival they'd both attended in China a couple of years before, Leslie had told her of his intentions, but she'd thought he'd been joking.[335] He had repeated this to her several times after that, but she had hoped to dissuade him, eventually only accepting the inevitability of his departure when his final Hong Kong concert was imminent and its tickets were ready for sale. To her and the rest of Hong Kong, the news that they were losing Leslie was inconceivable.

Why did he make up his mind to leave it all behind? The question fascinated Hong Kong at the time and has done so ever since. Over the years, Leslie gave many reasons for his decision, not all of which could have applied all of the time, particularly when he started leaking the plan back in 1986.

The reason he most often cited was a desire to leave his profession at the peak of his form.[336] On stage in his last concerts he told his fans that a clever artist would bow out at the top so that his sadness would be shared by many, and that he believed that those who only left after they had started to fall would be sorry for it. He claimed to be clever enough to leave while the sun still shone.[337]

On another occasion, he said that he had promised himself back in 1983 that he would allow himself five years to make and enjoy his success.[338] He was inspired in this, he said, by the retirement of the highly popular Japanese female singer and actress Momoe Yamaguchi, who had abandoned her singing career to huge public dismay in 1980 at the pinnacle of an eight-year career.[339] Leslie was also wont to mention in this context the less-encouraging case of the American film star, James Dean, who had died in a car crash whilst a legend and so had remained one—something, Leslie thought, which would not have been the case had his fans watched him grow old.[340]

Leslie sometimes extended this idea to state that he believed that he had achieved what he had set out to do back in 1977, sometimes going so far as to say that he had resolved on this course when he first started singing.[341] He added that he feared to make his fans bored by going on singing without changing (something that he had indeed seen happen to some of his rivals, and which was perhaps the motivation behind his frequent changes of style over the years). He later also mentioned that he feared losing himself in all the compromises necessary to match the expectations of his fans.[342] Yet, as had been the case till now, Leslie's future development of his singing, of his songwriting, and of his performance style in the years after he was to make his eventual comeback would never slacken, so his own subsequent career would prove these ideas false. He was always to stay ahead of the pack, and the pace of his transitions never faltered. As he had always possessed absolute confidence in his own abilities, it is hard to believe that the fear of failing to change could have driven him to retire. At one point in the late nineties he was even to claim that he had himself been bored by his own career, something frankly unbelievable in 1989.[343]

There was certainly an evident element of a desire to do something else, to meet other challenges. However, when he later returned to his singing career, he continued to balance both his acting and singing careers simultaneously, just as he had done before; he did not seem in need of time. Equally difficult to accept is his later claim (made in the mid '90s) that he needed a rest, an unlikely reason for the vigorous, fit young man that he was.[344] Leslie expressed a real wish to develop his film career, and in particular to direct, and to do this might conceivably have left less time to concentrate on his singing.[345] He said that he wished to study directing in either the USA or Canada.[346] Yet whilst the next few years of his life saw an explosion in his acting career, he was not to take up directing for many years, nor was he really to take seriously his idea of studying the profession, and he would drop this idea almost as soon as he reached Vancouver. There is no doubt, of course, that he wanted to direct films; he cited, for instance, the Taiwanese actress-singer-director Sylvia Chiang as an example to follow. He told the Hong Kong press in February that he was about to direct a thriller with John Woo which would show "a new definition of love" and in which he wanted the handsome and very new Hong Kong-born Taiwanese singer Dave Wong Kit to star, though this was not to happen.[347] At the end of the year, he told a press conference that he planned to return to Hong Kong in the summer of 1990 to direct a new movie called *The Story of Gangsters*.[348] He also said, earlier in the year, that he intended to buy up the rights to his past film and TV performances and re-produce them himself.[349] He did none of these things.

Another often-repeated reason he gave for retiring was that he felt the pressure of his position, always in the public eye, always the butt of abuse. He said he felt lonely, unable to communicate with anyone other than his manager; a star, he felt, was something of an alien, separate from the rest of mankind.[350] He also said on one occasion that the Hong Kong music industry had become too complicated, too political. On top of this, he claimed to be reacting to the threats he was receiving from the fans of his rival Alan Tam, and to be seeking to avoid the trouble they caused.[351] There was something in this; some incidents had been unpleasant, but he had always shrugged them off before, as did other stars. Leslie indicated elsewhere that he could no longer live any form of ordinary life in Hong Kong; he dreamed, he suggested, of being a normal person at the same time as being a superstar—incompatible goals, as he had found out.[352] His relations with the media had indeed soured due to their focus on his private life and the more scurrilous creation of stories about him by the gutter press. Yet this had not applied so much, of course, back in 1986 when he had first began to talk of retiring, though indeed by 1989 he was often angry with the press and preferred to keep them at arm's length. His choice of Canada as a place to live did support this reasoning, as the peaceful tranquility of Vancouver, to which he was much attracted, he said, allowed him to relax as he never could in Hong Kong.[353] He said that he had liked the space and quiet he had found in England when he had studied there and thought he could find that again in Canada. In reality, he was far too creative and energetic a man to fester in the provinces and was to find himself increasingly bored when he tried to live there.

The multiplicity of the reasons he gave for retirement indicate that he was searching for excuses to satisfy the public's insistence on knowing why he was leaving. It seems that he made use of whatever ideas were to hand. At times, for instance, Leslie blamed his fear of the Chinese Communist Party and its future control of Hong Kong.[354] This was an understandable fear, especially after the events in Tiananmen Square, and it was undeniable that his family had suffered much under Mao. Many others had emigrated for the same reason. Leslie put it rather crudely to writer Gerd Balke in 1989, saying that he would tell those in Hong Kong who felt they couldn't live under Chinese administration that they would be better off getting out and finding another place to live. If they couldn't or wouldn't do that, he added, they had better start studying politics.

Yet this can hardly have been a reason for retiring in 1989, with eight years left to go before the handover, and in any case he had made his decision long before the events of June the 4th.

In his conversation with Gerd Balke, who was in Hong Kong that year to conduct a series of interviews of eminent Hong Kongers (including Leslie's sister, Ophelia), Leslie brought up many of these ideas. Balke was seeking opinions about the forthcoming handover for his book *Hong Kong Voices*. On the subject of China, Leslie was forthright. He complained about having to write to apologise to the mainland government after his concerts in Taiwan, about which Beijing was always touchy, due to the mainland's claim that the island was part of China. He explained that he felt very insecure when he thought of Hong Kong's political future, and was blunt about the fact that he distrusted Hong Kong's home-grown politicians—all of whom, he said, had foreign passports with their escape routes already prepared. He added that he disliked what he had heard of corruption in China and gave the example of his last trip to Japan when he had met a man who said he had connections to Deng Xiaoping's family, and who had tried to set himself up as Leslie's agent in China. He wasn't, he emphasised, prepared to do such a thing and had no desire to break into China's entertainment market through someone's political connections.[355]

The sheer number of reasons Leslie cited for his decision gives grounds for pause. Whilst many of them undoubtedly had some force, they do not really explain why he made the decision to retire as early as 1985 or 1986, nor why he had fixed the year of retirement as 1989. There has to be the suspicion that there was more to this decision than he was prepared to say, that the many reasons he gave (almost a new one for every interviewer, it seems) were designed to cloud the issue. It is likely that the answer was rather obvious but was nevertheless one which could not, at the time, be stated. He hinted at what this might have been in his remarks to his friend, actress Tina Lau Tin-lan, saying that in other countries you could keep your private and professional lives separate, but that in Hong Kong that was not possible.[356]

Leslie and Daffy had been a couple since 1983. It was clear by 1989 that for both of them there was no one else. Yet they had to live apart in the pressure cooker that was Hong Kong. The media was increasingly trying to uncover details of Leslie's private life, enforcing complicated regimes of secrecy on them both. To make things more difficult, Leslie's mother was now living with him for much of the year and Luk Che for the rest. With mother, media, career, and the public all combining to make it impossible to live in Hong Kong as a couple, the only answer, if they wished to have a life together, must have been to leave. That automatically meant the end of Leslie's career as a singer, for although he could manage to maintain and even develop his acting career whilst he lived in Vancouver, he could not from there fulfil the continuous engagements necessary to retain superstar status in the febrile world of Hong Kong Cantopop. In short, it is seems most likely that Leslie and Daffy just wished to be together at last and that this was important enough a reason for Leslie to resolve to forfeit his stardom.

***

Leslie's withdrawal from the world of Cantopop had been planned well in advance and was very carefully managed. He would say goodbye in the most elaborate concert series he had staged to date. He would travel the world to bid a personal farewell to his fans in each of the countries where he was a star. The studio had begun to reveal this plan back in February, when it announced that his world tour would kick off in May.

The tour began with twenty days in Malaysia, where he opened with, surprisingly, Michael Lai and Connie Mak in the Putra World Trade Centre in Kuala Lumpur, travelling thereafter to venues in Ipoh, Penang, and Kota Kinabalu.[357] His Malaysian fans mobbed him everywhere he went, and he was forced to avoid them for most of the time by remaining in his hotel, so the first leg was one of the least comfortable of the series. On the one occasion he managed to go out to a shopping centre, the fans went so wild that the management were forced to close the mall, and Leslie beat a sad retreat to his hotel. The rain and humidity made working very difficult, and to cap it all Leslie went down with a stomach bug, though once on stage he ignored his discomfort and performed all his shows regardless. There was much unhappiness when Leslie closed his Malaysian fan club, which was a strong one and had opened as long ago as 1981; he advised his fans to join Anita's fan club instead. There was time off between gigs to relax when Leslie reached Sabah, where he recovered by snorkelling over the beautiful coral reefs off Sipadan Island, escorted by his concert crew.

The tour flew on to Australia and Singapore, then, after a ten-day break back in Hong Kong, crossed the Pacific to the US and Canada, after which it traversed the Atlantic to Europe, all in July. This was followed in August by performances on the other side of the world in South Korea, Thailand, Taiwan, and China. In each country, Leslie donated thirty percent of the profits to a local children's charity, writing into each concert a special event for the local children, which he called "the children's song."

Another element of the withdrawal plan became public in the summer as Cinepoly Records issued Leslie's personal farewell tribute to the stars he admired most. This was the album *Salute*, which went on sale on 29 August 1989.[358] Leslie had co-produced this, and on its cover he included his own dedication to the stars whose music he most admired, writing that it was far more difficult to sing other people's masterpieces than to sing his own songs. He saluted his favourite singers' contributions to music in ten Cantonese tracks, all songs well known in Hong Kong. Most were sentimental ballads, such as Anita Mui's "Flowing like Water." This was no rip-off album; Leslie put enormous effort into singing the numbers in his own style. All profits from this work were given to Hong Kong's college for artists, the Hong Kong Academy for Performing Arts, a gift commemorated on its auditorium landing to this day. *Salute* was a unique album, the first not-for-profit album ever issued by a Hong Kong star. After its issue, Leslie went to Japan to take part for the second time in the Tokyo Music Festival. *A Chinese Ghost Story* was showing in a Tokyo cinema while he was there.

This was a remarkably punishing schedule, as much emotionally as physically, for in each place Leslie had to say goodbye to his fans, and the continual effort drained him. After taking some time to draw breath in Hong Kong, he started his farewell there in December. On the 18th, just before his concert kicked off, Cinepoly Records brought out some of its songs in the album *Final Encounter*.[359] Leslie was billed as executive producer of its ten Cantonese tracks, which included the new songs "Miss You Much" and "Forever Love You," a version of a Bruce Springsteen number.

The heightened emotion of this long goodbye took its toll not only on Leslie, but also on his fans. The huge numbers who followed him in Hong Kong were devastated by the idea that they were about to lose their idol. The fan club organisations were dissolved officially, though many stayed in touch with each other. Leslie was to many of them the centre of much of their lives, someone whose music and, more crucially, his personal touch had given them a motivation and spirit they did not find elsewhere in Hong Kong. They bought tickets for his final concert with tremendous sadness.[360]

On 21 December 1989, the day at last came for Leslie's *Final Encounter of the Legend* concert to open in the Hong Kong Coliseum. The series was to run for a packed and record thirty-three nights and would close only on 22 January the following year.[361] It was the first farewell concert ever given by a Hong Kong star. The routine was always the same: on the days of his concert, Leslie took part in rehearsals from 2 pm to 6 pm, eating only a small bowl of beef and rice before starting the concert at 8.20 pm. His fans bought whistles and luminous sticks from vendors in the tunnels near the Coliseum, which they blew loudly and waved throughout the performances.[362] The concert kicked off on a transparent stage illuminated from below by lights, and surrounded by the audience on all four sides, as was usual at the Coliseum, the musicians below stage inside the square.[363] The chorus struck up with "The Wind Blows On" after which Leslie rose from the deep on a platform centre stage, dramatically dressed in a long, lush black cloak. He sang "Crazy for You," then "Madly in Love" and "Side Face," which he danced with the eminent Hong Kong choreographer Stanley Chu Wing-lung. This was Chu's first collaboration with Leslie and the beginning of a long history of working together. Leslie took great pains with his dance steps and movements, continually rehearsing with Chu and the other dancers. For "Side Face," both Leslie and Chu wore startling black and red evening clothes, laser lights pulsed to the rhythm of the music, and the ending of the routine saw them both clutching hands.[364]

This was followed by a medley of songs from *Salute*, in which Leslie sexily unbuttoned his shirt while singing "Thinking of You," winding his fans up in the vain hope that he'd take it off completely. Fast numbers like "I Can't Break Away" (for which he and his dancers wore heavy leather gear studded with metal zips and chains that flashed and sparkled in the lights) and "Don't Want to Sleep" were followed by "Miss You Much," a surprisingly lively number, which he told his fans was an appropriate song for saying goodbye. The poignant number "Starting from Zero" (with its English line "Will you remember me?") slowed the tempo, Leslie singing alone on a darkened stage. He added old favourites like "A Chinese Ghost Story," though this time without his famous costume, encouraging the audience to participate in the melody. Other celebrities, as always, were involved in the show. Michael Lai came on stage to bid his protégé farewell; Leslie had included three of his songs in the concert as a tribute, sitting and even standing on Lai's grand piano as he sang. Leslie also dedicated a song to Chow Yun-fat and at the end especially thanked Michael Lai and Florence Chan for all they'd done for his career.

For anyone who had doubted it before, in this farewell concert Leslie made it abundantly clear that he was in love with his audience. Despite the sorrow of the farewells, his smiles, his vivacious movements, his vigorous dancing, and his repartee all showed that he was still immensely enjoying his status as a superstar. Yet the pain of leaving it all was intense, and he could not prevent his tears falling. In his last speech from the stage, he reminded his fans that he'd come from nowhere and that he'd been called Bobby before—his fans screamed back "We love you, Bobby." He begged them to remember him and threw red carnations out into the audience. All through the shows he never stopped going around the four-sided stage taking flowers from his fans and touching their hands.

He cried visibly when he sang "The Wind Blows On" and balanced the song with another entitled "The Wind Blows Again," which he said he'd personally composed as a farewell to his fans. On the final night's performance, he especially requested the cast not to be as boisterous as they normally would have been on a last night. He wished, he said, to make this an especially solemn occasion, for on this the evening he was to perform the ceremony of hanging up his microphone. At the end of this last show, dressed in immaculate white from head to toe, scarcely able to look at the audience through his tears, he placed his microphone on its specially designed stand then walked out along the catwalk into the crowd. After one lingering, longing stare at his audience, he turned and disappeared down the stairs into the dark. Below, he barely greeted Chow Yun-fat and other stars who were awaiting him, fleeing past them without stopping. He entered his car, alone, and was away.[365]

That night he had never looked more beautiful or sung better. He had fulfilled his every intention and could not have bowed out at a higher point in his career or at a time when he could have been more loved by his fans. Now, without them, he had to remake his life. He had sacrificed the thing he had always wanted most and which he had finally achieved after so hard a struggle. Now, though, he and Daffy could be together at last.

CANADA

CHAPTER 10

DAYS OF BEING AWAY

1990 – 1992

The retreat across the Pacific to British Columbia was a drawn-out, lingering affair, which must have added to its poignancy. After the final farewell party organised by Florence Chan, Leslie and Daffy took six months to take a vacation to recover, pack, move, and set up home in Vancouver. By April, Leslie had moved out of Repulse Bay and set up home in a big house with a pool in its own grounds in Eyremont Drive in the smart suburb of West Vancouver.[366] Daffy had by then also resigned from his job in the bank, in effect retiring to go with Leslie, but even now they were still unable to go that one step further of publicly living together. So he also bought a house, near Leslie's, on Duchess Avenue.[367] Despite the unavoidable withdrawal symptoms they must have suffered, this was a time in which they could at last be together out of the glare of Hong Kong's spotlights. They had never been able to spend so much time in each other's company. After the stress, the high emotional octane, and the constant frenzy of the *Final Encounter* concerts, the quiet of Canada must have been strangely shattering.

At first, they hoped they could lead an ordinary life in Vancouver, but Leslie's star status was not so easily jettisoned. He entered a charity walk, along with Carol "Do Do" Cheng Yu-ling, another Hong Kong star who had emigrated to Vancouver, only to be mobbed by fans seeking his autograph or just trying to touch him, and he was forced to cut the walk short. Even his project of studying film directing was spoiled by his fame. As planned, he started a filmmaking course at Simon Fraser University, but found after nine months in Vancouver that he attracted so much attention that study became too uncomfortable.[368] With a year left to finish, he abandoned the project.[369]

There was in this perhaps also an element of Leslie's old reluctance to undertake formal education. He had never taken easily to the classroom. He had not, though, given up the idea of directing films and told the press in 1992 that he had written a script for a drama, and even mentally pencilled in a date for the start of production. He had hopes, he said, of being able to direct his movie debut around the end of 1994.[370] Nothing, though, was to come of this idea for a lot longer than that.

The personal contact which Leslie had kept with his Hong Kong fans was no longer possible in Canada. There was little chance now to meet informally for tea and, in the days before emails, letter-writing deterred keeping in touch in the way that is possible now.[371] The couple had not long been in Canada when news from Hong Kong darkened their lives: Luk Che had died. She had been ill for some time with cancer and by the time they had left Hong Kong had been walking only with difficulty. Now she had passed beyond her suffering. Leslie did not go back to Hong Kong for the funeral, though he helped her family with the cost of the funeral arrangements. Luk Che's death was one more break with the past. The woman he had loved since he was a child, and whom he had looked after in her old age, was gone.

So they settled down in Vancouver, living an uneventful, simple, even dull life. Friend Connie Chan Po-chu later spoke of this on Commercial Radio, telling audiences that whenever Leslie learnt that she was in Vancouver, he phoned her, picked her up, and drove her home to have dinner and play mahjong.[372]

Though he remained true to his word that he was retiring from his singing career, Leslie had made no such promise regarding his career as a film star. Indeed, he had justified his move to Canada in part by the idea that he could better concentrate on acting without the distraction of music. Now, he said, he wished to follow a career in which he could pick and choose his films, their directors, and his fellow stars. Given the nature of Hong Kong's film industry, things would not work out that way, but in future Leslie's name and earning power did give him greater scope to decide which projects he would accept. The years Leslie spent in Canada were punctuated by the making of a series of films, some of them among the best he ever made.

The first to be released after the move was, though, not one of these. *A Chinese Ghost Story 2*, this time a Golden Princess production, was released on 13 July 1990 as the long-awaited sequel to the 1987 movie. It had been made back in 1989, so had not involved Leslie in any work after his departure from Hong Kong.[373] Produced once more by Tsui Hark and directed by Ching Siu-tung,[374] the sequel re-assembled the key members of the original cast, Leslie in the role of student Ning, Joey Wong in the semi-new guise of Windy, a look-alike for her original character, Sian. Leslie still admired Joey's work greatly and told James Wong that he thought she was much better in the second *A Chinese Ghost Story* than in the first.[375]

The making of the film was fraught with difficulties. For financial reasons, it had been shot in two phases, the first six months before the second, and this had resulted in changes to the script. The first phase had more characters and stars, some of whom were cut to save money. One of the three script writers, Lam Gai-to, later described the tremendous difficulties they had rewriting the story to suit the new stars and budget, adding that he was tremendously grateful for the way Leslie listened carefully to his advice and quizzed him about the characters and plot. He also noted that the fraught atmosphere of the sets was too much at times even for Leslie's temper. Explosions of anger occurred all round, but Leslie always got over them quickly and apologised to anyone he had offended when he himself found it all getting too much. Leslie never put on airs, Lam said, and never hid his feelings.[376] It must have been a very trying time; Leslie's emotions were wound to breaking over his imminent departure from singing and Hong Kong, and the film was chaotic. It was rare indeed for anyone to see him lose his cool on set.

His music featured again, of course, the film once more ending to the strains of Leslie's original rendering of the *Chinese Ghost Story* theme. The sequel screened for nearly a month up until 10 August, making a good sum at the box office. It did not, however, earn much critical acclaim. Tsui Hark went on to make a third version, but Leslie rightly turned down a part in it.

Though Leslie was keeping carefully to his promise to neither sing nor record anything new, back in Hong Kong his music reverberated throughout 1990. His fans did not forget him and his albums carried on selling. Recordings of the *Final Encounter* concert were issued in 1990[377] and re-issued as DVDs and karaoke recordings the next year (and again in 1996 and 2002). Karaoke was by now an established pastime for Hong Kong's youth as mahjong had been for its older generations. Cinepoly Records made as much profit as they could from Leslie's continued popularity, putting out collections of his recordings in a three-volume set this year as well as the album *'90 New Mix Plus Hits Collection*. Later in the year, they issued another compilation, *Dreaming*, another ten-track Cantonese disc that included many favourites such as "Miss You Much," "Side Face," and "I Can't Break Away."[378] The title track, "Dreaming," evoked the album *Day Dreamin'* he'd issued at the start of his career in 1977—a deliberate reference, it seemed, to round off his career. Two more volumes of collections and remixes (*Miss You Mix* and the fortunately mis-named *Final Collection*) were to be issued during 1991.

In the second half of 1990, after the end of the six-month period Leslie had given himself to settle into Vancouver, the cinema took him back to Hong Kong. The film he now made, *Days of Being Wild*, Leslie's second collaboration with the director Wong Kar-wai (the first being *The Intellectual Trio*, for which Wong had written the script), would become a Hong Kong classic, a diffuse, languid, and difficult art film and a showcase of the darker side of Leslie's acting powers.[379] It was a film that would infuriate and alienate many of his old cinema fans, one quite unlike anything he had made before, but it was the one which at last established his name as an actor of the first class.

Days of Being Wild was a story of nihilistic alienation and of a fruitless quest for love set in the by now very out-of-date world of Hong Kong in the 1960s. It established Wong Kar-wai's unique style, which was one much more concerned with the emotions and motivations of his characters than with the story which binds them. It was a style characterised by long, lingering shots; very slow-moving storylines; confused chronology; dialogues with short, abbreviated speeches uttered by characters incapable of expressing their feelings; and weighty, melodramatic voiceovers.[380] *Days of Being Wild* was thus not only the first of Wong Kar-wai's stable of films but also the first of a new type of art-house film in Hong Kong.

The script, written by Wong himself, gave Leslie the perfect vehicle to project a characterisation including facets he had never before allowed to be seen on screen, things rooted in the sad experiences of his earlier life. Yuddi, the character he plays, is a tough young man whose magnetic physical attractiveness and amoral hedonism draws weaker characters to him like moths to a flame. Once caught, his victims burn in the cold fire of his refusal to yield to any kind of love. The truculent, selfish but stylish rebelliousness of Yuddi's character harks back consciously to James Dean's 1955 film *Rebel without a Cause*, a comparison even more visible in Wong's Cantonese title, which translates as *The Story of "A Fei"* (*a fei* being the Hong Kong term for the rebellious young males of the rock-and-roll era).

Yuddi has been brought up by his "auntie," a Shanghainese prostitute working in Hong Kong, with whom his real mother had abandoned him as a baby. Auntie has always refused to reveal to him his mother's identity, so Yuddi has become obsessed with finding her, and in the search for this unworthy object of unrequited love, he destroys himself. In one of his voiceovers, Yuddi speaks of a legendary bird with no legs that lands only once in its life and then dies. To him this is a metaphor for love. Making yourself vulnerable by allowing others to love you will kill you, he believes, and so it turns out when he tracks down his mother in the Philippines. She refuses him admittance to her house and hides behind the curtains of an upper room. He walks away guessing that she's watching him but refusing to look back and give her the pleasure of seeing his face. He dies meaninglessly shortly afterwards, just as he had always known he would.

Wong Kar-wai said later that he thought that Yuddi was a projection of Leslie's spirit, his lack of family love resonating with Leslie's memories of an empty childhood and of family indifference. There was much that was true in this remark. In this year, in which

Leslie had just abandoned the adoration of his fans and in which Luk Che had died, it was particularly easy for him to identify with Yuddi's deliberate rejection of, but continued fruitless search for, the love he didn't have.

Leslie took enormous pains working on this part. Maggie Cheung, who starred with him, recalled that she had heard him at the end of a tiring day's shooting session walking up a corridor to get the sound of his footsteps right.[381] Wong Kar-wai continually re-shot scenes, refusing to tell his actors what it was that he had not liked and filming again and again until he was satisfied; one scene in bed between Leslie and Maggie Cheung, for instance, needed thirty-nine takes. Wong refused to work to a script, improvising as he went along, and would assemble the film from the cutting floor so that none of its actors could fully recognise the result when they finally watched it.

Leslie's co-stars were a stellar group. Maggie Cheung, with whom Leslie had appeared most recently in *Sunset in Paris,* played a waitress in a cheap backstreet café who falls hopelessly for Yuddi. He snares her with some classic lines: when he first comes to her drinks counter, he tells her she will see him that night in her dreams. Next day he comes by again. Did she see him as he had predicted? "No," she says, but he is unfazed. "Naturally," he says, "you couldn't sleep at all." Looking at the clock on her wall, he says they will always remember that for one minute, at one minute to three on 16 April 1960, they were friends. They stay together for much longer than a minute but can never be friends, and she leaves him when she comes to realise his heartlessness. Another star was Tony Leung Chiu-wai, here in his first film appearance alongside Leslie. He is seen in an unexplained small cameo right at the close of the film; a sequel was planned but never made, and instead his character next appeared meeting Faye Wong in Wong Kar-wai's later film *Chungking Express.* Andy Lau also made an appearance, as a policeman. Jacky Cheung, who had played Autumn in *A Chinese Ghost Story 2*, took the part of Yuddi's young sidekick, a boy who idolises Yuddi and fancies his women but is abandoned with the rest when Yuddi goes off in search of his mother. Carina Lau Kar-ling played Mimi, a hard-bitten prostitute fatally ensnared by Yuddi, who inevitably throws her out when she gets too close to him.

The film was partially shot in the Philippines, with filming there starting in November, and the conditions were often bad. Yuddi stays in flea-bitten hotels, eats in scruffy cafes, and meets his death in the cheapest-class seats in a local train, so Leslie had to spend much time shooting repeatedly in the dingy, smelly, and cockroach-infested rooms and carriage. It is not, though, these foreign scenes which make this film, but rather the earlier shots of Yuddi in cheap Hong Kong restaurants and in his small, messy apartment. Here he preens himself and cha-chas in front of the mirror, forever combing back his Brylcreemed quiff. Leslie's Yuddi is a man who is hard and handsome and knows it well enough to make use of every one of his charms. There is nothing soft or effeminate here. He makes love violently, and the scenes of lust with Mimi are arousing and sadistic. Leslie is savagely, frighteningly violent in this film. He strikes fear through the icy intensity of his hatred and his total lack of any care for whether he himself lives or dies. In a scene where he attacks his auntie's boyfriend in a toilet, he reduces the man to a bloody pulp in a chilling, calculated, and horribly prolonged assault; Leslie had never before been called upon to be so vicious on screen. Yet Yuddi's eyes reveal that he loathes himself for the way he is. He pushes his women away as much to save them as to get rid of their entangling embraces. He is no shallow low-life.

When it was screened between 15 and 27 December 1990, *Days of Being Wild* was a failure at the box office in both Hong Kong and abroad. The company had pre-sold distribution rights across Asia, using the cash to make the film, which turned out to be one of the most expensive films made in Hong Kong to date, mostly due to its six very expensive stars. Distributors were horrified when they saw it, and audiences proved no more appreciative. The film went into the red to the tune of tens of millions of dollars and grossed only just over HK$9 million at the box office in Hong Kong.

Leslie, though, was hugely pleased with his performance. His friend Jimmy Ngai was with him when he did the voiceovers in Hong Kong in December; he did them perfectly first time. It was clear he felt he had done really well and mocked his friend's surprise at his skill, asking him how he dared doubt the "*Le Gin,*" the Legend he had become. He was right to be pleased with himself. Though the film made no money, it attracted the applause of the critics and won fistfuls of awards including the one Leslie so much coveted, that of Best Actor in the 1991 Hong Kong Annual Film Awards. *Days of Being Wild* would win the Special Award of Best Hong Kong Film of the Past 10 Years in the 1997 Hong Kong Film Festival and in 2005 was to be voted Most Favourite Film in the poll held in Hong Kong for the Centennial of Chinese Film History. Much more so than *Rouge*, it established Leslie's place in cinema history.

Hong Kong's cinema being what it was, the film made almost immediately after this was in nowhere the same league. *Once a Thief* (in Chinese, *Criss Cross over Four Seas* or *Vertical and Horizontal World*), was released in cinemas in Hong Kong on 2 February 1991.[382] It proved a hugely popular film and showed for more than a month to 6 March, over that year's Chinese New Year. The movie was directed by John Woo, who had clearly decided to have some fun while at the same time making money; he did, to the tune of over HK$33 million in box office takings in Hong Kong alone.[383]

Once a Thief pretended to look back to Hollywood films like Alfred Hitchcock's *To Catch a Thief* of 1955 and Jules Dassin's 1964 *Topkapi*, and took its title from the 1965 Ralph Nelson film noir starring Alain Delon, but the zany, disjointed plot set in the south of France was all Woo's own and is better reflected in its Chinese title, as it left common sense behind in a successful striving after the amusing and bizarre. Woo's hallmark violence is missing here and a love triangle replaces his usual all-male bonding. The film was panned by the critics but audiences lapped it all up. The soundtrack features Leslie singing "The Wind Blows On," a rare occasion on which his fans could hear his voice that year. He clearly loved the whole experience; it must have been a great relief to make after the sombre *Days of Being Wild*.

Amazingly, even now the industry and the media had not given up their attempts to provide a feminine interest for Leslie's life, and he had to deny to reporters during the making of *Once a Thief* that he had a girlfriend.

There was talk in the media around this time that Leslie might accept a role in a controversial new film planned by the Chinese director Chen Kaige, maker of the earlier critically acclaimed *Yellow Earth*.[384] The new film was to be the story of a male Peking opera star in love with his male co-star, with a script taken from a novel by Lilian Lee. She had hoped Leslie would star in the role a decade before, but the idea of a homosexual part had been too much to contemplate for the struggling artist he was then. It was still a highly controversial topic, and Tomson Films, the owners, found it impossible to put the package together at this stage. This was the first mention of the movie that would become *Farewell My Concubine*.

Strangely, after all the times he'd attended when he hadn't won, when the Hong Kong Film Awards ceremonies took place in April 1991, Leslie stayed in Vancouver and left Alan Tang, his producer, to pick up his award for Best Actor in *Days of Being Wild*. There was naturally considerable unhappiness in Hong Kong when he didn't show. The Best Actress winner, Do Do Cheng, and Best Supporting

Actor, Ng Mang-tat, were also absent. This led to reform of the Awards, which the industry now took out of the hands of the magazine *Film Bi-weekly*, which had hitherto run it, and restructured as a formal body representing all aspects of Hong Kong film. Stars began to attend once more in subsequent years.

Leslie and Daffy spent some of 1991 travelling around Canada. One of Leslie's sisters had settled there earlier as had his eighth brother, Didi Cheung, his wife Carol, and their son Christopher. At home in Vancouver, Leslie bought a border collie and attended a dog-training course so that he could look after it properly. He was visited by an occasional guest from Hong Kong. John Woo and his wife were with him when Vancouver suffered an unusual small earth tremor that caused Leslie's home no damage. The Woos had come in part to persuade Leslie to return to his old life in Hong Kong, but they found him immoveable.[385] They were followed in a similarly unsuccessful quest by Raymond Wong Pak-ming, who had just set up a new film company, Regal Films. Wong was more successful in another way, as Leslie did agree to sign a contract to make six films with his company, though Wong was unable to persuade him to move back home.

For much of the time, Daffy and Leslie stayed at home, going out with friends or visiting the rich wives of Hong Kong businessmen who lived nearby, taking high tea in the afternoons and eating out at Chinese restaurants in the evenings. It was a very relaxing life doing nothing in particular.[386] To enliven it, Leslie would ask his friends to lunch or to sing karaoke in the huge basement room he'd set up for the purpose in his house. The basement was actually a whole recreation floor which included a mahjong room. Some of the karaoke he and his friends sang featured his songs and concerts, and he'd sing and dance to the music with his guests. He also linked up with his female idol from the much earlier Cantonese opera world of the 1950s, Pak Suet-sin, who had a house in Vancouver. Leslie had learned the songs of Pak and her partner on stage and in life, Yam Kim-fei, since the days when he had been taken to see them by Luk Che, and he'd sing their numbers in his karaoke den. To his friends, though, he was clearly missing his old life, and although he would not say so at this stage, it often seemed to them that even after just a year in Canada, he was becoming bored away from the electric energy of Hong Kong.

Leslie made occasional appearances in these months, both in Canada and back in Hong Kong. On 17 August 1991, he acted as MC for two shows in Hong Kong's Convention Centre to raise funds for flood victims in eastern China. On this occasion, as it was for charity, Leslie relaxed his no-singing rule, and gave his audiences "The Wind Blows On" and "Bridge over Troubled Waters."

Leslie was back in Hong Kong later in the year to start work on his next film, *All's Well Ends Well* (in Chinese, *Family Has Happy Affairs*), his first of those promised to Raymond Wong. This was a comedy timed for release at the following year's Chinese New Year festival. Leslie also took a very small roll in *The Banquet*, a fundraiser for the victims of that year's floods in China.[387] This was a collaborative effort by four directors (Tsui Hark, Clifton Ko, Joe Cheung Tung Cho, and Alfred Cheung Kin-Ting) and about two hundred Hong Kong actors, including Anita Mui, Maggie Cheung, the two Tony Leungs, Jacky Cheung, Stephen Chow Sing-Chi, Karl Maka, Andy Lau, and—for the first time appearing with Leslie— Leon Lai Ming and Aaron Kwok Fu-shing, two young actor-singer stars of the next generation. This was almost all the stars in the Cantonese firmament. The film was rushed together in the space of a few weeks to screen on 30 November. Leslie, as did most of the others, appeared only for a matter of minutes playing himself in a crazy story focussing on property developers and an unlikely Kuwaiti prince played by George Lam.[388]

On 7 December 1991, Leslie was in Taipei for the Golden Horse Awards, held there that year jointly with the Asia Pacific Film Festival. He had hopes of winning Best Actor for *Days of Being Wild*, and his victory was in fact announced by presenter Brigitte Lin Ching-hsia, only for it to emerge that she'd made a mistake and that a Taiwanese actor had won instead. A Korean took the Asia Pacific prize. It was a long way to go to be so embarrassed.

Before they had emigrated, Leslie and Daffy had already lived a relatively quiet private life in Hong Kong, and this must have eased their passage to Canada. Leslie had long ago cut back on partying and always moderated his intake of food and drink. He had cut down his smoking and had never taken drugs. His looks and figure were vital to his image and he maintained them by exercising and playing games regularly. So, when he justly won a competition for a healthy lifestyle, it was something of which he could rightly be proud.[389] Commercial Radio's Chinese Channel II held a competition in 1991 in aid of the environmental group Green Power, and Leslie was voted one of ten stars with the healthiest looks and lifestyle. For each vote cast, HK$1 was donated by the sponsor, Pantene Pro-V, and the two-month-long competition raised a figure of HK$230,000, concluding with a concert and prize presentation in the Hong Kong Coliseum. Leslie was in Hong Kong at the time and so was able to collect this award in person.

***

The new year of 1992 started badly. Leslie was back in Hong Kong but this time under police protection.[390] For some as-yet-unexplained reason, a triad gang had targetted the production of *All's Well Ends Well*, perhaps seeking to extort money, perhaps seeking to pressurise an actor (it was rumoured to be Leslie, hence the police guard) to perform in a film they were financing. That the threat was not imaginary became clear on 9 January when two original reels from the film were stolen from Mandarin Films' laboratories in Kowloon by a gang of five masked men wielding pistols and knives.

This was one of the few times that the public were made aware of triad activity in the Hong Kong movie industry. Over the previous couple of years, a number of intimidating and violent incidents had occurred, including the kidnap of Carina Lau during the making of *Days of Being Wild* and the firebombing of the female assistant to comedian actor Stephen Chow Sing-Chi (the principal star of *All's Well Ends Well*).[391] Complaints to the police had got nowhere, so Regal's Raymond Wong and the president of the Hong Kong Directors' Guild Association, composer James Wong, took the very brave step of organising a public protest. They persuaded six movie industry organisations to place an anti-triad advertisement in Hong Kong's Chinese newspapers calling for the creation of an anti-triad task force. The next day, 14 January, Hong Kong was treated to the amazing spectacle of some 300 of its major stars and movie figures marching along the major thoroughfare of Queensway to the police headquarters in Arsenal Street to demand police protection.[392] The marchers included Andy Lau, Stephen Chow, and Jackie Chan, though not Leslie, who remained under guard. The colonial government was embarrassed and the police agreed to set up a special team to investigate triad activity in the industry. This succeeded in prosecuting the gang who had stolen the two reels of film, and the chief suspect in that case fled to China, but the police task force failed to get to grips with the masterminds behind triad activity in the industry. The violence did not abate. Anita Mui was involved in a series of incidents including chopping, shooting, and a murder in May 1992 and had to flee Hong Kong for a time. Jet Li and John Lone both suffered intimidation and Andy Lau's manager was forced at gunpoint to release the star to make a triad-financed film. The triad threat to the film industry was never properly dealt with, and the special investigation team was disbanded in 1994 without having achieved a major conviction. Triad activity only died down when the industry's profitability started to evaporate after 1993.

All's Well Ends Well was completed despite all the fuss. The film was directed by Clifton Ko, who had directed Leslie in the holiday movie *Merry Christmas* in 1984, and its principal stars were Stephen Chow and Maggie Cheung.[393] Leslie here played what can be seen as his first gay role (though at the time most did not see this). He took the part of Shang So, the family's effeminate younger brother, whose frighteningly masculine female cousin was played by Teresa Mo. The juxtaposition of these gay and lesbian stereotypes made it abundantly clear just what the film was poking fun at, and Leslie and Teresa were obviously not in the slightest confused about what was implied in their roles. They had great fun in either camping it up or butching it down, Teresa at one point riding her motorbike into the classroom in which Leslie is teaching flower-arranging and running over his flowers. It had already been reported in the media that Leslie would play a homosexual in *Farewell My Concubine*.[394] He was evidently not worried about the association of his name with homosexuality and was quite capable of having fun with the whole idea.

Despite the nastiness that surrounded its making, *All's Well Ends Well* proved outstandingly successful at the box office, making over HK$50 million during the six-week run it enjoyed between 25 January and 6 March 1992. It spawned a long line of Chinese New Year comedies.

By now, Leslie was making his next film, *Arrest the Restless*.[395] This Win's Movie film was directed by actor director Lawrence Lau Kwok-cheung, who had earlier made the well-known film *Gangs*, and Leslie's co-stars included Win's boss, Charles Heung, here playing the decent and only very slightly corrupt police Sergeant Lam ("Lam Sir"). Also starring was singer actress Vivian Chow

Wai-man, here in her only performance with Leslie.[396] The film harked nostalgically back to the 1960s (the era, of course, of *Days of Being Wild* as well as Leslie's very early films, such as *Encore*), and the sets, props, cars, and costumes were very carefully selected to fit the period. Leslie played A Fei, or Teddy, who runs a gang that keeps clear of drugs but is into chicks, rock and roll, and the occasional bit of violence. Made at a time when police inaction against triads in the movie business was big news, this film deliberately cocked a snoot at the colonial hierarchy. Every character is corrupt; every policeman, whether British or Chinese, is on the take. Leslie, now aged thirty-six, coasted along in this part, performing just as he had a decade earlier, though he looked at times just a little old for the role. While shooting *Arrest the Restless*, he wrote a song for his co-star Vivian Chow, a number named "My Hidden Reason" that she turned into a hit.

Arrest the Restless screened in May, after which Leslie flew to Cannes with producer Hsu Feng and director Chen Kaige, with whom he was to make *Farewell My Concubine* that year. The rest of 1992 was taken up with filming, Leslie being involved with three films that would come to the screen in 1993. One of these, *Farewell My Concubine*, was his first filmmaking foray into mainland China, and that year he spent many months in Beijing learning classical opera and perfecting his Mandarin. The second of these movies was another comedy, *All's Well Ends Well Too*, and the third the martial-arts parody *Eagle Shooting Heroes*.

By 1992, Leslie had accumulated enough time in Canada to achieve citizenship there, though he had never ceased to criss-cross the Pacific, flying back to Hong Kong repeatedly.[397] While there in February 1992, he was photographed with Danny Chan in Yin Yang, the new gay club on Ice House Street that had just replaced the defunct Disco Disco. Later in the year he was with friend Gary Ngan in the Hilton Hotel in Central, one of the classier venues used by Hong Kong's gay community, which used its Cat Street Cafe to drink coffee and hang out.[398] The gay community was becoming a bit more visible and self-confident, bolstered by the decriminalisation of homosexuality that had at last taken place in Hong Kong in 1991. The first gay magazine to be published in the city, *Contacts Magazine*, was founded around that time and first appeared in 1993.

Two more compilations of songs by Leslie were released in 1992 (one with another inappropriate title, *Ultimate Leslie*). At the end of the year, he appeared at the farewell concert given in Hong Kong by Sam Hui, who had collaborated with him in the song "Silence Is Golden" in 1987 and appeared with him in *Aces Go Places V* in 1989.[399] At his farewell concert, Hui credited Leslie with showing him how to retire and enjoy life. The concert, which had a star-studded cast, was one of the very rare occasions in these years in which Leslie broke his resolve not to sing in public other than for charity. He was, to everyone's great surprise and his fans' dismay, sticking to his word.

CHAPTER 11

PALME D'OR

1993

The year 1993 was the most productive and, in terms of both quality and financial gain, the most successful, year Leslie ever had in the film industry. It opened with the screening on New Year's Day of what was perhaps Leslie's greatest achievement, the film he had been working on for the last five months, *Farewell My Concubine*.[400] This was the movie through which he would achieve cinematic fame outside Asia and the wider Chinese world and which has, more than any other, become the monument to his talent.[401] Director Chen Kaige's masterpiece, it is an almost perfect film, breathtaking in its beauty and in the bravery of its making. Its visual impact is matched by the depth of the issues it plumbs and its highly detailed reconstruction of a story spanning fifty years of Chinese history. In *Farewell My Concubine*, Leslie's genius came to full flower.

The movie is based on a Chinese novel of similar name written in 1979 by Lilian Lee. There had long been plans to put the story on the big screen, though it had been made into a two-part miniseries by RTHK in 1981.[402] Leslie had been approached to star in it as far back as 1983, and Lee had always envisaged him playing its principal role, the Peking opera star Cheng Dieyi, who in the story is famous throughout China for his portrayal of female roles—in particular, that of the Concubine in the opera *Farewell My Concubine*. The film revolves around Cheng Dieyi's unrequited love for his lifelong friend Xiaolou, the male lead who plays the Concubine's King.

Rights to the film were owned by the Taiwanese-funded Tomson Company, whose boss and leading producer was Hsu Feng, female star of the kung-fu film *A Touch of Zen*. Hsu was a rich, dynamic, and creative woman, known in Hong Kong as the Goddess of Gamblers for her habit of placing huge bets at the casino table. She determined to make the story, initially asking the highly renowned mainland Chinese director Chen Kaige to direct. He was already renowned for films such as *Yellow Earth*, *The Big Parade*, *King of the Children*, and *Life on a String*, the last of which had been entered for the Cannes film festival, but he turned her down, as he thought that both the script and the novel were shallow and that they failed to handle the Cultural Revolution properly. Hsu Feng then turned to the director Ann Hui, who asked Golden Harvest to release Jackie Chan to star, but the studio feared his involvement in a story featuring homosexuality and refused her. An attempt was made to get John Lone, star of *The Last Emperor*, to play the principal role, but contractual terms could not be agreed. Ann Hui gave up, so Hsu approached Chen Kaige again, and this time he agreed, on the basis that he could have the script re-written to alter the ending and to widen what had hitherto been a story with two principal characters into a triangular tale.

Chen approached Leslie, who had by then become so secure in his career that he was willing this time round to risk the part of Cheng Dieyi. The two met in Hong Kong in July 1992 and discussed the part. Initially, Chen was not convinced that Leslie was really suitable, but Leslie had no doubts. He was attracted by the prospect of working with such a highly acclaimed director and the renowned Chinese co-stars he had recruited; this was exactly the sort of artistic endeavour to which he had aspired when he retired from singing. He was also attracted by the chance to work in a film that was a collaboration between the Hong Kong, Chinese, and Taiwanese industries. The film was a first in that respect, and Leslie believed that it would be highly significant both for the future of the Hong Kong industry and for his own career. Luckily, he had read the novel some ten or so years before and had loved it. Its themes of unrequited same-sex love, betrayal, and loss moved him strongly. From the start he saw himself as Cheng Dieyi, telling Chen Kaige that Dieyi was, like himself, a person who did not distinguish between acting and real life and who, also like him, was a man in whose soul both male and female components vied. Chen Kaige was persuaded and Leslie got the part.

There ensued the most intensive period of preparation that Leslie was ever to undertake for a film. He put aside fear of the Communist mainland to fly up to Beijing in August 1992 to join the cast and crew and to study both the Mandarin language in which the film was to be made and the techniques of Peking opera. He lived for six weeks with a Chinese family while studying for four hours every day with the top opera teachers in Beijing, Zhang Manling and Shi Yansheng. He was familiar with only Cantonese opera so far, and the music and highly stylised form of Peking opera were completely unknown to him. His part called for him to act the role of the Concubine in a believably professional manner, so by dint of vast patience and grinding practice he learned the body movements, the hand gestures, the footsteps, and above all, the mental attitude that were necessary for the role. He could not sing the part, as his tenor voice could not reach the high registers it required, but he lip-synched perfectly to match the professional singers who sang in his stead.

All this was despite Leslie's very real fears of venturing into the power of the Communist state, a system that only a few decades before had destroyed his family. He had neither colleagues nor friends in the Chinese film world and found himself cold-shouldered on his arrival in Beijing. His fellow actors and crew at first affected to despise this southern Chinese pop singer with no record, in their eyes, of serious acting. But his friendly, unassuming nature; the way he made no distinction between himself and others, whatever their status; and, above all, his professionalism won them over, and contempt soon turned to admiration and praise. His professionalism impressed the cast and crew, who noted that Leslie never forgot his lines; some of them commented later that he took more on his shoulders than the director. Lei Han, who played his apprentice Xaio Si, later remembered that there was no other actor on the set that respected his work as much as Leslie did and spoke of a scene in which Leslie played the concubine on stage. As his Mandarin was still not too good, he did it again and again. After a few takes, Chen Kaige was happy with the result, but Leslie himself was not and kept going till he felt it was perfect. It was only after more than thirty takes that he stepped down from the stage.[403] The cast and crew remarked that Leslie always treated his fellow actors with kindness, often feeding those living in hostel accommodation at his suite in the Shangri-la Hotel. He was admired for the ease and openness of his relationship with Daffy, for he responded honestly to questions about his partner and amazed everyone by not trying to hide the fact that they were lovers.

His most difficult relationships were with the two Chinese stars, Zhang Fengyi, whose part (the role Jackie Chan had turned down) was that of the actor Duan Xiaolou, who always played the King, and Gong Li, who played Juxian, Duan's prostitute wife. Zhang had a history of playing earthy peasant types and found it difficult to adapt to a role where he was the object of the affections of another man. It took a lot of effort on Leslie's part to break through his reserve, either on or off stage. Gong Li was a much more glamorous star who had made her name in films like *Red Sorghum* and *Raise the*

Red Lantern, and she could on occasion behave in ways more reminiscent of a Hollywood star, objecting to direction and absenting herself from the set. She did not take kindly at first to second billing behind Leslie, and it was in part to make her accept the role that Chen Kaige had expanded the script. Yet, as filming progressed and as she watched Leslie's dedication and attention to detail, she too warmed to him and the two became friends.[404]

The film traces the life and career of Cheng Dieyi from 1925, when his mother delivers him to an opera troupe in Peking. She abandons her son there and is never seen again. Dieyi is small, sweet-natured, and pretty as well as very talented. He is in need of protection, which he gets from the slightly older and bigger Duan Xiaolou. Dieyi's size and voice mark him out for the female roles (which were all, at the time, played by men), but initially he resists this, refusing to sing any line indicating that he is a woman and enduring much punishment as a result. Finally broken, he sings the female part. The two friends slowly establish themselves as stars, making their name particularly as the King and his Concubine, Ru Yi, in the classic opera *Farewell My Concubine*, a story in which the Concubine sacrifices herself by committing suicide with her King's sword as he loses his kingdom. Off stage, as Dieyi grows older he finds that he has fallen in love with his childhood friend Xiaolou, but only on stage as Concubine Ru Yi can he allow himself to show this love. In effect, his stage life takes over his real world. Offstage, all the joys of stardom ensue, but the idyll is smashed when Xiaolou marries the prostitute Juxian. Dieyi is shut out and in despair gives himself to a wealthy opera patron, a man with whom he begins an affair. This unhappy ménage survives the Japanese occupation, during which their troupe is forced to perform for their country's enemies, but it collapses after the fall of nationalist China. Dieyi is forced out of the opera by his own apprentice and, during the struggle sessions they endure during the Cultural Revolution, he, Xialou, and Juxian all betray each other. The film ends in Hong Kong, where Xialou and Deiyi, by now old men, once again find themselves preparing to re-enact their roles, this time presented in the Coliseum as relics of a bygone age. At the point in the story where the Concubine seizes the sword, Dieyi finally merges his two lives and wields it to kill himself.

The story can be seen on many levels. It tells vividly the tragic political history of China from the decades between the wars up until the late 1970s. The scenes of self-destruction it includes when it reaches the Cultural Revolution almost had it banned in China. It is also the story of a unique part of Chinese culture, Peking opera, and of its ruin by the Communists. On the personal level, it is a tale of loyalty, loss, and failure: all the major characters betray and are betrayed in their turn. It is a story of love and of the sacrifices love may require: both Dieyi and Juxian ultimately give their lives for Xialou. On top of all this, the film is a story in which the love of one man for another is shown to be just as deep, just as real as that of a woman. Though Chen Kaige often needed to play down the importance of his film's homosexual theme, for political or PR reasons, its message was clear, and in the China of 1993, his was a very brave film indeed.

Taking the part of Cheng Dieyi was also personally a brave act for Leslie, for he was placing his career on the line in playing an effeminate star of female opera parts who is in love with the masculine hero. To many, the link between actor and role was unavoidable, made more so by the double linkage of life and art as Leslie identified with Cheng Dieyi and Cheng Dieyi identified with the Concubine. As was noted in the press some four years later, the femininity he had sparingly displayed till then burst out on the screen. A line spoken of Dieyi in the film was often said later of Leslie: "Has he not blurred the distinction between theatre and life ... male and female?"[405] It was not Dieyi who hid under the Concubine's makeup, but Leslie.[406]

Leslie brought to this part all his experiences of love and loss in the gay world. He played his unrequited love for his partner as a tragedy of a high order, but at the same time illustrated his plight in every aspect of his daily life. The small ways in which Dieyi fusses about the insouciant object of his love are painful to watch. Until Juxian arrives on the scene, Dieyi tries to protect Xialou from all the minor problems that beset his life; he worries over him, he checks his clothes, he all but acts as his wife. None of this, of course, can survive Xialou's marriage, and the storms, tantrums, jealousies, pettiness, and the final despair in Dieyi's inevitable loss, well up out of Leslie's own experience. As does the radiant happiness that Dieyi but briefly enjoys when he has both the adoration of his fans that stardom brings and the companionship of the man he loves.

Farewell My Concubine was hugely expensive, costing some HK$30 million to make, and great attention was paid to detail. Filming was gruelling, the scenes on stage taken again and again at the instigation of both director and actors. The elaborate costumes and heavy makeup took two hours each day to prepare, and they made the street scenes, shot in Beijing in the heat and dust of the late summer, very hard to bear. The emotion that permeated every scene made the film psychologically very draining. Leslie threw his soul into the part. Chen Kaige recalled an incident at the end of the scene where, in despair at ever winning the love of Xiaolou, Dieyi gives his body to his wealthy opera patron, from whose house he returns home by rickshaw, broken by the sorrow and horror of what he has done. Chen cut the film as the rickshaw curtain was pulled back to expose the distraught Dieyi. The film stopped rolling, but Leslie sat motionless in the rickshaw, his makeup washed away by the tears which streamed down his cheeks, his eyes empty and black with despair. Chen had the studio lights turned off and the crew departed in silence, leaving Leslie alone with Dieyi in the dark.

It was not surprising that Leslie found making the film the hardest thing he'd ever done. To make things more difficult, during shooting he had news from Hong Kong that Danny Chan was in a coma in hospital. There was no official announcement of what had happened, but the word on the street was that Danny had overdosed on drugs. Leslie rang Danny's mother several times during the filming to check on his progress; sadly, there was to be none.

Farewell My Concubine was a huge success as soon as it opened in Hong Kong, taking over HK$5 million at the box office inside a few days. The critics raved and audiences flocked to see it. When it was released internationally, it rapidly won critical acclaim and was nominated for the *Palme d'Or* at that summer's Cannes Film Festival, the world's most prestigious celebration of current film. Leslie went there in July with Chen Kaige, Hsu Feng, Gong Li, and Zhang Fengyi. He made an immediate impression, his handsome appearance and his star quality attracting attention at every function. Being fluent in English and Mandarin, he acted as interpreter for the others. Tomson made an excellent job of the public relations and placed Leslie's face on huge posters all around the town.[407] It was the merit of the film itself, though, which drew huge praise from the audiences that saw it and ensured that *Farewell My Concubine* took the prize, jointly that year with Jane Campion's *The Piano*. It was the first time that a Chinese film had won the *Palme d'Or*.

The *Palme d'Or* was to do more than make the reputation of all those involved. In both China and Taiwan it prevented financial disaster, for in both countries, for varying reasons, the film came within an inch of being banned. Chen Kaige had feared that this might happen, having had his earlier film *Life on a String* banned in the mainland. The Chinese authorities initially cleared the film for distribution across China and Tomson arranged premieres in both Beijing and Shanghai, with the usual razzmatazz of accompanying events and press conferences. However, by the time Leslie reached Beijing for the August launch, the Chinese government had changed its mind. The Politburo itself was said to have watched the film at a special screening, and some of its members were said to have walked out before its end. The homosexual theme was not to their taste, the Cultural Revolution scenes offended, and the suicide, a depressing ending, was not felt to be in line with China's official optimism about the future. So when he arrived in Beijing for the premiere, Leslie was met by no welcoming delegation at the airport and with the news that the press conference had been cancelled. Screening had been restricted to one theatre for which tickets were on sale only by hand on the streets. Advertisements had been pulled, and fifty feet of the film with three scenes that found especial disfavour had been cut, though for some reason the final suicide had not been touched.[408]

Things were not quite so bad in Shanghai, where cinemas had already sold out, and where distributors prevailed on the authorities to let them go ahead, pleading the huge financial losses they faced, but even there the launch programme was curtailed and the press was instructed not to ask Leslie about the film. Despite repeated protestations that he was merely an actor and had no wish to get involved in politics, Leslie made it very clear that he was exceedingly angry with the treatment meted out by the Chinese authorities, telling the *South China Morning Post* that he was an artist who never attended rallies and hated politics. The Chinese reaction, he said, had stunned him.[409] The spectacle of China banning the first Chinese film that had won a *Palme d'Or* also invoked international criticism. It is said that this persuaded Deng Xiaoping himself to watch a private screening and that he, with the help of his daughter, Deng Ling, used his influence to have the film released. Eventually, the film was distributed in its uncut version all over China, and by September it was playing to packed houses in the capital.[410] Wherever it was shown, the film was a huge success. At its initial showing in Beijing, over a thousand stood in addition to the 2,700 who managed to get seats.

Across the straits in Taiwan, things were strangely the same. The film fell foul of a Taiwanese rule banning films with over half the actors from the mainland, and it was initially refused a licence. This would not only have prevented its showing in cinemas but also its sale as a video. The ridicule this attracted forced the Kuomintang government to amend the law, which they swiftly did to exempt any film that had won one of five specified international awards, one of them the *Palme d'Or*.[411] The film was then licensed and was put on show in over 100 cinemas round the clock, making over HK$6.1m inside three days.

This was the first and only film starring Leslie that received immediate, widespread international exposure. Across the Pacific, it was shown at film festivals in Toronto in September and New York in October. It was nominated (unsuccessfully, much to Leslie's disappointment) as Hong Kong's entry for an Oscar as Best Foreign Language Film—the film's entry in this category had enraged some Hong Kong film producers, who alleged it was a mainland production.[412] It went on to win BAFTA and Golden Globe awards for Best Foreign Language Film as well as awards at many international film festivals. The California state government threw a reception to celebrate the movie, and Madonna threw a party for Chen Kaige. Strangely, the only personal awards Leslie won for this film came from the Japanese Film Critics Society, which awarded him their Best Actor Award (Foreign Movie) in 1994, and in China, where he was given the Award for High Achievement by the Society for Performing Arts. He had been the first Hong Kong actor to take part in a mainland production. The omission of his name from the lists for Best Actor is strangely baffling.

Farewell My Concubine remains a great favourite worldwide. It was selected as one of the best 100 movies in the history of worldwide cinema by *Time Asia* in 2005, and, although the film was never entered for the Hong Kong Film Awards, as it was not considered in Hong Kong to be a local film, it was voted Most Favourite Film in the poll held in Hong Kong for the Centennial of Chinese Film History, also in 2005.

This success led to a flurry of speculation about Leslie's future acting career. Chen Kaige told the press that Leslie would star in his next film, a drama titled *Shadow of a Flower*, which was to be set in the 1930s; this was the script that eventually came to be titled *Temptress Moon*. One idea that did not work out was a plan by Canadian director David Cronenberg to cast Leslie for the part of Song Liling in *M Butterfly*. John Lone played this role when the movie was made in October that year. Leslie was also offered roles in Hollywood productions but declined them. He indicated many times that he was averse to going to Hollywood, where he feared he would be a minor figure and an Asian one at that. He mentioned derisively to the press that he had been asked to play a ninja in a film with Keanu Reeves. He preferred to be a star at home rather than play in B or C-grade movies in America.

While the furore over *Farewell My Concubine* was in full spate, Mandarin Films brought out the second of its *All's Well* series of films at the Chinese New Year of 1993, this one named *All's Well Ends Well Too*.[413] This was the usual slapstick movie directed by Clifton Ko, this time set in period costume spliced with modern jokes (seat belts in sedan chairs, pager frogs, traffic lights made of paper lamps, and the like). The cast included many with whom Leslie had worked in earlier comedies, and this time he played David Copper Feel, a travelling magician who wins the principal girl, Snow White, a role taken by Rosamund Kwan Chi-lam, who had worked before with him in both ATV's *Agency 24* and the charity show *The Banquet*.

Teresa Mo reprised her role as a butch tough girl, this time with a huge birthmark and hairy legs. Slight but fun, typical of the series, the show aired from 20 January and made number one on the box office list. It did well abroad, too, and Leslie flew to South Korea to promote it.

On 5 February, as *All's Well Ends Well Too* closed, the second comedy Leslie had made in late 1992 opened, this entitled *The Eagle Shooting Heroes* (or, in direct translation of the Chinese title, *Success Here and There*).[414] Directed by Jeffrey Lau Chun-wai, who had produced *Nomad* back in 1982, it was a parody of the trilogy of novels by Jin Yong, the pen name of the prolific Hong Kong writer, journalist and novelist Louis Cha, founder of *Ming Pao* newspaper.[415] The film was billed as a political allegory, but if it was so, it was a very distant one. It was a not hugely amusing comedy, though it had a star-studded cast: with Leslie were the two Tony Leungs, Jacky Cheung, Kenny Bee, Brigitte Lin, Maggie Cheung, Anita Yuen, Veronica Yip Yuk Hing , Carina Lau, Joey Wong, and more. Leslie's character, one of his series of innocent and naïve young men, wears the kind of silky, effeminate, and brightly coloured clothes he first donned in the TV dramas of his early days. He is pursued by a very gay prince played by Tony Leung Ka-fai, who seeks to become an immortal by getting Leslie to say "I love you." There are amusing scenes where Leslie fends him off. His line "We're both men. How can I fall in love with you?" must have been deliberately ironic. At one point he is subject to an operatic seduction by the prince who is dressed outrageously in female clothes. In the end, unsurprisingly, Leslie says "I love you" and Tony Leung's prince ascends to heaven. This film was made, of course, to tap the Chinese New Year market and duly, if amazingly, made number three at the box office. Most of the cast, including Leslie, went across to Taiwan to promote the film when it came out there.

The year 1993 turned out to be a busy one for Leslie. His hectic pace of filmmaking (five movies starring him screened during the year) reflected closely the state of the Hong Kong film industry, which was just passing the never-to-be-surpassed peak it had reached in 1992, when the local box office takings for Hong Kong films were a huge HK$1.240 billion.[416] Leslie's growing international status also let him in for more work. In October, he flew to Japan to join the jury for the Young Cinema Competition at the Tokyo International Film Festival.

Ticket sales had begun to drop in Hong Kong, however, and now commenced what was eventually to be a catastrophic decline in the Hong Kong film industry's fortunes. Low-cost VCDs, many pirated, had begun to flood the market at a time when the growing audience sophistication caused by Hong Kong's increased wealth, its status as a world financial centre, and the better education and improved levels of English of its people, had led to an increased demand for US movies. Hong Kong studios, fragmented as they had been over the last decade, were not capable of matching the big budgets deployed by Hollywood and failed to counter Hollywood's aggressive public relations machines.

There were qualitative factors at work here, too. The large number of independent studios making films needed to make a lot of them in order to survive, but the more films that were made, the less time they aired and the less market share they won. Even the well-established studios were trapped in the cycle of financial investment and return, and believed that they needed to make as much money as possible before the 1997 handover to China put a final end, they feared, to the merry-go-round. There was a huge element of pure greed here, particularly from the industry's triad participants, and few cared that quality was given less weight than quantity. Costs were rising, too: Hong Kong's stars were not slow to recognise their earning potential, and the fees they charged put increasing pressure on budgets. As a result, they ended up working at a pace which reduced the standard of their work, some of the key actors working on up to five films simultaneously and making up to ten films in a year. Producers and directors chasing cash returns also took on too much work, and found themselves forced to delegate much of it to less-talented subordinates. The triads were not long in working out that there was now more money to be made in VCDs than in the filmmaking they had earlier invaded. Whilst this slowly reduced the sort of unpleasant pressure the industry had been subjected to before, it worsened the pressure on its finances as triad distribution of pirated VCDs was efficient and international.

This trend was worsened by the fact that much of the profitability of the industry was increasingly dependent on foreign sales, especially in Taiwan and Japan, with the results that the demands of these overseas markets came to dominate the industry. Their viewers were often less sophisticated than Hong Kong audiences and wanted big stars and simple, formulaic stories. Even so, these foreign markets also began to collapse. A vicious cycle of overexploitation of the video rental business set in. Hong Kong studios would pre-sell films to overseas distributors, especially in Taiwan. These would both distribute films to cinemas and sell packages of videos to shops, sandwiching perhaps ten A-grade movies with thirty to forty B or C-grade movies. This called for a large supply of films of any quality, so most of them were bad and swamped the few good movies among them. Worsening this process was the fact that Taiwan rapidly installed cable TV channels in the nineties, creating an insatiable demand for films. Quantity rose, quality dropped, and the demand for Hong Kong films fell with it. Distributors made less and less money, so they demanded lower prices from Hong Kong filmmakers. Taiwanese distributors and theatre owners started a boycott of Hong Kong films in 1993 to force the Hong Kong industry's hand, and prices for Hong Kong movies started a free fall. In 1995, Taiwanese distributors agreed amongst themselves to cap Chinese movie rights at HK$125k per film; this was 20% of the previous highest prices and a huge blow to the Hong Kong industry, which could only respond with cheaper films, which in turn reduced demand. Nor were Taiwanese audiences long behind in catching up Hong Kong audiences in terms of sophistication and desire for the Hollywood product. Japan, Singapore, Malaysia, and Thailand soon followed Taiwan. For a time there was hope that China would provide a replacement market, but this was dashed when China imposed stiffer rules for co-productions, both to shield its own industry and for political reasons. The Hong Kong film industry started a long descent into an abyss.

But in 1993, all this was just beginning, and Leslie's filmmaking career continued to flourish. During the spring and summer, under the direction of the long-established Hong Kong film director, Ronny Yu Yan-tai, he made another of the films for which he would be remembered. *The Bride with White Hair* was screened first in Hong Kong on 26 August 1993 and was an immediate success.[417] The film was another Mandarin Films production, co-produced by the Company's founder Raymond Wong and by Clifton Ko, director of the *All's Well* series.[418] It was a highly expensive production, costing over HK$30 million to make, though it was completed swiftly, in about two months. Leslie's co-star was Brigitte Lin, with whom he had just worked in *Eagle Shooting Heroes*. She was a Taiwanese actress who had moved into Hong Kong films and had a reputation for playing gender-crossing parts. The film, which became a classic of the fantasy swordplay genre, was loosely based on the 1954 *wu xia* novel *Bride* by Leung Yu-sang. It follows the ill-fated love story of swordsman Cho Yi-hang (played by Leslie) and the top assassin of a rival cult, Lien Ni-chang (played by Brigitte Lin). The movie was beautifully shot in dark blue colours, matched by dramatic music and sombre acting: wind whips dark hair across pale white faces, sword-strokes shower flower petals, waterfalls drench lovers in sparkling cascades. This is a film as striking in its cinematography as *A Chinese Ghost Story*, but darker, much more sinister in its plot. Leslie's character smoulders and erupts at times, and at others lapses laconically into indolence, a man who wishes to avoid killing but only succeeds in creating more bloodshed and the destruction of all that he holds dear. Wada Emi, the Japanese costume designer, suggested that Leslie cover his face with his hair in the film, which he did for many of his scenes, and this drove his fans into paroxysms of frenzy, disrupting screening in cinemas with cries for him to show his face.

The movie was notable too, as one of the two beginnings mooted for the adoption of the nickname Gor Gor for Leslie (Joey Wong had been first recorded as calling him this during the making of *A Chinese Ghost Story* six years before). When he himself used that phrase, Leslie always used it to refer to Daffy. Now, during shooting, Leslie praised Brigitte Lin's wearing of Japanese designer Wada Emi's costumes, and she replied, "Leslie Gor Gor, you are stunningly beautiful."

Critics were quick to notice the treatment of gender in the film. Leslie's character is psychologically averse to waging war. Since his childhood, he's been in love with a female "wolf child" who surpasses him in aggressiveness and fighting spirit, though he manages to disarm her with his passive love. Even Leslie's clan sister in the film has more apparent martial spirit than he does, and he voluntarily cedes leadership of the army to her. Yet Leslie still manages to be the most masculine man in the film, and the strong, sultry, and melancholy character he portrays makes the rest look like children. These paradoxes were matched by Brigitte Lin's character, which is magnificently steely, coldly insane in her hatred of men. She can be defeated in battle by neither man nor woman, but she nevertheless remains beautiful and very much a woman. Their enemies in the film, a pair of Siamese twins, are a diabolical combination of genders, joined at their backs, with the female the more dominant of the two (the male figure is rather like the demon in *A Chinese Ghost Story 2)*. The conjoined twins are kinkily sexy, especially in a scene where the male half of the duo tries to rape Lien.

The making of the film was marred by yet another of the triad-related incidents of violence that Leslie had last encountered when making *All's Well Ends Well*. Mandarin Films' leading personalities were clearly subject to some pressure at this time. On this occasion, two bombs were thrown onto the set while filming was underway at a country location in the New Territories.[419] Luckily, no one was hurt. The attack was believed to have been an attempt at extortion, as two men had earlier approached the film crew demanding *tor dei* ("tea money"). One bomb exploded but the second, three sticks of explosive taped with a timer inside, did not. There was talk, too, that Brigitte Lin was on a blacklist of Taiwanese stars, as she had demanded HK$3.5m for making the film, causing its Taiwanese financiers to fear losing money.

Ronny Yu later warmly recalled his experience of working with Leslie on this film and its sequel. He praised Leslie's positive outlook and the way he kept his own spirits up by telling his director not to worry. Leslie would say "It's only a movie" and then ask how he could help. He worked over and over again on all the difficult martial arts sequences until he got them right, ending up with cut hands and feet in the process but never complaining. When the rest of the cast moaned about their work, Leslie told them to respect their profession and stop complaining. To Ronny Yu, Leslie was "a good comrade."[420]

Leslie wrote and performed the movie's theme song, "Red Face White Hair." He still would not break his vow not to sing and agreed to on this occasion only on the condition that the soundtrack would not be released. This drove up attendance in cinemas as fans watched the film to hear the song.

The Bride with White Hair won both box office success and critical acclaim. At the 13th Hong Kong Film Awards in 1994, Leslie's song was nominated for, though failed to win, Best Original Film Song. It succeeded, though, at the Golden Horse Awards that year in Taiwan, winning Best Original Song. The film did well abroad, too, winning several prizes.

When he wasn't involved in filmmaking, Leslie continued his quiet life with Daffy in Canada throughout 1993. Maybe even now thinking of coming back to Hong Kong, or perhaps because he just wanted a base there while he was there filmmaking, Leslie now bought an apartment on Hong Kong's Peak.[421] He discussed his life when he gave what was by this time a rare interview to the *South China Morning Post* in May. He told the reporter that he was much more relaxed and no longer wanted the old pop-idol image. The anonymous interviewer characterised Leslie as "fussy as a feline" in his choice of film work and reported that he was going to reduce his rate of filmmaking to one movie a year. Singing, though, still seemed to be ruled out.[422] Leslie was now, though, making it clear elsewhere that he was finding Canada dull and that he felt that fate was continuing to bring him back to Hong Kong to make films.

When back in Hong Kong during the year, Leslie had the sad duty of paying several visits to Danny Chan's bedside. Danny had remained in hospital in a coma, and he never recovered consciousness. Leslie spoke to him when he visited, though there was no way of telling whether Danny heard him. His old friend and rival wasted away during the summer, lingering on until he finally died on 25 October. It was a sad end to a friendship that had lasted through ups and downs since the beginning of Leslie's career. Now, of the three young men who had set out together in the late seventies, both Danny Chan and Paul Chung were dead. Leslie was only thirty-seven.[423]

On 22 December, timed for the Christmas holiday peak season, the sequel *Bride with White Hair 2* hit the screens.[424] Mandarin Films had managed to get only a small amount of Ronny Yu's time for this film, so most of the work was done by the credited director, David Wu Dai-wai, an American-born actor and TV personality, who had played small parts with Leslie in many films. Brigitte Lin and Leslie starred again, though Leslie made only rather brief appearances at the beginning and the end of the film.[425] The sequel was neither as deep nor as interesting as its predecessor, though it contained the same moody music, striking sets, and dark cinematography. Most of the supporting characters had much less substance than those of the two principal stars. When Leslie reappears to reclaim his lost love, the film moves up several notches, but it is for a very short time. The movie won no awards and there was not to be another sequel, rightly so.

Sticking still to his resolve, Leslie made no more music in 1993, though his record company brought out a new edition of *Salute* in a *24k Gold Collection*. He was still claiming that this secluded Canadian lifestyle was what he wanted.[426] It was, though, becoming increasingly difficult to believe.

CHAPTER 12

HE'S THE MAN

1994

While living in Canada, Leslie did not go back on his word to desist from performing as a singer. He continued to maintain during 1994 that he would not sing again, but he could not escape the music industry entirely.[427] The year opened with something like a sense of déjà vu on Saturday 8 January when he was at RTHK's 16th Annual Chinese Gold Songs Awards at the Hong Kong Coliseum, this time to present one of the prizes to Leon Lai Ming, whose single award that night was overshadowed by the three won by Andy Lau Tak-wah.[428] Lai's fans did not like this, and in an incident reminiscent of the days when Leslie's fans had scuffled with Alan Tam's, Andy Lau's spot was spoiled when his rival's fans opened up a cacophony of catcalls and boos and threw a shower of luminous sticks at him on the stage.[429] Rather than just two Canto-pop "Kings," as there had been in the days of Leslie and Alan Tam, Hong Kong now boasted "Four Heavenly Kings": Andy Lau, Leon Lai, Jacky Cheung, and Aaron Kwok. Leslie's fans, who had never given up hope that their hero would return, saw this as a distinct deterioration in quality. He, however, used his unusual appearance that night to repeat that he would be sticking to his resolution not to sing.

In 1994, Chinese New Year fell in February, and on the 6th of that month, the latest annual offering from Mandarin Film's Raymond Wong and Clifford Ko reached Hong Kong's cinemas. This, the usual silly comedy, was entitled *It's a Wonderful Life* (in Chinese, *Big Rich Family*).[430] It was a film in no respect similar to Frank Capra's 1946 film of that title starring James Stewart (though it also opens at Christmas and aims for the same heart-warming glow).[431] Leslie had a key, if often absent, presence in this film, playing a stranger who rights all the ills of the warring family and brings them together at their New Year reunion dinner. It is one of his nicest roles, that of a gentleman with a conscience who is also a dispenser of help and advice. He spends most of the film in bohemian style, bearded for a change and wearing jeans, his hair tied up in a pigtail or left long. Though still only thirty-seven, Leslie on screen seems far more mature than anyone else around him. The film is good-natured and warm, leaving its audiences the simple message: "treasure your family." It was perfect for the New Year and highly popular, running to 10 March and making over HK$37 million.

Shortly after the film's release, Leslie was a co-presenter at the year's Hong Kong Film Awards and, with Tony Leung Ka-fai, presented Anita Yuen the year's Best Actress award for her role in Derek Yee Tung-sing's *Till the End of Time*. In an interview in the middle of the year, he told the media that he wanted to extend his career into the international market, but by that he did not mean Hollywood. He said he'd rather work in Chinese films as their quality attracted him. Conversely, he was disparaging about the quality of the average Hong Kong movie.[432] He was, he added, in his own view a serious actor, not a movie idol.

On 23 July, Leslie's latest film opened in Hong Kong cinemas, screened during the 19th Hong Kong International Film Festival. *He's a Woman, She's a Man* (in Chinese, *Golden Branch, Jade Leaf*—an earlier age's euphemism for female aristocracy) was a United Film

Organisation (UFO) film directed by Peter Chan Ho-sun.[433] Chan had founded UFO with other Hong Kong filmmakers in 1992 to make quality Hong Kong films which were not driven solely by the profit motive but which aimed to bring sophisticated Asian audiences back to Hong Kong film. They believed that romantic comedies would do the trick. Theirs was exactly the sort of scheme that suited Leslie and he was to make three films with them over the next four years. One of Peter Chan's partners was the actor Eric Tsang Chi-wai, who often starred in UFO's films, and he did so in this, taking the part of the stereo-typically camp Auntie, the film's conscience and gay mouthpiece.

He's a Woman, She's a Man was an amusing, snappily-paced, and sophisticated comedy of manners boldly focussing on Hong Kong's attitude to homosexuality.[434] The plot was, perhaps, an unlikely one, but it managed to be a clever satire of the Hong Kong film and music industries and their attitudes. The movie had a gay actor (Leslie) playing a homophobic heterosexual man who falls in love with a woman who's pretending to be a man, and so in the process comes to realise that it doesn't matter what type of person you love, only that you love them.

Peter Chan let Leslie direct two scenes in the movie, his first attempt at fulfilling his directing dream, and Chan was highly complimentary of his meticulous filming, modestly saying that the parts made by Leslie were the best things in the film. Later comment on these scenes agreed:

> They [the two scenes Leslie directed] were probably the best things in the film. But you were caught in the conflict of characters between the meticulous precision of a director and the wild temperament of an actor. How I wished and how I've always waited for you to make that giant leap of transition.[435]

Leslie starred as songwriter and producer Sam Koo Kah-ming, the finder and still the minder of singing star Rose, played by Carina Lau. Anita Yuen played Lam Chi-wing (the Wing here not, this time, being the same in Chinese pronunciation as Leslie's name), the adoring and naïve fan of the two stars. Sam is living in a slowly fraying relationship with Rose, occupying the flat above hers and making love to her when they both feel like it, something which is by now happening less and less. He's in the doldrums, failing as a composer, so, feeling the need to break away from Rose in both his business and his personal life, he holds auditions to find a new "Mr Ordinary" to turn into a star. All the applicants he listens to are terrible. Rose flies into a tantrum when she finds out what he's doing, arriving in the studio just as Wing, who has dressed as a man for the audition, takes her turn. Wing is an appalling singer, and Rose challenges Sam to make something of this "Mr Ordinary."

Sam signs Wing on through pique, allowing her to worm her way into his life as well as into his flat, where she ends up as a non-paying lodger. Pretty early on, Sam's crew, many of whom are themselves gay, jump to the conclusion that the very effeminate Wing is one of them, something initially that Sam (who, despite his closeness to Auntie, has homophobic opinions) finds hard to stomach. He tries to be open-minded and asks Wing directly if she's gay. Wing denies it, but by chance finds herself chased into a corner by the sexually rampant Rose, who has been so driven to frustration by Sam that she descends to fancying the man Wing is pretending to be. To escape Rose, Wing now pretends she really is gay, but her "confession" is overheard by Sam, who reacts with horror and locks himself in his room. Emerging, he finds Wing playing a new tune on the piano, finds his muse reawakened, and writes "Chase" (a song which in real life was to be a huge hit for Leslie).

To his mortification and confusion, Sam finds himself falling in love with Wing. Their first passionate kiss at the piano leads the horrified Wing (whose only wish as a fan was for Rose and Sam to marry) to run away. With Wing in hiding, Sam is forced to face the fact that he's in love with a man and, deciding that this must mean he's gay, breaks up finally with Rose. When Wing returns, Sam finds she's a woman after all. The key point, of course, is that he's been attracted by Wing as a man in the first place, so he's forced to face the failure of his beliefs about gender and sexuality. By the end of the film, he has so switched position from his earlier revulsion at gay sex that, when he finds Auntie under his piano in the embrace of a man, he leaves them to it, announcing (in English), "It's none of my fucking business." In the final scene, Sam admits to Wing: "Whether you are a boy or a girl doesn't matter. I only know I love you."

Leslie was by far the most impressive performer in this movie (though once again it was not to win him any award). He showed a stature and deftness of comedy which easily made him the focus of the highly talented cast, and (rather as in *The Bride with White Hair*) his character, if not his face, had a maturity which stood out from the rest.

Despite the unlikelihood of the story (an unlikelihood compounded by the fact that Anita Yuen was not really convincing as a boy) and the unrealism of the continual switching of genders, the film is nevertheless a neat vehicle for an open discussion of the sort of sexual orientation issues that weren't aired in Hong Kong at that time. In this film, men of all types, some effeminate, some not, touch, hold hands, are found in bed together, and talk about it openly. At its time, this was quite a staggering advance for Hong Kong and, despite his earlier roles, it was a brave thing for Leslie to draw attention to his own still publicly ambivalent sexuality in this way. His own indeterminate orientation gave the film an edge it would otherwise have lacked, consideration of which must have brought the audiences to focus a little more closely on the reality of the issues, if not the plot. Although Hong Kong law had, though only three years before in 1991, legalised sex in private between adult males, newspaper surveys published at the time still showed that the homosexual community in Hong Kong remained "largely underground, unfocussed, and locked in the closet." The film is a telling commentary on the hypocrisy of Hong Kong's entertainment industry, so many of whose stars and supporting cast and crew were gay or lesbian, but none of whom, at that point, had been brave enough to say so.

The film's soundtrack was the only oasis for Leslie's fans in this year's musical desert. *He's a Woman, She's a Man* included his new song, "Chase," composed by Dick Lee Dik-man, the Singaporean singer-composer. It soon became a very popular number and entered Leslie's favourite repertoire. In the film he also sang a very energetic version of the Beatles' "Twist and Shout" as well as a version of "In this Lifetime." This time the soundtrack was released, in two versions, one sung by the stars, including, of course, Leslie, the other by relative unknowns, in line with the film's story of the discovery of talent amongst "the ordinary." The soundtrack had itself had a more than usually important place in establishing the film's message, the opening and closing sequences being accompanied by Dean Martin's classic romance, "Amore." Dick Lee's song "In My Life," also on the soundtrack, was to become another of Leslie's concert staples.

Leslie took the opportunity of the film's release to make very plain his own view of life, suggesting, perhaps tongue in cheek, that love between a man and a woman lasted for but a moment like a firework and was something that easily disappeared. Making it last was very hard. Love between two men, though, he thought was different. It was generous, kind, and based on solid trust. That was about as obvious a hint of his sexuality as it would have been possible for Leslie to make in 1994. It is clear that he intended the film to be seen as a serious comment on the views on this issue prevalent in

Hong Kong. He was not happy, and said so, that the film contained some of the old homosexual stereotypes, objecting, for instance, to Eric Tsang's role of Auntie.[436]

The movie was hugely popular. *He's a Woman, She's a Man* became the 8th biggest grossing film of the year, making over HK$29 million in its run of nearly four weeks, and at the time it showed was number two at the box office. At next year's 14th Hong Kong Film Awards, Leslie was nominated for, but did not win, Best Actor.[437]

Leslie was very heavily engaged in filming in early 1994. As he was making *He's a Woman, She's a Man*, he was also making the much less distinguished *Long & Winding Road*, dashing from one set to the other to do so and tiring himself out in the process.[438] This second film screened just under two weeks after the first, starting on 4 August, and despite its insipid and actually rather boring story, managed to run for three weeks and make over HK$17 million, reaching number three at the box office at the time.[439] Leslie once again played a character named Wing, but this was a tired office drama that allowed Leslie no chance to act or even to be very funny; it even managed to make him (for the only time on the screen) dull in appearance: his hair lank, his skin greasy, his suit unfashionable, his spectacles unattractive, and his smoking continuous. This was a movie that had pretensions to being a satire on Hong Kong's materialism and ruthless business style, but it hardly deserved to be taken that seriously. Despite its success at the box office at the time, it has rightly sunk without trace since.

As both these films were being filmed, Leslie took another role, though this was only a very small walk-on part, in a film that was released on 31 August. This was UFO's *Over the Rainbow under the Skirt*, a comedy in which Leslie appeared briefly as himself. Though the star of the film was John Tang Yat-kwan, who had appeared with Leslie in *Once a Thief*, Leslie was very much the senior figure here.[440]

The year 1994, as were the previous four, was a year free of any new music (save for the numbers from *He's a Woman, She's a Man*), though as usual two remix discs were issued by the record companies. Leslie spent a lot of the early part of the year in Canada, but he was growing increasingly restless there, though he still said he enjoyed staying at home. He mentioned again to the press the idea of opening a coffee shop in Vancouver, though he hadn't done so in the four years he'd lived there and would never actually do so.[441] His real feelings were made plain in a tourist guidebook entitled *My Visitor*, which was published that year by the *South China Morning Post*, compiled from much earlier interviews.[442] Leslie is quoted as saying that he was born in Hong Kong and had grown up there. His roots meant that he was most comfortable there. He could not, it seems, get over this feeling no matter how long he stayed in Vancouver. In 1994 for the first time in an interview, he no longer ruled out the possibility of a return to both home and music. An indication of what was in the wind was the foundation of his Internet fan club, the first fan club he'd countenanced in Hong Kong since he'd dissolved the original clubs back in 1989.

Leslie's last film to screen that year was one he had spent a very large part of 1992 and 1993 making, though its production had been so slow that the final product only reached cinemas on 17 September 1994. *Ashes of Time* was his second film under the direction of Wong Kar-wai, and was even more of a strange and almost incomprehensible art-house production than the first. It was the major film of the pair made simultaneously by Jet Tone Productions (the other being *The Eagle Shooting Heroes* released the year before) based on the novel *The Legend of the Condor Heroes* by the Hong Kong novelist Jin Yong (Louis Cha),[443] though this version forms a prequel and ends where the novel starts.[444] It was financed in part by the Taiwanese company Scholar Films and the Japanese Pony Canyon Inc. All were to make large losses, for the studio allowed Wong Kar-wai and his team of cameraman Christopher Doyle and Art Director William Chang Suk-ping full rein to indulge their artistic talents, and as a result the film took two years to make and cost a cool HK$47 million. Unsurprisingly, it ran out of cash and had to be rescued before it could be completed.

The film is riven by a fragmented approach to time, frequent disjointed flashbacks of memory, and dense story line. Each of its many characters has a history which hangs like a pall over the present. It is, though, also a vivid work of visual art, its cinematography, dialogue, sonorous voiceovers, and moody music drenched in melancholy and malaise. So complicated a movie is it that it is impossible to comprehend at the first sitting. The film was packed with stars. Led by Leslie as its principal character, the swordsman turned assassination agent Ouyang Feng (Malicious West), these included both Tony Leungs, Jacky Cheung, Maggie Cheung, Brigitte Lin (the latter typically playing both a brother and sister), and Carina Lau.

Initially, Leslie spent much time playing a part that was later taken over by Tony Leung Kar-fai; when the two actors arrived on location in western China, they found that Wong had reversed their roles, causing all the earlier shooting to be jettisoned. The subsequent filming went slowly, horribly behind schedule, and reel after reel of film was re-shot so that Wong could achieve the perfect vision he sought. The actors became as frustrated with this as they did with Wong's habit of working without a script (he was also the script writer). Every morning, he would hand them a sheet with acting directions, then demand that they improvise their roles. Much of the dialogue that was spoken in the action ended up as voiceovers, leading Leslie, for one, to complain that he had not been given much chance to act.

The shooting on location took place in the arid north of Shaanxi province around Yulin, where it was mostly dusty and hot but at other times depressingly wet. Drizzle dampened spirits; torrential downpours washed out roads. Filming took place in ruined shacks or caves, in one of which Leslie was bitten on the neck by a scorpion. The crew rushed him to the clinic in the nearest town and awoke the local doctor in the middle of the night only to find he had no treatment for scorpion bites. Leslie was left to recover on his own. The hard conditions and the length of shooting enraged the stars, all of whom had other films to shoot, one of them the film's sister comedy, *The Eagle Shooting Heroes*, for which they were at times whisked away by Jet Tone.

Leslie admired Wong Kar-wai, whom he and the others called "Tall Man," and was proud of the fact that he picked him first for his favourite films, but he found his way of working incredibly frustrating. He was to speak of his experiences in this film in a lecture he and Brigitte Lin gave at Hong Kong University in 1999. He said then that Wong had given his actors wonderful guidelines, then confused them by switching them all later. He compared Wong to a master painter, who took months to make a single stroke with his brush. It was, he thought, "a very selfish way of making a movie," wasting money as well as the time of the roughly forty crew and actors on site. "He's talented but no one knows exactly what he wants; you only see what you did at the premiere," he said.[445] The discomfort and frustration of the actors, though, suited the mood of the film and thereby paradoxically assisted in calling forth the requisite feelings of despair, ennui, and depression.

These fitted the story well. The tale revolves around the familiar Wong themes of loss, betrayal, and failure amongst characters for whom desire is always ill-chosen and self-destructive, and whose fates are capricious. The film is a meditation on remembering and forgetting, each character unable to forget the past but desperately trying to cast it aside. The result is the loss of hope, particularly by Ouyang Feng, whom Leslie played as hard, nihilistic, and blasted by a vastly unattractive cynicism. There is nothing likeable at all about his character, which exploits others' weaknesses whilst carefully avoiding the destruction he leads them to. He is akin to the dusty wind that whips and tears the tattered cloths that hang from the eaves of his mud hovel and adorn the bodies of both heroes and baddies alike. Ouyang Feng is a fine swordsman, a giant among the heroes he fights, but he has lost his honour. Sensual with failure, his presence broods over the whole film. Leslie was magnetic throughout: tough, masculine, unforgiving, and unforgivable.

Unsurprisingly, all this made the film an immediate flop at the box office. Cinemas kept it on their screens until 12 October, a period of some three weeks, but it was greeted with incomprehension and dismay by its audiences, many of whom left cinemas halfway through the performance, and later audiences were very thin indeed. The film grossed only HK$9 million in Hong Kong, and both the studio and its backers made a huge loss.

While the public rejected the film, the critics adored it. Though Leslie himself was not to win anything for his part in it, the movie won three awards at the 14th Hong Kong Film Awards in 1995 and many prizes overseas. *Ashes of Time* has attracted critics and repelled audiences ever since.

***

At the end of 1994, as was usual by now, Leslie indulged in a comedy for Mandarin Films for the Chinese New Year of 1995, this one entitled *The Chinese Feast* (in Chinese, *Gold Jade Full Hall*), directed by Tsui Hark.[446] Leslie had been asked by Clifton Ko to star in his New Year film, and had even had a cheque from him in payment, but, giving as reason that the filming of *Temptress Moon* then going on in China made this impossible, Leslie didn't cash the cheque. This upset Ko, who never really forgave him, but didn't worry the studio as it was making both films. Raymond Wong himself had a small part in *The Chinese Feast* so would not have objected to Leslie's choice. One factor in this choice may have been that Leslie got star billing that year, something he rightly deserved as he was now, at HK$5 million a film, the top-earning Hong Kong star.

The film centred on a competition to make the best Imperial Manchu Han Feast, and Leslie played a very scruffy chef, a part he much enjoyed.[447] When he spoke of it to the press, he made pointed comments about how easy it was to work with a director as clear in his intent as Tsui Hark and with a script always in front of him. Perhaps not surprisingly, the film was very popular, staying on screens from 28 January to 3 March 1995 and grossing HK$31 million.

The year 1994 was a very quiet one socially, whatever time off available between films spent in Vancouver, though Daffy joined Leslie at Teresa Mo's wedding in Hong Kong. Although he didn't name him, Leslie spoke that year about his love for Daffy in a radio interview with Sandra Ng.[448] Having told her that there was only one person in his life, he replied to her question about what kind of dreams he would like by saying:

> I want to dream about the person I love the most [...] That is the person I'm referring to.

ON TOP OF THE WORLD

CHAPTER 13

YIN AND YANG

1995 – 1996

In February 1995, at a press conference held in the ballroom of the Si Hua Hotel in Taipei, Leslie told the world that he was resuming his singing career and that he had signed a contract with the Taiwanese company Rock Records.[449] The news brought joy to countless fans worldwide and relief to his friends. Whilst unexpected, the news was not a shock, just a pleasant surprise. Only a few journalists in Hong Kong's gutter press cavilled at his change of mind. Everyone else was too pleased to want to criticise any inconsistency.

Leslie had met Rock Records long before while with Capital Artists, and he now signed with them for three albums and three videos, at rumoured earnings of a cool HK$50 million. Now that he had made the decision to resume his pop career, he said, he had chosen Rock because they were prepared to honour his desire for greater artistic freedom.[450] He told the press that he was under a lot less pressure now and that his status gave him a freedom to suit himself that he had not had before.[451] He promised himself and his public that henceforth he would focus on being original in his music, as he had some time ago announced that he intended to be in his choice of films. From now on, he would choose the composers and lyricists who suited him. He was coming home, but on his own terms. Surprisingly for him, though not for the Taiwanese Rock Records, he said that he was intending to concentrate on Mandarin songs, which would have a market beyond Hong Kong. This idea lasted hardly beyond the press conference.

Lest his fans be disappointed by any absence from the public eye, he deliberately made it clear that he was going to adopt a lower profile than before. He might be abandoning the seclusion of Vancouver, but he did not intend to return to the old maelstrom he had hated in Hong Kong. From now on, he would engage in less promotional activity and attend no musical award ceremonies. Nor did he, he added, intend to indulge the media in the way young singers were obliged to; the press were, he thought, spoilt. What he would do now was focus on quality rather than the "packaging" (like all the others did, he implied). He and his fans were now, he believed, a bit older and more mature, and he wanted to reflect that in his music. He wanted to make his songs more socially relevant, too.

Straight away, these remarks got him off to a bad start with the two hundred or so reporters assembled in the ball room, who wrote catty remarks in their subsequent articles about his retirement and return, which in return Leslie made plain he didn't like. There was soon more to come of this sort of antagonism. Leslie's old war with the media had resumed before he had set foot back in Hong Kong.

Although he was to give fewer explanations of this change of mind than he did of his initial decision to retire, he nevertheless broadcast quite a few. Initially, as early as 1993, he had revealed that film industry friends like John Woo had tried to persuade him to return, though their arguments had proved insufficient to break his resolve.[452] He teasingly said some years later that he could not afford to live in Canada on the money he had earned earlier; on what he was earning as a film star, one has to doubt that he was serious in giving this explanation.[453]

Nor could it have been that he was persuaded that the political situation had changed for the better. With the handover to China now only two years away, the last British governor of Hong Kong, Chris Patten, had so fallen out with Beijing that it was clear that the Chinese would not accept the political system the British intended to leave behind and were already making their own arrangements.[454] This was alarming many, and large numbers of those who could do so were leaving. Doubtless, though, Leslie was less worried about the Communists than when he had emigrated. His work had given him a personal knowledge of China he had not had before; starting with the time he'd spent there making *Farewell My Concubine*, he had travelled there often. He was a well-established star there by now, and this is likely to have quietened some of the anxieties he retained. He did say that he had come to realise that the grass was not all that greener in Canada. As he nicely put it in a magazine interview, he thought the moon seen from a place abroad might seem round and beautiful, but he found out that it was the same as the moon you saw from China.[455]

Despite all this, it seems very clear that he had become more than bored at home in Vancouver, which was then still a somewhat placid town. Some years later he related to a Japanese writer that he had woken up one morning and found that he couldn't take his lifestyle anymore, that it was all too boring.[456] He had discovered that something was missing in his life and had come to realize that at the age of thirty-three he had been far too young to retire.[457] A seminal moment, he explained, had happened by chance in Hong Kong, when he had come across Chris Babida, the musician with whom he'd earlier collaborated whilst with Cinepoly, playing at a concert given by Emil Chow Hua-jian. The atmosphere had been such fun that he thought it was wonderful and wanted it all again for himself.[458]

It is scarcely surprising that Leslie would miss the excitement of his old life and the relationships he had achieved with his audiences. He was, perhaps, beginning to worry about getting older. The fear of gradually losing these looks, and a desire not to waste them while he had them, could well have taken hold in the isolation of Canada, which seems also to have become, ironically, stressful in itself. When he returned this year to Hong Kong it was noticed that he was looking thinner and that he had lost some hair, not it seemed through baldness, but from some other cause.[459] The press reported that he was so concerned about his thinning hair that he was spending HK$2,000 a month on treatment. Whatever was troubling him, though, soon passed. His hair returned to normal and he retained almost exactly the looks that he had always had.

Leslie was, in any case, as he characterised himself to the press, addicted to work and could not find the stimulation he needed in the quiet of British Columbia. As he told the Hong Kong press later in the year, he had decided to return "to fulfil himself."

The first fruit of his new collaboration with Rock Records naturally took some time to ripen, some five months in all. This was the ten track album *Love* (also known as *Strong Love, Beloved, Fondness*, or *Love Leslie*) which soon became the bestselling album of the year after its release on 7 July.[460] The huge splash the album achieved was all that Leslie could have hoped for. It was a collection of his movie songs, including the theme from the long-awaited *Temptress Moon*, as well as "A Thousand Dreams of You" and three Mandarin songs he'd composed for his film *The Phantom Lover* (including his and Leslie Mok's "Midnight Song"). All these new songs were destined to join the list of favourites with his fans and were added to well-known numbers from *Farewell My Concubine*, *Days of Being Wild*, and *The Bride with White Hair*. He also included "Chase" from *He's a Woman, She's a Man*. Rock spent a hefty HK$4 million on promoting this album and as a result over 210,000 copies were sold very swiftly in Hong Kong, making it one of the IFPI's top five selling albums of the year.[461] Leslie travelled abroad to market it in some of the locations of his earlier triumphs, finding himself greeted ecstatically by fans who turned out in their tens of thousands to clog airports and theatres. He visited three locations in Taiwan and in South Korea, where he also appeared on a popular TV show.

So a triumphant revival it was, though one mostly based on a look back at the past rather than on any new music or style. His old record companies jumped on the bandwagon with several re-issues of his earlier music during 1995 (one was entitled *Always in My Heart*). However, just as he had resolved, he did not resume the hectic speed his musical career had reached in the eighties. From now on, he would take it all at his own pace, and at the start it was a slow one.

In the summer, he flew to Tokyo to take part in a Hong Kong Movie Festival, part of the industry's efforts to boost their flagging markets. He was determined that year to keep stress levels under control and managed this so well that he succeeded in giving up smoking completely.[462] At a time when other stars were still making a dozen or so films every year, Leslie managed to carry out his pledge to limit himself to films in which he was interested. He was to star in only two movies screened in 1995.[463]

The second of these (the first being *The Chinese Feast* which came out at Chinese New Year) hit cinemas on 22 July.[464] *The Phantom Lover* was a Mandarin Films remake of a very old Shanghai movie, *Song at Midnight*, China's first horror film made in 1936 by Ma-xu Weibang.[465] This had been based on Gaston Leroux's French novel of 1909, *The Phantom of the Opera* (so despite its apparent similarities, this film is not based on Andrew Lloyd Webber's 1986 musical *Phantom of the Opera*, though maybe not so coincidentally this was showing in Hong Kong at the time). *The Phantom Lover* was directed by Ronny Yu, who had directed and produced both films in the *The Bride with White Hair* series and had also produced *All's Well Ends Well Too*. He chose Leslie as the male lead because of his fluent Mandarin and his experience of Beijing filmmaking, and Leslie became the fulcrum around which the film turned. Its plot included the live performance of a musical play, and Yu allowed Leslie to take charge of the music for this and for the film as a whole (allowing him to be credited as co-producer). Leslie wrote three Mandarin songs for the film, one of which, "Midnight Song," was nominated for Best Song at the next Hong Kong Film Awards. He was also given some experience in script-writing, as Ronny Yu let him write some of the dialogue, including that for a key scene.

There was some penalty to having Leslie in the principal role in this film, however, as his phantom character's face needed to be disfigured, something that Yu knew the fans would not tolerate. Yu solved this by disfiguring only one side of Leslie's face so that his fans could still gaze at his perfect side. He made certain that it was the beautiful side of his face that was seen more often seen than the not-so-horrible mask.

Ronny Yu enjoyed working with Leslie, later praising him for his professionalism and the fearless way he took on the part.[466] Leslie was, Yu said, the only actor in Hong Kong who could have played it. He was, in truth, well suited to the role, with just the right amount of narcissism to make the tremendously selfish hero acceptable to the audience, and with the ability to carry off the stage performances and songs. Yet Leslie himself did not find the film convincing, and, when interviewed a year later by Stanley Kwan for his film *Yang-Yin*, was to be critical of the shallowness of the character he played and the undeveloped storyline.

The music from the film became part of the Leslie repertoire but the film itself was not a success. In a year when Leslie was seeking special vehicles for his talent, it was something of an anticlimax.

Leslie's return to resume his status as a Hong Kong superstar once more made him easy game for the Hong Kong media. His relations with the press resumed a downward trajectory as reporters took pictures of him and Daffy together and suggested publicly that they were lovers. He denied the report, complaining that people were trying to set him up as a homosexual.[467] The media were not deterred and carried the story that Daffy was living in the dream house that Leslie had purchased for HK$26 million at Number 2, Turtle Cove Bay on the south side of Hong Kong Island. Reporters were soon following Daffy around. On one occasion, Leslie spotted some cameramen trying to take photos of the two of them together. Infuriated, he gave pursuit in his Porsche, and the cars collided, damaging the Porsche.[468] Magazines started to publish photos of the house at Turtle Cove Bay and of his mother's flat in May Tower, the expensive block of flats in Tregunter Path, Mid-Levels, where Leslie had set her up; she had not resumed living with him when he returned from Canada. Leslie was very disturbed by the resulting harassment from fans and tourists and sold his house two years later (though for HK$42 million, so at a good profit). All this confirmed his fears that his return to Hong Kong was to be the end of the very real privacy he and Daffy had carved out for themselves in Vancouver.

***

RTHK's 18th Top Ten Chinese Gold Songs Award Presentation Concert was held on 31 January 1996 in front of 10,000 fans in the Hong Kong Coliseum, raising some HK$3.8 million for the Yan Chai Hospital in Tsuen Wan.[469] The show was groundbreaking as it was broadcast live for the first time on the Internet, with viewers also casting votes online, followed by a screening on ATV on 10 February. In all, it was watched worldwide by an estimated 5.7 million people. Leslie, who was not there, of course, following his new policy of refusing to attend award ceremonies, won the new category of Best Selling Artist, along with Jacky Cheung, Andy Lau, and two others.

Another year, another Lunar New Year comedy. In 1996 it was *Tri-star*, the title of which made more sense in Cantonese, from which it translates as *Big Three Round* (a perfect hand in mahjong).[470] The New Year fell in February that year and the film opened on the 15th. This was one of several movies made at the time by the local industry in an attempt to revive its flagging fortunes, which were now declining fast.[471] The press reported that takings at the 1995 Lunar New Year had dropped to HK$31 million from the HK$36 million achieved in 1994, and that local films now formed only sixty percent of Hong Kong cinema screenings. There was little analysis, though, of the fundamental malaise affecting the Hong Kong industry, as was indicated by the hopes pinned on the insubstantial prospects of a film like this one. Yet *Tri-star*, despite being a mediocre comedy, went down well at the box office. Leslie starred, not very convincingly, as a Roman Catholic priest. The film ran for a full month till 15 March and grossed over HK$25 million.

The year turned out to be an immensely busy one after 1995's slow start back to life in Hong Kong. Leslie added to his load when in April he fulfilled a dream he'd had as far back as the late eighties by opening a coffee shop.[472] Located in Sung Lan Mansion on Matheson Street in Causeway Bay, the café was called *Wei Nin Zhong Qin*, or For Your Heart Only (after his film of that name), and was a joint venture with a professional restaurateur named Mr Yu, the boss of Queen's Café. On the opening day, his mother, sister Ophelia and niece Ayesha, Chen Kaige, and several Hong Kong actresses assembled at the café. The place was described in the press as: "intriguing and quirky: monochromatic in the extreme, with darkened wood panelling and recessed wall-lighting. The decor resolutely recalls '60s art-crowd hipness." Leslie's own photo was on the walls as was his Golden Disc Award for *The Wind Blows On*. But it was not a very successful enterprise, as the reports of his friends indicate:

> The service wasn't particularly outstanding and the food sucked and even a glass of ice lemon tea was worse than what you could get elsewhere; I don't know why anyone would go there. The décor was OK but not brilliant, all so so ... He wanted to be like other famous stars like Robert de Niro with Nobu in New York, or a friend who was an old time Cantonese movie star of the '60s who moved to Thailand and her daughter opened up a restaurant. Alan Tam, Eric Tsang and the gang had their own hotpot restaurants in the '80s and '90s. I guess he felt he should open one. It drew a lot of fans, from Korea, Japan, Taiwan, they thought they'd bump into him. To me, a wrong move.[473]

Leslie had made a promise during his farewell concert in 1989 that holders of his concert tickets would be able to get a free cup of coffee or tea at the restaurant and he made that good now. He tried hard to be involved in the café in its early stages, but this couldn't last. Interest waned all round and the restaurant was to last only a few years.

Another of the Hong Kong film industry's attempts to find a way out of their declining returns was to make expensive historical epics, and Leslie, with the team of Tomson Films and Chen Kaige, had been making one of these now for some two years. This was *Temptress Moon*, which was finally released on 9 May.[474] The public had been expecting its release since at least October 1994, when the press had reported that Leslie was busy shooting it in Shanghai.[475]

Two months into production, the leading lady, Taiwanese actress Jean Wong Ching-ying, departed; it was rumoured that she'd been fired. Production schedules were rocked by an abortion, two attempted rapes, and two attempted suicides. Who was involved in these incidents was not made public, but the delays and resulting dislocation set everything back. Gong Li joined the team to take the female lead in December 1994.

Despite the skilled director and its big cast, and despite the studio's intention of producing another exquisite period piece to rival *Farewell My Concubine*, when *Temptress Moon* emerged from the studio, it seemed to audiences and critics that it had somehow lost its way.[476] The film was 130 minutes long, and Chen Kaige was criticised heavily for self-indulgence as well as for the movie's stylised "China's Fifth Wave" concentration on rottenness, loss, and betrayal by unattractive characters who were doomed to disaster. Reactions were so antagonistic that when it was screened later at Cannes, crowds were said to have jeered.

During the long making of this film, Leslie, as usual, had charmed the cast and crew with his professionalism and his simple, unassuming ways. They later spoke warmly of their appreciation of the way he mucked in with everyone, no matter how small a role they were playing. Leslie found Chen Kaige as demanding a director as ever and exhausted himself in the making of every scene, following his usual practice of rehearsing everything, no matter how insignificant, until he was perfect. The cast remembered him missing lunch to run up and down the stairs to perfect the sound of his footfalls. Richard Corliss, the film critic, reported watching him on set, and related later that just before a scene was about to be shot, he would retreat into his character. Corliss remembered a scene that required Leslie to burst through a door, cast an eye on some domestic mischief, and exit in high dudgeon. Leslie did it perfectly, and at the end bowed to the crew's applause. "One Take Leslie!" he announced proudly.

Leslie built up a long-lasting rapport with the young Ren Lei, who played his character as a child. Leslie gradually adopted the boy, who was twenty-four years his junior, helped him with his role, looked after him off set, fed him, and gave him lifts and, on occasion, gifts of money. Leslie seemed to recognise in Ren Lei a boy much like he had been himself, with a quiet character formed in a difficult childhood in which he had found no love. Ren Lei certainly found love in Leslie, who became his godfather and whom Ren Lei came to call "Papa." After filming was finished, Leslie continued to look after the boy, visiting him whenever he was in his area and telephoning him often. It was a relationship which was to last until Leslie's death.

The soundtrack of *Temptress Moon* included Leslie singing "A Thousand Dreams of You," but even this was not enough to save the movie financially. Banned in China, despite Chen Kaige's hopes that its theme was so apolitical that it would evade the censors, the film made only a few million dollars in Hong Kong, despite running for nearly a month until 5 June. It was a financial disaster. Nor was it a critical success, locally or internationally. *Time Magazine* alone rated the film highly, awarding it the accolade of one of the best films of the year.

About a month later, on 13 July 1996, the third of Leslie's films to screen this year opened at Hong Kong cinemas. This was *Shanghai Grand*,[477] a remake of *The Bund* and *The Bund Part II*,[478] a 1980s TVB serial which had already been repackaged as a highly popular two-part film starring Chow Yun-fat. This helped to attract audiences, as did the stars in the new production, the others being Andy Lau and an attractive mainland actress named Ning Jing (or Ling Jing). As a result, *Shanghai Grand* eventually grossed nearly HK$21 million at the box office. It was not, though, a vehicle in which any of the actors were able to show their abilities. Its mishmash of music, styles, and themes from many different eras was laughable. Leslie was suitably tough and virile; his character is beaten and shot on frequent occasions, gets to make rather unconvincing love to Ning Jing, and dies in a hail of bullets at the end, all for no real discernible reason. The taciturn character gave Leslie little scope to lift this film out of the mire.

During the film's shooting in Hong Kong and Shanghai, the media carried reports of a deterioration in the relationship between its two male leads. Andy Lau sang the two songs on the soundtrack and had his name placed first on the billing. His agent managed to arrange for a party of journalists and fans to visit the film set at the same time, and the media hacks wrote up the encounter to indicate that Andy Lau was highly popular—in contrast, they indicated, to Leslie, whom they claimed to have spotted sitting alone in a corner. This was very foolish stuff, typical of much of Hong Kong's muck-raking journalism. On the other hand, the director, Poon Man-kit, was very complimentary about Leslie when he spoke to the press, praising him for listening to his advice and suggestions and for compromising with the other actors in a way unusual for a superstar. When she spoke to the press, Ning Jing, embarrassingly, made no bones about which of the male leads she preferred. She praised Leslie's looks and acting and omitted to mention Andy Lau altogether. Leslie held his peace, only commenting (some two years later) that Andy Lau, with whom he had to dance one short number at arm's length in the film, hadn't liked this at all and had been shaking when he did it. There was, though, little reality in any of this talk about friction, and the pair got on well enough to go later to Taiwan together to make a charitable commercial for disabled children.

On 15 August 1996, just a week after *Shanghai Grand* closed,

Leslie's fourth film of the year opened at cinemas. This was *Who's the Woman, Who's the Man* (in Chinese, *Golden Branch, Jade Leaf 2*), sequel to *He's a Woman, She's a Man*, the major hit of two years before.[479] Peter Chan again directed this gender-bending parody of the pop industry in which Leslie reprised his role as music producer, Sam, and Anita Mui played more or less herself.[480] It was a less light-hearted movie than the first and suffered the usual difficulties for a sequel of having little to say that was new. There are, though, some notable moments, and the film opens with the line from the earlier film, "I don't care if you're a man or a woman. All I know is that I love you." Later in the film, Leslie tells the two gay painters decorating his apartment, "You shouldn't worry how others look at you. Love can't be explained." The film included a new song written by Leslie, "Man with Intentions," a song that became one of his most popular numbers. After the movie was released, Peter Chan's company UFO was taken over by Golden Harvest. UFO had been too indebted to survive prior to the making of the film, and had been forced to make it part of the deal to attract Golden Harvest. Independent filmmaking in Hong Kong was dying.

The issue of sexual orientation was in the air for much of 1996. Leslie took part in a film entitled *Yang-Yin: Gender in Chinese Cinema*, which had been commissioned by the British Film Institute as part of their 100 Years of Cinema celebration.[481] Director Stanley Kwan put together a celluloid examination of the homoerotic themes in Chinese cinema, looking as far back as the 1930s and interviewing in the process a series of modern Chinese filmmakers, including Leslie—who was, of course, an obvious choice given the common knowledge about him and Daffy current in the Hong Kong film industry, not to mention the rumours about them which continued to surface in the press.[482] Anyway, Leslie had a history of starring in films which were either directly about sexual diversity or in which the sexual orientation of the characters he played was in doubt. Yet none of this was raised in Kwan's documentary and Leslie's appearance was disappointing. Unlike Stanley Kwan, who was also gay and used the vehicle of this film to come out to the world and to speak openly of his own sexuality, Leslie still preferred to remain ambiguous on the subject. Not that he was subjected to any searching interrogation, for Kwan focussed only on Leslie's characteristic narcissism and his cross-dressing in *Farewell My Concubine*, all of which fell far short of the real points he could have raised. Leslie was allowed to say only that Chinese culture found it hard to accept the idea of men playing women, but that it had no such problem the other way around, and to admit to the "unique quality" which his audiences identified with in his acting, "a kind of sensitivity," he said, "something soft." Making this even more ironic was the fact that Leslie was about to leap into the making of *Happy Together*, his most true-to-life gay film.

Elsewhere, he was still making excuses about why he didn't want a family. He told *Next Magazine* that he wouldn't think of having children as it would be too scary. He recalled the time when his sister Ophelia Cheung Luk-ping was having a baby and she went into shock and her heart stopped beating. This had set him against being a father, he alleged. He was happy, he laughed at the reporter, playing with his teddy bear.[483] It is difficult to think that he thought anyone would any longer believe such stuff.

At times over the last couple of years, he had seemed to be working towards being open about himself, yet at others he had drawn back. He was, it seems, conflicted about the difficult, embarrassing process of coming out, and though he was to go further than he did in 1996, he never quite managed to throw aside in public the cloud with which he enveloped his secret private life. Yet what was not in doubt was his rock-solid relationship with Daffy. If there had been any doubts in their minds about each other before, the experience of all those years together alone in Canada, then of the disrupting return to the Hong Kong spotlight, had put their relationship through the fire. It had emerged unscathed.

Work went on steadily at Rock Records through the year for the release of Leslie's first album of new songs, though the end of the year was left free for Leslie's comeback Christmas-and-New-Year concert, *Crossover 97*. Rock Records timed the release of the new album for a few weeks before the opening of the concert series. *Red* came out on 26 November.[484] It was an album very carefully put together by Leslie himself (with the help of song writer Lam Jik, who wrote many of the lyrics and contributed the name of the album).[485] The ten and a half tracks were in Cantonese (bucking the recent trend for Mandarin songs or "Mandopop" in Hong Kong, and running counter to the intentions Leslie had expressed the previous year). They were a fusion of tracks similar to Leslie's old styles with some new departures.[486] At times in the slow numbers his voice sounded gravelly and hoarse, especially in the deeper registers, and the rock numbers did not make for easy listening. Some of the songs were taken from the film he was making that year, *Viva Erotica*. Two music videos, Leslie's first, were made to promote the CD. "Red" was the track with the sexiest beat, music, and atmosphere and was to be used for the notorious red shoes routine in his forthcoming concert (where he sang it better live than he did on the recording). The CD was, of course, a success, and has even been called his "most highly proclaimed album," but as the first example of his new music, it lacked much pizzazz and any unity of theme. The record companies released several other recordings (one called *Listening*, another *Love with All My Heart*) during the year, including a karaoke LCD and VCDs as well as an album in Japan.

The fever for the *Crossover '97* concert eclipsed all else in Leslie's life through the end of 1996 and would carry on doing so right up until June 1997. Despite the fact that *Crossover* was to be Leslie's most successful concert series to date, some would say his most successful ever, he was apparently reluctant to return to the stage.[487] The concert was planned to run at the Hong Kong Coliseum for twenty-two shows, later extended to twenty-four, for each of which Leslie was reportedly paid the princely sum of HK$1 million.[488] The title of the concert was nuanced; Leslie claimed he'd wanted to call the concert "Red '97," as in Chinese tradition red was an auspicious colour with connotations of popularity and fame (as well as being a homonym for the word "Hung" in Hung Hom, the district in which the Hong Kong Coliseum was situated). He had, though, he said, been away filming *Happy Together* in Argentina before October and so had not been present when the name had been chosen. This seems a little disingenuous. 1997 was the year of the handover of Hong Kong to China and so could certainly be characterised as a crossover, as could the timing of the concert, which straddled the New Year of 1997.

There was more to the title, though, than a play on words and dates. For Leslie personally, this concert marked an emotional crossover. It was his return to the big stage after an absence of seven years, and it was his intention to use the concert to make statements about sexuality, statements that would inevitably be taken to be about his own sexual orientation. He personally placed cross-dressing and camp routines at the heart of the show. This, it seems, was the point at which he had decided to come as far out of the closet in public as he was ever to do. He wanted, too, for the first time to acknowledge Daffy's place in his life, and he would do so in this concert.

The first tickets put on sale sold out within two days, and this was even before Leslie came back from filming *Happy Together* to promote the show at a press conference in October.[489] On that occasion, he looked very gaunt due to the amoebic dysentery he'd picked up in Argentina; he weighed only 58 kilograms. The concert was managed in Hong Kong and abroad by Cheung Yiu-wing, as before, and Rock Records, a huge task as it was the most carefully designed and choreographed show in which Leslie had starred so far. He started to rehearse with his dancers in November, and the show opened at the Coliseum on 12 December, closing there on 4 January the following year.

No expense was spared to make this an outstanding success: the sets, lighting, and costumes all were lavish.[490] Leslie, its focus, wore a series of glittering and stylish outfits designed by art director William Chiang Suk-ping.[491] The sets were imaginative; at the start, Leslie appeared inside a glass pyramid akin to the pyramid at the Louvre, which opened then lifted to leave him standing dramatically in a long, shaggy, red-and-black coat over a red tie and glittering suit, his face initially hidden for a short time by an elaborate mask held in his hand. His numbers varied throughout the series and included the full repertoire of favourites going back to Capital Artists days (including "Thanks, Monica") as well as a few new numbers, most in Cantonese, a few in Mandarin. Eight children from the Beijing opera school where he had studied for *Farewell My Concubine*, brought to Hong Kong by his teachers Shi Yansheng and his wife Zhang Manling, performed a routine recalling the film (Leslie was to take the trouble later to visit the children in Beijing and during the period of the concert he entertained the Chinese couple to dinner at his house; they recalled later how kindly he treated them and how he personally took them back to their hotel after supper).[492] Filling in the spaces between Leslie's numbers came a series of female guest stars, including Karen Mok and Shu Qui, the female lead in his forthcoming film *Viva Erotica*. None of these was allowed to detract from the centrality of the fact that the show was Leslie's and that he was the most beautiful person in it. "Am I beautiful?" he teased the crowd, "Am I sparkling, am I gorgeous, am I too hot to handle?"[493]

Leslie brought in dance maestro Chu Wing-lung to put together the routines which formed such an important vehicle for the messages he intended to impart through the show, and in which, particularly in the rendition of "Red," he set out successfully to shock his audiences. At the start of the number, the smoke parted to reveal Leslie in a sparkling blue matador jacket, matching trousers cut off at the calf, and a pair of scarlet women's high-heeled shoes.[494] In these, he pirouetted and camped amongst dancers who wore black masks, long black gloves, tightly fitting black-and-silver costumes, and black boots, their butch sado-masochistic look contrasting vividly with Leslie's flirtatious effeminacy. Chu, the more macho of the pair, joined Leslie in an erotic-dancing flirtation in which Leslie wrapped his leg around him then languidly waved a yellow rose in his face, tossing the flower to Chu as the number ended.

The red shoes were a sensation, as Leslie had hoped they would be. He stated at the time that he was deliberately making reference to David Bowie's wearing red shoes many years before, but this did not prevent a barrage of reactions in the press so acerbic that Leslie was taken aback. He resented the criticism and the assumptions of his own effeminacy which the tabloids drew from what they (and almost everyone else) saw as a "gay" dance routine. Choreographer Chu bravely maintained to the press that the performance had been intended to be "gender-neutral," but this line was impossible to take at face value. Leslie later commented that perhaps he had been trying to express the fact that he could be a woman, but this was also difficult to accept. It was not at all a woman's persona that he had adopted here, rather that of an effeminate gay man. His every gesture indicated same-sex attraction. He set out deliberately to tease his audiences and succeeded in arousing them. He really should not have been surprised at the resulting furore. The *South China Morning Post* reported that Leslie had been more daring than ever before, no longer afraid to transcend the boundaries of sexuality. "Leslie Cheung has no fixed image," he said on stage. "He can be a good-looking man, and he can be a very beautiful woman."[495] Cantopop, as the *Hong Kong Standard* put it, had finally come of age in this routine, and it was rather pointless to try to turn the clock back.

Leslie's was also a performance attuned with a very personal purpose, the culmination of quite a succession of revealing performances in shows like *All's Well Ends Well*, *Farewell My Concubine*, and *He's a Woman, She's a Man*, not to forget all the semi-revealing comments he'd made in public. This concert, it seems, was a fulfilment of a deliberate process, and it culminated on New Year's Eve with the most dramatic statement he had made so far. Late at night, at the end of a performance deliberately delayed so that the New Year could be ushered in onstage, Leslie stood before the audience, divested of all his glitter and in sober black tie, and, as "a dutiful son," thanked his mother, who was in the audience with his sister Ophelia and her family. He'd sung for over ten years now, and his mother, he said, had attended all his concerts, so he had always sung a song for her. With the spotlight upon his embarrassed but delighted mother, he asked her, "How did you give birth to such a cute and gorgeous son? Were you very happy with Daddy?" He then turned towards his companion for the last thirteen years, the partner whom he had never before acknowledged in public, Daffy Tong. Leslie looked directly at his mother and said he wished to thank:

> Another person who is very close to my heart [he used the Cantonese words ho pangyau, best friend], your Godson. At my lowest point he gave me several months' salary to help me through the rough times. He is my great friend Mr Tong. Now I would like to dedicate this song to my dearest friend and family.

And so Leslie ended all the years of speculation, all the times when he had teased his fans and bemused the public.[496]

There was, of course, immediate reaction in the press. As the *Hong Kong Standard* commented, if Leslie had meant to make a statement about his own sexuality, nothing could have been clearer than his world tour.[497] Leslie, as usual, did not take kindly to this and complained bitterly that the media had forgotten his dedication to his mother and had concentrated only on his words about Daffy, a complaint he could not have meant seriously, for dedications to parents were scarcely newsworthy in showbiz.[498] He can scarcely have expected that the media would *not* believe that he had given them open season on this topic. He went further later and complained that he had lost several markets due to adverse press coverage of his dedication (though without saying where these were, and no evidence has ever been adduced to show that this happened). In his responses to this media frenzy, Leslie repeated the words *best friend* when he spoke of Daffy, and was careful to avoid any more emotive word. Speaking to *Oriental Sunday* much later in 2001, he was much braver when he complained to his interviewer that the press had said he was singing that night for only one man. Of course, he said, he was singing for everybody. Had he really wanted to sing for him, he could do so at any time, before going to sleep at night and again in the morning.[499]

Which in itself, of course, was a lovely way of admitting that he and Daffy were living together, and had been as true in 1997 as it was in 2001. They had not taken separate houses when they got back to Hong Kong.

***

On 28 November, his final film of 1996 opened. This was *Viva Erotica*, a satire on the by-then-parlous state of the Hong Kong film industry.[500] It proved popular enough to stay on screens until 8 January the next year, though in all this time it only managed to gross the below-average sum (for a Leslie film) of HK$11.6 million.[501] Leslie played Sing, a washed-up Hong Kong film director who has artistic pretensions but is forced by lack of work into making a soft-porn movie. Leslie took the role after Jacky Cheung and Stephen Chow had both turned it down because of the nude scenes and its controversial subject. Karen Mok starred as Sing's girlfriend, a role which involved some fairly erotic scenes with Leslie, scenes which she found very hard to act; Leslie was said to have loosened her up by tickling her toes. *Viva Erotica* could itself be said to have been soft porn, and it received a Category III (the most restrictive) certificate from the Hong Kong censor. The star of the film, surprisingly, turned out to be the Taiwanese actress Shu Qi, who played the gangster's moll turned film star, Mango. She won both Best New Performer and Best Supporting Actress for the role at the next year's Hong Kong Film Awards. Leslie was nominated for, but once more failed to win, Best Actor, among the five other nominations the film garnered. Elsewhere, at Berlin in February 1997, *Viva Erotica* was nominated for a Golden Bear and in Movie Express Japan's Hong Kong film category, Leslie won runner-up for Best Actor for the role.

Two years had gone by since his return to Hong Kong. Had he achieved all that he had hoped? There is little doubt that he was back at the pinnacle of his musical career, though the old issue of just what exactly was his style had resurfaced and had yet to be answered. His film work, though frenetic, had not achieved the same success. There was work still to do.

CHAPTER 14

HAPPY TOGETHER

1997-1998

By the time the last *Crossover '97* concert ended in Hong Kong, Leslie had become the first star to have held one hundred concerts at the Coliseum. He did not stop there, and now launched the most gruelling world tour he'd ever undertaken. He took his show back to the places where he'd bade his fans farewell all those years before, as well as to new locations where his fame had now spread. In many, in the politically more conservative places like China or Singapore, or the religiously sensitive ones like Malaysia, the raunchier parts of the show had to be toned down, but in the rest, apart from changes to make the songs more effective locally, the show stayed much the same.

The tour opened between 25 and 28 January 1997 in Tokyo and Osaka, with Karen Mok also in attendance. Leslie broke local concert custom by shaking hands with as many fans as he could reach from the stage.[502] At the end of January, he reached Singapore, where he had some trouble with the press, which mocked him for returning after having said a final goodbye seven years before. The *Straits Times* acidly commented on what it characterised as an outrageous show in which the star wore red stilettos and touched his private parts.[503] After this, in February, Leslie travelled to China to appear before 20,000 fans in Zongshan, moving on to Shantou, Foshan, Zhanjiang, and other Chinese cities on a tour that lasted till early March, in each place toning down the show's dance routines to comply with local expectations.[504] After that, he flew across the Pacific, appearing at the end of March at the Trump Taj Mahal Casino in Atlantic City, where he performed his show in English, so successfully that he had the usually staid audience dancing in front of the stage.[505]

In Hong Kong again for the Chinese New Year of 1997, Leslie was back on the big screen, carrying on his usual tradition of appearing in a seasonal comedy. This one, including Leslie in a literally two-minute walk-on part as himself, was Raymond Wong's latest offering from Mandarin Films, *All's Well, Ends Well '97*.[506]

In April, his world tour reached Toronto and Vancouver, where he went back to have a look at the house he had earlier sold. He flew south that month to San Francisco and Los Angeles, where it was not surprisingly reported that his voice had become rather tired and dry. At the end of April he flew back across the Pacific to Taiwan for appearances in Taipei, Taichung, and Kaohsiung. May saw him on the other side of the globe in Manchester and a few days later he played at Wembley Arena in London, where tickets for his show were reported to have been selling for almost twice the price of those for Michael Jackson's recent concert. Then it was on to Amsterdam, after which he went home briefly to Hong Kong, to be there at the opening of the second of his two films that screened that year.

This was *Happy Together*, which reached cinemas on 30 May.[507] It was to be Leslie's last major art-house film and the last movie that would win him international critical acclaim.[508] The times were very bad to bring forth a difficult local film. The Hong Kong film industry was in steep decline. To get by, it had reverted to squeezing the most out of what were characterised at the time as "the most raucous and least contemplative films on the planet."[509] Only a few directors, including Wong Kar-wai, stood out against this trend, but by now Wong had a reputation for turning away local audiences, which often found his works indecipherable, slow, and boring. The economic crisis that was to hit Hong Kong shortly after the handover to China in the summer of that year would add further woes to the industry. Many filmmakers turned to cheap independent films as a way out, but these could not compete with Hollywood and made little money. That *Happy Together* managed to take HK$8.6 million in Hong Kong in these circumstances was good going, and largely a tribute to the drawing power of its two stars, Leslie and Tony Leung Chiu-wai, whose international career it launched.

That *Happy Together* was so successful was also surprising given the controversial nature of its theme, a tortured love affair between two men, Lai Yiu-fai (the film's pivotal character, played by Tony Leung) and his feckless on-and-off lover Ho Po-wing (played by Leslie). In his public pronouncements, Wong Kar-wai played down the gay elements in the film, preferring rather to stress the bleak universal themes of betrayal, disillusion, and abandonment in love that marked all his works, but the Category III movie he made left little to the imagination, featuring the Hong Kong screen's first full-on scenes of gay lovemaking. The homosexuality of the film was, for Hong Kong at that time, stunning.

Leslie played a gay man with few redeeming features doing his worst to keep, then lose, his relationship. In public, as usual, Leslie played down what he had done: "I don't play many gay films anymore, a modern one and an ancient one, it's enough," he told the press, saying the issue was too sensitive to do more—managing, of course, to skip over the other films with similar themes and the myriad references to homosexuality in his earlier work. The accounts of the making of *Happy Together* make it plain, though, that Leslie had never had any illusions about what the film was about and was typically open about his own sexuality on set, especially with his fellow star Tony Leung, who was not at all happy with what he had let himself in for. The achievement of this movie, and this must have attracted Leslie to it, was that it treated a love affair between two men as just another love affair—one which failed, of course, but failed because of the incompatible personalities of the two lovers, rather than because they were gay.

The story opens with the couple making love on a narrow bed, Yiu-fai fucking Po-wing vigorously. Wong had not revealed this scene to the actors before he took them to Argentina to shoot the movie, and when Tony Leung discovered that he had to make love to Leslie, he withdrew to his room for two days. It took a good deal of persuasion, mostly by Leslie, to get him back on set. Leslie told him (according to cameraman Chris Doyle, who later produced a book about the making of the film), "Now you know how bad I've felt all these years pretending I want to put my thing into that extra hole that women have."[510] Leslie put this line more politely when he gave his own version of the event to the press some time later, saying that he'd told Tony Leung to think of how he'd had to touch all those breasts over the years and that in any case he "was not [his] type." The message was the same.[511] Yet when back in Hong Kong, Leslie was to pretend, rather speciously after his revelatory remarks about Daffy at his New Year's Eve concert that year, that he too was unhappy about being cast in such a gay film.

More honestly, Leslie also said later that homosexuality was a hot topic at the time in Hong Kong and he thought it might be interesting to play a homosexual. Before making the film, he had told Wong Kar-wai that if he wanted to tell a gay love story, he'd see how far he dared go. The film's timing, of course, fitted perfectly with his resolve to open himself up to the public.

It also fitted well into what was happening then in Hong Kong's art scene, where a steadily growing openness about all things gay was beginning.[512] The local independent theatre had taken the subject up. That year, on the radio, RTHK presenter Dino Mahoney discussed gay theatre shows at the Fringe Club in a programme called "When the Fringe Goes Mainstream: Gay Theatre in the Nineties." A local Cantonese play, *Bedtime Stories*, showing at the City Hall in Central, focussed on homosexuality. Pioneering local playwright, writer, and dramatist Edward Lam Yick-wah was in the middle of a run of shows in local theatres focussing on gay sexuality. The film *A Queer Story* starring George Lam had just hit local cinemas. At the handover to China in the summer of 1997, the gay community threw a mega-rave called *Unity*, which attracted 8,000 revellers and featured music by Grace Jones and Boy George. The club scene was expanding. A whole series of venues had emerged in place of Disco Disco—some to remain, others to fade swiftly. *Contacts Magazine* was being published to the city's gay readership. As Mao might have put it, a hundred flowers were blossoming in Hong Kong, at least for a time.

The shooting of *Happy Together* had started back in the August of 1996 in Buenos Aires and, as usual with Wong Kar-wai, went on longer than planned. As ever, Wong had no real script, improvised as he went along, trashed much of the 400,000 feet of film he shot, removed in the cutting stage all vestiges of the principal female role played by singer Shirley Kwan Suk Yee, and got way behind schedule. The six weeks planned for shooting in Argentina expanded to three months. This gave the press the opportunity to accuse Leslie of demanding large sums of money in overtime to finish the film. He indignantly denied this in a later interview, becoming so agitated with the interviewer that he knocked over his coffee, but there is no doubt that, by the end of the film, he and Wong were no longer getting on, and this was to be the last film they made together. They made light of this in public, Wong later saying that they were closest in *Happy Together*, but Leslie confessed in later interviews that it was the most difficult film he'd ever made and that he was very unhappy while making it. It was not helped by the fact that he fell ill with dysentery in Buenos Aires and had to work while feeling groggy. He spent his fortieth birthday rather unhappily there. But he felt he had done well, and though he was not to win an award for the film, he was proud of his performance. It was the one film, he said, in which he would not alter his performance one jot.[513]

His was neither an easy part to bring to life nor one that audiences found easy to stomach. Po-wing is a wastrel, a man who continually lets down and cheats on his lover, Yiu-fai, who cares for him when he's been beaten up and who has to put up with his whining and sluttish ways, yet finds it almost impossible to break the attraction that he holds over him. They break up over and over again, and each time Po-wing is down on his luck, he crawls back saying, "We could start over." He drinks and steals, prostitutes himself with Caucasian men, and behaves outrageously in bars. He is aimless, dissatisfied, lost, and when Yiu-fai finally leaves him, he finds himself distraught and alone. Leslie was perfect in this louche, immoral, sexy role. Every now and then, when Po-wing is in his gentlest of moods, his vulnerability makes it quite clear why Yiu-fai loves him to distraction and disaster. Mostly, he is just a heel. In scenes cut from the final three-hour version, when Yiu-fai finally ditches him, he puts on drag, paints his face, and goes out to sell himself over again.

The film was doomed to be censored and duly was, banned in China and all of Southeast Asia, as well as in South Korea until the 1998 election brought its democrats to power. Yet it made up for this by the critical acclaim it won. At the 17th Hong Kong Film Awards in 1998, Tony Leung won Best Actor, beating Leslie, who was also nominated for the award. The film garnered a sprinkling of foreign awards, too. Much later, in a 2005 film survey in Hong Kong, *Happy Together* was placed in the top ten films of all time. It was, indeed, a film of which Leslie could be proud.

After the film was released, Leslie took his concert to Australia, to play in Perth and Sydney at the end of May and Melbourne in June. There, reporter Kathryn Bird commented on the reaction of the audience to Leslie's bejewelled red high-heeled shoes, what she described as a "collective intake of breath." Never, she added, had she felt so many people so deeply uncomfortable.[514]

Leslie then returned to Japan, performing in Tokyo on 5 June and Osaka on the 9th, thereby becoming the first foreign star to hold two concerts in Japan inside a six-month period. Here he again performed in English, though he promised his fans he'd give them half his next concert in Japanese. The tour came to a finale once again in China, this time in Guangzhou, where the concert was staged from 13 to 15 June.

A series of albums was released in different countries around the world tour, including recordings of his *Crossover '97* concert,[515] a Japanese disc titled *Double Fantasy*, and *Legend*, a karaoke disc on LD and VCD. The video accompanying this was, for Hong Kong, dramatic: leopards, erotic images of Leslie lashed to a bedpost and abused as an office boy by his boss (played by supermodel Janet Ma, who sacks Leslie for ogling at Taiwanese film star Shu Qi, only to pair up with her herself), and Leslie flirting and more with Karen Mok whilst looking at the face of hunky model and actor Jimmy Wong Ka-lok.[516] The music was a lively mix of his Rock Records songs. Despite the lack of musical novelty, this ensured Leslie the prize of a place among the Top Ten Asian Singers for Asian Pops that year.

By the time the tour ended, he was clearly very tired. He'd performed fifty-five concerts and announced, not surprisingly, that he was taking the rest of the year off. It was as well that he kept himself in trim. He told the press that year that he enjoyed life more and laughed at those who kept gossiping about lamb placenta injections. He said that nowadays he rarely went out, instead going to bed before midnight. He worked out at home, practised the Chinese breathing and meditative exercise *qigong*, and looked after his health. He was not interested, he added, in competing with others anymore, and ruefully recalled the days when he and Alan Tam had gone head to head. His life was filled with pleasures now.[517]

It was, though, not yet quite time to relax, for a larger event than any of these was looming in Hong Kong, something for which he really did have to be back home again.[518] The event, of course, was the handover of Hong Kong to China. In the newly built hall of the Hong Kong Convention Centre in Wan Chai, the territory was handed back to the motherland on the night of 30 June-1 July in a ceremony at which a galaxy of luminaries attended to watch the Prince of Wales relinquish government to Jiang Zemin, the Chinese president. Leslie, though, was not in Hong Kong on that day, but instead was in Beijing, where, at the invitation of the Chinese government, he performed in a celebrity concert to celebrate the event at the Beijing Workers' Sports Stadium on 1 July. This show immediately generated a sour note in the world of entertainment. Allegations surfaced in the press that the stars had been pressured to appear. Four other Hong Kong stars had appeared with Leslie and others had performed back in Hong Kong at the Coliseum.[519] Many of the top singing stars, though, had refused to appear. Those who went to Beijing denied that political pressure had been applied, but it was not a felicitous start to the new regime.

In Hong Kong, there was huge apprehension. No one knew what the new government would bring. The People's Liberation

Army drove over the border just after midnight and occupied all the old British barracks. Flags and cap badges changed overnight. No one had any idea whether the "One Country Two Systems" formula agreed by the Chinese would work or indeed whether they would keep their word to leave Hong Kong its freedoms and rule of law. Many Hong Kong residents had already emigrated abroad. Those who stayed, many of whom had themselves fled Communist China decades before, could not feel optimistic at the outcome of the political experiment now being conducted.

Leslie wasn't sure of his own feelings. Despite having worked in China over the preceding years, indeed more than had almost any other Hong Kong celebrity, he had recently been quoted in the Los Angeles media as saying he was thinking of living in London.[520]

Leslie's by-now-traditional bad relations with the media continued unaffected by the change of regime. *Apple Daily* stalked him with what were locally known as "puppy squads" of photographers; one of these harassments culminated in a car chase from which he had to be rescued by the police. The newspaper published pictures of him talking to the police after an incident they themselves had instigated.[521] Now that he had spoken of him at his *Crossover* concert, Leslie was, though, becoming a little more comfortable in speaking to the press about Daffy. In an interview, he denied he felt pressure any longer on this subject and said that he didn't mind what the press printed about it as long as they didn't invade his privacy. He told *Next* magazine that when he loved someone, he wouldn't care if it was a man or a woman.[522]

On 20 July, Leslie attended the premiere of Tsui Hark's cartoon version of *A Chinese Ghost Story*, a film for which he had been asked to speak the voice of his old character Ning, though he had not been able to find the time to do so. The film contained some clearly allegorical passages aimed at China, something possibly risky at this early stage of the new regime. Leslie also flew over to Taiwan to cut the ribbon for the film in Taipei. He was back in Hong Kong to celebrate his godson Justin's birthday in August. Justin, or Ah Jen, was the son of a close friend and was at the time studying in England. Leslie was very fond of the boy and supported his studies financially.[523]

Leslie fulfilled his intention of taking it easier at the end of 1997. There was little film work for the time being and there were no more album releases. It was, in any case, not a good time to bring out new music. Cantopop was entering the dire straits that the Hong Kong film industry had entered some years before. The Hong Kong press lamented its decline and the rise of Mandopop, as well as the fact that new talent just didn't seem to be entering the field; the old faces were alleged to be looking tired.[524] This compounded (and maybe, as with the film industry, was the result of) the drop in music revenues. The seventy percent of sales which the local music industry had been accustomed to winning annually dropped that year to fifty percent. New releases were gradually more often Western than local; Celine Dion was 1996's bestselling artist in Hong Kong's HMV Megastore. Mandarin, a language becoming more popular than in the past due to the handover to China that year, and a language much more marketable abroad, was being used more and more, and this allowed Taiwanese competition to enter the Hong Kong market. Local artists began releasing more numbers in Mandarin than Cantonese.

As the year ended, bird flu hit Hong Kong and the government slaughtered all the territory's chickens. This sombre event occurred while considerable political anxiety about the handover remained in the air and at a time when Hong Kong was experiencing the economic downturn just then beginning to hit Asia. Leslie welcomed the New Year at a friend's wedding. There was no chicken on the menu. [525]

✱✱✱

1998 began with an event that marked the international apogee of Leslie's lifetime of work as a movie star. Between 11 and 12 February, he served as a member of the jury at that year's Berlin Film Festival, a first for an Asian actor. The eleven-person jury was led by Ben Kingsley and included Santa Berger.[526] At the awards, Leslie presented the Golden Bear for the best feature film to Walter Salles, the director of *Central do Brasil*, and the Silver Bear for best actress to Fernanda Montenegro, the film's leading lady. Later, with Maggie Cheung, he was also invited to Berlin's Gay Teddy Night to present Stanley Kwan with awards for his film *Hold You Tight*. Despite the obvious attraction of the recognition and all this highly enjoyable glitz, Leslie had almost not gone to Berlin, as it had been planned that he would be in the middle of filming *A Time to Remember* in Shanghai at the time. The European trip needed about a fortnight of his time, but having responded negatively in a radio interview to the question as to whether he should go, he consulted the film's producer, Huen Ga-ling, who was present in the studio, and they agreed on the spot that he should take part. It was a fortunate decision, as it gave Leslie the chance to demonstrate his superstar aura on an international stage, and he duly charmed everyone he met in Berlin.

Leslie's desire to become a film director had so far remained unsatisfied, as he mentioned when interviewed in 1998 in Berlin by the magazine *Positif*.[527] Leslie told the reporter that he wanted to be a director, since, he said, "a director is the soul of a movie." It seems he had at last begun to make concrete plans. Elsewhere that year, he told the media that he planned to direct a love story starring Karen Mok. He had, he said, considered Shu Qi (his co-star in *Viva Erotica*) for the role but had rejected her because she did not have strong enough Cantonese.[528] Whatever this project was, it never came to fruition. Nine years after first making clear his aims, Leslie had still not made any concrete moves to fulfil his dream of directing films.

Back in Hong Kong, Leslie's Lunar New Year film, *Ninth Happiness*, was screened from 14 February, the annual comedy offering by Mandarin Films producer Raymond Wong and director Clifton Ko.[529] It was to be Leslie's last New Year film, for as he made it clear at the time, he had tired of the sort of frivolous comedies that were the staple of the festive season and indeed of most of Hong Kong cinema at that time.[530] From now on, he made it clear in the media, he wanted to cherry-pick serious projects (by which he said he also meant comedies with a message) that suited him. Yet Leslie told an interviewer from the newspaper *Ming Pao* that he knew the film would be a financial success from the start, and he was right.

After the film was shown, Leslie was among the many celebrities entertained by Mandarin Films to their annual spring dinner, and he used the opportunity to reiterate that he had no intention of going to Hollywood. He sang on stage that night accompanied at the keyboard by his old godfather, Michael Lai. They all waited in vain for Alan Tam to join them; he arrived some two hours late, lamely blaming traffic. Something of the old rivalry between the two perhaps lingered even at this late stage.

In mainland China, whilst filming his next film, then known as *The Red Lover* (later re-titled *A Time to Remember*), Leslie took the opportunity to make his current view of his country clear. His opinion had changed over the years, and he now stated clearly that he was proud of being Chinese and that he'd finally got a sense of belonging and peace of mind. It was Chinese blood running through his veins.[531] He even thought, he said (though he was never to show any sign of doing so) of moving to mainland China as it was better to live there than in Hong Kong, where prices were so high. A line somewhat overdone for local consumption, perhaps, but Leslie does seem to have undergone a genuine change of heart about China, starting with his making of *Farewell My Concubine*, and to have come around to the view that he was, above all, a Chinese actor. He took every possible opportunity from then on to reject the idea of following Jackie Chan and Chow Yun-fat to Hollywood.[532] Why be a small fish confined by race and language in a small pond when you could be a superstar back home? It was his duty, he said, to make the Chinese and Hong Kong film industries vibrant, not to dash off to make money in the USA.

Musically, 1998 was a productive year, one in which Leslie's new styles started to come through strongly. On Valentine's Day, the same day that *Ninth Happiness* was released, Rock Records released an EP, *All These Years*, a collection of Cantonese songs, which also featured the Taiwanese artist Liu Chi Hung. This gave it a distinctive Taiwanese flavour, which was strengthened by the addition of songs by Hong Kong lyricist Lam Jik and Taiwanese composer Chen Xiu Xia.[533] Leslie himself composed "The Future," one of the Cantonese numbers. A karaoke compilation was also issued. In March, Leslie was in Kyoto to make a music video for his forthcoming Mandarin album, *Printemps*,[534] and whilst in Japan, he made several of what were by now very rare TV and radio appearances, one on the TV show, the "Leslie Cheung Night," and two on radio shows on Tokyo FM, "Toyota Weekly Album Top 10" and "Ashahi Wonda Golden Hits," both on 4 April.

All this formed the usual PR lead-up for the release of Leslie's new album, *Printemps*, the fruit of his search for a new personal style. It was very different from anything he had done before, with subtler lyrics; gentler, more sensitive music; interesting melodies; and more evident use of instrumentalists in a well-recorded set of ten Mandarin tracks.[535] The eleventh track, an extra, was sung by Leslie in Japanese; this was "Love Like Magic," a song written by the Japanese singer song-writer duo Chage and Aska (or Asuka). The album proved a tremendous success. The songs were good listening no matter what the language and exactly suited Leslie's vocal and emotional range. The CD was issued with an attractive small hard-covered booklet in white, which contained a series of shots of Leslie in contemplative mood taken amidst, appropriately, the serene greenery of Japanese gardens. The booklet (its title, like the CD, being French for *spring*) was prefaced and closed by the words *il fait un (print) temps printanier*. Leslie was reaching out here to his older, more sophisticated public. The album sold 2.5 million copies.

Rock Records also brought out an album entitled *Gift* especially for the Japanese market; this was released shortly afterwards, on 21 April. This had more songs by Chage and Aska, and the album included a Japanese song, "Marshmallow." It, too, proved a great success, reaching the Toyota Weekly Top Ten Segment. The album also went down well in Taiwan, its track "Everybody" reaching number two in the Asia Top 20 list, and another track, "The Truth," reaching first position on Cashbox KTV. Another track, "Keeping Company," became number two in CSMTV's Best MTVs of 1998. A separate release, *Everybody*, also came out in Japan.

After the appearance of *Printemps*, Leslie travelled to Taiwan, where he was interviewed on the Taiwanese channel TVBS-G. Here, while making a music video directed by the Taiwanese director Ma Yi Jung, one of the six he was contracted to Rock Records to produce, he slipped and injured his leg and had to return hastily to Hong Kong for treatment.[536] He was back in Taiwan to finish the shooting a week later, this time with Daffy in support, though he was still in pain. His second film of the year, *A Time to Remember*, opened in Tokyo on 18 April (it would not be released in Hong Kong until the next year), and Leslie went there for the premiere, staying to appear on a talk show broadcast from the Shinjuku Mirano-za theatre.[537]

He was still hobbling badly from the leg injury he'd received in Taiwan, and at times he was forced to use a wheelchair. Still in pain, he flew on to Seoul between 14 and 16 May to attend an event for his fans. Tickets for this were sold as a benefit for Korean children, and he also appeared there at an autograph session for *Printemps*.

In preparation for his trip to Taiwan, he had allowed a rare interview by reporter June Lam Bing for *City Entertainment*'s 5-13 February issue.[538] Lam took the bull by the horns and asked him about his gay roles in *Farewell My Concubine* and *Happy Together*, as well as the role in *M Butterfly* he hadn't taken. In reply, Leslie was surprisingly cagey at this late stage, remarking that the theme of homosexuality was too sensitive to allow him to play in any more gay films. He had, perhaps, had second thoughts after all the publicity his openness had aroused, or maybe was just reverting to his old media tease.

Back in Hong Kong again, Leslie was among a galaxy of stars that appeared in the *Joseph Koo & James Wong True Friendship Concert* at the Hong Kong Coliseum, all of them singers who had come to fame singing songs written by the composer Joseph Koo Ka-fai and the lyricist James Wong Jim.[539] Leslie performed on their opening night on 17 May and their last show on 25 May.

Despite the musical success he achieved in 1998, Leslie was already growing restless at Rock Records and the year was to be his last with them. *Printemps* was not to be the spring of a new wave of music with that record company; the pattern of his departure from Capital Artists a decade before was about to be repeated.

That summer, Leslie sold his house in Kwai Pui Wan (Turtle Cove), and he and Daffy moved to what was to be Leslie's final residence, a detached house in a walled garden in the exclusive Kadoorie Hill area of Kowloon.[540] They moved in with a new dog, a German shepherd named Bingo. It was a smart move financially: Leslie made a good deal of money on the sale of the old house as prices in Hong Kong's property market were still higher than when he'd bought it, despite the economic downturn. He used the occasion of his move to take a swipe at Lai Chi-ying, proprietor of Next Media and its newspaper *Apple Daily*, whose reporters had bamboozled their way into the Turtle Cove house shortly before and had tried to dig up dirt on Daffy. Lai Chi-ying was a *bête noire* of Leslie's, and in an interview with *Ming Pao*, Leslie thanked him sarcastically for being the cause of the profit he'd made selling his house.

Further plans to travel to Taiwan that year to attend film and musical award ceremonies had to be abandoned because Leslie's mother fell dangerously ill.[541] She was seventy-eight years old and had developed cancer. It seemed she had little time left to live. This was not the only death which became imminent at this time: Leslie's Beijing opera teacher, Shi Yansheng, was also dying of cancer, and he flew to Beijing to be with him before he died.

Leslie's final film release of the year was *Anna Magdalena*, in which he took a cameo role to help out the production company and his old friend, the film's director, Hai Chung-man, who was making his first movie.[542] This was the first of a number of films in which Leslie did what he could to save the ailing industry. Leslie had known Hai since the latter had been artistic director for *A Chinese Ghost Story*.

Leslie's mother lingered on, ailing slowly, and his 42nd birthday party was a sombre affair overshadowed by her imminent death.[543] She finally died on 18 November. Leslie was stricken, the years of estrangement and his inability to love her making him guilty now at her loss. He organised her funeral according to Buddhist rites. Anita Mui, Jackie Chan, and Karen Mok were there, as, of course, was Daffy, both to support Leslie and because Madam Cheung had been his godmother. Leslie was bitter at the time about the way the Hong Kong media focussed much of its attention on Daffy, largely ignoring his mother and, he thought, taking the opportunity to attack him through his partner.[544] This was the first public ceremony which Daffy had attended at Leslie's side, and it was not surprising that the press had found that newsworthy.

Speaking around this time to the Japanese writer Chitose Shima, who was interviewing him for the book of photographs she was producing,[545] he was strangely melancholy in his response to her questions (perhaps not unconnected with the fact that the night before this interview took place he had awoken to find a crazed fan in his house at the foot of his bed). She asked him what happy memories he had of his childhood, to which he coldly replied that he had no happy memories at all. He seemed to Shima to be depressed, and she was surprised at the end of the interview when he said that sometimes he thought he could not love anyone and that perhaps he had never loved anyone seriously. She asked him whether he had anyone then whom he loved, to which he replied that there was no one, and that he had always been lonely, and was lonely even now.[546]

About Daffy, all he could bring himself to say was that Mr Tong was his best friend, like his younger brother, a person whom he could trust and talk to. He would be grateful to him for the rest of his life. Leslie related the story of the time many years before when he had been in financial difficulties and Daffy had lent him the money without a word. Later on, Leslie had learned from friends that, as a result, Daffy had been forced to eat cheap lunch boxes for months. Daffy was the only man who would stand by him. Leslie said he treated him as his lifelong friend, not only a friend but his very special and important friend.[547]

Chitose Shima asked him forthrightly whether the question of homosexuality was a taboo subject. It wasn't, Leslie said, but hastily denied that he was gay, then went on to say that it didn't matter to him what sex a person was and that he was happy with either sex. He asked why it was necessary to choose, and suggested that everyone should accept the universality of love. Shima rather openly baulked at this, and Leslie hastily went on to say that it was very difficult to make people understand what he really wanted to say, though he still didn't think he was gay. Yet he immediately cast doubts on this assertion by asking her whether all Japanese fans thought he was gay. Maybe not all, but many, she told him, at which Leslie confessed jokingly that many fans at every one of his events in Japan gave him bags full of books on homosexuality, which he confessed made him blush. The idea of a beautiful young girl buying such books just to please him made him so embarrassed! [548]

For both Leslie and Daffy the public enunciation of their relationship was uncharted territory. It would have been too much to have expected any full disclosure or consistency in what they said (and Daffy has never spoken in public on this subject). No one had ever done so in Hong Kong. For Leslie and Daffy, there was no guide on how to cope with their circumstances, no precedent to fall back on. It was a minefield they had to negotiate together, and they had to live with the consequences of whatever was said. Ultimately they would not say or do anything to endanger their relationship. Unlike Lai Yiu-fai and Ho Po-wing, they really were happy together and meant to stay that way.

CHAPTER 15

TIME TO REMEMBER

1999-2000

The film that Leslie had started work on back in early 1998, *A Time to Remember*, screened in Hong Kong on 18 January 1999.[549] It was a Chinese production made in Shanghai (though financed by investors in Hong Kong, Taiwan, Japan, and Malaysia) and was directed by the up-and-coming Chinese director Ye Da Ying, who had won fame with his film *Red Cherry* five years before.[550] The movie was still, at the time, an unusual enterprise for a Hong Kong star like Leslie, not only as it was a Chinese film, but also as it was a romance with a Communist hero. Leslie played Jin, an idealistic member of the People's Liberation Army in the early 1930s who falls in love with the daughter of the Kuomintang policeman who is hunting him. This gave the film the alternative title it was known by throughout 1998, *The Red Lover*. To help get around the difficulties posed by the film's subject, the Communist struggle against Chiang Kai Shek's Nationalists, the film is narrated by the third character in the love triangle, an American surgeon named Payne, played by Todd Bancroft. Much of the film is spoken in English, and this gave Leslie a chance for once to show off his cultivated English accent, which, strangely enough, somehow suited the role.

The film was only mildly successful in Hong Kong—the subject matter was a difficult one there still—but it was a huge success in China, where it played for over a month in Beijing alone. Across the country it was number two to *Titanic* at the box office that year. When it screened in Hong Kong, it had already been shown in 1998 in several Chinese provincial cities, including Shenzhen and Shanghai, as well as in the capital. Leslie went to some of the places the film was showing, including Chengdu, and while in China managed time to call to see the young Lei Han (his apprentice in *Farewell My Concubine*).

Leslie's character dominates the film, even though spending much of it wounded or as a prisoner. He has some sadly prophetic lines, one spoken of the wife who had killed herself before the tale commences by throwing herself from the window of their home to warn him that he was about to be captured: "It was a tall building and she was in the air for a long time … The sun rises, an eagle flies toward heaven … It's so awful and so beautiful."

The part of a dedicated revolutionary was a first for Leslie, who must have had mixed feelings about taking it on. Once he had agreed to do it, though, he followed his usual habit of immersing himself completely in the role. While making the film, he told an interviewer (somewhat disingenuously given his family's history and what he'd said in the past) that he knew nothing of Communism, and that both as a Hong Konger and as an artist he wasn't interested in politics. He went on to claim that for the three months it had taken to make the film, he had needed to rely on the director to tell him how to be a Communist. He added that one of the reasons he had taken on the part was that he now regarded himself "as completely Chinese."[551] So the film was a challenge for him as well as a statement about his place in the world. It was clear that, unlike many of his contemporary artists, he had decided to embrace the motherland now that Hong Kong had rejoined it.

Beijing clearly took note of this and was pleased. The film made him an even bigger star in China than he had been before, and Leslie was interviewed on Beijing TV during its making. His popularity was evident daily around the set. Todd Bancroft watched him in Shanghai signing autographs and giving fans photo opportunities, only taking his leave when the hordes of screaming girls got too close for safety. Bancroft admired Leslie and was pleasantly surprised how easy he was to get on with. When they relaxed together he tried unsuccessfully to get Leslie to break his vow not to smoke. The female lead, Mei Ting, told the media that she had much enjoyed working with Leslie, whose sensible, professional approach she found very attractive.[552]

On 29 March, Leslie and Brigitte Lin were guests at Hong Kong University, where a seminar gathered to discuss *Ashes of Time*.[553] This was organised by Professor Ackbar Abbas, who two decades before had been married to Leslie's sister, Ophelia.[554] Leslie was asked about his views of the current state of the Hong Kong film industry, which he characterised in his reply as "almost dead," blaming not only copyright piracy but also the fact that moviemakers had forgotten quality. He did not wish, he said, repeating his usual line, to go to Hollywood; he had no desire to play in kung-fu movies and disliked the stereotypical way Americans always mixed up Asian races. He said he still believed that Hong Kong movies had a future. A movie with a heart would stimulate the market again, he suggested. It was a fond thought but sadly wishful thinking.

It was this view that lay behind his participation in his remaining two films that were released in 1999. *Moonlight Express*, the film which opened shortly after this talk, gave proof, if any were needed still, of the moribund state of the Hong Kong film industry.[555] It was almost entirely foreign, made with Japanese money and a Japanese TV star, Takako Takiwa.[556] Some of the scenes were shot in Japan, much of the music was Japanese, and in the opening scenes, Leslie speaks Japanese. The story was a shallow one which did not call for much subtlety of acting; Leslie did what he could with the limitations of the part.

Daniel Lee, its director, like many of his predecessors who had worked with Leslie, spoke very highly of his professionalism and hard work, remarking that, unlike most stars, he didn't ask for a double in the scenes where his back was to the camera, no matter how many takes it took.[557] Takako Takiwa, the female lead, also spoke warmly of Leslie, saying that she had come to regard him as a brother and had not worked before with someone who took such care of people. Leslie had tasked his maid with making soup for her during the shooting to help her upset stomach. She later wrote that he was a "near-perfect" star and that though she was not the type of person to have crushes on anybody in showbiz, "Leslie was an exception. He was my number one star in the world." He remained friends with her, as he did with many with whom he worked, and afterwards, when she visited Hong Kong secretly, he always took her out for meals. "He was like a dependable big brother," she told the media.[558] Another happy relationship was established during the filming; Leslie was introduced to a young man named Kenneth Wong Chin-man. Leslie hired him as his personal assistant, in which capacity Kenneth stayed with him for the remainder of Leslie's life.

Moonlight Express opened in March in South Korea and Japan, earlier than in Hong Kong, where it was released only on 1 April, and Leslie went to both countries to promote it. His visit to Japan was the occasion for more of the usual scurrilous press reporting, this time a story appearing about his allegedly kissing an unknown man in the back streets of the Ginza district. Nothing was substantiated, of course, but the story was typical of the way the Hong Kong press would make up a story if they couldn't find a true one. *Moonlight Express* was not a lucky film in terms of press relations. Back in July 1998, at the conference held in Hong Kong to mark the commencement of shooting, the Hong Kong and Japanese photographers there had fallen out with each other and a fracas had ensued. Leslie, unaware of what was happening, left the hall, and the Hong Kong press criticised him for leaving without doing anything about the disturbance. There was no way he could win with some of them.

For the Hong Kong premiere, the Hong Kong Tourist Association brought a plane-load of Japanese fans to Hong Kong, but this did nothing to increase the film's popularity; it received only a lukewarm reception and hardly any critical acclaim. The film was nevertheless chosen to open the Hong Kong Film Week held in Vancouver on 16 June. The Hong Kong Chief Secretary for Administration, Anson Chan Fang On-sang, and the Malaysian-born Hong Kong star Michelle Yeoh Chooh-Kheng were present with Leslie and his director, Daniel Lee Yan-Kong, and producer, Catherine Hun. Whilst in Vancouver, Leslie took time to visit his sister.

Apart from the numerous music videos he was making at the time (one of which was a provocative film of Leslie as androgyne—half man, half woman), Leslie was also very visible in a small number of concerts during the year.[559] Between 30 April and 8 May, he appeared as the special guest of Anita Mui in her Hong Kong Coliseum concert.[560] This was yet another occasion marked by friction with the media, which reacted badly to Leslie's curt refusal to give interviews by throwing in their columns what they described as his "coldness" back in his face.[561] Leslie had appeared with Anita out of friendship. The other concerts in which Leslie performed this year were for charity. Children's Day was 4 April, and in a concert jointly organised by the End Child Sexual Abuse Foundation and UN Life International, Leslie performed with Jacky Cheung, Hong Kong film star Josephine Siao Fong-Fong, and Michelle Yeoh.[562]

Even if there were no directing projects in the immediate

pipeline, life was very good, and the year 1999 was full of enjoyable and interesting events. In February, Leslie was shown the proofs for *All about Leslie*, the book of photographs and accompanying texts in which he had cooperated with its Japanese author, Chitose Shima, over some two weeks during 1998.[563] He was so pleased with these that in April he and Daffy flew to Japan for the launch of the book. Shima was not part of any commercial entity, only a private individual, so she had been unable to make the kind of arrangements for his reception to which he was accustomed. At the airport, the crowd got out of hand, forcing Leslie and Daffy to escape the crush by diving into the car which was to take them into town. They were immediately pursued by a couple of taxis full of female fans. Their driver tried unsuccessfully to shake these off, so they were forced to stop in a side street to enable a member of staff to get out and run back to shout at their pursuers, who only then shamefacedly ended the chase. Leslie had become very angry by this stage and had to be calmed down by Daffy. Back in Hong Kong, more mishaps occurred. The book was due to be released in the shops on 23 April, but one bookshop put it on sale on the 8th and the next day the *Sun* newspaper published unauthorised extracts, including ten photographs. As usual, the paper focussed on Leslie's relationship with Daffy, and, despite protests, apologies were not forthcoming. The book was eventually released three days early on the 20th, simultaneously in Hong Kong, Taiwan, and Singapore. On that day, long queues built up at the book signings. Leslie had volunteered to attend the Hong Kong event, and he wearily signed all the copies presented to him. He seemed to view the issue as one of the duties that came with maturity; he had told Chitose Shima that he thought he was too old to be an idol.[564]

On 3 July, Leslie's contract with Rock Records expired. He had been increasingly unhappy with them since the previous year, and he had decided not to seek a renewal. The arrangements to which he then came made it clear that what he was seeking now was his independence. He signed a two-year contract with the Universal Music Group (UMG), which had earlier been known as Polygram and was the recording company for his erstwhile rival, Alan Tam (as a result, Leslie and Tam found themselves singing a duet, the first time they had sung together since the eighties). Chan Siu-po, the managing director of UMG, had been managing director of Cinepoly Records when Leslie had been with them, so this was a return, if not to a friend, at least to familiar management. This time, though, Leslie signed a contract only for publicity and distribution.[565] What was more important artistically was that, with his old music producer, Alvin Leong, known in Hong Kong as the "Ace Producer," Leslie himself now set up APEX Music Production to record his own music. The launch of their new venture was broadcast live over the Internet from the Hong Kong Convention and Exhibition Centre.

What time he gave to performing was still being devoted to good causes. Late that summer, on 21 August, he sang in the Peace Concert in Hiroshima and, one month later, he joined a multitude of stars on TV to record a charity song, "There Is Love in This City," to raise money for the victims of the earthquake that had struck Taiwan on 21 September. On the show that night, he purchased a bowl of rice for HK$250,000. At a later charity event, he appeared with Maggie Cheung and Tony Leung Ka-fai for the same cause. On 1 October, he played in a charity concert in Singapore, this for Media Corporation's All Star Charity Show.[566]

It was not until the autumn that his new musical contracts resulted in the issue of a new album, *Countdown with You*. This was named for the countdown to the new millennium, and appeared in October with Leslie billed as its executive producer.[567] It sold in large numbers and soon started taking awards. The track "Left/Right Hand" (or "Left and Right Hands") was one of RTHK's Top Ten songs by Christmas and became Top Ten Gold Song of the Year.

Leslie was to use it often from then on as a sort of signature tune, and it was a song often taken to have been meant by him as an indication of his sexual orientation. Lyricist Lam Jik later denied that this was the case, saying that he himself had suggested the use of hands for the music video, one hugging, one waving goodbye.[568] One of *Countdown with You*'s songs, "Little Star" was taken from Leslie's forthcoming film, *The Kid*. The last track, "Loneliness Is Harmful," was a fast-tempo song by Leslie himself, arranged by C.Y. Kong with lyrics by Lam Jik. Leslie held an autograph session for the launch of the album at HMV, his first public autograph session for a music album in Hong Kong, and a sign of the different working conditions his contract with UMG made necessary. *Countdown with You* became IFPI and RTHK's Top Best Selling Album of the Year.

Though it was still very early days, Leslie's relationship with UMG was rumoured in the media to be less than ideal. Stories were current that he believed he was being treated with less than the appreciation he believed he deserved, and he was said to have been particularly unimpressed by being asked to participate in publicity for Alan Tam's new album. In reality, Leslie had been in Hiroshima when Tam's album was released so could not have been present had he wanted to be. The loose talk was encouraged, though, by the guarded answers he gave to the press about his willingness to appear with Tam, saying that he would do so if Tam asked him to, thereby putting the ball back in Tam's court. They had never warmed to each other since the rivalry of the eighties.

The record companies, as always, capitalised on his name by putting out a handful of remixes and karaoke discs in several countries (including, in Japan, *The Best of Leslie Cheung*), and Leslie was Special Guest at the China MTV Awards. To cap his musical successes in 1999, RTHK gave "Thanks, Monica" its Gold Song of the Millennium Award.

To some small degree, Leslie overcame his earlier aversion to working on TV that year, appearing on ATV's *Celebrity Talk Show 30* in a programme called "All about Leslie."[569] On another occasion, he sang an excerpt from a Cantonese opera in a TVB tribute to opera star Yam Kim-fai. One slightly more substantial TV project came off in September, when he went back to Paris to shoot his third drama, the second for TV, in that city. The new one was TVB's *Leslie Cheung Special '99*, the first for a decade, a musical made with UMG help titled, unoriginally, *Left Right Love Destiny*.[570] Leslie wrote and in part directed this story, and it was credited as a "Leslie Cheung Production" when shown. This was his most creative film work since *The Phantom Lover* four years before.[571]

During the making of this TV drama, Leslie was very much the senior member of the team, who regarded him as a father figure. He shepherded them all around Paris, buying them hot dogs during the shooting. They were all still there for his forty-third birthday, so the cast bought him a cake and he gave them dinner in a Chinese restaurant. Shooting continued back in Hong Kong, where Alan Tam and others appeared in scenes in Leslie's restaurant. The show was shown on TVB on 10 October and later featured as in-flight entertainment on Cathay Pacific's aircraft. Leslie's production role in this show encouraged talk that he intended to direct the romantic movie he'd first mentioned the year before, and he now allowed some details of this to emerge. It was said to be about three couples of different ages, and it had been pencilled in for production for the autumn. Leslie even started to look for a leading actress to star, but the project was not taken forward.

The Kid, a film that Leslie had made back in 1998, hit Hong Kong screens on 12 October 1999.[572] The circumstances surrounding its making were yet another indication of the dire state of the Hong Kong film industry. Like his other two films that first screened in 1999, this was not a mainstream Hong Kong movie, but was made by a consortium of five directors who had formed a new company, the inaptly named Midas Films, to make cheap-budget local movies.[573] They had conceived the idea that the way to resurrect the moribund Hong Kong film industry was to make inexpensive films that would appeal to the public. Leslie helped the consortium, which was operating on a shoestring, with accommodation and cars, and himself persuaded Ti Lung (who had played his brother in *Better Tomorrow*) to join the cast. He even forfeited his salary to make the movie possible, taking only HK$1 for the role. The film, however, was still not a success, and it bombed in Hong Kong (though it did better abroad). The concept was obviously unrealistic. The company made no more movies, and the Hong Kong film industry as a whole continued its sorry decline.

The times were highly inauspicious as well, as the film had been made in the teeth of the 1998 Asian financial crisis, which itself formed the backdrop to the film. In the story, the economic downturn propels stock broker Wing (played by Leslie in another role using his own name, though only in English, for the Chinese name is different) from riches to poverty, setting in train the course of events which lead him to bring up baby Ming, who has been abandoned on his houseboat by its mother. It is a rather unlikely story, though occasionally a tear-jerker. Leslie acted beautifully with the engaging Ming and gave one of his most likeable and natural performances. His character's appearance is very different from that of his usual roles: he's scruffy (he usually wears a reversed baseball cap, torn jeans, and stubble) and has reverted to a very local way of life. Clearly, Leslie didn't give a damn about being shown in a less-than-glamorous light. Though it may have been an unrealistic tale, it clearly affected Leslie and brought out something of the gently paternal in him. When Leslie and the child are together on screen, the film is a joy to watch.

Director Jacob Cheung became very fond of his star during the making of this film, remarking how Leslie took huge care of the little boy and also of the rest of the cast, particularly of the young TV actor Lam Ka-tung, who was here working in his first film.[574] He later recounted how Leslie helped Lam learn the techniques of movie-making. After the screening of *The Kid*, Leslie felt enough at ease to make some very open comments to the press about himself, ones very similar to those he'd made in private during the making of *Happy Together*. He told the local gossip magazine *City Entertainment* that there was no love story in the film save between adopted father and son, a fact that gave rise to his obvious pleasure that he had not had to "cuddle a woman!"[575]

Earlier in the year, on 8 March, while presenting the Best Actor award at the Hong Kong Film Critics Society's ceremony at Planet Hong Kong, he had joked about his lack of success in actually winning awards, saying he hoped he'd be on the other side of the podium the next year. The three films in which he starred in 1999 had given him little chance of that.

On New Year's Eve, the eve of the new millennium, the Hong Kong government held a Millennium Gold Songs Concert at the Happy Valley Race Course attended by Chief Executive Tung Chee-hwa and Chief Secretary Anson Chan. Leslie was one of a large number of celebrities, including Jackie Chan, Alan Tam, Andy Lau, Leon Lai, Aaron Kwok, Sammi Cheng Sau-Man, and Faye Wong (Wong Fei), who played in the new millennium despite the rather difficult open-air circumstances of the race course.[576]

***

The new millennium opened well. On 21 January, Leslie attended a ceremony at which RTHK honoured him with their Golden Needle Award for lifetime achievement in the Cantopop industry. For this unique award, he broke his resolution to attend no more award ceremonies and so was there in person to perform "Left/Right Hand," the song of the year. He did not, though, go to receive RTHK's Top Ten Chinese Gold Songs Award for the same song, nor to ceremonies to receive the other awards the song won him this year, Commercial Radio's Ultimate Song Chart Gold Song of the Year and Metro Radio's Song Chart of the Year and Gold Song of the Year. His appearance on 21 January, of course, gave the press the opportunity to criticise him for breaking his word, this time for actually appearing at the ceremony.[577] He would never do right in some of their eyes.

As Leslie had resolved, the year 2000 was the first for many years in which he starred in no film screening over the Chinese New Year. He and Daffy stayed quietly at home for the festival playing mahjong with their friends.[578]

The early part of 2000 was a relatively quiet time until 2 March, when Leslie took part for a single day in the FM 903 Live Concert at the Hong Kong Convention and Exhibition Centre.[579] This was to be the first of that radio station's series of six concerts, each featuring different artists. The jeans that he wore that day, which sported a hole torn somewhere near his crotch, were duly noted in the press; Leslie teasingly claimed not to have noticed this as his jeans were, he said, "vintage seventies." The concert was known thereafter as "the Pillow Concert" as Leslie did a routine with a pillow, tearing it apart to release its feathers while he sang the song "Pillow" from his new EP, *Untitled*. The concert was a fundraiser for charity and tickets were free, redeemed by credit card holders, Leslie on this occasion achieving the sum of over HK$210,000 for the Children's Cancer Foundation. He sang many of his own songs, including "Stand Up" (for which the audience stood up and danced), "H2O," "For Your Heart Only," and "I Honestly Love You," as well as a song by Sandy Lam Yik Lin and old favourites like "Country

Road." There were no dancers or special effects, just Leslie alone on the stage.

Untitled, an EP with five romantic tracks, was released at the time of the concert.[580] True to his contract with UMG, he held an autograph session for its launch in Causeway Bay. Its first track, "Passing Dragonfly," was a song composed by Taiwanese composer Diane Chen with lyrics by Lam Jik and was based around a triangle between two men and a girl. He had sung this twice in the FM 903 concert (the second time as an encore, telling the audience he wasn't satisfied with his performance the first time). Lam Jik also wrote the lyrics for the second track, "You Hate Me Like That." The third track was a re-arrangement of "Left/Right Hand," the fourth "Pillow,"[581] and the fifth "I Honestly Love You," the old Olivia Newton-John number.[582] "Passing by Dragonfly" was to win and "Pillow" was to be runner-up for Best TV Serial Soundtrack that year. To complete this list of accolades, the album was awarded an unusual Joint Award by RTHK, CR, TVB, and Metro Radio as Best Album of the Year.

More charity work engaged Leslie on 3 April, when he appeared together with Anita Mui on TVB's Children's Charity Drive, for once not singing but dressed in a fencing costume and fighting a mock bout with Anita, initially anonymously, hidden by their masks. Nine other celebrities were there lending their most prized collections for the night, others doing crazy things like knitting a sweater.[583] On the 28th of April, Leslie and Anita were again together, this time to present prizes at the Taiwanese Golden Melody awards ceremony.[584] There was no Hong Kong music honoured that night, but other Hong Kong stars were also there, including the group Grasshopper. Leslie found more time for charity work on 6 May when a benefit arranged by Health Express was held at the Hong Kong Convention and Exhibition Centre. He sang two songs to raise money for surgery for the blind. Leslie had been appointed ambassador of Bright, an organisation working with other charities to improve the independence of those who could not see, and he received a medal on this occasion.

Despite his occasional honesty, Leslie would never let himself be brought to state in plain words what was by now obvious to the public. In May 2000, when questioned as to whether he was gay or not by the critic Richard Corliss, he replied that it was more appropriate to say that he was bisexual. In the same interview, he gave the Hong Kong press a broadside, complaining that they knew his car numbers and were there whether he was at the Mandarin Hotel Coffee Shop or at Propaganda; the latter was by then Hong Kong's gay disco and so his remark was in itself something of a give-away.[585]

On 19 May, in the evening of the day on which he had launched his next concert tour in a press conference in Hong Kong's Conrad Hotel, Leslie attended the premiere of his new movie, *Double Tap*, accompanied by his co-star, Ruby Wong Cheuk-ling, as well as by Takako Tokiwa, who had flown in from Japan for the event.[586] In this film, Leslie was again under the direction of Bruce Law Chi-leung, co-director and writer of *Viva Erotica*.[587] Leslie played Rick Pang, marksman and manager of a firing range, who has mastered the art of "double tapping," squeezing the trigger in such quick succession that the shots hit exactly the same spot. Forced to shoot a disturbed man threatening to kill others on his range, Rick finds he has a taste for killing and starts to indulge it. This psychologically disturbed character—hard, cold, indifferent, and fuelled by bloodlust—was different from any Leslie had played before; he said that he took the role because he wanted a new challenge. He told an interviewer at the time that he had been able to accomplish a breakthrough in his acting by taking the part. He commented that not many actors were willing to play that kind of role through fear that their image might be damaged, but that he didn't really care as he liked to try out different roles.[588]

The film called for skills in weapon-handling that Leslie had not hitherto possessed, and he had to spend a month learning how to hold, use, and dismantle a pistol. The hero of the film, a policeman named Inspector Miu, also a firearms expert, was played by Alex Fong Chung-sun, a highly experienced actor with scores of films to his credit. When Leslie heard that the film had overshot its budget, he volunteered to reduce his fee by half on the grounds that the film had two male leads, he and Fong, and the film was able to go ahead. It was said that the stars had been left to decide who played the hero, who the villain, and that Leslie had deliberately taken the latter part, seeking to escape his "idol" image; at times he deliberately appeared on film without makeup. The director later told the press of his admiration for Leslie's professionalism, commenting that Leslie had insisted on acting his lines in full, even when not on camera, so that his fellow actors could react properly when they were being filmed.[589] He went on to add the jarring note that he was less happy with the way he said Leslie had showed his displeasure at having to act beyond the ten hours a day specified in his contract. When forced to work for sixteen hours on set, he had upset Law by doing so with a scowl on his face. An untypical remark; there was something personal here that neither made public in explanation, but then what, one might wonder, could Law have expected, demanding sixteen hours' work for only half a fee?

The film was released on 27 May and proved a modest success, though it attracted no critical attention. Leslie was accused in the press of melodramatic overacting, which, it may be said fairly, is the case in some scenes of the film. He was at his best when portraying the frozen, controlling gunsmith, coach turned killer, as iron-willed and cold as the weapons he wields.

Before *Double Tap* was released, Leslie flew to Japan to make *Okinawa Rendez-vous*, his second feature film of 2000, this for Charles Heung, who was now running movie company China

Star.[590] The film was a light summer comedy with little in the way of plot or characterisation.[591] The cast, Leslie included, had a romp making it in under two months—it was a very rushed job, without even a full script to start it off—but none of them was really called upon to act. It is difficult to see why Leslie took on this film. It was not a film that had a serious intent or message, or which called for real acting—the only types, he had pledged, he would take part in from now on. Charles Heung tried to place the film in these categories, stating to the press that Leslie had been attracted because this was a film that satisfied his exacting parameters, as well as one which had other major stars. But it wasn't really so. It was especially surprising as Leslie was about to embark (in July) on his next concert tour and needed time to prepare. Perhaps the money was too good to turn down. The film did, though, provide the occasion for another Leslie song, this one entitled "Without Love," which would feature in his 2000 album *Big Heat*.

Producer-Director Gordon Chan Kar-Seung, though, was yet another filmmaker who was very complimentary about his star: "He was so professional, so laid-back, I can't see him as a legend. When I panicked or was frustrated he always said, "Don't worry about it!" He pointed out what I'd overlooked. He was very creative."[592]

The fact that his resolve to concentrate on good films was being foiled by the problems in Hong Kong's film industry must have worried Leslie, but he had, at this point, little time to sit and fret, for he had been preparing for his next big series of concerts during the first half of the year. He had invested much of his creativity and a huge amount of his time and energy into this. He was about to embark on his last world tour.

CHAPTER 16

PASSION

2000 - 2001

Before the *Passion Tour* concert series kicked off, *Big Heat*, Leslie's second major album of 2000, was released in July, timed just before the first of the performances that would include many of its numbers.[593] Several tracks swiftly became hits: "Big Heat," the title track, and most memorably, the song "I," which Leslie said later was his self-portrait, its lyrics containing lines in which Leslie sang that he forever liked the way he was, open and upright, and that he believed that people had to respect one another as well as to respect and love themselves.

Leslie had specified to his lyricist, Lam Jik, that the first line of the song had to be "I am what I am." Lam Jik later commented that "I" was the song in which Leslie wanted to state his gay orientation and that the opening line "I love myself forever" was taken from a song in a movie he had seen.[594] The song in question must have been the gay anthem, "I Am What I Am," Jerry Herman's defiant song from the 1983 Broadway musical and later film *La Cage aux Folles*, a song that defied the world and its prejudices, particularly those expressed by the gutter press which had afflicted Leslie all his working life.

Leslie described his purpose in this song during one of his forthcoming Hong Kong concerts:

> Please listen to what I have to say... both Lam Jik and I composed this song. What we mean to say is that God made all mankind equal regardless of whether they are black or white. Some people like cats ... some people love dogs, but I know there are some people who like others that are different. They feel that they can find happiness in this way. As that is so, why can't we let them be? Each one is free to choose his own way of living as long as it makes him happy. No one has the right to question this! I am not here to preach because I feel I am not a saint but all I want to say is, no matter what, I will always treat people with kindness even though it may never be reciprocated. My fate [...] is that I am a person who treats people with the utmost sincerity but in return people use this virtue of mine against me to insult me. All these many years in the entertainment world, it has always been this way. I am so used to it and I DON'T BLOODY CARE! Let me tell you here that I will always be myself, Cheung Kwok-wing... I will always be me.[595]

That was about as explicit a statement about his life as he could ever have been expected to give in public. And his fans didn't seem to care. The video he made later in the Australian desert for this album reinforced his message.[596] He appears in the Garden of Eden, with a feminine man and a masculine woman, releasing the dove of sexual liberation from his own hands. He himself cross-dresses in the video, all of which is aimed at showing the mutability of the boundaries of gender and sexuality. It was released on 11 August.

On 31 July 2000, Leslie opened what was to be the first of forty-three concerts in his *Passion Tour* series, the first thirteen of which were to be held at the Hong Kong Coliseum. He had taken immense care with the design of this show, which was produced by Florence Chan and a huge team, and choreographed by Stanley

Chu Wing-lung. The series was sponsored by a Hong Kong media company, Tom.com, and was planned to take the cutting edge of the *Crossover* concerts to another level.[597] Leslie was still, at the age of forty-three, intent on leading the Cantopop field.

This time he'd been offered the once-in-a-lifetime chance of a set of eight costumes by Jean-Paul Gaultier, unique and eccentric, at times beautiful, on occasion shocking.[598] The costumes were worn beneath a long, dark wig with hair pieces, and Leslie kept his moustache and beard unshaven for the series, which added a strongly masculine touch to costumes which transcended all gender and challenged the given notions of what was suitable for either a man or a woman. There was no hint of femininity this time, despite one of the costumes including a long, sarong-style skirt. A good deal of sexuality was in evidence on stage—he'd made himself very sexy for the show, reducing his waistline to an astonishing twenty-seven inches, it was said, by a regime of three hundred push-ups a day—but it was all safely hetero this time, and Leslie kissed and held only the female dancers. Gone was the effeminacy of the "Red" sequences of the last concert; in its place was something provocative but something much more difficult to understand.

The Hong Kong press, of course, were to find it *impossible* to understand, had they wanted to.[599] They attacked his costumes and what they described as his "dirty dancing." The controversy they stirred up deeply offended Jean-Paul Gaultier, who, from sending Leslie a huge bouquet of flowers on the first night (as well as placing the designs for Leslie's costumes on his website), was reduced to paroxysms of fury. He sent Leslie an email on the concert's third day melodramatically saying, "You Hong Kongers are absolutely ridiculous! From now on, international designers will never collaborate with Hong Kong ever again!"[600] This hurt Leslie badly, though the attack should really have been directed at the media. The designs disappeared shortly afterwards from Gaultier's website. As a result of all this, the concert promoters in Taiwan and Singapore cancelled the shows that were planned there. The Hong Kong press also made fun of Leslie's facial appearance, offensively likening him to Ching Che, a character in *The Ring*, a Japanese horror film then showing in local cinemas, whose name translates as "horrible" in Cantonese. The foreign press were amazed at the way the Hong Kong media devoured their own, the Japanese media in particular openly wondering why their Hong Kong colleagues savaged, rather than promoted, their country's premier star.

Leslie intended the concerts to have a serious theme and was heartbroken when no one in Hong Kong seemed to notice. He deliberately closed the concert with the song "I" to give his audiences the message that there should be no discrimination because all human beings are equal. By wearing clothes designed to break down prejudices and stereotypes, it seemed to him that he had succeeded only in reinforcing them. He became very depressed by the whole experience, so much so that Florence Chan later identified this as the start of his later clinical depression and blamed the media's attacks for his death. That may have been an exaggeration, but the furore over the *Passion Tour* can be seen as the first step in a series that led to Leslie's decline. Even the photographs taken of him surreptitiously during the show, then published in the press—one, for instance, a close-up of his thigh while he was wearing the skirt—seemed to him aimed only at titillating people and at bringing him down. He couldn't get the subject out of his mind and was to raise it again and again in future, making himself (it seemed to those around him) ill in the process, continually saying how hurt he had been and attacking the Hong Kong media's propensity to look for breasts rather than brains. It was all very sad and seemingly very silly, but it was typical of Hong Kong and the effect was real.

The show, though, was spectacular.[601] Though the songs changed in each location, the concert was executed as a packaged set, with

Leslie appearing at the start surrounded by blue and frosted white light in a huge column illuminated by lasers, wearing white feathered wings and a white suit, appearing as if he were an angel descended from heaven. The light show was the most spectacular ever before achieved in any of his concerts, and this added glamour to what was in some respects a simpler concert. Leslie performed alone for most of the time, and the dance routines were less dramatic than those of earlier concerts. A montage of Leslie's films showed throughout the performance as a backdrop to the stage. The show's central section was designed as a rave party, for which audiences were asked to get up out of their seats and dance in the aisles. They often crowded the stage and were difficult to get back in their places afterwards, but the high levels of emotion this engendered made this a concert series that lifted the roof (or the open skies) off everywhere it played. At many times, especially at the close of the concert when he sang "I," Leslie was reduced to weeping, and he often ended the show with tears streaming down his cheeks.

The concert series, though, was designed to be less stressful this time, spread over a longer period than had been the *Crossover* series and lasting until the April of the following year. Longer breaks and fewer locations were scheduled, and this allowed Leslie to complete other engagements during it, and to come home to Hong Kong to recuperate before setting off again on tour.

On 17 August, the first such opportunity in between shows, he started to make a short film for RTHK and the Council on Smoking and Health (COSH), a body set up by the Hong Kong Government as part of its anti-smoking campaign.[602] Leslie, who had given up smoking some years before, was an active supporter of COSH. The film now planned was produced by Jacob Cheung, with whom Leslie had worked on *The Kid*, and Leslie was asked to direct.[603] Named appropriately *Ashes to Ashes*, this was Leslie's debut as a film director (though he had taken a hand directing scenes in some of his earlier films, as we have seen). Though this was a film of only thirty-nine minutes, it was at last the start of what he hoped would be the fulfilment of his dream of becoming a director.

Leslie had high intentions for the film. He intended, as he put it in a TV interview given after the film was completed, to give something back to society after all the years he had enjoyed in the business. Actors, he thought, often seemed aloof and were believed to be in showbiz only for the money. He wanted to correct that impression.[604] To this end, Leslie pulled together a group of his friends, including Anita Mui and Karen Mok, and dragged Teresa Mo, who was pregnant at the time, out of her temporary semi-retirement. The film was made cheaply on a budget of only HK$700,000 and was completed in only five and a half days, enabling it to fit neatly between concerts. He himself took the male lead. The cast included the up-and-coming Chinese American actor/singer Wang Lee-hom, whom Leslie had met the year before in the Green Spot nightclub in Hong Kong. That night Leslie had taken Wang up on stage to sing Elton John's "Don't Let the Sun Go Down on Me" as a duet.

Leslie did pretty much everything for this film, writing the script, acting, directing, and editing the film. Getting the cast together to act for free was not so easy. He had begun to lose touch with some of his old friends and had to re-establish ties, as one of his friends related later:

> He particularly wanted to get Anita Mui to do the film with him. So he put a call through to Grasshopper, the three-man boy band of the eighties. One of them was her manager. Leslie called and got hold of the manager, and he said she was busy, she didn't have time, there were scheduling problems, there'd be no way without a budget, "no; no budget, no time." Leslie was at the Ambient Bistro having a drink and told us, "Who the hell does he think he

is, I knew Anita long before he did, when we knew each other he was nothing, how dare he talk to me like that," so Leslie told him, "You tell Anita to call me back, I don't want to talk to you." When Anita called he said, "How dare you? You have no time for me? What is this bullshit?" "Of course not," she replied, and ended up starring in the movie.[605]

Ashes to Ashes was the story of a mother and father played by Anita and Leslie, both smokers who lose their young son to cancer caused by passive smoking. As he had while making *The Kid*, Leslie worked charmingly with the young boy who played his son, and was completely natural as a father. The film, though, was less natural and tended to the melodramatic—unsurprisingly, perhaps, given the purposes for which it was made. The scene where Leslie breaks down in the hospital after the death of his son is harrowing but a trifle overdone, reminiscent of similar scenes he'd played in *Temptress Moon* and *Double Tap*. The characters, of course, all smoke like chimneys. Aside from its main purpose of illustrating the harmful effects of smoking, the movie took a few gentle pokes at Hong Kong's entertainment industry and its star cults. It had a very lively, rhythmic soundtrack, chosen by Leslie himself. He was typically modest about the film when interviewed by RTHK, apologising to the fans of all the stars who'd had such small roles and to all his audience if he hadn't met their expectations, hoping nevertheless that they would like every shot and that the story would move them. He ended the interview saying he hoped that all would get the message of the film, as there was only one take in real life.[606] TVB aired it on 7 January 2001. It was Leslie's penultimate film.

As there was not much time for making films in 2000, the next year was inevitably to be a dry year cinematographically. Some projects were mooted only to fall by the wayside, one being *Crouching Tiger Hidden Dragon*, whose director Ang Lee had earlier contacted Leslie and did so again now to discuss his taking the supporting part of Lo Xiou Hu, or "Dark Cloud." Leslie read the script and was interested, but the discussions were not fruitful and the role was later taken by Chen Chang.

After *Ashes to Ashes* was in the can, Leslie returned to the *Passion Tour*. The first stop outside Hong Kong was Kuala Lumpur, where the show was staged between 7 and 8 September. This was Leslie's first appearance in Malaysia for eleven years.[607] He played at the Merdeka Stadium, without the hair pieces and skirt to adjust for local sensibilities, in a concert sponsored (ironically in the light of the film Leslie had just finished making) by Peter Stuyvesant. He opened up to the local press about his frustration with all the criticism his concert had received from the Hong Kong media, getting quite carried away in the process: "No matter how much they criticize me, I'm still here, aren't I? They are finished, not me, OK?"[608] The local press were kinder, likened the show to the drama of a Madonna concert and admired the way the forty-three year old strutted like a supermodel who loved his audience and was loved by them in return. They quoted him asking them about his costume, in his own inimitable style: "Do you like it? Pretty, isn't it? It's a Jean-Paul Gaultier design; of course it's nice!" Not all were quite so polite. Brian Cheong wrote in *The Star* that Leslie was extremely suspicious, defensive, and just a bit big-headed at his press conference, though he admitted that he also showed himself charming, suave, and boyishly handsome.[609] Despite his carping, Cheong had the grace to write that he felt Leslie was a pop superstar in every sense of the word and that the performance was a triumph.

Leaving Malaysia, Leslie stopped off in Bangkok and stayed at one of his and Daffy's favourite hotels, the Mandarin Oriental, in order to celebrate his forty-fourth birthday with twenty of his friends, whom he had invited specially for the evening. He had often stayed in the Mandarin Oriental since he had been taken there by his friend Ka Ling, the Hong Kong actress of the sixties.

Transitting once more through Hong Kong, Leslie managed to find some time for charity work. On 3 September, in Causeway Bay for the Mid-Autumn Festival, Leslie took a turn selling the traditional moon cakes to benefit local NGOs. He was then off again to China, the next country on the tour, where he opened in Shanghai on 16 and 17 September. Strangely, this was the first time he had staged a concert in the city. This was an open-air event in a sports stadium with a capacity of 80,000, and Leslie set a record by holding concerts on two consecutive nights there, selling over 100,000 tickets in all. The first night's concert was held the day after a typhoon had passed, so the stage could only be set up at the last minute and everything was soggy and wet. For a time, the Chinese government, which had taken note of the media furore surrounding the concert in Hong Kong, had considered banning the show, but eventually allowed it to go ahead, though once again without the wig and skirt. The huge crowds went wild and screamed throughout the performances, each of which lasted a full 150 minutes. Leslie became very emotional at times and had to re-start the number "Going through Winter Together" after breaking down halfway.

A week later, on 22 September, the tour reached Hangzhou, where Leslie was awarded the Zhi Jiang Media Eternal Charisma Award then performed the next day in the Zhi Jiang stadium before a crowd of 20,000 fans. On 29 September he reached Kunming, a location where things turned rather sour due to a dispute about crowd control with the local government. Officials would not let the crowd anywhere near the stage, and Leslie threatened to cancel the concert rather than spoil its rave party; in response, local officials threatened to arrest him. So the show went ahead, though Leslie said he'd never perform in Kunming again. Some weeks later, on 14 October, the tour reached Guangzhou for a performance at the Tianhe Sports Stadium. It rained hard during the concert, drenching both star and 40,000 fans alike. Leslie was moved to tears several times by the high-octane emotion in the stadium and the ecstatic welcome the crowd gave him.

Interviewed around this time in China, he said:

> Hong Kong doesn't have any reporters, only a bunch of authors. They have no qualifications to be reporters [...] In my song "I," there are the lyrics: "I forever like the way I am [...] open and upright." Giving Hong Kong media interviews is a waste of my time. They don't prepare, they ask questions they should know the answers to (like "how many years have you been in show biz?") and only want photos so they can go back and make up stories. I open my heart to tell the truth and they make up false statements. I am cheated! All I can do is to hide in my house all day. It's become a game I don't want to play anymore.[610]

On 18 October, once more back in Hong Kong to catch his breath between *Passion Tour* appearances, Leslie became the first local celebrity to donate three items to be auctioned for charity in a series of events organised by *The Sun* newspaper. He selected from his house a fragrant Australian candle, an antique Chinese vase, and a wooden mahjong box. [611] This was followed by a trip to Japan on 30 October, where he once again accompanied Hong Kong's chief secretary, Anson Chan, who took a group of Hong Kong stars to open the largest Hong Kong film festival ever held there.[612]

Partly to capitalise on the tour, the record companies made other issues of Leslie's music during the year. In addition to the *Passion Tour* music on CD and karaoke DVD issued at the end of the year, there were compilation and karaoke releases in Hong Kong and Japan (including the albums *Big Heat*, *Leslie Best of Music Videos*, and *Untitled*). Awards flowed, too, Leslie winning this year: the 2nd CCTV-MTV (Beijing) Music Award Outstanding Artist in Asia; first place in RTHK's Top Ten Popular Artists of the '90s; and TVB

Jade's Solid Gold Best Ten Award (Honorary Award). Uniquely, he was appointed Music Ambassador of the Composers and Authors Society of Hong Kong (CASH). Later in the year, he composed the number "Noah's Ark" as a theme song for their Golden Sail Awards.[613]

Some weeks later, on 4 November, Leslie took the *Passion Tour* to a venue just across the border from Hong Kong in the new industrial city of Shenzhen. He asked his audience, most of whom were local Cantonese speakers, whether he should speak in Mandarin or Cantonese—the crowd shouted "Mandarin," which he then spoke for the rest of the evening. During the singing of "I," the fans rushed forward and the security guards lost control, causing Leslie to retreat temporarily to the rear of the stage until order was restored. On 11 November the show arrived in Nanjing, where winter had set in. Icy rain swept across the open stadium onto the stage, drenching Leslie, who carried out the entire show in his thin costumes with no cuts to the programme. His nose turned red, he trembled with the cold, and his breath hung in the air in front of him. The fans could see this and were so concerned that they shouted to him to put some clothes on. One threw his coat onto the stage for him to wear. At the local hotel there was some embarrassment when Daffy was questioned by the security guards. He was staying in the same room as Leslie, but they failed to recognise him, and he had to explain who he was. At the same hotel, Leslie staged a photo op for his local fans, who had formed the strangely named group, Leslie Inn. On 15 November, the last stop on the mainland was reached at Ningbo.

After another short break back in Hong Kong, Leslie crossed the Pacific, reaching the States in late November. On the 23rd and 26th, he played once more at the Trump Taj Mahal Casino Resort in Atlantic City. During this show, he backed into a speaker and fell off the stage, hurting his arm, but he carried on singing and climbed back onto the stage to audience applause. On the second day, he made the strange, but prophetic, announcement that he would not return to Atlantic City "for the rest of my life." What prompted that remark is unclear, but it turned out to be all too true.

Then it was back west across the States and the Pacific, this time to Japan, where he opened on 29 November before 5,000 fans at the Kanagawa Kenmin Hall in Yokohama, his hand still painful from his fall in Atlantic City.[614] On 1 and 2 December, he was at the Osaka Festival Hall, followed on the 5th by a performance at the Sonic City in Saitama. The Japanese leg of the tour ended on 6 and 7 December, when he performed in the Tokyo International Forum Hall. These performances, taken together with those of his '97 *Crossover* series, meant that Leslie had given a total of sixteen concerts in Japan, giving him the title of the foreigner who had played the greatest number of concerts in the country.

Leslie's Japanese shows were notably different from those in other places: he included more of his most recent songs and deliberately made the performances sexier. His T-shirts were tighter and shorter; he made his routines with the female dancers raunchier (kissing one with bright red shoes, almost in a heterosexual reversal of his "Red" performance of three years before). He clearly felt safer expressing himself in Japan, and loved the Japanese crowds. "I'm in my mid-forties and it's really something, you know, to keep a figure like this," he teased them in Tokyo. The fans liked his long hair and went really wild when he let it down from the bun in which he tied it for some of the show. He threw them roses and kissed all his female dancers (but only shook the men's hands). Japan seemed to appreciate all that Hong Kong had not.

Then, exhaustingly, he flew back across the Pacific, this time to Canada. On 21 December Leslie performed at the Hershey Centre in Toronto. During the concert someone shouted, "I love you, Leslie"; Leslie replied with a reference to his 1994 film, *He's a Woman, She's a Man*, "I love you too, whether you're a boy or a girl." The rave party was a huge success here, and the fans showered Leslie with flowers and toys. He had been collecting cuddly toys from his fans throughout the whole tour and by now had a large collection. Then the tour moved once more to the United States, and in the run-up to Christmas, on 23 December, Leslie played at the ballroom at Caesar's Palace in Las Vegas. Tickets for this concert were said to be going for over US$230 each. The house was filled almost entirely by wildly enthusiastic Asian fans, but the front rows had been reserved for some rather more staid VIP ticket holders. This made it a lot harder for Leslie to liven up his audience, but he managed it, and the seating plan did not prevent the fans from swamping the aisles and the area near the stage during the rave party.[615]

The New Year of 2001 opened with the final overseas leg of the *Passion Tour*, once again in Japan, which had long been one of Leslie's favorite countries. Between 14 and 18 January, he played in Tokyo, then in Nagoya, Osaka, and Fukuoka, travelling between them on the bullet train. The Tokyo concert, which was held before 6,000 fans, was broadcast live on Hong Kong TVB. The Osaka concert proved the most emotional of them all, Leslie using tissues to wipe away his tears. He told his fans that he would dedicate everything to them except his private life, and asked them not to knock on his door or take tours to find his house. He needed space, he pleaded, to live the way he wanted. He was remembering here, quite clearly, what had happened to him in Turtle Cove. In Fukuoka, he told his fans he wasn't sure when he'd be back to see them as he planned to be very busy making films. Perhaps he did have in mind the idea that his concert days were drawing to a close.

***

Back in Hong Kong again, Leslie presented Jacky Cheung

with his Golden Needle award at RTHK's Top Ten Chinese Gold Song awards on 21 January.[616] His *Leslie Cheung Passion Tour* CD went on sale on 14 February[617] and shortly thereafter, on 24 February, Leslie went up to Guangzhou to collect China's Original Music Outstanding Achievement Award for the song "Fever" (the Mandarin version of "Big Heat"), receiving at the same time the amazingly named 2000 Most Successful Person in China award.

2001 was a year in which he opened himself up to the media in a way he had long shied away from. When he appeared with Teresa Mo on her cable TV show at the end of February, he found himself forced to fend off her playful but pointed remarks about their earlier relationship. He parried that if she'd agreed to marry him when he'd asked her, his life might have changed totally. Teresa Mo tweaked him back with the way he continued to cover up of his relationship with Daffy, whom she said she liked very much, adding that it seemed that Leslie's friends liked Daffy more than Leslie did. Leslie responded that Daffy knew his role well; as an artist, he himself was constantly under pressure, so he had to rely totally on Daffy's support. Teresa asked Leslie if Daffy would be his lifelong companion, a question which Leslie partially dodged. Daffy was like Teresa, he said, his forever lover, friend, and family member [...] a blessing, a gift from God.[618]

2001 was also a year of ceremonies, public events, and attendance at other people's concerts, the mark of a star at the peak of his popularity. Everyone and every organisation wanted a piece of Leslie's fame and glamour. Some events he did gladly, such as attending Karen Mok's first concert at the Hong Kong Coliseum in March.[619] Mok had long been a friend; Leslie had been known to her mother since 1977, when she had been in the audience when he first sang "American Pie."

His life was so busy now that he decided to give up the coffee shop in Causeway Bay. He could hardly ever be there, and without a personal connection, there seemed little point in keeping it.

The *Passion Tour* concluded in Hong Kong with six shows held at the usual venue of the Coliseum between 11 and 16 April. Leslie intended, as he said in Hong Kong at the time, that this would be his last concert for a while; as he had told his Japanese fans, what he wanted to do now was to spend more time making films. The concerts were sold out and made a rousing finale to the series.

Whilst keeping the overall shape of the show unchanged, Leslie made some changes for his final concerts. He invited the Japanese dancer Kazuhiro Nishijima (who was usually known as Kazu), whom he had met on the last leg of the Japanese tour, to perform a dance sequence to the number "Dreaming of the Inner River" from the new album *Leslie Forever*.[620] Leslie and Kazu had appeared together the previous month in a music video called *Bewildered*, which Leslie had directed and featured the song. This had been banned almost as soon as it was shown in Hong Kong on the grounds that it portrayed a gay love affair.[621] The artists denied this, saying rather disingenuously that the couple portrayed could have been "brothers" or "close friends." Kazu commented on Leslie's direction of the video, which he said that he much appreciated, as Leslie had seen the essence of what he was trying to do and used it in the film. When questioned by Stephen Short of *Time Magazine*, Leslie denied that the production had indicated a personal message, but the video speaks for itself.

Hong Kong stars attended each of Leslie's closing concerts and Leslie's sister, Ophelia, attended the last show with her family, as did his brother, Eddie Cheung Fat-wing. The final concert was a particularly emotional event, extended by half an hour so that Leslie could take three encores and sing a punishing forty-two songs. He'd added different numbers for this final show, had put together a new montage from his old films, and had lengthened the rave party to thirty minutes. He teased one of his male chorus with having no girlfriend and characteristically flirted with his audience: "Are you saying I am very handsome?" he asked them. "Of course I am. If you had wanted to see an ugly guy, you wouldn't have come to see me." He included the song "I," telling his audiences that "this song is the one I love most, it's written by Lam Jik, he knows very well now what I am. There's no need to say any more, you all know." He thanked the editor-in-chief of the newspaper *Ming Pao*, Lung Kung-cheong, for the Grand Salute Award they'd just given him for the concerts and "for giving me back my dignity and encouragement" after all the other negative Hong Kong press reports he'd received. These continued to sting him. Interviewed on TV after the concerts ended, he said that there was no point in his doing any more; he'd had such negative comments.[622] Once again, there is an echo here of an idea that he might give no more concerts.

After the performances were over, Leslie held a celebratory end-of-concert party for the whole cast and crew in Happy Valley's Hong Kong Jockey Club.[623] James Wong recalled that at the party he handed out presents and addressed everyone by their names, no matter whether they were senior or junior staff. There were two crew members who happened to have the same names, but Leslie managed to distinguish between them without making a mistake.[624] After it was all over, a documentary film about the concert was begun but was never completed. The acclaim, though, continued, as Leslie was awarded the Music Salute Award from the Pop Music Media Association of China for his work on the *Passion Tour*.

The album *Leslie Forever* had been released on 21 March to coincide with the last phase of the concert series.[625] It was another collaboration with lyricist Lam Jik and, with the concert tour itself, garnered another crop of music awards, including RTHK's Top Pick Award and TVB Jade's Solid Gold Best Ten Salute Award.

The record companies continued to churn out remixes, dance mixes, karaoke, and DVD albums in Japan and Hong Kong throughout 2001, titles including *Music Box* and *Dear Leslie* going on sale during the year. China Music Awards also gave Leslie the Millennium Best Award at their ceremony that year.

In April 2001, Leslie once again performed the role of presenter at the Hong Kong Film Awards. Charity work seemed more and more on his mind at this time, and, in May, he attended a charity clothes auction held for the Tung Wah Group of Hospitals at the Marco Polo Prince Hotel, donating many of his own clothes to be sold. In August, he attended a press conference as the ambassador of CASH, promoting their forthcoming music award (from which he had ruled himself out). In the same month, he presented prizes at a dog show in the Wan Chai Convention Centre.[626]

There was still not the film work that Leslie had hoped for. The parlous state of the industry meant that little was emerging; Leslie made only one film that year. In the summer, he flew to Japan for the rather belated premiere there of *Okinawa Rendez-vous*, after which he commenced work on his part in *Inner Senses*, a film that would be released in 2002.[627] The Hong Kong film industry's sorry plight was very much on his mind at the time. With other stars, he made a brief appearance in a Hong Kong government short made to support the ailing industry. Talk of Leslie directing his own film grew, centred on a movie which was later to be called *Stealing Heart*, and, though nothing was done about it yet, the idea of making this came increasingly to dominate his thinking.

In September, Leslie flew again to Japan for two signing sessions for his new photo book, *Passion in China*, which had just been published there by Wing Shya.[628] In October, he acted as presenter at the CASH Golden Sail Awards at the Wan Chai Convention Centre, the evening being the first time that his song "Noah's Ark" was heard. Leslie had not had time to rehearse, so did not sing it himself. On 15 December, he attended the premiere of Stanley Kwan's new gay film, *Lan Yu*, and met one of its stars, the mainland Chinese actor Liu Ye, whom he made a friend. That month, he was with Anita Mui at the premiere of her movie *Dance of a Dream*, a film that had caused bad blood between Anita and its male lead, Andy Lau, whom she blamed for inviting her to perform in a film in which she was given second billing behind another actress. Leslie went along to support her. It was a hectic, if disjointed life he was leading that year.[629]

Despite his attempts to be more open with the media, his relations with the Hong Kong press failed to improve, and by 2001 he had become very bitter indeed about them. When *Sudden Weekly* published a photograph of him hand-in-hand with Daffy, Leslie found himself forced to comment. He told *Oriental Sunday* that though he thought the photograph rather beautiful, it was not what it appeared. When it had been taken, he had been a bit drunk and Daffy had been holding his hand to support him. The cigarette that the press alleged he was smoking at the time was actually a rolled-up cinema ticket. The media would always keep doubling their abuse until their victim was damned and dead, he told the reporter, but claimed (though from the interview it seemed to be far from the case) that he was now more relaxed about the false reports the media made about him. He found himself, though, still saddened and even damaged by them. He alleged that he'd lost some of his markets due to adverse press comment (presumably referring here to the cancellations of the *Passion Tour*). He said that his biggest blow had been when he dedicated "The Moon Represents My Heart" to his mother and Daffy in the *Crossover '97* concert and had been attacked for it by the media. He adversely compared the Japanese media with those of Hong Kong. They were better educated, he thought, and not so interested in cheap sensation. He just wanted to be true to his heart, he said; that was his character, as was the fact that once someone became his friend, that person would be his friend forever. He was only sorry that the paparazzi bothered his friends.[630]

His friends were with him that December, when he made a music video at his and Daffy's house. In this he sang a duet with Anita Mui, the first they'd sang together since they had released the song "Fate" seventeen years before.[631] The video was released on Christmas Eve on the huge public screen at Times Square in Causeway Bay.

The year, though it had been testing and exhausting, had been a triumphant one. At its close, Leslie was a star at the peak of his powers. His popularity and fame were unrivalled. He was at the very centre of Hong Kong's popular culture and, to many, his face and his music represented what Hong Kong meant to them and to the world. He held a position that other stars could only envy; none came close to him. At the end of 2001, Leslie really did have the world at his feet.

DECLINE AND FALL

CHAPTER 17

INNER TURMOIL

2002

At the opening of the year 2002, Leslie was at the top of his profession and held an unrivalled position in Hong Kong. He was still setting the pace in musical innovation, he was getting what parts were still to be had in Hong Kong movies, and he had begun to fulfil his dream of becoming a director. He was in demand and on display everywhere, he had a firm place in the hearts of his still-growing number of fans, and he was putting a good deal back into society through his work for charity. He and Daffy were together in a fantastic house where they surrounded themselves with friends. They threw a party there for a large number of them to bring in the New Year.[632]

The unpleasant rivalries of the past had also been left behind. On 13 January, Leslie was at the TV Jade Solid Gold Awards, singing, for once, with Alan Tam and with the younger songwriter and singer Anthony Wong Yiu-ming.[633] The three of them sang "Going through Winter Together," a song which had been released successfully the previous December as a duet between Leslie and Wong. The two men had found then that they enjoyed working with each other, and this had encouraged them to start work together on a new album. At the TV Jade ceremony, Leslie had the pleasant duty of presenting an award to his greatest friend, Anita Mui.

He turned in earnest now towards preparing for the film he planned to direct himself. He continued to describe this as a romance (for he had never given up on his earlier conception) but now revealed that it was to be a drama set in China in the 1940s; at this stage it was referred to as "L Production."[634] Work began under the mantle of the new film production company he had created, which he called Dream League. He had named it thus, he said, as he intended to assemble a "dream team" of talent to create serious films in Hong Kong. He now set about finding the funding that was all-important to bring his dream to life, and he began to reach out to financial backers. They were not easy to find, especially as he announced that he did not want to star in the film himself; potential sources of funding were less interested in the film than in who would star in it.[635] Those with money, in typical Hong Kong style, were not slow to suggest casting bankable names inappropriate for the plot. Leslie had long promised that he would avoid all these old bad routines, which seemed to him to be indicative of the shallowness and short-sightedness of the Hong Kong film industry, so he refused to accept these terms. Perhaps he was being over-idealistic, but he was not prepared to compromise.

Instead, he was sufficiently business-like to go to China in late January 2002 to use his contacts, which were now considerable there, to find mainland backers. By now the film had developed a title, *Stealing Heart* (sometimes translated as *Stolen Heart*). In Beijing, Leslie offered the lead female role to Ning Jing, the actress who'd worked with him in *Shanghai Grand*, and spent a whole afternoon relating the film's plot to her. It was a tale of hopeless love involving a girl who'd married her cousin but instead loved a pianist, only to find that he was in love with another girl from a rich family.[636]

For his male lead, Leslie tried to bring onboard the very talented Chinese writer, director, and actor Jiang Wen, who had starred opposite Gong Li in *Red Sorghum*, but Jiang put him off, saying he'd star in Leslie's second film, presumably wanting to see whether Leslie could make a success of his first. Leslie had more success in finding financial backing.[637] The Precious Stone Film Company offered him HK$20 million in cash, and the remainder of the sum required was put up by a Japanese, South Korean, and French consortium put together by his old friend Wada Emi, the costume designer of the *Bride with White Hair*, who also agreed to design the costumes for the new project.[638] This was excellent progress, and Leslie went so far as to fly to Qingdao in eastern China to scout sites for the shooting. His team made attempts to keep all this under wraps, but the news leaked to the press while he was in China.

The next month, Leslie flew to South Korea in an unsuccessful attempt to persuade the new and very popular Korean actor Song Seung-heon to act as his male lead. Song had been a model before taking up acting and was a highly attractive man. He turned Leslie down, though. After two serious attempts to find his leading man, Leslie had drawn a blank and he felt he had little alternative but to break his resolution and take the role himself. He had decided by now that the rest of his actors would have to come from the mainland, not a bad thing as the film was to be shot in Mandarin and as he had always intended to make a Chinese film for Chinese audiences. The production team would be professionals, however, from a mix of countries: China, Japan, South Korea, and Taiwan. For the screenplay he turned to Hong Kong and brought in Lam Gai-to, the screenwriter and film critic who had written *A Chinese Ghost Story II* and *The Bride with White Hair*. Lam went ahead and completed the script, saying later that the idea for the story was drawn from Leslie's own world, and that it was intended to be a vehicle for him to express his views towards the news media and showbiz, though how this would have fitted into the plot, he did not explain.[639]

Leslie had taken a huge amount on his shoulders in this enterprise. He had not only the lead role and the position of director, but was in effect producing the film as well. The heavy workload this entailed ate into his time and precluded his accepting offers of roles in other people's work. He had to turn down a part offered him in the film *Duel to the Death*, also known as *The Sword of Master Three*; its director, Derek Yee, was never to make this film as he believed that the role could only be played by Leslie and he would not offer it to anyone else.[640] Zhang Yimou, the renowned Chinese director of films like *Raise the Red Lantern*, also invited Leslie to consider a part in the film *Hero*, in which Jet Li was to star. Leslie got as far as reading the script, but realised he couldn't devote enough time to it. In this case, Zhang went ahead with his film, which went on to win international acclaim and to be the highest grossing picture in Chinese history at that time.[641]

Leslie took time out from preparing for his film to go to the Chinese University in Sha Tin on 22 February to deliver a talk on characterisation in Lilian Lee's novels, this as part of a programme to mark the retirement of his friend, Professor Lo Wai-yuen.[642] The professor was also a friend of the idol of Leslie's youth and his fellow exile in Vancouver, Pak Suet-sin. The talk was billed as part of a study programme entitled A Comparison of Literature and Image. On the day of the talk, Leslie was in typical form: charming, humorous, and effortlessly a star. The place was packed not only with students but with almost every professor in the university.

Lilian Lee later remembered Leslie at this time, still highly excited about his new role of director. She told *Next Magazine* that as they were having tea in the courtyard of his house, Leslie served his guests with chocolates from the Mandarin Hotel. He told her that the day before, Ah Mui [Anita Mui] had called him. She had, he said, moaned and cried, yelling about committing suicide. She talked, he said, of killing herself every day. He had scolded her and told her that if she didn't sort herself out, then she'd better die![643]

Leslie and Daffy spent Chinese New Year quietly at home that year, inviting Wada Emi as a guest and taking tea with Teresa Mo in the Mandarin Oriental in Central. Wada Emi rather cruelly told Leslie that his house in the Kadoorie Estate, which he had spent many millions of dollars refurbishing, was not the home of a director but that of an actor playing a director. It was all too neat, too beautiful, she said.[644] Leslie's reaction to this effrontery is not recorded. Leslie rang his godson, Ren-lei, to wish him a happy New Year. "Son, don't worry," Leslie told him, "I shall see you again."[645]

In early March, Leslie travelled to China to attend the birthday party of actor Hu Jun, star of *East Palace West Palace* and *Lan Yu*. It was a perfect time to ask Hu to take a part in his film, and it seemed in the euphoria surrounding the party that Hu had accepted. Things were less happy when Leslie reached Hong Kong again, as the press found yet another occasion to make mischief. They photographed his assistant, Kenneth, who was travelling with him, and printed a story that he was Leslie's mystery lover, making out he was a rich mainland Chinese. Leslie felt sufficiently enraged by this to call a conference to present Kenneth to the press and show them his ID card. While this nonsense was still in the air, the media, baulked now of any mystery to plumb surrounding Leslie's relationship with Daffy, turned to making up stories about Daffy, snapping photos of him outside their house with a man they alleged was his lover, but who turned out to be their driver of many years, Ah Kang.[646]

Around this time, Leslie embarked on what for him could be described as a PR offensive, giving a large number of interviews, both to the Hong Kong and foreign media in what seems to have been planned as the run-up to the start of making his film. In February, he repeated to the Japanese Magazine *Pop Asia* that he viewed going to Hollywood as a cop-out for a Chinese actor and told their reporter of the importance he placed in his new film project and his desire to direct.[647] So important was this to him now, he said, that he had turned down an offer by a Japanese concert promoter to put on shows in Japan later in the year. He expressed the hope to the Hong Kong magazine *City Entertainment* that although he was now forty-five and less agile than he had been, he was ageing gracefully. Which, in fact, he was: he had retained his youthful looks and figure to an amazing degree. Wada Emi measured him for costumes for his new film this year and confirmed that he was still the same size as he had been twenty years before.[648]

On 23 March, Leslie gave an interview to *Hong Kong Commercial Daily*. He told them of his neutral attitude to awards, of how he loved to coach junior actors, how he exercised self-control, and how he coped with failure. He also discussed Wong Kar-wai's approach to filmmaking and his own falling-out with the media over his concerts. He was in good spirits that day, boasting to their reporter that he remained Hong Kong's pop trend-setter and that his songs and shows had taken Hong Kong's art to a higher plane.[649]

The film that Leslie had made in 2001, *Inner Senses*, premiered on the night of 22 March 2002.[650] Leslie was at the opening, accompanied by Teresa Mo and evidently on very good form. Public screenings commenced six days later during the 26th Hong Kong International Film Festival.[651] The film's director was Bruce Law, who had directed Leslie earlier in *Double Tap*. Part psychological thriller and part ghost story, *Inner Senses* has been seen as echoing *The Sixth Sense*, the 1999 Hollywood movie starring Bruce Willis. At the start of the film, leading lady Karena Lam Gayan's character Yan sees the spirits of a dead mother and children in her apartment and is driven to find help. This takes her to workaholic psychologist Jim Law (played by Leslie). Any slight similarity with *The Sixth Sense* ends there. Law is a man with no time for anything that cannot be explained by science, but he is a man with a past—one which, after he has rescued Yan from her "haunted" flat, and then fallen into a highly unprofessional relationship with her, starts to bubble forth. He begins to suffer visions in the harrowing form of a childhood sweetheart who had killed herself when he jilted her, jumping from a roof to land on a car near the spot where he was standing. Law fears that she is out for revenge and starts to lose his sanity.

This largely unsympathetic character was a challenging and atypical role for a Hong Kong film star, and Leslie, in his first part after his role as a damaged man in *Double Tap*, had once more taken on a role as a challenge. He told the reporter from *Hong Kong Commercial Daily* that he had got into the character of his part by visiting a friend who was a psychotherapist. Normally, Leslie said, his friend wouldn't give anyone any information about his work, but Leslie had loved watching him practise as a psychotherapist. Leslie had allowed himself to be interviewed and, as he told his friend his childhood experiences, he had watched his movements carefully and later adopted them in the film.

Leslie was stretching himself in this movie. Whilst there was a good deal of the melodramatic in his part, he was credited by many as having turned in a fine performance. *Asia Week* commented, "There has never been an actor, at least a Hong Kong actor, who, like Leslie, without hesitation makes acting a medium of discovering or even redeeming oneself." Yet Leslie had not, during the making of this movie, considered that the part contained anything of the personal. Contrary to the legend that built up after his death, at the time the film was made, there was no sign that he had become "possessed" by some malevolent force nor that he had descended into any self-tortured hell. On the contrary, at the launch of the film, Bruce Law mentioned to the media the way Leslie had been able to switch off after a harrowing scene and return to his usual playful self. Leslie himself also commented after making the film that acting was hard work but such fun! He had, while making the film, been very helpful to the director and crew. At one stage when Karena Lam was having difficulties with a scene, Leslie asked everyone to go out and leave them to rehearse together. After an hour they were ready, and they shot the scene again in just one take.[652]

Indeed, it was only many months after the making of this film that Leslie began to suffer from any medical or psychological condition. Though even his friends like Teresa Mo later remembered the film as being significant in the timing of his first problems, it seems that this was purely coincidental.

Inner Senses was a considerable success, both commercially and critically. In the following year's Hong Kong Film Awards, Leslie was nominated for Best Actor, though he once again failed to win. At the 2003 Hong Kong Film Critics Society Awards, *Inner Senses* achieved Film of Merit. Leslie was also nominated for, but didn't win, Best Actor at the Taiwan Golden Horse Awards later in that year. *Ming Pao Weekly* chipped in again on his side, giving him their award of Most Outstanding Actor 2002 for his part in the film.

All was well with Leslie at the Hong Kong opening of *Inner Senses*, but it no longer would be by the screening of the film at the Puchon International Fantastic Film Festival in Bucheon, South Korea. By then, he had become too ill to travel, and Karena Lam had to attend by herself.

Leslie was still fine, though, when he and Anita Mui, to whom Dior was providing costumes for her forthcoming concert, attended Dior's fashion show on 23 March. That night, Leslie met with four hundred Japanese fans who had flown into Hong Kong to support the opening of *Inner Senses*. On 28 March, he still seemed in good spirits at the premiere of Edison Chen Koon-hei's new film, *Princess D*. The Director, Sylvia Chang Ai Chi, was a friend of Leslie's, and she took the opportunity of meeting him that night to ask him to co-direct her forthcoming film, *20-30-40*.[653]

At the very end of March, Leslie's health first began to give cause for concern. Something began to trouble him, and it was not clear quite what. He and Daffy took some time out to fly down to Thailand to shake off his malaise, but the trip did not appear to clear the air.[654] Leslie returned tired, suffering from stomach pains and an unpleasant complaint in which his stomach acid regurgitated and on occasion caused him to retch. He later told a reporter from *Ming Pao*, who on a rare occasion managed to get straight through to him on the phone at his house, that this was diagnosed as gastric acid reflux, a nasty though not uncommon condition in which stomach acid rises to the mouth, burning the tissues in the throat.[655] He became unable to sleep or to concentrate and became highly emotional, weeping profusely in front of his mother's tomb when he went there with his nieces during the spring Ching Ming (tomb-sweeping) festival that took place that year between 5 and 7 April. He told the girls then that he was depressed and that his condition was "quite severe." They thought he was in very low in spirits, and they were rather disturbed when he told them that if anything happened to him, they must continue to live well.[656]

Florence Chan spoke later about the onset and possible cause of Leslie's depression. She was of the opinion that there were many reasons, the biggest being the reaction to his *Passion Tour* concerts, which had hurt him a lot. He had spent so much effort to make the concert perfect, but the attacks in the media, she thought, had caused him to suffer a great blow. He had become upset, just bottling up his feelings, unable to speak them out loud. At first, when he'd started to suffer from depression, she explained, he hadn't been aware of it, and only became so later when symptoms appeared, things like trembling hands, insomnia, and cold sweats. He felt weird; if he wasn't ill, then why was it that he couldn't sleep at night? Why did he suffer such symptoms? Leslie had always been very concerned about his health—he did not smoke, drink, or go out much at night—so why should a healthy man be sick? Yet he had at first not thought of seeing a psychiatrist. When he was suffering his worst moments, his friends had all been very worried. He was in such deep pain that it seemed as if all his flesh was going to tear apart. He suffered different pain at different stages, and it really tortured him. Nobody knew, she said, how terribly Leslie suffered.[657]

Leslie tried at first to press on with life, but it was a hard and increasingly hopeless struggle. On 6 April, as they arrived at a wedding party, he and Daffy were jostled by the press and public, which seemed to upset Leslie badly; they stayed only for a short time. Leslie told Maggie Cheung, who was also a guest, that he wasn't fit to play in films with her as he was no longer handsome enough to play her lover. She was amazed at this remark. This seemed so unlike the Leslie she knew, but he left before she could respond to him properly.[658] Leslie and Daffy went straight on that night to the Hong Kong Coliseum, where Anita Mui was giving her own comeback concert series, her 20th anniversary concert entitled Fantasy Gig 2002.[659] She had apparently got over whatever had been ailing her earlier, but had been disturbed that she couldn't get hold of Leslie throughout that day. There was relief all round when he appeared onstage. Anita later told the press that Leslie had promised to be her guest from the very first day she had started planning her concert. When he turned up at the Coliseum on that day he told her he wasn't feeling well, as he had a stomachache, but he shrugged it all off when he reached the stage. Leslie's duets with Anita proved he was still able to overcome his stomach pain to perform, but he couldn't bear to stay and left immediately to the crowd's chants of "Gor Gor, Gor Gor." He left without saying goodbye and without giving Anita the chance to thank him personally.[660]

Even now, Leslie was still managing to give interviews to the press. The latest by Winnie Chung appeared in the *South China Morning Post* on 10 April.[661] Leslie had taken the precaution of limiting the questions beforehand to areas in which he felt safe. Two of the several conditions attached to the interview were that no questions be asked about "rumours" surrounding his private life and that no questions be asked about his directorial debut. Leslie told her of his film *Stealing Heart* and his company Dream League, so named because he wanted to create a dream team not only for movies, but also for concerts and showbiz. He was downbeat about the state of the Hong Kong film industry and confessed that it was depressing and discouraging. He had, he said, given an outline of his film to Hong Kong investors, but all they were interested in was who would star in it. They only wanted him in the lead and he had initially refused to take it as he didn't want to be both director and star. He claimed that the budget for the film was HK$20 million, quite a sum for a new director. Moving on to more personal matters, Leslie made the typical remark that he had a very clear mind about one thing: that a job was a job, privacy was privacy, and that he would not accept any blending of the two. Despite the preconditions, Chung took the chance to ask him about his sexual orientation and his admission to *Time* magazine in May of 2001 that "It's more appropriate to say I'm bisexual." Was that a coming-out statement? He reacted strongly to this and denied it. It was not, he suggested, the first time he'd said something so daring, but he was now able to go further than he had before, saying things he wouldn't have dared say in earlier days when his personal identity could never have been allowed to overshadow his image as an idol. It would have upset his fans, not just because of his sexual orientation but just because being attached to one person would have shattered so many dreams.

During April, Leslie's condition deteriorated and he began to decline work, seeking a break until he had recovered from whatever it was that was ailing him. One of the parts he refused now was a role in a story about the Chinese poet Xu Zhimo and his love for his friend's wife, Lu Xiaoman. Billionaire Chinese property developer Zhang Xin floated a script to Leslie, asking if he'd play the poet, but though Leslie was interested, his health was not up to the task.[662] He forced himself to travel in pursuit of his own film, but his deteriorating physical condition and loss of concentration started to adversely affect the project. As reported the following year in *Ming Pao* by filmmaker Alex Law Kai-yu, who was there at the time, Leslie was spotted around now in Beijing at Club Banana. The room that night was crowded with people and Leslie was singing dispiritedly all by himself, one song after another. Then he suddenly stopped singing and unhappily threw away the microphone. Everybody turned quiet.[663]

Shortly after this, Shek Suk of Precious Stone, the major investor for *Stealing Heart*, was arrested in China on charges of corruption. This dashed all the hopes placed in his company as a source of funds for the film. Leslie was left adrift. He was no longer in a fit state to go out on the road again to find other backers, and without money planning ground to a halt. It was a disastrous time for this to have happened.

He battled his baffling ailment, trying to maintain a schedule, less busy now as preparations for his film had ceased, but still working as normally as he could. He attended the Hong Kong Film Awards on 21 April and presented Stephen Chow with the prize for Young Talented Director, an unfortunate choice of award that must have rubbed home the failure of his own project.[664] He had to recognise that his long-dreamed-of film would not go ahead, and he began the difficult job of telephoning the actors and key crew members he'd enlisted to tell them. Wada Emi recalled later that "his film was on the rocks."[665] Leslie phoned her one night at midnight, saying he couldn't sleep because of the pain in his body caused by stress.

People began to distance themselves; Hu Jun denied to the press that he'd ever accepted a role in the film.

Attempts were made by Leslie's friends to interest him in new projects now that his own had failed. Lilian Lee and Hsu Feng (writer and producer respectively of *Farewell My Concubine* and *Temptress Moon*) invited him to Hsu's house on 1 May to discuss re-making for the big screen the old TV series *The Young Concubine*.[666] Lilian Lee wrote later that while at the Chinese University, Leslie had mentioned to Professor Lo Wai-yuen and Pak Suet-sin that he had really liked the tale of *The Young Concubine*, in which he'd starred twenty years before, and that he wanted to reshoot it. Both tried hard to interest him, promising a rewrite of the script to suit him, but they could see he wasn't really interested.[667] Hsu Feng advised him not to waste time with exorcisms (which he'd been reduced to considering) but to get professional help. Lee comforted him, telling him that if he hadn't hurt anyone or done anything bad, anyone who wanted to set evil spells against him would only have such an evil deed rebound on him. Evil could not defeat good. She told Leslie that he wouldn't need more than a year to recover and that she'd wait for him till the next Labour Day. But Leslie was still depressed and gloomy, his stomach acid was still troublesome, and he had lost his motivation. He didn't even want to meet anyone.[668]

Leslie had earlier accepted the invitation given him by Sylvia Chang to co-direct her forthcoming movie, *20-30-40*.[669] Chang had written the film in three sections and had asked Leslie to direct the part entitled *40*. When she heard he was depressed, she altered the script to create a happier version in order to attract him. Yet he was no longer able to honour his promise and the film went ahead with Chang as sole director. Leslie was also forced to withdraw from a part in *Shanghai Family* (also known as *Shanghai Story*), a film for which he had been offered the leading role.[670] He had several other offers at the time, all of which he declined. His friends were rallying to him but he was unable to respond.

Word was not long in getting around the town that all was not well. The local press began to speculate about Leslie's demeanour, and rumours surfaced of Leslie and Daffy arguing so noisily that they had been heard by their neighbours.[671] Speculation in the press was rife about the strength of their relationship.

Leslie's symptoms worsened, and as his public appearances diminished and his appearance deteriorated, rumours began to circulate that he believed he was being pursued by some malevolent force and that he was seeking an exorcist.[672] Some of this may have originated with Leslie himself; Florence Chan later said that Leslie told her he had been told by a "master" (a fortune-teller or necromancer) that he had a curse upon him. Some of his friends tried to help him by getting advice from other such "masters." More sensibly, Daffy persuaded him to see a series of doctors to examine the real state of his health and to find out what was wrong. This was difficult, as Leslie didn't want to be seen going to a doctor.[673] When he finally did, although his symptoms were becoming plain for all to see, including shaking hands and sweating, the doctors could find nothing physically wrong. Daffy, speaking to the press much later, indicated that Leslie's health and emotional problems had separate causes. What those emotional problems were, Daffy refused to confirm, saying only that "something didn't go smoothly which caused him some problems."[674] It was about then that Leslie made a will.[675]

The early part of May was horribly unhappy. Leslie was grappling with whatever it that was afflicting him and could not work, though he did manage to get to a Japanese show in Hong Kong and to appear at two charity events, at one of which (an event in a shopping centre for the End Child Sexual Abuse Foundation) he handed out donation forms to the crowd in person.[676] It was noted that day that his movements seemed sluggish and that he was not in his usual ebullient spirits. Nokia presented him with a star at an event in Hong Kong on 23 May, when he said he was very stressed at the moment from working on the script of his film—clearly an excuse, as work on this had already stopped. By late May, though, he seemed to be recovering. Leslie evidently craved to believe that he was, and forced himself to go back to work. "You can never imagine how much Leslie yearned to recover," Florence Chan said later.[677]

It was partly music that kept him going. On 4 June, flanked by Daffy and Kenneth, Leslie held a press conference to announce the commencement of work on a new album, for which he was to sing alongside Anthony Wong.[678] This had been delayed for a month due to Leslie's illness, but he was now determined to go ahead. He spoke of his stomach "inflammation" to the press and made light of the earlier talk of "possession" by some evil spirit. When Leslie left rather rapidly after the conference, Anthony Wong fielded more questions, some about Leslie's health. Leslie, he suggested, had insomnia. Both he and Lam Jik also suffered from insomnia, he said; it was not, after all, an uncommon problem in the city.

So work began on a fresh album to be called *Crossover*, which was not planned as a collection of the songs of his *Crossover* concert of 1997 but as a totally new creation.[679] It included a duet for Leslie and Anthony Wong entitled "Dream in the Night," which had themes of insomnia and stress, something that was clearly on all their minds at the time. Lam Jik later said that he regretted very much including this, as it had been his intention to write the song about his own inability to sleep, but he hadn't told Leslie that, and he thought later that he should have done so. He obviously feared that Leslie had believed the song was about him.[680]

Leslie was indeed affected by the serious tone of much of the music. He was unsure about including "Dreaming of the Inner River" (the second song in the album *Leslie Forever*), thinking its atmosphere too heavy and sad, but eventually was persuaded by Wong to include it. Another track, "Happy Together," was not music from Leslie's film of that name, though the lyrics, music, and instrumentals referred to it; the number featured the well-known guitarist Tommy Ho, who gave the song a South American feel. "So Far, So Close," written by Leslie for Anthony to sing, though with some words spoken by Leslie himself, also had a Latin feel. Anthony Wong's song "Typhoon No 10" had appeared the year before, but was included here as Leslie liked it. "If You Knew My Hidden Reason" was the old song written by Leslie for Vivian Chow Wai-man, the Cantopop singer and actress who had been popular for much of Leslie's working life. Leslie and Anthony had picked two songs each from the other's repertoire, one old, one new.

Though redolent of the earlier successful tour (and not the seemingly painful—to Leslie—*Passion Tour*), the meaning of the album's title remains unclear. It was perhaps intended to refer to the "crossover" choice of songs by the two singers. The cover was an interesting melding of both their faces, Anthony's on the left merging into Leslie's on the right.

By the time *Crossover* was issued, Leslie's condition had again deteriorated, and he was no longer fit enough to promote the album. His voice had developed a hoarseness that made singing and talking difficult, and Anthony Wong was left to promote it on his own. Leslie was also unable to help make the accompanying music video they'd planned. Despite all this, the album was a success. "So Far, So Close" made it to number one in the FM903 chart and number three on the Metro Showbiz chart. *Crossover* was to be the last album Leslie ever completed. With a record of his last concert released that year in Japan, that was all of Leslie's music to emerge in that depressing year, but it was enough to make Leslie Number One Artist of the year for Universal Records.

By the summer of 2002, Daffy and Florence Chan were sufficiently alarmed by Leslie's state of health and by the failure of his doctors to find a physical cause for his ailments that they persuaded him to consult a psychiatrist.[681] They went with him and listened to the psychiatrist's advice. This was a big step, for mental illness was, and remains, one of Hong Kong's big taboos, being traditionally considered a personal failure in Chinese society, something that brings shame both on the person who is suffering it and on his or her relatives. Families do not wish to admit publicly that any one of their number is mentally sick. Leslie himself felt this way; earlier, he had objected to the press reporting his problems as psychological, and to have to admit now that this might have been so all along must have been galling, even frightening.

Sensibly, they chose to consult the most pre-eminent psychiatrist in the field in Hong Kong, Professor Felice Leih-Mak (known locally as Dr Mak Lit Fei-fei). Professor Leih-Mak had only just retired from Hong Kong University as a Professor Emeritus after a lifelong career in which she had founded the study of psychiatry in Hong Kong. Leslie could not have found a more distinguished psychiatrist. She commenced a course of interviews and treatment. This was not easy, as Leslie felt he could not afford to be seen visiting her clinic and as she similarly could not be seen visiting Leslie and Daffy's house. The solution was to meet and hold sessions at the house of Leslie's sister, Ophelia, in as much secrecy as could be managed.

What exactly was wrong with Leslie? It is unlikely that we will ever have access to his medical papers, so for an evaluation, we are reduced to relying on witness reports, and therefore can reach only what have to be tentative conclusions. It does seem, though, from the evidence of the time and from what Daffy later told the press, that Leslie was afflicted with depression. There was speculation later in the media that this had been a lifelong affliction (a period of twenty years was mentioned), but there seems to be no evidence for this, nor is it possible to identify the source of this idea. Apart from the operation on his hands in 1978 and a few minor accidents, and from the one incidence of what looks to have been some kind of breakdown in the depths of the seeming failure of his career in 1981, when he was advised to rest, Leslie had been physically healthy for all his life. There is no evidence that he suffered from, or was treated for, depression until 2002.

Depression can manifest itself in many ways, but is often said to be of two major types: major depressive disorders, where depressed moods last for over two weeks and include a loss of interest in socializing, eating, and sleeping; and bipolar disorders, where swings of mood (mood cycling) are manifested, from exultant euphoria on the upside to very low, manic moods on the downside.[682] Highly creative people often suffer from the latter (well-known examples are Virginia Woolf, Tennessee Williams, and Stephen Fry), but there is no clear evidence that this is what afflicted Leslie, whose usual cheerful equanimity was famed, and whose current depressed state seemed not to fluctuate but to be long-lasting. It is noteworthy, though, that at least one of his friends mentioned later that they were used to his swings in mood.

Depressive disorders can occur for no obvious reason (though ageing, the loss of a loved one, illness, or medication can be the immediate cause). It is considered nowadays that biological factors can contribute to depression as it has been discovered that some people are slightly more predisposed to the affliction by their genetic makeup. Psychological factors can also be a sole cause or can work together with physical factors; failures at work, relationship problems, criticism, or attacks by others can lead to self-defeating thought patterns, chronic feelings of inadequacy, despair, sadness, frustration, and emptiness. The tendency for withdrawal from family and friends at the moment of crisis worsens the effects and self-destructive behaviours compound the problem. On top of this, it has also been found that gay men often suffer depression due to the societal pressures affecting them.[683]

Symptoms of this type of depression are usually listed as affecting a person for most of the day almost every day, and include sadness or irritability; loss of interest or pleasure in daily activities; difficulty in falling asleep (or conversely, sleeping too much); unusual restlessness or sluggishness; feeling excessively tired; feeling worthless; unreasonable or excessive guilt; difficulty concentrating, thinking, or making decisions; and thoughts of death, dying, or suicide. Sufferers often avoid social encounters, preferring solitude, and are impatient with, or lash out at, others. These reactions serve only to bring on feelings of remorse, shame, or guilt. There is an increase in negative thinking and a tendency to cry frequently and effortlessly (or, again conversely, an inability to cry at all). Physical symptoms of headaches, backaches, stomach aches, and nausea are common.

Leslie showed many of these symptoms during this time. He seemed to withdraw from his friends (Anita Mui, Teresa Mo, and Maggie Cheung all commented on this)[684] and to find it impossible to concentrate enough to carry on his normal productive life. At one point during the making of *Crossover*, he told Lam Jik he could not read the lyrics of a song he had sent him. He could not concentrate enough to sing at the Banana Club in Beijing and abandoned the stage to sit morosely alone.[685] He was reported as losing his temper repeatedly with Daffy; the press published reports of the noise of violent rows heard coming from inside their house.[686] He told Maggie Cheung that he was no longer fit to play alongside her as he had lost his looks. He indicated to his friends and nieces that he was thinking of his death and gave them what could have been interpreted as farewell blessings; similarly, he asked Florence Chan to take care of Daffy if anything happened to him. He developed physical ailments, including a stomach complaint for which physical causes could not be found. He wept uncontrollably in front of his mother's grave.

His psychologically induced physical illnesses were nonetheless disturbingly real. Leslie suffered for many months of 2002 from a hoarse voice that at times made him sound quite unlike himself.[687] He also seems to have suffered from sleeplessness and pains in many areas of his body.[688] Florence Chan later said that he had difficulty controlling his limbs and trembling hands and that he suffered from insomnia and cold sweats.[689] She said he was very ashamed of what was afflicting him and yearned to be better. He suffered terribly because he could not work.

What had set this off is impossible to say. There may have been some incident, or a combination of them, that began his slide into depression. These could have been the death of his mother or the hostile press criticism he received—we have already seen that Florence Chan believed that this was so. It could also have been accentuated by a self-perception of ageing, of no longer being the "legend" that he once had been. That Leslie had these sorts of feelings is evident by the pride he took in fending off the signs of age; this had been perceptively picked up by Stephen Short back in 2001:

> Leslie had become the outsider—still talented, beautiful, wealthy, relatively young and beloved, but an outsider nonetheless. His era had passed, and he seemed wistfully aware of the fact.[690]

***

Professor Leih-Mak commenced treatment and it seemed to work. Encouraged by the success of *Crossover*, a new album was planned and preparations for it began. Leslie was sufficiently recovered to compose four new songs. He asked Lam Jik to write the lyrics for the gentle track, "Glass Love" and invited the famed Hong Kong composer C.Y. Kong (who wrote often for the very popular singer Faye Wong) to compose the first track planned, "Thousand Tenderness, Hundred Beauty." The lyrics for one number were contributed by another eminent Hong Kong lyricist, Chan Siu-kei, writer of over 3,000 songs in a career that had started back in 1984. Chan had written something poignant, but Leslie asked for a more upbeat number, so Chan suggested a song to commemorate Leslie's love for Daffy. Leslie gladly accepted, and thus was composed "I Know You Are Good," the only song ever specially written by Leslie for his lover. Some sombre music was included on the album, one the track "Red Butterfly." UMG also planned to issue a double CD later with many old tracks from his recordings owned by his earlier record companies as well as three new songs, going so far as to spend about HK$2 million on the rights to these songs.[691]

Despite this activity, after the making of *Crossover*, Leslie withdrew into his home and was little seen by his public. He avoided meeting his friends; Anita Mui later recalled that while she had been on overseas tour after her concert in Hong Kong, she had become very unhappy with her work and had wanted to talk to him. She had become angry with him as she thought he was ignoring her. When she tried to call, she found that he had even changed his telephone number. It was only later that she realised he hadn't wanted her to worry about him. She was guilt-stricken that she had not, she thought, done enough to help him.[692] Teresa Mo sensed that Leslie needed help and offered to be with him through his rough patch, but he refused her offer.[693] Others of his friends, like Chow Yun-fat, were kept at such a distance that they didn't even sense there was anything wrong.

In September, Leslie celebrated his 46th birthday. Reporters assembled outside the Kadoorie Estate house, and he distributed chocolates to them. Friends joined him at home that evening and gave him birthday gifts, some giving him cash for the charity he was then helping, the End Child Sexual Abuse Foundation, of which his friend, actress Josephine Siao Fong-Fong, was the chairperson.

Yet despite the treatment he was now receiving, his condition did not improve, and other programmes had to be abandoned. In October, Florence Chan told the public that Leslie would not be going to the 11th Golden Rooster Awards and the Hundred Flowers Film Festival in China, nor to the Tokyo Film Festival where *Behind the Yellow Line* was to be screened on 26 October.[694] That month, however, Leslie did manage to resume some public engagements that did not involve travel outside Hong Kong. He presented prizes at the annual CASH awards ceremony, sitting next to Alan Tam, with whom he was seen to have a long conversation.[695] His voice had recovered, though he gave no interviews that day. He was seen out again on the 11th of that month at the opening of Dunhill's new store in the Prince's Building in Central, and replied to reporters' questions about what he was then working on, saying that he was "recording songs."[696] This was true and although he had not yet fully recovered from the reflux syndrome, he was again recording music.

His isolation was increased, though, by events which occurred around that time. Leslie was devastated when he heard on 18 October that Roman Tam, his mentor in his earliest showbiz days, had died of liver cancer. He was reported to have cried uncontrollably at his friend Pak Suet-sin's house when he heard the news.

Back in August, Leslie had added his name to a proposal made to the Hong Kong government by the Hong Kong Performing Artistes' Guild that greater legal protection be given to stars from intrusive reporters and photographers.[697] The Guild proposed that photographs should only be allowed to be taken of the public working life of stars, and not of their private lives. This was a cause close to his heart, though it was one doomed to failure. That there was a need for some protection was indicated later in the year when, on 30 October, photographs were published in *East Week* magazine of actress Carina Lau, nude and distressed, after she had been kidnapped from the film set of *Days of Being Wild* and reportedly raped by triads. On 3 November, Leslie managed to join many of his colleagues in the film world to demonstrate outside the Government Secretariat building in Central to protest this outrage.[698] He was photographed there standing with Anita Yuen, looking distraught and depressed. He managed to get to Jackie Chan's birthday banquet that month, but left halfway through without anyone noticing.

On 11 November, Leslie attended the *Ming Pao* awards ceremony, where Anita Mui presented him the title of Most Outstanding Actor for his role in *Inner Senses*.[699] On that occasion, he told the media that he had yet to decide finally whether to direct Sylvia Chang's *20-30-40*, but he confirmed that he would not be going to the Golden Horse Award ceremony in Taipei on the 16th because of his health. Nor would he be well enough to travel to Taipei with Karena Lam and Bruce Law for the promotion of *Inner Senses* on 26 December.

That month, probably after the *Ming Pao* ceremony, it is possible that Leslie made his first attempt to commit suicide.[700] If this did occur, it went unreported at the time and was carefully and successfully kept from the public. The circumstances of the incident are unclear as is the story of how his life was saved. One unconfirmed account, which appeared in the press the following year, was that he had taken an overdose of sleeping pills and had been found in time by Daffy.

Whatever the treatment he was receiving, Leslie was not getting better. His lack of progress threw him further into despair. Would he ever be able to go back to being the star he still had been only nine months before? He was losing hope that he would. In December, compounding the gloom, Brigitte Lin's mother jumped to her death from her apartment on the 12th floor.[701] Leslie sent flowers to her funeral. Maggie Cheung met him for the last time that month at a dinner party given by Jackie Chan:

> I went to the toilet and Leslie came with me. At last, we had the chance to have a long talk. It was a strange place for a strange conversation, but Leslie was like that. The next day, at the end of the morning, he asked my assistant Teresa to get me to call him back. We continued our conversation—a conversation which he told me to keep secret. At the end, he told me that I deserved a wonderful life and that I must take good care of myself. We said good-bye and we put down the telephone.[702]

It was to be the last time they talked.

CHAPTER 18

ASHES OF TIME

2003

There had been no improvement in Leslie's health by the time the New Year of 2003 dawned. He had been sick now for nearly nine agonising months. He and Daffy flew down to Bangkok to stay at the Mandarin Oriental, their usual home-away-from-home there.[703] Leslie surprised Paitoon, the manager of the hotel's function department, who customarily looked after him in Bangkok and with whom he was very friendly, by asking whether he thought he had been bewitched. Paitoon was non-plussed and suggested that Leslie visit a Buddhist monk, but Leslie wouldn't do that. It was not evident to Paitoon that Leslie was depressed, though he could see he was unwell. Sometime around then, Leslie took up smoking again.

On 17 January, Leslie made an appearance at RTHK's 25th Top Ten Gold Songs presentation ceremony to receive their Silver Jubilee Award. He managed to sing along with the other stars, but his voice was not up to performing solo. He apologised to his fans and told them he hoped to be able to give them more songs in future. For a second time he sat next to Alan Tam; at this late stage in Leslie's career, they seem to have got on a lot better, and they were seen teasing each other good-humouredly.

Leslie also managed what was by now becoming a rare public performance, appearing on 27 January on the TVB Chinese New Year show of a girl band known as The Twins (Gillian Chung Jan-tung and Charlene Choi Cheuk-lin), two naïve and very young girls who were very much in awe of working with him.[704] Despite their nerves, the programme went well and Leslie looked better, but it was to be his last TV appearance. The Chinese New Year (which fell on 1 February that year) was spent by Leslie and Daffy quietly at home, visited by family and a few friends, including Karen Mok and Stanley Kwan.

Offers of film work continued to come in, but as before none were to lead anywhere. The principal male role in the movie *New Police Story*, a hard-bitten and partially failed policeman named Chan Kwok-wing, was written with Leslie in mind, but he had to relinquish the role to Jackie Chan.[705] During these months when Leslie was too ill to work, producer Nansun Shi suggested to her husband, Tsui Hark, that he invite Leslie to take a part in one of his movies, hoping thereby to pull him out of his depression. They finalised a script in March and Tsui Hark planned to give it personally to Leslie, but he was never to have the opportunity to do so. This film was not given a name and has never been made. A film by Chinese director Chen Guoxing, a romance story intended to be made as a joint Hong Kong and Japanese project, was offered to Leslie, but it too came to nothing. Another missed opportunity was one suggested by Jacky Cheung, the actor-singer, who suggested to Leslie that they put together a stage opera for which he already had a script ready. Like the other projects, this one was stillborn.

When Bruce Law telephoned to tell Leslie the good news of his nomination for Best Actor in the Hong Kong Film Awards for his role in *Inner Senses*, he found that Leslie was too depressed to take any pleasure from the news.[706] Nor was his mood lightened when he heard that an unusually enlightened award had come his way from South Korea, where he and Tony Leung were voted third in a competition to find the best couple in a film. It was around this time that a reporter from the newspaper *Ming Pao* somehow got through to Leslie on their house phone and asked him whether he would attend the film awards ceremony scheduled for 6 April.[707] Ominously, Leslie replied that he would if he was in Hong Kong at the time.

Rock Records were confident that Leslie would return to work and chased him to sign a contract with them. They asked him to perform in their 10th Anniversary concert planned for April. He accepted neither invitation. He kept to his contract with UMG and tried to keep recording music, working with Lam Jik on tracks for the album that they planned to release later in the year. Lam Jik said later that three songs were recorded of the five lyrics he'd submitted, but that Leslie had found it hard to concentrate.[708] Sometime in March, Leslie called Lam Jik from the studio, saying he couldn't read the lyrics clearly and asked him to go over and help him read them. When the album was issued after his death as *Everything Follows the Wind*, it contained four numbers composed by Leslie himself.

Unmarked at the time, on 8 March Leslie managed to participate in a concert organised by Pepsico; he had been their first Pepsi Superstar, and he was there with those who had followed him. Sad memories of better days must have made this a very bitter event for him. Once more he was unable to sing and his hands were seen to be shaking uncontrollably.[709] No one there that night realised it, but it was to be his last professional appearance.

Four days later, it was announced that Leslie had been the first donor to the End Child Sexual Abuse Foundation's charity night, donating the substantial sum of HK$100,000.[710] When he went out one night with Brigitte Lin to the cinema to see *Gangs of New York*, she noticed that he was tense and trembling. Yet, strangely, Tsui Hark saw Leslie several times during the month to talk about his film projects and the film script he was preparing and remarked later that he had never seen Leslie so much at peace.[711] He felt Leslie was very different, quite changed, and that he had never felt so close to him before. He took encouragement from Leslie's serene demeanour and said later that he had felt he was witnessing the best years of Leslie's life. Father Lionel Xavier Brown also remembered meeting him at this time, walking with his sister and her partner on the path that winds around Hong Kong's Victoria Peak. They greeted each other warmly and agreed to stay in touch. "He seemed to be very normal then," said Father Xavier.[712] Given the other reports of this time, one has to wonder whether this was the effect of anti-depressant drugs. Daffy was seen by reporters picking up medicine for Leslie from his psychiatrist's consulting rooms.

An invitation was given to Leslie to attend the United Nations' Love Forever concert on 12 April in Shenyang, the old city of Mukden in northeast China, a concert held in aid of Asia's disabled, but he felt forced to decline. However, he pushed himself to continue to go about the town with Daffy. They were not about to give up on pulling Leslie through this bad time. On 22 March they went to see the film *Confessions of a Dangerous Mind* at the UA Cinema in Admiralty. Leslie was seen by reporters, who noted that he was very pale and that Daffy seemed worried about him. On 26 March, the couple ate dinner in a Wan Chai restaurant, passing Hong Kong's then Chief Executive, Tung Chee-hwa, in the lift there and spending some minutes chatting with him.[713]

For anyone to go out in public at that time was a brave act, for the SARS epidemic that had hit Hong Kong was now at its height. Hong Kong was going through a very depressing time as SARS had struck in the middle of the financial crisis that had started with the bursting of the dot.com bubble and had turned into a stock-market crash. Businesses folded, unemployment rose, and a deflation of the currency began which lasted several years. The gloom of the economic slump was worsened by the outbreak of the fearsome disease which was carried into the city by a mainland Chinese doctor who had been treating SARS patients in China before travelling to Hong Kong, where he collapsed in a hotel on 11 March and subsequently died. The disease was proving both highly contagious and lethal, and the fear that it aroused had shut down a lot of the city's activity. By the end of the epidemic, 1,750 people had been infected in Hong Kong, of whom nearly 300 died. While it raged, entire flat blocks were quarantined. Most people went about wearing masks. Schools closed and restaurants and places of entertainment stood empty. Travellers from abroad stopped coming, flights into Hong Kong arrived largely unoccupied or were cancelled, and outbound flights were full of expatriates escaping to their homes. Fear was in the air. In Leslie's condition, to have forced himself go out to public places in this climate must have required a very large effort of will. Sadly, in the face of crippling depression, that effort could not be maintained.

On the afternoon of 31 March, Leslie and Daffy held a mahjong party at their home. With them were their old mahjong buddies Elisa Chan, Nansun Shi, and Suzie Wong. The party went on into the small hours. The next day, 1 April, Daffy saw Leslie off from their house somewhere between 11 am and 12 noon.[714] He later told reporters that Leslie said he wanted to go out for a ride and that he seemed normal.

He and Leslie kept in touch with each other by phone on and off during the day, as was their custom. Daffy was clearly checking up on him. Leslie wanted to go to the gym to exercise. Daffy told the driver to phone him and ask if he needed his clothes to be brought to him. He said there was no need for that.

At 1 pm, Leslie lunched with Alfred Mok Wa Ping, the interior designer of Leslie and Daffy's house and a long-time friend. They met in Fusion, his favourite restaurant in Causeway Bay. The general manager, Deborah Li Kit-ming, saw him leave around 4 pm after a late lunch. She told the press that Leslie had come in dressed in a linen suit and was as friendly as ever and seemed both happy and normal. She told him that he looked great. There was a private party on in the area he normally occupied, so she moved him to a table near the window. The restaurant closed at 3 pm, but the pair stayed on there. Someone sneezed and Leslie put his hands over his face, laughing, saying that he didn't want to die. He was, she thought, in good spirits.[715] Leslie reminded Mok to wear a mask because of SARS. What Deborah Li thought she saw, though, was an impression gained at a distance. All was not well.

Alfred Mok was disturbed by what he saw of Leslie that afternoon. He described his unease to the press much later.[716] Leslie, he said, had talked to him about his feelings and told him that when he had called him at 10 am that day, he had been driving around aimlessly in his Porsche (meaning that he had been out earlier and gone home to change cars and say goodbye to Daffy). Leslie revealed that he had felt very tired that morning and had had thoughts of speeding to his death in his car. However, he had remembered his appointment with Mok and had abandoned the idea. Mok asked him not to be silly and tried to steer the subject away from Leslie's suicidal thoughts. Describing the atmosphere later, Mok said that he felt that Leslie was very nervous; his hands were fidgeting all the way through lunch. Leslie had also talked over lunch of leaving Mok a small gift in his will.

When they left the restaurant, Leslie drove Mok back to his office in his Mercedes-Benz. As Leslie dropped him off, he told Mok that he didn't have to call him anymore. At first, Mok did not catch his meaning, but once in his office he remembered a similar episode in the past when Leslie had said the same words, confessing then that he had had suicidal intentions. On that occasion, fortunately, Leslie had found the windows at his hotel could not be opened. Fearing a repeat incident, Mok contacted Leslie's sister, who returned his call at 6 pm, saying that all was right, and that Leslie was window shopping in Central.[717]

All was far from right. Leslie drove on to Central, leaving the car in the car park next to the Star Ferry piers. He walked under the underpass to the Mandarin Oriental and went up to the private health club on the 24th floor. There was a balcony there which looked out over the harbour where guests could sit outside, relax, and enjoy the view; Leslie often took tea there. This time, around 4.30 pm, he ordered a drink inside, then asked the waiter to move it to a table on the balcony.[718] He was seen at one point standing, staring out over Victoria Harbour. Using his mobile phone, he rang Li Yi-mei, a female friend on the marketing staff of the China Star Entertainment Group, whom he'd known for twenty years, and told her he was suffering from depression, that it was very painful, and that he needed time for a cure. He told her that he thanked Daffy and his friends for taking care of him.

He spoke to Daffy on the phone at about 5 pm. Daffy later told the press that they had arranged to play badminton, agreeing to meet at 7 pm. Leslie asked Daffy to bring his stuff to the court, where he would drive himself.[719]

Leslie also arranged to meet Florence Chan in the coffee shop on the ground floor of the hotel. Much later, in 2004, Chan told the Shanghai journal *Xinmin Weekly* that she called him but it was Daffy who picked up the phone. She asked where Leslie was, and Daffy replied that he'd said he wanted to go for a walk, and that they were going to play badminton together at 7 pm. Daffy told her Leslie was in Central having tea with some friends. So she called

Leslie but no one answered the phone. She left a message in his mailbox and asked him to call back when he was free. He rang her back immediately and said he was in Central. She asked him what he was doing, and he replied that he was drinking tea alone at the Mandarin. Chan chided him that he should have asked her to join him rather than drink tea by himself. She suggested that she should go and find him, but he replied that he was leaving to go shopping. She told him that she wanted to tag along and he agreed.

When she was about to hang up the phone, Leslie told her he wanted to use this time to take a good look at Hong Kong. It was then that she sensed something was not right. She took a cab to the Mandarin Oriental but couldn't find him in the lobby, so she went to the coffee house where they often met. When she got there, the staff said he wasn't there, so she walked around searching for him, but to no avail.[720] Florence Chan was also clearly checking up on Leslie and watching out for him. She then phoned him again. This time he picked up the call and told her he'd just gone out, then asked her to drink some tea first as he would be there very soon. So she waited for about half an hour but he didn't appear.

Leslie was making up his mind to die. He had not expected Florence to show at the hotel, but maybe now was thinking that her arrival was providential. At about 6.15 pm, he went back inside, borrowed a pen and paper from the waiter, who noticed that his hands were shaking, and wrote a short suicide note in Chinese, which he kept on his person. Translated, it said:

Depression.
Thank you to all my friends, thank you to Professor Mak Lit Fei-fei.
This year has been too tough, cannot stand it anymore.
Thank you Mr. Tong, thank you family, thank you Fei Jeh [Lydia Sum].

I haven't done anything bad in my life, why does it have to be like this?"[721]

Florence Chan continued to wait downstairs. After waiting for forty minutes, she got a call from him. He said that she would see him in five minutes and told her to go to the front door and wait for him there. She looked at her watch and saw that it was nearly 6.30 pm. She knew that he was supposed to play badminton at 7 pm, so she immediately paid the bill and left. She got outside fast and stood at the front door waiting but there was no sign of Leslie.[722] She rang Daffy again and told him that she didn't think Leslie sounded too good.

At 6.41 pm, Leslie mounted the rail of the balcony and jumped. He landed in front of the hotel on the railings that divided the car pick up point from the main thoroughfare of Connaught Road, just by the spot where Florence Chan was waiting for him.

She heard a very loud noise, as if something had dropped; and looked in the direction of the sound; and saw that something had fallen to the ground. She thought she saw a man. There was a bus next to him, and she thought there had been a traffic accident. She immediately turned around and asked the people in the hotel to call an ambulance. At the time, she was thinking that Leslie was suffering from depression and was afraid that if he witnessed such a scene it would be bad for him, so she ran, thinking that she should go and stop his car before he arrived. She called his phone but it was set to voice message. She sensed then that something was wrong, so she ran back to take a look, not daring to go very close.[723]

Leslie's fall had been reported by a Caucasian man standing nearby, who had summoned an ambulance. His badly injured body was taken to the Queen Mary Hospital at Pok Fu Lam, some fifteen to twenty minutes away on the west side of Hong Kong Island. He was pronounced dead shortly after arrival at 7.06 pm.[724]

Chan clearly suspected what Leslie had done, and acted on her feelings. She followed the ambulance to the hospital and asked the police officer on duty there how the man was. The officer knew her and asked her whether it was Leslie. At that point, she was sure what had happened. She called Daffy and her security immediately, wanting to protect Leslie and not give the media any chance to take pictures, as she knew that Leslie would be very angry if that happened.

Daffy was about to leave for the badminton game. He rushed to the hospital, where he found Florence Chan.[725] They were shortly joined by Leslie's brother-in-law, by Professor Leih-Mak, and by Leslie's assistant, Kenneth. They identified the body, which was transferred to the morgue in the Western District by 9.25 pm. By then, fans had begun to lay flowers on the spot outside the hotel where he had fallen and which had by then been cleaned up by the hotel staff. Crowds of the public and press soon gathered outside the morgue, and police had to cordon it off.[726]

Daffy somehow got home to meet those closest to Leslie, amongst them Nansun Shi and Elisa Chan, who said later that she had been shocked by his death but not surprised that he had committed suicide. He was, she said, so severely depressed that he was no longer himself anymore. When they had all finally gone, Daffy took sleeping pills, but was unable to sleep, and, at 3.45 am, still drowsy, he opened the door to find the press outside their house.[727] Accompanied only by their driver, he answered questions for about thirty minutes.[728] His eyes were swollen but he managed to remain coherent. He made a statement that revealed what he knew of the suicide. He told them that Leslie had been suffering from depression and had attempted suicide the previous November.[729] He said:

All these years I have loved him very much. Our relationship has always been very good all these years. There was definitely no "third person" between us, and my feelings for Leslie have never changed. I know he had been depressed, I've spent a lot of time accompanying him, comforting him.

Asked why Leslie had committed suicide, Daffy replied:

Some obstructions in work ... well, it's because of a combination of many factors, it's very complicated. I know why, but I can't say. I'll see if his family want to reveal it. We will give an explanation to his fans and the public later on.[730]

Even after these horrifying and harrowing events, some elements among the Hong Kong press repeated the accounts they'd previously fabricated that Leslie had been having an affair with his assistant, Kenneth, and others repeated their story that Daffy had taken a new lover.[731]

Daffy visited the funeral parlour where Leslie's body was laid every night until the ceremony.

Florence Chan later gave an account of the reasons why she thought Leslie had committed suicide. She blamed the criticism his last concert had attracted and the way he had allowed it to prey on his mind. She said that he really didn't know when he would recover, as even the doctor couldn't tell him. His condition had worsened and he couldn't control himself. He was afraid that if he appeared in public and did something wrong, reporters would write a lot about it. He really didn't want this to happen to him, so he made the choice to kill himself. He was, she knew, very, very reluctant to do that and wanted so badly to recover. He wanted to get well but he had only got worse.[732]

In Leslie's death certificate, the recorded cause of death was given as "Multiple injuries. Intentional self-harm by jumping from a high place."[733]

Leslie Cheung was forty-six when he died. Though in despair, he was still beautiful. His life had been one long legend in the making. Most of that legend had been a creation of his own spirit. It was tragic that, by his last, harrowing act of will, he had himself placed the seal on that legend forever.

BIBLIOGRAPHY

NEWSPAPERS AND PERIODICALS

100 Marks' Magazine (a magazine published in Hong Kong), 1986 ('Side story of Leslie in Concert '86', *http://lesliecheung. cc/Magazine/1986/sidestory/info.htm*); 1987 ('Leslie's 'Best Companion' at home', *http://lesliecheung.cc/Magazine/1987/10 0marks6/100marks6.htm*).

Advocate, The, 13 May 2003 (Lawrence Ferber, 'Leslie Cheung – Actor Singer').

Aera Magazine, 3 April 1998 (Hiro Ugaya, 'I'm a Perfectionist Either with Movies or Songs').

Age, The, 29 October 2003 (Philippa Hawker, 'Listening for a Footfall').

All Music Shop Newsletter, May 2003.

Apple Daily, 6 April 2003 (Lam Jik, 'Interview', *http:// clubstar.sina.com.hk/cgi-bin/user/news_search. cgi?type=detail&id=2827&news_id=990083*).

Asia Week, ('In Acting He Draws from Experiences of the Pains in Real Life, *http://lesliecheung.cc/memories/leepikwah_eng.htm*).

Asian Cinema, 10 (1), Fall 1998, 62-70 (Juanita-Huan Zhou, 'Ashes of Time: The Tragedy and salvation of the Chinese Intelligentsia'); 198-207 (Denise Tang, 'Popular Dialogues of a 'Discreet' Nature').

Asian Cult Cinema, #42, 2003 (David Aaron Clark, 'Farewell to a Friend').

Asia Weekly, April 2003 (Perry Lam Pui-li, 'In acting he draws from experiences of the pains in real life').

Austin American Statesman, 14 January 1994 ("M' Butterfly is Unconvincing Poor Casting').

Body & Society, 8.1, 2002, 29-48 (S.K. Travis Kong, 'The Seduction of the Golden Boy: The Body Politics of Hong Kong Gay men').

BOMB, 62, Winter 1998, 48-54 (Han Ong, 'Wong Kar-Wai').

Business Week, 14 April 2003 (Bruce Einhorn, 'Hong Kong: A City in Mourning').

Cahiers Du Cinema, no. 579, May 2003 (Maggie Cheung, 'Leslie Cheung's Days Of Being Wild').

Canadian Folklore, 19.1, 1997, 55-68 (Mikel J. Koven, 'My Brother, My Lover, My self: Traditional Masculinity in the Hong Kong Action Cinema of John Woo').

Cashflow, no. 41, June 2003 (James Wong, 'In Fond Memory of Leslie Cheung').

China Daily, 12 April 2003 (Xiao Hua, 'Making a Choice to Cherish Life'), 15 May 2004 ('Guangzhou Concerts'), 5 April 2005 ('Tomb Sweeping Moving High Tech'), 2 May 2006 (Meeting Stars Face-to-Face in Shanghai').

Cinema Journal, 37.2, 1998, 18-34 (Jenny Kwok-wah Lau, 'Besides Fists and Blood: Hong Kong Comedy and Its Master of the Eighties').

Cinemaya, 23 (Spring, 1994), 28-32, (Stephen teo, 'The Hong Kong New Wave: Before and After'); 39-40 (1998): 10-16, 15 (Richard Havis, 'A Better Today.)

City Entertainment, 11 August 1991 (Ngai Siu-yun. 'A Living Legend from 23 to 34 Years Old'); 1999, no. 520 ('A Story behind the Legend', *http://lesliecheung.cc/Magazine/1999/city-entertainment_moonlight/cityenter520.htm*); April 2004 (Chu Wing Lung, 'Cheung Kwok Wing – A Movement Free Dance Act', *http://lesliecheung.cc/memories/magazines/one_and_only/index.htm*).

City Magazine, 1985 (Mak Uen Shou, 'Cheung Kwok-wing Cohabited with a Love Swindler'); 1985 (Zha Hsiaohsin, 'Cheung Kwok Wing Boldly Thrusts Forward to Refute Kai Yee Lin', *http://lesliecheung.cc/Magazine/1985/metropolitan/text.htm*).

Cut, no. 172, November 2004 (Shino Kokawa, 'Leslie, It's You Who Caused the Wind to Blow in Asia').

Daily Trojan, (Interview with Chen Kaige).

Dallas Morning News, 12 November 1993 ('Top Attraction: Farewell To My Concubine').

Elle, May 2003 (Lui Zhu-lian, 'In Loving Memory of Leslie Cheung', *http://lesliecheung.cc/memories/magazines/ELLE/article_eng.htm*).

ET, a weekly magazine published in China, (April 2003, by Xiao Si, 'Farewell My Concubine', *http://lesliecheung.cc/memories/luihan.htm*; Ren Li, 'Goodbye Leslie Cheung', *http://lesliecheung.cc/memories/yanlui_eng.htm*; Zhang Man-ling, 'My heart aches, My heart really aches', *http://lesliecheung.cc/memories/zhangmaning.htm*).

Film Bi-weekly

Film-Dienst, 52, 1999, no. 21, pp. 16 – 17 (Andrea Bette, 'Masculine-feminine: Hong Kong's Androgynous Superstar Leslie Cheung').

Film Quarterly, 49.4, 1996, 23, (Jillian Sandell, 'Reinventing Masculinity: The Spectacle of Male Intimacy in the Films of John Woo').

Film TV (Italian), no. 15, 2003, (Alberto Crespi, 'Leslie Cheung, the Underestimated Superstar'); no. 16, 2003 (Pier Maria Bocchi, 'Digital Memories').

Galaxy Production, 7 September 2000 (Thomas Huong, 'Leslie tells

Malaysia, 'They are not worth it!!', *http://www.galaxy.com.my/press/musicnet.htm*).

Hollywood Online, 4, 30 November 1997 (Nina Davidson, 'Wong Kar-wai Tackles Controversy in *Happy Together*').

Hong Kong Commercial Daily, March 23, 2002 (Economic News, 'Cheung Kwok Wing - The Trend-Setting Superstar').

Hong Kong Entertainment News in Review, 2 April 2003 ('Leslie Cheung Kwok-Wing Commits Suicide').

Hong Kong iMail, 28 September 2000 (Clarence Tsui, 'Can't See the Stars for the Smoke'); 20 October 2000 (Tyronne Henricus, 'Trucking Illegals fall for Chassis Charm'); 22 January 2001 (Paul Goddard, 'Canto Popstars Go for Gold').

Hong Kong Standard, 16 May 1977 ('Who Will Win Tonight's Contest is Anyone's Guess'), 11 July 1981 ('The Man Who Dies For a Living'), 4 April 1982 (Evans Chan, 'Leslie Chang, Rich, Young, Famous'), 2 August 1985 ('Leslie Gets Injunction'), 7 August 1985 (Jenny Leung, 'Leslie Charm Thrills fans'), 12 August 1985 (Ken Martinus, 'Return of a Superstar'), 11 October 1985 ('Macau Calls Local Rocker'), 23 November 1985 ('Leslie's First in Macau'), 21 April 1986 (Sophia Morgan, 'Leslie Cheung Fans Stand Up for Star'), 1 August 1986 (Ann Mercer, 'We're Not Lovers'), 8 September 1986 ('No Clash'), 18 August 1986 ('Aussies, Here They Come'), 23 September 1986 ('Giants to Clash in Concerts?'), 29 September 1986 ('Les' Christmas Present'), 20 October 1986 ('Brains & Not Beauty is What Leslie Looks for in his Ideal Girl'), 30 December 1986 (Ella Yu, 'A Night to Come

Closer'), 28 February 1987 ('Leslie Cheung to Leave CA?'),
9 April 1987 (Elven Ho, 'Leslie Leaves Capital Artists'),
29 April 1987 ('Leslie Explains Reasons Behind Move
to Cinepoly'), 23 July 1987 (Shirley Chan), 3 September
1987 (Shirley Chan, 'Leslie Keeps His Cool at Hot Gig'), 5
October 1987 ('Hey fans! Win Leslie's new Summer LP!),
14 November 1987 (Michele Trewick), 20 February 1988 ('I
want $10 Million'), 2 April 1988 ('Will Leslie Bail Out?'),
23 April 1988 ('In Concert Leslie Cheung'), 21 May 1988
('Leslie Launches Pepsi Campaign'), 6 August 1988 (Sally
Ratcliffe, 'A Star in the Making'; 'Leslie Lends a Helping
Hand'), 27 August 1988 (Shirley Chan, 'Record Maker,
Record Breaker'), 3 September 1988 ('Go West Young Man'),
15 October 1988 ('Cheung Charity'), 25 February 1989
(Shirley Chan, 'Buzz: A Change in Cheung'), 23 April 1989
('Triangle Without Adventure'), 29 April 1989 (Shirley Chan,
'Fast Action – Thin Plot'), 16 December 1989 (Anita Fung, '33
Final Encounters with Leslie'), 14 January 1990 (Anita Fung,
'Bobby's Star Shines Bright'), 19 May 1991 ('Homosexual
Film Role for Leslie'), 18 December 1991 (May Fung,
'Exemplary Pop Singers Rewarded'), 15 January 1992 (Elven
Ho & Max Kong, 'Top Actor Given Police Protection'), 13
March 1994 ('Controversial Chinese Film Nears Ultimate
Movie Accolade'), 24 June 1994 ('No More Sad Songs for
Youthful Actor Cheung'), 19 February 1995 (May Fung,
'Cheung's Point on Pressure'), 16 July 1995 (May Fung,
'Another Phantom Stakes His Claim'), 22 December 1996
('Cheung Flirts With New Image'), 13 March 1997 (Playing
It Shy, 'Cheung's Got It, But He Won't Be Flaunting It'), 20
July 1998 ('The Show Just Had To Go On'), 9 August 1998
('Cheung at Ease in Tsuen Wan'), 16 August 1998 ('Stars Kick

in Despite Slump'), 14 September 1998 ('Sultry Coco Steals Show'), 6 October 1998 ('Hui in the Shade'), 26 October 1998 ('Jacky Plans Gig'), 27 November 1998 ('Musical Ghost'), 4 December 1998 ('Party for Carina'), 15 January 1999 ('Money talks for Leung'), 10 March 1999 (David Poon, 'Stars Join Child Sexual Abuse Fight'), 1 June 1999 (Hiram To, 'Tribute to Paternal Love'), 18 June 1999 ("Chan Praises Film Industry's Health'), 22 October 1999 ('Leslie Cheung Seems Unhappy with Reporters'), 11 December 1999 (Michelle Lee, '$20 m Bill'), 28 January 2000 ('Show Biz'), 11 February 2000 ('Leslie Cheung'), 3 May 2003 ('SARS in Their Eyes'), 24 June 2003 ('Leslie Sang Andy's Song'), 27 June 2003 (Nicholas, 'To Those Who Remember Leslie'), 10 July 2003 ('Going Up and Down and Then Out'), 5 April 2004 (Teddy Ng, 'Delay in Getting Help 'Could Prove Deadly'.'), 9 November 2004 (Cally Chang, 'Media Helps Encourage Copy Cats'), 18 October 2005 (Stamp Tribute to Stars').

Inter-Asia Cultural Studies, 1 (2), 2000, 251-64 (Audrey Yue, 'What's So Queer about *Happy Together*? a.k.a. Queer (N) Asian: Interface, Community, Belonging').

Irasia.com, 4 April 2001 (TOM.COM Ltd, 'Annual Report 2001).

IS Department, Government of the Hong Kong Special Administrative Region, 31 October 2000 (CS Promotes Hong Kong Film Festival in Japan'), 26 August 2004 ('Treasures of Music Exhibition'), 26 January 2005 (Hong Kong Film Archive's 'Cityscape in Film'.').

Journal of Homosexuality, 39 (3-4), 2000, 187-200 (Chris Barry, 'Happy Alone? Sad Young Men in East Asian Gay Cinema').

Kinejun, no. 1384, 2003 (Wada Emi, 'Leslie Cheung As A Star And His Art-Mind').

KPS Entertainment Express, 1998.

Kuai Bao, 28 February 2006 (Xun Yi, 'Florence Chan Reveals The Cause Of Leslie Cheung's Death – He Was Killed By The Paparazzi', *http://www.kuaibao.net/cdsb/ GB/2006/02/28/73261.html, http://www.leslietong.com/lovehouse/dispbbs.asp?boardID=331&ID=29821&page=1*).

Los Angeles City Beat, 2003, (A. Klein, 'Farewell, Leslie Cheung').

Los Angeles Times, 22 June 1997 (Kevin Thomas, 'A Career in Full Bloom'); December 2003 (Kevin Thomas, 'Premiere Caps Leslie Cheung Tribute').

Men's Uno, April 2004 (Ngan Luen, 'Remembrance of Our Beloved Idol').

Metro, 126, Summer 2001, 92-7 (Jo Law, 'Wong Kar-Wai's Cinema).

Metropolis Daily, 1 April 2004 (Jelly Tse, 'Madame Tussaud's Hong Kong Unveils Leslie').

Ming Pao Weekly/ Ming Chow, 30 August 1986 (Sek Kei, 'Film Teahouse'); 901, 1986 ('Leslie is Afraid of Getting Married', *http://lesliecheung.cc/Magazine/1986/mingpao901/ mingpao901.htm*); 22 September 1994 (Sek Kei, 'Brand Names Create Dummy Audience'); 28 October 1995 ('Leslie Cheung's *Beloved* has sold more than 300,000'); 1998 (Lam

Bing, 'If Destiny Wants Them To Be Together, Leslie and Wong Kar-wai Will Meet Again', *http://lesliecheung.cc/ Magazine/1998/mingpao/interview/interview.htm*); 2003 (Eunice Lam, SCMP Book Publishing Limited 2003, *http:// lesliecheung.cc/memories/eunice/mingpaowkly.htm*); 6 April 2003 ('Interview with Florence Chan'); April 2003 (Law Kai Yu, 'Songs Behind the Door', *http://lesliecheung.cc/memories/lawkaiyui2.htm*); 12 April 2003 (Anita Mui, 'No More Unjustice To Gorgor Please', *http://lesliecheung.cc/memories/ anitamui_eng.htm*); no. 1820, 2003, (*Wong Lai Ling*, interview with Florence Chan); 17 July 2003 (Too Kit, 'Bo Gorgor'); 23 September 2004 (Sek kei, 'The Confused Malicious West'); 9 October 2004 ('Leslie's Footprints in Oriental Bangkok', *http://www.mingpaoweekly.com/htm/1874/BB01_6.htm*); 26 March 2011 ('Six Hours before the Death of Leslie Cheung – Last Lunch with Best Friend').

Movie Stories, 1995 (Chiu Wing, 'Cheung Kwok Wing: It Won't Be Long For Us To Meet Again').

Music Net, 7 September 2000 (Thomas Huang, 'The Legend Arrives').

New Paper, The (Singapore), 9 July 2005 (Ton Theon Loon, 'Desperados and the Dead').

New Republic, 14 and 21 July 1997 (Fredric Dannen, 'Making all the Right Moves').

Next Magazine, 1997 ('Interview With Leslie', http://lesliecheung.

cc/Magazine/1997/next97/next97.htm); 10 April 2003 (Lee Pik-wah, http://lesliecheung.cc/memories/leepikwah.htm); no. 795, 2005 (Lilian Lee Pik Wah, 'It Came Too Late', *LeslieTong.com*).

Oriental Sunday, no. 201, 2001 ('Leslie is always found guilty of unsound accusations').

Pop Asia, 'Interview', April 2002; 'Never Forget Leslie' by Wang Lee Hom, 2003.

Positif, 1998 ('Berlin Film Festival', *http://xoomer.virgilio.it/nguidett/berlin.htm*); no. 455, 1999 ('Michael Ciment and Hugo Niogret interview', 21 February 1998); June 2003 (*Lorenzo Codelli and Hubert Niogret*, 'Leslie Cheung 1956 - 2003', *http://www.jeanmichelplace.com/fr/revues/detail.cfm?ProduitID=607&ProduitCode=1*).

Positions, 9.2, Fall 2001, 423-47 (Helen Hok-sze Leung, 'Queerscapes in Contemporary Hong Kong Cinema').

POTS, 23 April 2004 (Charles Leary, 'Ana and the Others').

Ready, Steady, Go, 2 August 1985.

Shanghai Daily, 19 November 2003 (Canto-pop Lyricist Lam Dies, 56'); 2 April 2004 (Claudia Sunday, 'Shanghai Commemoration of Leslie'), 12 May 2005 (Michelle Zhang).

Shenzhen Daily, 25 March 2005 (Law Chi-leung interview, *http://www.sznews.com/jb/20050325/ca1507377.htm*).

Sight and Sound, 6(9), September 1996, 6-9 (Larry Grose, 'Nonchalant Grace'); 7 (5), May 1997, 14-7 (Tony Rayns, 'To the End of the World')..

Sing Pao, 7 April 2003, (Song Song, 'Big Brother Gor Gor', *http:// lesliecheung.cc/memories/singpao6.htm*).

Sing Tao Daily, 31 March 2004(?) ('Fans Volunteer to Help Depression Patients, *http://www.leslietong.com/lovehouse/ dispbbs.asp?boardID=286&ID=16862*).

Sino, (Interview with Mei Ting).

Sohu.com, 31 March 2005 (Interview with Florence Chan).

South China Morning Post, 16 May 1977 ('A Song for Asia); ? 1986 ('A Night to Come Closer); ? 1987 ('Leslie Cheung wins TV ad deal'); ? 1988 (Sally Ratcliffe, 'A Star in the Making: Leslie Lends a Helping Hand'); 23 December 1990 (Ambrose Aw, 'Wong's Wild Way'); 13 December 1992 ('Chen's Farewell to Taboo; Farewell To My Concubine'); 1 January 1993 ('Cheung, the Concubine, Tiptoes Past the Censors'); 14 January 1993 ('Immersed in World of Chinese Opera'); 14 February 1993 (Paul Fonoroff, 'Pointed View of the Swashbuckling Sagas'); 16 May 1993 (Thea Klapwald, 'Leslie Cheung Gets Real/It's the Real Me At Last'); 23 May 1993 (Scarlet Cheng, 'Gong Li and Company The Centre of Attention'); 27 June 1993 (Chris Dobson, 'Bombs Hurled in Movie Set 'Extortion Bid"); 25 July 1993 (Scarlet Cheng, 'The Concubine Controversy'; 'Beijing Silences a Prodigal Son and His Concubine'); 29 July 1993 (John Kohut, 'Hello and Farewell to Winning Movie'); 1 August 1993 ('The Day When the Movie Industry Thumbed Its Nose at China's Leaders'); 15 August 1993 (Scarlet Cheng, 'A Director's Dream, and Actor's Nightmare'); 16 August 1993 (Chris Yeung, 'Controversial Film to be Shown'); 27 August 1993 (Paul Fonoroff, 'One for the Birds'); 29 August 1993 (Elven Ho, 'Cut and Thrust of Classic Swordplay'); 2 September 1993 (Geoffrey Crothall, 'Farewell to Concubine Drawing in Audiences'); 19 December 1993 ('Taiwan Embraces Concubine'); 10 April 2002 (Winnie Chung, 'Inner Secrets'); 14 January 1994 (Winnie Chung, 'Star Wars Leave Singers on Sidelines'); 30 October 1994 (John Dykes, 'Storms Halt Tempest'); 11 December 1994 (John Dykes, 'Eclipse of the Moon'); 3 February 1995 (Paul Fonorroff, 'Romance Takes a Backseat as Kenny Bee Gets Cooking'); 1 March 1995 (Wanda Szeto, 'Love in the Air at Film Awards'); 16 April 1995 ('Yu Got It Made'); 23 April 1995 ('Showbiz Polishes Its Act'); 14 July 1995 (Winnie Chung, 'Ghostly Lover Breaks Movie Sound Barrier'; 'Resembling the Phantom'); 21 July 1995 (Paul Fonoroff, 'Shallow Phantom Love'); 27 July 1995 ('Phantom Role Fits Like a Glove'); 6 August 1995 ('That's Show Business'); 8 October 1995 (Winnie Chung, 'Rap! Rap!'); 31 January 1996 (Thomas Chang, 'Solid Gold Stuff from the Stars'); 11 February 1996 (Glenn Schloss, 'Films Fight for New Year Success'); 23 February 1996 (Paul Fonoroff, 'One Star for a Gifted Director'); 2 June 1996 ('Manda Pop Muscles In'); 19 July 1996 (Paul Fonoroff, 'Banality By the Bag-load in Tsui's Shanghai Stinker'); 28 July 1996 ('Stars Top the Bill with Young Volunteers'); 6 October 1996 (Winnie Chung, 'Leslie's New Year Present'); 20 October 1996 ('Gay Icons of Our Time'); 6 December 1996 (Paul Fonoroff, 'Yee So-So On Soft Core'); 16 December 2006 (Winnie Chung, 'Leslie Proves

He's Still A Showman'); 20 December 1996 (Winnie Chung, 'Leslie Cheung Kwok-wing'); 29 December 1996 ('Pushing the Gay Envelope'); I January 1997 (Winnie Chung, 'Local Artists Heed warning Note and See Regional Audience'); 5 January 1997 (Anthony Woo, 'Not a Gay day'); 30 May 1997 (Alice Cairns, 'Views of Gay Theatre'); 14 June 1997 (Wanda Szeto, 'Pressure on Stars to Sing in China'); 2 September 1997 (Andy Ho, 'Time for Restraint'); 9 November 1997 ('A Gay Old Time'); November [?] 1997 ('Leslie Cheung Flirts with New Image'); 31 March 2004 ('Mathew Scott Interview with Fans'); 3 March 2001 (Vivienne Chow, 'Mok's Star Turnout'); 10 April 2002 (Winnie Chung, 'Inner Secrets'); 1 August 2002 (Albert Cheng, 'Suddenly Shy Stars Biting the Hand that Feeds Them'), 21 April 2003 ('Shops Shunned as Online Sales Soar on Sars'), 22 April 2003 (Peter Michael, 'Driver's Death Leap Highlights Tragic Trend'), 24 April 2003 (Alisha Macpherson, letter 'No Trend'), 28 April 2003 ('Taiwan gets Ready for *Apple* Daily'), 28 April 2003 (Winnie Chung, 'Festival of Leslie Cheung Films Organised in a Tribute to Dead Star'), 1 May 2003 (Winnie Chung, 'Singer Leaves Behind Grief and Inspiration'), 26 May 2003 (Denise Tsang, 'Favourite Gymnasiums'), 24 June 2003 (Caryn Yap, 'Tough Times Highlight Mixed Fortunes of Iconic Restaurants'), 25 June 2003 (Jane Cai, 'Authors Top Poll of Icons of Century'), 14 July 2003 (Tim Cribb, 'Legal Row Looms on Same-Sex Wedlock'), 17 July 2003 (Magdalen Chow, 'Suit Filed Over Late Singer's Musical Legacy'), 25 October 2003 (Magdalen Chow, 'Court Asked to Lift Order on Singer's Legacy'), 12 November 2003 (Sara Bradford, 'Leslie Cheung Producer Gets Control of Recordings as Judge Overturns Injunction'), 30 March 2003 (Vivienne Chow, 'Menu Pays Homage to

Leslie's Memory'), 31 March 2004 (Vivienne Cow, 'Mainland Glamour for Hong Kong's Oscars'; Matthew Scott, 'If We Knew More'), 1 April 2004 (Carrie Chan, 'Hong Kong Music Industry Gets Top Billing'; 'Curtain Rises Again on the Immortal Leslie'), 2 April 2004 (Louisa Yan, 'Thousands Remember Leslie'), 5 April 2004 (Vivienne Chow, 'Hong Kong Film Awards'), 7 April 2004 ('Hottest Tickets in Town'), 29 April 2004 (Elaine Wu, 'Avenue Visitors Hand it to Stars'), 13 September 2004 (Scarlett Chiang, 'Fans pay Homage to Leslie Cheung'), 23 September 2004 (Paul Fonoroff, 'Nothing More than Images of Beauty'), 18 March 2005 (Vivienne Chow, 'Film Awards Chief Pans Property Giant'), 23 March 2005 (Vivienne Chow, 'Music Sales Awards Led by Warning on Piracy'), 1 April 2005 (Vivienne Chow, 'More depressives Seeking Help Since Singer's Suicide'), 2 April 2005 (Chandra Wong, 'Grey Sky Reflects Mood as Star's Fans Remember'), 8 April 2005 ('Life is No Longer a Sweet Musical Journey for Cookies'), 23 June 2005 ('The Skin I'm In'), 6 July 2005 ('Asia Style'), 21 July 2005 (Vivienne Chow, 'Early Birds Give Book Fair Stamp of Approval'), 7 September 2005 ('Clever Ploy Stirs Up Tribute for Leslie Cheung'), 9 September 2005 ('City Briefs'), 17 September 2005 ('Headlines'), 25 September 2005 (Anthony Holden, 'Cracker of a Showcase Highlights the Best of Asian Cinema'), 20 October 2005 ('Stamps Honour Singers'), 10 November 2005 ('Curse Celebre'), 5 January 2006 (Felix Chan), 22 March 2006 (Vivienne Chow, 'Music Fair Gives Fans an Intimate Look at Their Idols'), 25 March 2006 ('Tam on Comeback').

Star, The, 13 September 2000 ('Leslie's Last Fling').

Straits Times, 25 April 1997 ('Organiser of Leslie Cheung's Concerts Sued').

Sudden Weekly (photo of Leslie Cheung hand-in-hand with Tong).

Tai Pei Times, 10 April 2003 (Yu Sen-lun, 'The Leslie Cheung Legend Lives on').

Tai Sing Pao, 20 March 1994 ('Ang Lee's *Young Lady Siao Yue*).

Time, 3 May 2000 (Stephen Short, 'Bedroom Pinup').

Time Asia, 7 May 2001 (Richard Corliss/Stephen Short, 'Forever Leslie'); 3 April 2003 (Richard Corliss, 'That Old Feeling: Days of Being Leslie'); 14 April 2003 (Richard Corliss, 'To Fall from a Great Height').

TV and Entertainment Times, 6-12 July 1992 (James Giddings, 'Leslie Cheung A Man's Woman Reversing the Roles in Chen Kaige's New Movie).

Vancouver Sun, 14 March 1994 (Peter Birnie, 'Star Turn').

Varsity, (Interview with Wing Shya).

Vitality, April 2004 ('Post-Cheung Kwok Wing Phenomenon').

WBI, 27 October 1997 (Khoi Lebinh and David Eng, 'Interview with Wong Kar-wai').

World Movies, no. 413, (Chiu Hung Ping, 'Falling Like Cherry Blossoms').

Xinhua, 2 April 2005 ('Activities to Commemorate Leslie Cheung').

Xinmin Za Zhi, 1 April 2004 (Florence Chan interview).

BOOKS

1990-99 Box Office Ranking for Chinese Movies in Hong Kong.

Abbas, Ackbar, *Hong Kong: Culture and the Politics of Disappearance* (Minneapolis: University of Minnesota Press, 1997).

Abbas, Ackbar, Jean-Marc Lalanne, David Martinez and Jimmy Ngai, *Wong Kar-wai* (Paris: Dis Voir, 1997).

Baker, Rick, and Toby Russell, *The Essential Guide to Hong Kong Movies* (Hong Kong: made in Hong Kong, 1994).

Balke, Gerd, *Hong Kong Voices* (Hong Kong: ?, 1989).

Berry, Chris, ed., *Perspectives on Chinese Cinema* (London: British Film Institute, 1991).

Bliss, Michael, *Between the Bullets: The Spiritual Cinema of John Woo* (Lanham, Maryland: Scarecrow Press, 2002).

Bordwell, David, *Planet Hong Kong: Popular Cinema and the Art of Entertainment* (Cambridge, Massachusetts: Harvard University Press, 2000).

Browne, Nick, ed., *New Chinese Cinemas: Forms, Identities, Politics* (Cambridge: Cambridge University Press, 1994).

Brownell, Susan, and Jeffrey N. Wasserstrom, *Chinese Femininities/ Chinese Masculinities: A Reader* (Berkeley: University of California Press, 2002).

Broughton, Simon, and Mark Ellingham, *World Music Volume 2: Latin and North America, Caribbean, India, Asia and Pacific* (London: BBC Radio, 2000).

Capital Artists, compilation with four CDs, *His Story* (Hong Kong: Capital Artists, 2005).

Chan, Ching-wai, *The Structure and Marketing Analysis of Hong Kong Films* (Hong Kong: Film Biweekly, 2000).

Chan, Eric, Chi Wai, *Happy Birthday to Our Dearest Leslie; 50, 1956-2006* (Hong Kong: Red Mission, 2006).

Chang, Natalia Sui-hung, *Butterfly of Forbidden Colors: The Artistic Image of Leslie Cheung* (Hong Kong: Joint Publishing, 2008) (Chinese).

Chong, Milan, *Pop Stars in Hong Kong* (Hong Kong: Sing Tao Educational Publications, 1989).

City Entertainment, *A Time to Remember: Leslie Cheung Kwok-wing* (Hong Kong: City Entertainment, 2009) (Chinese).

City Entertainment, *Leslie Cheung* (Hong Kong: City Entertainment, no date) (Chinese).

City Entertainment, *The One and Only* (City Entertainment: Hong Kong, 2004) (Chinese).

City Entertainment, *Leslie Cheung's Movie World, Volume 1, 1978–1991* (City Entertainment: Hong Kong, 2005) (Chinese).

City Entertainment, *Leslie Cheung's Movie World, Volume 2, 1991–1995* (Hong Kong: City Entertainment, 2006) (Chinese).

Coldstream, John, *Dirk Bogarde: the Authorised Biography* (London: Wiedenfeld & Nicolson, 2004).

Curtin, Michael, *Playing to the World's Biggest Audience: The Globalization of Chinese Film and TV* (Berkeley: University of California Press, 2007).

Dannen, Fredric and Barry Long, *Hong Kong Babylon: An Insider's Guide to the Hollywood of the East* (London: Faber and Faber, 1997).

Dissanayake, Wimal, *Wong Kar-wai's Ashes of Time* (Hong Kong: Hong Kong University Press, 2003).

Doty, Alexander, *Flaming Classics: Queering the Film Canon* (London: Routledge, 2000).

Doyle, Christopher, *Don't Try for Me Argentina: Photographic Journal of 'Happy Together', a Wong Kar-Wai Film* (Hong Kong: City Entertainment, 1997).

Fang, Karen, *John Woo's A Better Tomorrow* (Hong Kong: Hong Kong University Press, 2004).

Film Biweekly, *The Legacy of Leslie Cheung: A Soul on Film* (Hong Kong: Film Biweekly, 2010) (Chinese).

Fitzgerald, Martin, and Paul Duncan, *Hong Kong's Heroic Bloodshed* (Harpenden, Herts: Pocket Essentials, 2000).

Fonoroff, Paul, *At the Hong Kong Movies: 600 reviews from 1988 till the Handover* (Hong Kong: Film Biweekly, 1998).

Fu Poshek and Davis Desser, eds, *The Cinema of Hong Kong: History, Arts, Identity* (Cambridge: Cambridge University Press, 2000).

Fu, Winnie, ed., *The Making of Martial Arts Films – As Told By Filmmakers and Stars* (Hong Kong: Hong Kong Film Archive, 1999).

Gammond, Peter, *The Oxford Guide to Popular Music* (Oxford: Oxford University Press, 1991).

Hall, Kenneth, *John Woo: The Films* (Jefferson, NC: McFarland & Company, 1997).

Hammond, Stefan, and Mike Wilkens, *Sex and Zen & A Bullet in the Head: the Essential Guide to Hong Kong's Mind-bending Films* (New York: Simon and Schuster, 1996).

Hammond, Stefan, *Hollywood East: Hong Kong Movies and the People Who Make Them* (Lincolnwood, Illinois: Contemporary Books, 2000).

Hardin, Kimeron and Marny Hall, *Queer Blues* (Oakland: New Harbinger, 2001).

Heard, Christopher, *Ten Thousand Bullets: The Cinematic Journey of John Woo* (Los Angeles: Lone Eagle, 2000).

Hill, John and Pamela Gibson, eds, *World Cinema: Critical Approaches* (New York: Oxford University Press, 2000).

Hong Kong Film Archive, *Fifty Years of the Hong Kong Film Production and Distribution Industries: An Exhibition* (Hong Kong: Urban Council, 1997).

Hong Kong Film Critics Society, *Review on Hong Kong Movies* (Hong Kong: Hong Kong Film Critics Society, 1994-99).

The 22nd Hong Kong International Film Festivals, *Hong Kong Panorama, 97-98* ('Home is Where the Heart Is; Wong Kar-wai and Christopher Doyle on *Happy Together*').

Hong Kong Twenty-first International Film Festival, *Hong Kong Cinema Retrospective: Fifty Years of Electric Shadows* (Hong Kong: Urban Council, 1997).

Hong Kong Twenty-third International Film Festival, *Hong Kong New Wave: Twenty Years After* (Hong Kong: Urban Council, 1999).

In Memory of Leslie Cheung Kwok-wing, 1956-2003 (Hong Kong: no publisher, no date).

Jarvie, I.C., *Window on Hong Kong: A Sociological Study of the Hong Kong Film Industry and Its Audience* (Hong Kong: Centre of Asian Studies, University of Hong Kong, 1977).

Jeffries, Stan, *Encyclopedia of World Pop Music: 1980-2001*(Westport, Connecticut: Greenwood Press, Oryx, 2003).

Law Kar, ed., *Hong Kong Cinema in the Eighties: A Comparative Study with Western Cinema* (Hong Kong: Urban Council, 1991).

Law Kar and Frank Bren, *Hong Kong Cinema: A Cross Cultural View* (Lanham, Maryland: Scarecrow Press, 2004).

Lent, John, *The Asian Film Industry* (Austin: University of Texas Press, 1990).

Leslie (Beijing: Shi Xian dai chu ban she, 2003) (Chinese).

Leslie Cheung (Xianggang: nan hua chuan mei chu ban you xian gong si, 2004) (Chinese).

Leslie Cheung, 1956 – 2003 (Hong Kong: S C Media, ?) (Chinese).

Leslie Cheung Artist Studies, *A Time to Remember: Leslie Chueng Kwok Wing* (Hong Kong: City Entertainment, no date).

Leslie Cheung, Forever Love: In Memory of Leslie Cheung (?) (Chinese).

Leslie Cheung in Concert (Xiang-gang: Di yi guang gao, 1985) (Chinese).

Leslie Cheung: Legend Forever, 1956 - 2003 (Hong Kong: Ming Pao, ?) Chinese).

Leslie Legacy: His Charm, Charisma and Craft Remembered in Celluloid (Memorial booklet, Hong Kong film commemoration in the Hong Kong Cultural Centre and the Hong Kong City Hall, 11-12 May 2003).

Leslie Cheung Cyberworld, *The One and Only Leslie Cheung* (City Entertainment: Hong Kong, no date, pre April 2004).

Leung, Helen Hok-Sze, 'In Queer Memory: Leslie Cheung (1956-2003)', *Undercurrents: Queer Culture and Postcolonial Hong Kong* (Hong Kong: Hong Kong University Press, 2008).

Leung, Helen Hok-Sze, *Farewell My Concubine: A Queer Film Classic* (Vancouver: Arsenal Pulp Press, 2010).

Leung, K.P., and Teresa Y.C. Wong, eds, *25 Years of Social and Economic Development in Hong Kong* (Hong Kong: University of Hong Kong, 1994).

Leung, Victor, [a biography by year] (Hong Kong: City Entertainment, no date) (Chinese).

Lilley, Rozanna, *Staging Hong Kong: Gender and Performance in Transition* (Richmond, Surrey: Curzon, 1998).

Logan, Bey, *Hong Kong Action Cinema* (London: Titan Books, 1995).

Lu, Sheldon, ed., *Transnational Chinese Cinemas: Identity, Nationhood, Gender* (Honolulu: University of Hawaii Press, 1994).

McClure, Steve, *Nipponpop* (Tokyo: Tuttle Publishing, 1998).

Morton, Lisa, *The Cinema of Tsui Hark* (Jefferson, NC: McFarland and Company, 2001).

Nowell-Smith, Geoffrey, ed., *The Oxford History of World Cinema* (Oxford: Oxford University Press, 1996).

Pang, Laikwan and Day Wong, eds, *Masculinities and Hong Kong Cinema* (Hong Kong: Hong Kong University Press, 2005).

Pomerance, Murray, ed., *Ladies and Gentlemen, Boys and Girls: Gender in Film at the End of the Twentieth Century* (Albany: SUNY Press, 2001).

Red Mission (Enid), (Hong Kong:) (Chinese: ISBN 962-8114-90-5).

Red Mission, *50: 1956-2006* (Hong Kong: Red Mission, 2006). (Chinese).

Ryker, Harrison, *New Music in the Orient* (Buren: Frits Knuf, 1991).

Salute to Leslie Cheung (Huhehaote shi: Yuan fang chu ban she, 2003) (Chinese).

Server, Lee, *Asian Pop Cinema: Bombay to Tokyo* (San Francisco: Chronicle Books, 1999).

Shi Yonggang, (Beijing: Zuo Jia chu ban she, 2003) (Chinese).

Shi Yonggang, *Leslie Cheung: Legend Forever, 1956-2003*

(Xianggang: Ming bao chu ban she you xian gong si, 2004) (Chinese).

Shi Yonggang, *Leslie* (Beijing: Zhong xin chu ban she, 2005).

Chitose Shima, *All About Leslie* (Tokyo: Sangyo Henshu Center Co., 1999).

Chitose Shima, *The Time of Leslie* (Tokyo: Sangyo Henshu Center Co., 2004).

Situ Peiqi, (Chongqing Shi: Chongqing chu ban she, 2005) (Chinese).

Smith, Richard, *Seduced and Abandoned: Essays on Gay Men and Popular Music* (London: Cassell, 1995).

South China Morning Post. *Hong Kong Visitor* (Hong Kong: South China Morning Post, 1994).

Starlight, *Golden Music of Always: Leslie* (Hong Kong: Starlight, no date).

Stewart, Clare, and Philippa Hawker, eds, *Leslie Cheung* (Flinders Lane, Australia: Australian Centre for the Moving Image, 2003).

Stokes, Lisa Odham, and Michael Hoover, *City on Fire: Hong Kong Cinema* (London: Verso, 1999).

Stokes, Lisa Odham, *Peter Ho-Sun Chan's 'He's a Woman, She's a Man'* (Hong Kong: Hong Kong University Press, 2009).

Tambling, Jeremy, *Wong Kar-wai's Happy Together* (Hong Kong: Hong Kong University Press, 2003).

Teo, Stephen, *Hong Kong Cinema: The Extra Dimensions* (London: British Film Institute Press, 1997).

Thompson, Clifford, ed., *Contemporary World Musicians* (Chicago: Fitzroy Dearborn, 1999).

Wang, W., *Hong Kong Cinema POV* (Taipei: Yang Zhi Wen Hua Shi Ye Gu Fen You Xian Gong Si, 2002).

Weisser, Thomas, *Asian Trash Cinema: The Book* (Miami: ATC ETC Publications, 1994).

Weisser, Thomas, *Asian Trash Cinema: The Book (Part 2)* (Miami: Vital Sounds Inc, ATC Publications, 1995).

Welsh, Frank, *A History of Hong Kong* (London: Harper Collins, 1997).

Will You Remember (: Publications (Holdings) Ltd, 1989) (Chinese).

Wood, Miles, *Cine East: Hong Kong Cinema Through the Looking Glass* (Guildford: FAB Press, 1998).

Wu Minghong, *Leslie: Voice in Heaven* (Beijing: Zhi shi chu ban she, post 2003) (Chinese)

Yao, Ashley (a Leslie fan in China), (a book about Leslie's movies)

Yau, Esther C.M., ed., *At Full Speed: Hong Kong Cinema in a*

Borderless World (Minneapolis: University of Minnesota Press, 2001).

(Taibei Shi: Shi bao wen hua chu ban qi ye gu fen you xian gong si, 2003) (Chinese).

(Xiangang: Dian ying shuang zhou kan chu ban she, 2003) (Chinese).

(Xiangang: Xing wen she chu ban you xian gong si, 2003) (Chinese).

Zhuo, Botang and Cheuk Pak Tong, *Hong Kong New Wave Cinema (1978-2000)* (Bristol: Intellect Books, 2008).

: *1956-2003* (Hong Kong: Oriental Sunday, 2003) (Chinese, with four postcards).

ARTICLES

'1998 Major Events', Julie Ng, Red Mission.

All Music Shop Newsletter May 2003, 'Forever Leslie (1956-2003) – The Legend Lives On......' (net site).

Babcock, Todd, letter, 'Time to Remember', 30 November 1998.

Chow Shui Yum, 'Okinawa Rendez-vous' (May 2004) (net site).

Friedland, Lucy, 'Journey Into the East – An Ongoing Travel Journal', Part 3 (net blog).

Hammond, Stefan, 'Leslie's Demons', *goldsea.com*, 1997.

Hawker, Philippa, Australian Centre for the Moving Image, 'Forever Cheung' (2003) (net site).

Kelly, Stephen, 'Why Does It Have to Be Like This?': Leslie Cheung, 1956-2003', 2003.

Lam, Eunice, tribute article, no date, Ming Pao Weekly.

'Leslie's Footprints in Oriental Bangkok' (net site).

'Love Gorgor', interview with Lam Jik (net site).

Morton, Lisa, in *Leslie Cheung Tribute*, Asian Film Foundation booklet produced for the commemorative programme in Los Angeles on 6 and 7 December 2003.

National University of Defense Technology, Los Angeles, Alumni Website, Huang Lo, 1 April 2005, '2005 Sound of the Wind and Shadow of the Moon, Fondly Remembers Leslie Cheung' (net site).

S.F.L., 'Gentleman Leslie', *Hong Kong - Orient Extrême Cinéma*, No. 1, January 1997, pp 14-19.

Takako Tokiwa, website blog, 7 April 2003.

Tang Oi Lam, 'Leslie Cheung Has Great Vitality, More Than Any Ordinary Person', ?, 29 May 1987.

Wang Lee Hom, 'Uncle Leslie Has Taught Me The Important Thing As An Artist' in *Never Forget Leslie* (Japanese

Magazine), p.20, http://lesliecheungforever.net/Leehom-e.html.

'What People Have Said about Leslie', Red Mission.

Yao, Ashley, 'Only in Eden Would You Know Spring', 6 February 2006 (net site).

Yim, ieven, 'Cheung Woos Fans with a Bubbling Extravaganza', 1988 (net site).

THESES AND PAPERS

Erni, John Nguyet, 'Moving with It, Move by It: Gender and Cantopop' in *Perspectives* vol.16 Issue 2, Fall 2004, City University of Hong Kong.

Lau, Man-chun, 'A Study of the Hong Kong Popular Music Industry, 1930-2000', MA dissertation for the University of Hong Kong, 2003, MA 03 L18.

Ng, Brenda Pong-wai, 'The Development in Hong Kong of Commercial Popular Songs in Cantonese', MPhil dissertation for the University of Hong Kong, 1996.

Wong, Elvin Chi-chung, 'Making and Using Pop Music in Hong Kong', MPhil dissertation for the University of Hong Kong, 1997, XM Phil 97 W12.

Wong, James Jum-sum, 'The Rise and Decline of Cantopop', PhD thesis for the University of Hong Kong, 2003, PhD 03 W22.

Yip Ka-man, 'A Study of Hong Kong Popular Song Lyrics from 1970s to 1990s', MA dissertation for the University of Hong Kong, 2000.

DOCUMENTARIES

Kwan, Stanley, *Yang & Yin: Gender in Chinese Cinema* (1994/6).

Ming Pao Weekly, 1 April 2004, ('VCD in Remembrance of Cheung Kwok Wing', track 2, part 2).

TELEVISION PROGRAMMES

ATV Channel V, 25 June 1989, 'Interview with Leslie Cheung' by James Wong and two others.

RADIO PROGRAMMES

'A Time to Remember', 1998.

BBC, 1 April 2003 ('Actor Leslie Cheung found dead').

Commercial Radio Hong Kong, 1985, 'Leslie Cheung's Autobiography'.

Commercial Radio Hong Kong, 29 December 2005, 'Who Will Understand', Dicky Cheung Wai Kin, 'GorGor Leslie Cheung'; 9 January 2006, 'Who Will Understand', Connie Chan Bo Chu; January 2006, Lam Jik, 'Leslie's Passing and his Songs'.

HKVP Radio, 'Leslie Cheung: Larger than Life'.

Metro Radio, 'Touching Fans' Stories', *http://lesliecheung.cc/memories/fanstories.htm*.

Radio Television Hong Kong, October 1996 (Chow Kwok Fung, Interview with Leslie on 'Crossover 97' concert).

WEBSITES
(AS AT 1-17 AUGUST 2010)

3sat.de (German TV station), Andrea Bette. 'The Gender of the Stars: On the Actor and Pop Star Leslie Cheung', *http://www.3sat.de/3sat.php?http://3sat.de/film/reihen/71798/index.html*, *www.leslie-cheung.de*, trans. Bianca Patzelt, *http://february87.de/das_geschlecht_der_sterne.htm*.

'All About Leslie Blogspot; My Eternal Love for Leslie Cheung', http://all-about-leslie.blogspot.com/.

Chen Kaige, 'The Eyes of Leslie Cheung', *http://lesliecheung.cc/memories/eyes_of_leslie_cheung.htm*, *http://ent.563.net/article/2003/2003-4-30/37553.html (30 Apr 2003)*.

Depression drug company, http://www.depressionhurts.com/stories/stories.jsp?reqNavId=3.

Entertainment on Line, mm52.com, *http://www.mm52.com/chineseidols/zhangguorong/*.

'Fans' Stories' *http://lesliecheung.cc/memories/fanstories.htm*.

'Father of Yeung Lok-si Told Leslie: 'My Daughter Has a New Boyfriend', *Mingpao Weekly*, 1988: http://www.lesliecheung.cc/Magazine/1988/mingpao1988/English.htm.

'Feeling as if Stabbed by a Knife', **15 January 2005,** http://ashesoftime.tianyablog.com/blogger/view_blog.asp?blogID=16419&CategoryID=0&idWriter=0&Key=0&NextPostID=1068651&PageNo=2.

Gaultier, Jean Paul, *http://212.180.4.184/www.jeanpaulgaultier.com/.*

Golden Harvest, *www.goldenharvest.com*

Hitchcock, Lori, 'Leslie Cheung', IMDb mini-biography, *lhitch@lib.bekkoame.or.jp.*

Hong Kong Cinemagic, *www.hkcinemagic.com*

Hong Kong Entertainment News in Review, *www.hkentreview.com/2003/april/ckw.html.*

Hong Kong Vintage Pop Radio, 'Leslie Cheung: Larger Than Life', www.hkvpradio.com/artists/lesliecheung/ .

iLike, Leslie and Anita Mui on TVB: http://www.ilike.com/artist/Leslie+Cheung+%26+Anita+Mui/track/TVB+-+Leslie+Cheung+%26+Anita+Mui+-+Destiny?from=imeem.

Law Kai-yui, 'Songs Behind the Door', *http://lesliecheung.cc/memories/songs_behind_the_door.htm.*

Law Kai-yui, 'The Singer's Shirt', <u>http://lesliecheung.cc/memories/singer.htm</u>.

Lee Pik-wah, <u>http://lesliecheung.cc/memories/leepikwah_eng.htm</u>.

'Legendary Years of Our Leslie; A Biography', Eunike, 18 February 2006, http://xoomer.virgilio.it/nguidett/biography01.htm.

'Leslie and Brigitte Lin in Discussion Forum at HKU - *Ashes of Time*', <u>http://lesliecheung.cc/Special/hku/part1_eng.htm</u>.

'Leslie Cheung', <u>http://www.imdb.com/name/nm0002000/</u>.

'Leslie Cheung Artists Studies Website', 'Never Wanna Be Apart from Leslie: In Reminiscence of Leslie Cheung's Artistic Life' 30 April 2003, Hong Kong Baptist University, http://www.leslie-cheung.com/leslie/2004/5-31/14148.html, http://www.leslie-cheung.com 2004-5-31 1:39:28; 17 Aug 2004.

'Leslie Cheung Autobiography', Commercial radio, 1985: http://all-about-leslie.blogspot.com/2007/12/autobiography-by-leslie-1985-commercial.html.

'Leslie Cheung Dream World', http://www.lesliecheung-dream-world.com/index.html.

Leslie Cheung Fan Club of China, http://www.lesliecheung.com.cn/music/.

'Leslie Cheung Internet Fan Club', *www.lesliecheung.com*; <u>http://forum.lesliecheung.com/Forum62/HTML/000054.html</u>.

'Leslie Cheung Kwok-wing', <u>http://www.brns.com/hkactors/pages/page23.html</u>.

'Leslie Cheung Memorial', *www.geocities.com/yannipoo/LeslieCheung2.html*.

Leslie Cheung Special '85 on My Veoh: http://www.veoh.com/browse/videos/category/entertainment/watch/v1393014KhpPrN9t.

'Lesliecheung Cyberworld', <u>http://lesliecheung.cc/</u>.

'Leslie-Cheung.net', *www.leslie-cheung.net/*.

'Leslie Legacy Association', http://xoomer.virgilio.it/nguidett/legacy.htm.

'Leslie Legacy - His Charm, Charisma and Craft Remembered on Celluloid', http://lesliecheung.cc/memories/magazines/legacy/happytogether.htm. [and various other film names before the htm].

'Leslie's Pillow', <u>http://xoomer.virgilio.it/nguidett/index.htm</u>.

'Live Performance at Academy Hall, 10 August 1982', <u>http://www.seewise.net/CyberAudio/Live.html</u>.

Lok Bing, 'My Musical World of Cheung Kwok Wing - The Sparkle Of Fireworks On That Night', 10 September 2003, <u>http://books.educhn.com/detail.asp?BBS_ID=2618010</u>.

'Love Hong Kong Film', *www.lovehkfilm.com/people/cheung_leslie. htm*.

'Ma Yi Jung Regrets She is not Able to Direct Her Idol's Movie' (3 April 2003), *http://www.ttnn.com/cna/news.cfm/030403/98*.

Man Hong interview in China, 2000, *http://www.lesliesky.com/cgi-bin/topic.cgi?forum=35&topic=379&show=0*.

Mandarin Entertainment (Holdings) Ltd, *www.mandarin.films.com*

'Messages from the Stars', *http://lesliecheung.cc/memories/magazines/legacy/stars.htm.mm52.com*, *http://www.mm52.com/chineseidols/zhangguorong/*.

Morton, Lisa, 'Leslie Cheung Tribute 2003', *http://www.asianfilm.org/modules.php?name=Encyclopedia&op=content&tid=58*, *http://www.lisamorton.com/leslietrib.html*.

Morton, Lisa, 'Leslie Cheung Kwok-wing' (2003), *http://www.asianfilm.org/modules.php?name=Encyclopedia&op=content&tid=59*.

Mui, Anita, 'Statement to Ming Pao: No More Injustice to Gorgor Please', *http://lesliecheung.cc/memories/leepikwah_eng.htm*.

'*Mystery Love*; The Story', http://www.lesliecheung.cc/musicdrama/mysterylove/story/story.htm.

Nakagawa Yosuke, November 20, 2005, *http://blog.livedoor.jp/yoyogi2222/archives/50151785*.

html, http://bbs.ent.163.com/board/rep.
jsp?b=zhangguorong&i=147380.

'Never Wanna Be Apart from Leslie: In Reminiscence of Leslie Cheung's Artistic Life', HK Baptist University, Leslie Cheung Artist Studies, Seminar, 30 April, 2003, *http://www. leslie-cheung.com/leslie/2004/5-31/14148.html*, http://www. leslie-cheung.com 2004-5-31 1:39:28.

Ngai, Jimmy, 'Nomad', *http://lesliecheung.cc/memories/magazines/ legacy/nomad.htm*.

'People who support Leslie', *http://www.bbs6.netease.com* (Date of publication and author unknown).

Priceless is a Cavalier, Brilliant his Blossoms', *http://lesliecheung.cc/ memories/magazines/legacy/priceless_is_a_cavalier.htm*.

Red Forum, Tai Sing Pao, 20 March 2004, 'Movies Which Leslie Did Not Star In Or Have Failed To Finish', *http://bbs6.netease. com/ent/*.

Red Mission, April 2004 Commemoration, *http://lesliecheung. cc/Redmission/401_05/salute.htm*, *http://www.lesliecheung.cc/ Redmission/401_05/Index.htm*.

Ren-lei, 'Ren-Lei Talking About God-Father Gor-Gor', *http:// lesliecheung.cc/memories/yanlui_eng.htm*.

Shaw Brothers, *www.shawstudios.com*

'The Shining Star – In Reminiscence of Leslie's Artistic Life',

Seminar, 3 April 2005, Hong Kong International Trade & Exhibition Centre, Lam Kay To, *http://www.leslie-cheung. info/20050403.html.*

SPCNET TV, review of *Gone With the Wind* : http://www.spcnet. tv/ATV-TV-Series/Gone-With-the-Wind-review-r2112.html.

'Teresa Mo Cable TV Interview with Leslie Cheung', March 2001: http://www.lesliecheung.cc/Special/translation/teresamo.htm.

'Tribute to a Legend' ; Leslie Exhibit Opens at Madame Tussaud's : http://xoomer.virgilio.it/nguidett/tussaud.htm.

Ugaya, Hiromichi, interview, *http://forever.lesliecheung.cn/nindex. htm* (30 November 2003).

Wikipedia, 'Leslie Cheung', http://en.wikipedia.org/wiki/ Leslie_Cheung.

Wu Xia Society, Leslie's shows: http://wuxiasociety.org/forum/ viewtopic.php?t=199.

YOUTUBE OR SIMILAR SITES
(AS AT 1-17 AUGUST 2010)

1977 - Leslie singing 'American Pie' in the singing competition in 1977: http://www.youtube.com/watch?v=aDiUac4UZ_Y.

1977 – Photos from around the time of *Daydreamin'*: http://www.youtube.com/watch?gl=HK&feature=related&hl=zh-TW&v=GLug-yYF6yU; http://www.youtube.com/watch?v=GLug-yYF6yU&feature=related.

1978 – RTV's programme *Crocodile Tears:* http://www.youtube.com/watch?v=AplCUhW8OG0&feature=PlayList&p=1ED21090ADA4AD42&playnext=1&index=92

1978 – Photos from 1978: http://www.youtube.com/watch?v=NVkNm-C35o8&feature=related; http://www.youtube.com/watch?v=ijLhr6ZCgNc&feature=related.

1979 - Photos from 1979: http://www.youtube.com/watch?v=M-D8atxBnAw&feature=related.

1980 – RTV's programme *Gone with the Wind*: http://www.youtube.com/watch?v=NGVZG6SsOOc.

1981 - Episodes from *Pairing*: http://www.youtube.com/watch?v=Q3RxrbsIh7g; http://www.youtube.com/watch?v=lFKSK-DDk_I.

1981 – *On Trial*: http://www.youtube.com/watch?gl=HK&hl=zh-TW&v=pHnEExpsBK0.

1982 – Photos from 1978-1982: http://www.youtube.com/watch?v=IjlsPXhp3Y4&feature=related.

1984 – 'Thanks, Monica': http://www.youtube.com/watch?v=UD92ECnCrTc.

1985 – Leslie Cheung in Concert: http://www.tudou.com/programs/view/JGboQxDbGFw/.

1985 – Leslie Cheung in Concert with Danny Chan: http://www.youtube.com/watch?gl=HK&feature=related&hl=zh-TW&v=1D-wP2audUU.

1985 – Café de Coral advertisement: http://www.youtube.com/watch?v=MNTfvlFaPoU.

Leslie's MV of *A Better Tomorrow*: http://www.youtube.com/watch?v=u6lXDSbwHXg.

'Stand Up': http://www.youtube.com/watch?v=BmhtFcB9m3o.

Leslie's pop MVs: http://www.youtube.com/watch?v=1vzLRFedteQ; http://www.youtube.com/watch?v=Dn6cbQeS2Is.

1986 – Leslie and Anita in concert: http://vids.myspace.com/index.cfm?fuseaction=vids.individual&videoid=51470001.

1986 – Leslie at the Vancouver Expo: http://www.tudou.com/programs/view/JGboQxDbGFw/.

1986 – Leslie's Konica advertisement: http://www.videomeli.com/video/XdNukN5rTUw/leslie-konica-commercial-1986.html.

1986 – Leslie Cheung in Concert: http://www.lesliecheung-dreamworld.com/Concerts/Concert1986/Concert1986.htm.

1986 – Leslie at Hong Kong Beauty Pageant: http://www.

youtube.com/watch?v=JYzCSOuET1o&feature=related; http://www.youtube.com/watch?v=0oIMQiWvRlw&feature=related; http://www.youtube.com/watch?v=nuejpEC5sHk&feature=related.

1987 – Leslie's Pepsi advertisement: http://www.youtube.com/watch?v=2La-7TLhag0.

1987 – Leslie's interview with Michael Lai: http://www.youtube.com/watch?v=ngStshBHTwE&feature=related.

1987 – Leslie in Malaysia: http://www.youtube.com/watch?v=ZIlk_6lTouM&feature=related; http://www.youtube.com/watch?v=Eh8UuxNN9Fo&feature=related; http://www.youtube.com/watch?v=XJgR7bqH7ug&feature=related.

1988 - *Rouge*: http://www.youtube.com/watch?v=-L_yGHrzi54.

1988 – Leslie's Pepsi advertisement: http://www.dailymotion.com/video/xwrrm_pepsi-89_ads.

1988 – Leslie in Xaioyan's Mandarin talkshow, 'Windows': http://www.youtube.com/watch?v=hgPCVRpfnSI&feature=related; http://www.youtube.com/watch?v=CeBXq2sihco&feature=related. http://www.youtube.com/watch?v=wsgvh-Q-URU&feature=related.

1988 – Leslie Cheung in Concert '88: http://www.youtube.com/watch?gl=GB&hl=en-GB&v=foLXtvzIwa4; http://www.youtube.com/watch?v=lrACl6vCJ48.

1989 - 'Sideface': http://www.youtube.com/watch?v=4UeE122WoI8.

1989 – Leslie's performance at the ATV Miss Asia Pageant: http://www.youtube.com/watch?v=h3Nt9fnPcMQ.

1989 – Leslie's Korean chocolate advertisement: http://www.lesliecheung-dreamworld.com/Video/Advertisements.htm#KoreanAdvertToYou.

1989 – 'Final Encounter' concert: http://www.youtube.com/watch?v=gdkM1a14PaI.

1990 – Leslie in China flood fundraising concert in Vancouver: http://www.youtube.com/watch?v=qgNkGk36NMI&feature=related.

1991 – Leslie in *The Banquet: http://www.youtube.com/watch?v=Mw4DgFV7aMI*.

1993 – MV of *Farewell My Concubine*: http://www.youtube.com/watch?v=lGWRoVrBwx8.

1993 – *A Chinese Ghost Story*: http://www.youtube.com/watch?v=72gIFY7cyRk.

1994 – MV of 'Chase': http://www.youtube.com/watch?v=0_LmHKbIUEI.

? - Leslie with Anita Mui in 'Fongwah': http://www.youtube.com/watch?v=g5Q-05uCXYY.

1995 - 'A Thousand Dreams of You': http://www.youtube.com/watch?v=E4_WbwwPweo.

1996 - 'Red': http://www.youtube.com/watch?v=xDC9HQsbuN4.

1998 - 'Printemps': http://www.youtube.com/watch?v=S16YOGZHyqE.

1998 - 'The Truth' - http://www.youtube.com/watch?v=1syaAuu2vsE.

1997 – MV of *Happy Together*: http://www.youtube.com/watch?v=gb0u3bmflII&feature=related.

1998 – *Anna Magdalena* (9 parts): http://www.iidrama.com/Chinese_movie/Anna_Magdalena-994-1.html.

1999 - *Moonlight Express*: http://www.youtube.com/watch?v=IS0XC7fpXzA

1999 – *Buenos Aires Zero Degrees* (3 parts): http://www.youtube.com/watch?v=sFeFGBvpdd4.

1999 - *Stark Impressions*: http://www.youtube.com/watch?v=zCJS0M1XCsU.

1999 – Singapore charity concert: http://www.youtube.com/watch?v=7FMcFPjVilk&feature=related; http://www.youtube.com/watch?v=UB30-3E0vqg&feature=related; http://www.youtube.com/watch?v=DMMl7LFQTwk&feature=related; http://www.youtube.com/watch?v=radMRmHNvDM&feature=related; http://www.youtube.com/watch?v=uXtuZO9OdQU&feature=

related and http://www.youtube.com/watch?v=5P0Ll8efTdg&feature=related.

1999 - Leslie in Hiroshima: http://www.youtube.com/watch?v=SyL1JuobzDQ&feature=related; http://www.youtube.com/watch?v=Xk3RxXEYsFQ&feature=related; http://www.youtube.com/watch?v=ijn3rs9N5oM&feature=related.

2000 – 'Pillow Song': : http://www.youtube.com/watch?v=qg-3ymesKTY.

2000 - 'I Honestly Love You': http://www.youtube.com/watch?v=NuFUAJnUAYc.

2000 – Leslie in *Okinawa Rendez-ous*: http://www.youtube.com/watch?v=9Ws5yU66lUM. 'Without Love': http://www.youtube.com/watch?v=eaHzDfNHGbY.

2001 – Leslie at the CASH ceremony: http://www.youtube.com/watch?v=BdMITSPTMvA&feature=related.

2001 – Leslie on Teresa Mo's Cable TV talk show: http://www.youtube.com/watch?v=SXcchppDujM&feature=related; http://www.youtube.com/watch?v=UsNQwV6vogU&feature=related; http://www.youtube.com/watch?v=0Di6BfOigMI&feature=related;

2001 – Leslie and Kazuhiro Nishijima in 'Bewildered': http://www.youtube.com/watch?v=Tt0iAHS8pe8.

2001 – Leslie and Anita Mui 'Yuenfen': http://www.youtube.com/

watch?v=XIiWR8E1SZs&p=33DE254C60D185C4&playnext=1&index=18.

2002 – Leslie at the Hong Kong Film Academy Awards: http://www.youtube.com/watch?v=Qsg_sY2_rg4&feature=related.

2002 - Leslie interview with Stephen Chow: http://www.youtube.com/watch?v=WK7RSmR_WAU&feature=related.

2003 – The Twins with Leslie in a cameo role: http://www.youtube.com/watch?v=TjVnQzkcqGo.

2003 – Leslie's funeral: http://www.youtube.com/watch?v=Y7JMXSC1AgE&feature=related; http://www.youtube.com/watch?v=h-fwv5K5lew&feature=related; http://www.youtube.com/watch?v=p5Iit8LV_Z4&feature=related.

2003 – 'Walking Through The Shadows; A Tribute to Leslie Cheung', Bey Logan, http://www.youtube.com/watch?gl=HK&hl=zh-TW&v=zRSef-4CvZg.

CDS, DVDS, VCDS

A Better Tomorrow, Deltamac, Fortune Star DVD78007.

A Better Tomorrow II, Deltamac, Fortune Star VCD 7104.

A Chinese Ghost Story, Deltamac, Fortune Star DVD78035.

A Chinese Ghost Story II, Deltamac, Fortune Star VCD7004.

A Time to Remember, City Connection DVD, CL-DVD 379.

Aces Go Places V, part of the boxed set, *Aces Go Places Series*, Intercontinental Video, Fortune Star, digitally remastered, no serial number.

Agency 24, Asiaview Entertainment (US) YesAsia VCD 1001906026 issued 23 October 2002.

'All about Leslie' (*Celebrity Talk Show 30, Off-guard Tonight*, Asia Television Ltd, Universe Laser & Video).

All's Well Ends Well, Wide Sight VCD WSVCD1158.

All's Well Ends Well Too, Wide Sight DVD, no number.

All's Well End's Well '97, Garry's Trading Co DVD GAD200465.

Arrest the Restless, Deltamac, Fortune Star DVD 78089.

Ashes of Time, Mei Ah Entertainment VCD075.

Ashes to Ashes, in RTHK, Intercontinental Video DVD 010927.

Behind the Yellow Line, SB Celestial Pictures, Intercontinental Video VCD 612459.

Cheung Kwok-wing, Cinepoly CD 174352-6.

Collective Memories of Leslie Cheung; the Works of 1970s-2000s (Hong Kong: RTHK, DVD 010927).

Crazy Romance, Fortune Star, Deltamac Hong Kong DVD 78077.

Days of Being Wild, Media Asia, Megastar Video Distribution VCD MS/VCD/663/Hong Kong.

Double Tap, Universe Laser & Video Co VCD 2497.

Dreaming, Cinepoly CD 982544-8.

Energetic 21, Fortune Star Legendary Collection, Joy Sales Films and Video Distributors VCD, JS/VCD/3050/HK.

Erotic Dream of Red Chamber, Seasonal Film Corporation, Fine Arts DVD, FADS-00054.

Farewell My Concubine, Miramax Classics DVD 17368.

Fatal Love, Deltamac, Fortune Star VCD 7240.

For Your Heart Only, Deltamac, Fortune Star VCD 7186.

Final Encounter, Cinepoly CD 17359-9.

Final Encounter of the Legend Karaoke, New Century Workshop, Corrys DVDNC0102D.

Happy Together, Mei Ah Laser Disc Co VCD795.

He's a Woman, She's a Man, Fitto Mobile Laser Disc Distribution Co, VCD FMO10 A&B.

History: His Story, Capital Artists 4 disc compilation VCD CD-03-1333, 2004.

Hot Summer, Cinepoly CD 170835-0.

Inner Senses, Universe Laser & Video Co, VCD 3611.

It's a Wonderful Life, Wide Sight VCD WSVCD1225.

Leslie Cheung Final Encounter with the Legend, Cinepoly CD 846 301-2.

Leslie Cheung Kwok-wing, Cineploy CD 173628-4.

Leslie Cheung Kwok-wing (Allure Me), Capital Artists re-issue CD 1 December 2005.

Leslie Cheung Live in Concert 97, Rock (Hong Kong) Co, ROL 5150.

Leslie Cheung Live in Concert 97, Rock Records CD ROD 515.

Leslie, His Story (Hong Kong: Noel Music Publishing, 2006).

Leslie Cheung Passion Tour, Universal Cd 548 591-2.

Leslie in Concert '88, Cinepoly CDs 980922-78 and 88.

Little Dragon Maiden, SB Celestial Pictures, Intercontinental Video VCD 100536.

Long & Winding Road, Mei Ah Entertainment VCD CF 40245V.

Love, Rock Records CD RD 1319.

Make a Wish, Asia Television Ltd and Fat Kee records Ltd DVD FADVD7007 and VCD FAVCD8088.

Merry Christmas, Fortune Star, Deltamac Hong Kong VCD, 7174.

Moonlight Express, Mei Ah Entertainment DVD-579 with CD MMCD87003.

Ninth Happiness, Mei Ah Entertainment VCD1050.

Nomad, Hong Kong Movie, Mei Ah Entertainment DVD, DVD-283.

Okinawa Rendez-vous, Mei Ah Entertainment VCD 1956.

On Trial, Wing Artist Entertainment, Winson Entertainment Distribution DVD, WDV 34058, 34060.

Once a Thief, Deltamac, Fortune Star DVD 78118.

Once upon an Ordinary Girl, Sensasian.com, Modern Audio VCD V0920H.

Over the Rainbow, Under the Skirt, Fitto Entertainment (Hong Kong) VCD.

Pairing, Panorama Entertainment 10 VCD Boxset, PANCD304067.

Passion Tour, Universal DVD 060-839-9.

Printemps, Rock Records CD RD 1468.

Red, Rock Records CD ROD 5132.

Rouge, Intercontinental Video, Fortune Star DVD, digitally remastered, no serial number.

Shanghai Grand, Mei Ah Laser Disc Co VCD0475.

Stand Up, Capital Artists CD 03-1352.

Summer Romance '87, Cinepoly CD 983364-7.

Tai Chi Master I & II; East Media Entertainment Inc, YesAsia DVD 1012162133 issued 15 November 2008.

Teenage Dreamers, SB Celestial Pictures, Intercontinental Video Ltd VCD 611438.

Temptress Moon, Mei Ah Entertainment DVD-199.

The Banquet, Pan-Asia, Inc, VHS; Mei Ah Laser Disc VCD.

The Bride with White Hair, Universe Laser & Video Co, VCD 1215.

The Bride with White Hair 2, Wide Sight VCD WSVCD1217.

The Cheap Detective, Asia Television and Fat Kee Recordings DVD FADVD7008, and VCD FAVCD8089.

The Chinese Feast, Wide Sight VCD WSVCD1242.

The Drummer (Japanese version), Broadway, Yeasasia DVD, 1003627638, issued 8 October 2004. There is an older Cantonese version on VCD no longer available.

The Eagle Shooting Heroes, Mei Ah Entertainment VCD035.

The Fallen Family, TVB VCD, 2005.

The Intellectual Trio, Fortune Star, Deltamac Hong Kong VCD 7097.

The Kid, Mei Ah Laser Disc Co, DVD-246.

The Phantom Lover, Wide Sight VCD WSVCD1264.

The Spirit of the Sword; Asiaview Entertainment YesAsia DVD 1005053622 issued 8 October 2007.

The Wind Blows On, Capital Artists CD-03-1004.

Tristar, Wide Sight VCD WSVCD1268.

Virgin Snow, Cinepoly CD 170834-9.

Viva Erotica, Universe DVD 5023.

Who's the Woman, Who's the Man, Mei Ah Entertainment DVD-592.

Notes to pages 11-23

[1] Press summary in 'Leslie Cheung Internet Fan Club', www.lesliecheung.com; http://forum.lesliecheung.com/Forum62/HTML/000054.html.

[2] Press summary in 'Leslie Cheung Internet Fan Club', www.lesliecheung.com; http://forum.lesliecheung.com/Forum62/HTML/000054.html.

[3] Press summary in 'Leslie Cheung Internet Fan Club', www.lesliecheung.com; http://forum.lesliecheung.com/Forum62/HTML/000054.html.

[4] Stewart, Clare, and Philippa Hawker, eds, *Leslie Cheung* (Flinders Lane, Australia: Australian Centre for the Moving Image, 2003).

[5] *South China Morning Post*, 14 July 2003.

[6] *South China Morning Post*, 28 April 2003.

[7] *Cashflow*, no. 41, June 2003 (James Wong, 'In Fond Memory of Leslie Cheung').

[8] Press summary in 'Leslie Cheung Internet Fan Club', www.lesliecheung.com; http://forum.lesliecheung.com/Forum62/HTML/000054.html.

[9] Press summary in 'Leslie Cheung Internet Fan Club', www.lesliecheung.com; http://forum.lesliecheung.com/Forum62/HTML/000054.html.

[10] *South China Morning Post*, 28 April 2003.

[11] Entry in a register of births, Hong Kong, dated 18 September 1956, reference 13012 B&D.

[12] Leslie interviews: *City Magazine*, 1985 (Mak Uen Shou, 'Cheung Kwok-wing Cohabited with a Love Swindler'); *Time Asia*, 3 April 2003 (Richard Corliss, 'That Old Feeling: Days of Being Leslie').

[13] Leslie interviews: *Hong Kong Visitor* (Hong Kong: *South China Morning Post*, 1994), *Aera Magazine*, 1998 (Hiro Ugaya, 'I'm a Perfectionist Either with Movies or Songs'); Chitose Shima, *All About Leslie* (Tokyo: Sangyo Henshu Center Co., 1999).

[14] Leslie interviews: *Positif*, 1998 ('Berlin Film Festival', http://xoomer.virgilio.it/nguidett/berlin.htm); no. 455, 1999 ('Michael Ciment and Hugo Niogret interview').

[15] Autobiography by Leslie (1985) Commercial Radio.

[16] Autobiography by Leslie (1985) Commercial Radio.

[17] *City Magazine*, 1985 (Mak Uen Shou, 'Cheung Kwok-wing Cohabited with a Love Swindler'); *Hong Kong Visitor* (Hong Kong: *South China Morning Post*, 1994).

[18] Autobiography by Leslie (1985) Commercial Radio; *Ming Pao Weekly/ Ming Chow*, 901, 1986 ('Leslie is Afraid of Getting Married'); *Los Angeles Times*, 22 June 1997 (Kevin Thomas, 'A Career in Full Bloom'); Chitose Shima, *All About Leslie* (Tokyo: Sangyo Henshu Center Co., 1999); *Time Asia*, 3 April 2003 (Richard Corliss, 'That Old Feeling: Days of Being Leslie'), quoting an article by Stephen Short, May 2001.

Notes to pages 23-28

[19] *City Magazine*, 1985 (Mak Uen Shou, 'Cheung Kwok-wing Cohabited with a Love Swindler'); Chitose Shima, *All About Leslie* (Tokyo: Sangyo Henshu Center Co., 1999).

[20] Autobiography by Leslie (1985) Commercial Radio; Chitose Shima, *All About Leslie* (Tokyo: Sangyo Henshu Center Co., 1999).

[21] Autobiography by Leslie (1985) Commercial Radio; *City Magazine*, 1985 (Mak Uen Shou, 'Cheung Kwok-wing Cohabited with a Love Swindler').

[22] Autobiography by Leslie (1985) Commercial Radio; *City Magazine*, 1985 (Mak Uen Shou, 'Cheung Kwok-wing Cohabited with a Love Swindler').

[23] *City Magazine*, 1985 (Mak Uen Shou, 'Cheung Kwok-wing Cohabited with a Love Swindler'); Chitose Shima, *All About Leslie* (Tokyo: Sangyo Henshu Center Co., 1999).

[24] Autobiography by Leslie (1985) Commercial Radio; Chitose Shima, *All About Leslie* (Tokyo: Sangyo Henshu Center Co., 1999); *Time Asia*, 3 April 2003 (Richard Corliss, 'That Old Feeling: Days of Being Leslie').

[25] Autobiography by Leslie (1985) Commercial Radio; Chitose Shima, *All About Leslie* (Tokyo: Sangyo Henshu Center Co., 1999).

[26] Welsh, Frank, *A History of Hong Kong* (London: Harper Collins, 1997), pp. 448-466.

[27] Autobiography by Leslie (1985) Commercial Radio.

[28] Balke, Gerd, *Hong Kong Voices* (Hong Kong: ?, 1989); *Civil Service Newsletter Editorial Board* (undated) 'The Pioneering Administrative Officer Duo'; *Next Magazine*, 1997 ('Interview With Leslie', http://lesliecheung.cc/Magazine/1997/next97/next97.htm).

[29] Autobiography by Leslie (1985) Commercial Radio.

[30] Chitose Shima, *All About Leslie* (Tokyo: Sangyo Henshu Center Co., 1999); 'Legendary Years of Our Leslie: A Biography', by Eunike, http://xoomer.virgilio.it/nguidett/biography01.htm.

[31] Chitose Shima, *All About Leslie* (Tokyo: Sangyo Henshu Center Co., 1999).

[32] Entry in a register of births, Hong Kong, dated 18 September 1956, reference 13012 B&D, alteration dated 10 March 1964.

[33] Autobiography by Leslie (1985) Commercial Radio.

[34] Balke, Gerd, *Hong Kong Voices* (Hong Kong: ?, 1989); Welsh, Frank, A History of Hong Kong (London: Harper Collins, 1997), pp. 461-491; *Aera Magazine*, 1998 (Hiro Ugaya, 'I'm a Perfectionist Either With Movies or Songs'); *Time Asia*, 3 April 2003 (Richard Corliss, 'That Old Feeling: Days of Being Leslie').

[35] The detail of Leslie's life at Rosaryhill is taken from his own words in the Autobiography by Leslie (1985) Commercial Radio; Chitose Shima, *All About Leslie* (Tokyo: Sangyo Henshu Center Co., 1999); author interview with Father Francisco de las Heras, Supervisor and Principal, Rosaryhill School, 13 June 2006.

Notes to pages 30-34

[36] Leslie participated in a speaking contest, according to Mr Robert Kwan, one of his fellow pupils; email from Mr Robert Kwan to the author, 15 June 2006.

[37] Private email communication between the author and Father Lionel Xavier O.P., 13 June 2006

[38] Information from Father Francisco de las Hoeras, Supervisor and Principal, Rosaryhill School, 13 June 206.

[39] Email to the author from Mr Edward Ng, Chairman of Rosaryhill's Old Students' Association, 13 June 2006.

[40] *City Magazine*, 1985 (Mak Uen Shou, 'Cheung Kwok-wing Cohabited with a Love Swindler').

[41] *City Magazine*, 1985 (Mak Uen Shou, 'Cheung Kwok-wing Cohabited with a Love Swindler').

[42] 'Did you have any love affairs while you were studying?' 'Yes, but those were puppy love', *City Magazine*, 1985 (Mak Uen Shou, 'Cheung Kwok-wing Cohabited with a Love Swindler'),

[43] Author interview with anonymous informant, Hong Kong, 27 October 2008.

[44] Author interview with Ms Anna Sum, teacher, Buddhist Wong Fung Ling College, 18 November 2006.

[45] Buddhist Wong Fung Ling College Examination report for 1972/73 in the possession of New Eccles Hall School.

[46] Chitose Shima, *All About Leslie* (Tokyo: Sangyo Henshu Center Co., 1999).

[47] Leslie usually referred to them as 'relatives' but Mr B. Simington makes plain in his letter to Leslie's father of 25 April 1974 (in the possession of New Eccles Hall School) that they were friends of Leslie's father.

[48] *Time*, 3 May 2000 (Stephen Short, 'Bedroom Pinup').

[49] Letter from Bobby K.W. Cheung to Mr Simington, Eccles Hall, dated 15 July 1973, in the possession of New Eccles Hall School; Autobiography by Leslie (1985) Commercial Radio; *Positif*, 1998 ('Berlin Film Festival', http://xoomer. virgilio.it/nguidett/berlin.htm); no. 455, 1999 ('Michael Ciment and Hugo Niogret interview', 21 February 1998); *Time Asia*, 3 April 2003 (Richard Corliss, 'That Old Feeling: Days of Being Leslie').

[50] Leslie is confused about the order in which the English exam system then worked, writing first of A levels and then of G.C.E.s (which were O Levels and actually preceded A levels); letter from Frankie Bobby K.W. Cheung to the Principal, Eccles Hall School, dated 25 July 1973, in the possession of New Eccles Hall School. His form of application for admission to the school, dated 7 August 1973, gives his name as Frankie Bobby CHEUNG.

Notes to pages 34-38

[51] Letter from Frankie Bobby Cheung Kwok Wing to Mr B. Simington dated 7 August 1973. The change was complete before he left Hong Kong; in his letter to Mr Simington of 28 August, announcing that he would arrive in London on 8 September, he signs himself Frankie Cheung; letter from Frankie Cheung to Mr Simington dated 28 August. All letters in the possession of New Eccles Hall School.

[52] Author interview Mr Sean Symington, Proprietor, New Eccles Hall School, Norfolk, 29 September 2006.

[53] Leslie later described his experiences at Eccles Hall in: Autobiography by Leslie (1985) Commercial Radio; *Hong Kong Standard* (20 October 1986*); Positif*, 1998 ('Berlin Film Festival', http://xoomer.virgilio.it/nguidett/berlin.htm); no. 455, 1999 ('Michael Ciment and Hugo Niogret interview', 21 February 1998); *Time*, 3 May 2000 (Stephen Short, 'Bedroom Pinup'); *Time Asia*, 3 April 2003 (Richard Corliss, 'That Old Feeling: Days of Being Leslie').

[54] Eccles Hall School report for the summer term 1974, in the possession of New Eccles Hall School.

[55] Chitose Shima, *All About Leslie* (Tokyo: Sangyo Henshu Center Co., 1999).

[56] *Time Asia*, vol. 157, No. 18, May 2001 (Richard Corliss, 'Forever Leslie').

[57] Eccles Hall School report for the summer term 1974, in the possession of New Eccles Hall School.

[58] Letter S.3/P from Mr S. Semple, Chief Education Officer, London Borough of Bexley, to the Head Master, Eccles Hall School, 5 April 1974, including a typed transcript of Mrs Kelly's letter.

[59] File note on the correspondence by Mr. Mortimer B. Simington.

[60] Letter from Mr Mortimer B. Simington to Leslie's father dated 25 April 1974, in the possession of New Eccles Hall School.

[61] Letter to the Head Master from Mr W.H. Cheung, tailor Cheung, Yip Fung Building, 18 D'Aguilar St, dated 11 May 1974, in the possession of New Eccles Hall School.

[62] Term report on Frankie Cheung for Summer Term 1974, Eccles Hall School. Letter from Mr W.H. Cheung to the school dated 7 October 1974 enquiring about Leslie's luggage 'from the time Frankie arrived, it has been already three and a half months', in the possession of New Eccles Hall School. The School possesses also a copy of an HSBC bank remittance of £50 sent to Frankie at the school on 5 June 1974, presumably to fund his return.

Notes to pages 39-41

[63] Leslie gave differing accounts in: Autobiography by Leslie (1985) Commercial Radio; ATV, 25 June 1989, 'Interview with Leslie Cheung' by James Wong and two others; *Positif*, 1998 ('Berlin Film Festival', http://xoomer.virgilio.it/nguidett/berlin.htm); no. 455, 1999 ('Michael Ciment and Hugo Niogret interview', 21 February 1998); Chitose Shima, *All About Leslie* (Tokyo: Sangyo Henshu Center Co., 1999). By the time he made his 1985 radio autobiography in which he claimed that he had been to Leeds University, he had clearly forgotten the interview he gave Evans Chan of the *Hong Kong Standard* (4 April 1982) in which he had said he had been brought back to Hong Kong *before* going to Leeds as his father had 'had a stroke and became half-paralysed.'

[64] Inquiries to King Edward VI Grammar School, Chelmsford, the only school in that town likely to have taken foreign boarders then, received the following reply by email to the author on 22 July 2006 from Mrs Lindsey Clarke: 'The above named did not attend King Edward VI Grammar School, Chelmsford.'

[65] Personal email communications on 21 June 2006 and 8 August 2006 between the author and Mr James Anthony Smith, Education/Access Officer, University of Leeds International Textiles Archive, who was on the staff in the Department of Textile Industries in 1974 and 1975. Mr Smith states that: 'We are all rather perturbed here at Leeds, because we cannot find any trace of Leslie Cheung Kwok-wing either in the departmental records or those held in the University Archive' in the period 1972-1978. There was one Chinese student there in the late seventies, Leslie Yip Sai-chung, who went on to become Professor at the Polytechnic University of Hong Kong.' In an email of 17 October 2006 to the author, Professor Yip states: 'I have never seen him or even heard of him. At that time, there were very few Chinese students studying undergraduate programmes in Textiles at Leeds. I know all the few who came after me to Leeds and there is only one Chinese from Indonesia called Kimmy Buhan before me in 1975 and 1976 class in Textile Management.'

[66] Leslie actually stated that this was so in: Autobiography by Leslie (1985) Commercial Radio. Several photographs of him at the College exist dated 1976.

[67] Email to the author from Ms Alice Leung, Principal Assistant Secretary, Education and Manpower Bureau, dated 20 June 2007: 'We have tried but failed to trace the record of individual student of the school.' No other record of Wellington College exists either in the Bureau or the Public Records Office; email to the author from Mr Bernard Hui, Assistant Archivist, Public Records Office, 13 November 2006.

[68] Autobiography by Leslie (1985) Commercial Radio.

[69] This age is incorrect. This was after Leslie returned from England, making Leslie about 18 or 19.

[70] Chitose Shima, *All About Leslie* (Tokyo: Sangyo Henshu Center Co., 1999).

[71] ATV, 25 June 1989, 'Interview with Leslie Cheung' by James Wong and two others.

Notes to pages 41-49

[72] Autobiography by Leslie (1985) Commercial Radio.

[73] *Hong Kong Standard* (14 November 1987).

[74] ATV, 25 June 1989, 'Interview with Leslie Cheung' by James Wong and two others.

[75] See ATV, 25 June 1989, 'Interview with Leslie Cheung' by James Wong and two others; *Los Angeles Times*, 22 June 1997 (Kevin Thomas, 'A Career in Full Bloom'); *Positif*, 1998 ('Berlin Film Festival', http://xoomer.virgilio.it/nguidett/berlin.htm); no. 455, 1999 ('Michael Ciment and Hugo Niogret interview', 21 February 1998).

[76] Leslie told the tale of his entry to the singing competition in: Autobiography by Leslie (1985) Commercial Radio; ATV, 25 June 1989, 'Interview with Leslie Cheung' by James Wong and two others. Florence Chan gave her version in: Chitose Shima, *All About Leslie* (Tokyo: Sangyo Henshu Center Co., 1999). Other details are found in: *Hong Kong Standard*, 12 August 1985; 16 December 1989; 14 January 1990; 22 December 1996.

[77] 'Who Will Win Tonight's Contest is Anyone's Guess', *Hong Kong Standard*, 16 May 1977; 'A Song for Asia', *South China Morning Post*, 16 May 1977.

[78] Leslie's performance can be viewed on Youtube at: http://www.youtube.com/watch?v=aDiUac4UZ_Y.

[79] Autobiography by Leslie (1985) Commercial Radio.

[80] *City Magazine*, 1985 (Mak Uen Shou, 'Cheung Kwok-wing Cohabited with a Love Swindler'); ATV, 25 June 1989, 'Interview with Leslie Cheung' by James Wong and two others.

[81] Autobiography by Leslie (1985) Commercial Radio.

[82] Chong, Milan, *Pop Stars in Hong Kong* (Hong Kong: Sing Tao Educational Publications, 1989).

[83] Autobiography by Leslie (1985) Commercial Radio. Lai Wan was shortly thereafter developed into the huge Mei Foo housing estate. Lai Wan station was built on the new underground Mass Transit Railway line in 1982-85, and this later was renamed Lai Chi Kok.

[84] Welsh, Frank, A History of Hong Kong (London: Harper Collins, 1997), pp. 466-504.

[85] Detail on Hong Kong's TV culture is from: 'The Absorption and Indigenisation of Foreign Media Cultures; Hong Kong as a Meeting Point of East and West' by Paul S.N. Lee, in Law Kar, ed., *Hong Kong Cinema in the Eighties: A Comparative Study with Western Cinema* (Hong Kong: Urban Council, 1991), p. 78.

Notes to pages 49-52

[86] 'Television in the 70s: Its State of Being' by Cheuk pak-tong., in *Hong Kong Twenty-third International Film Festival, Hong Kong New Wave: Twenty Years After* (Hong Kong: Urban Council, 1999), p. 28; Zhuo, Botang and Cheuk Pak Tong, *Hong Kong New Wave Cinema (1978-2000)* (Bristol: Intellect Books, 2008), p. 35; Yau, Esther C.M., ed., *At Full Speed: Hong Kong Cinema in a Borderless World* (Minneapolis: University of Minnesota Press, 2001), p. 44.

[87] *Hong Kong Standard* 11 July 1981 and 12 August 1983.

[88] *City Magazine*, 1985 (Mak Uen Shou, 'Cheung Kwok-wing Cohabited with a Love Swindler').

[89] Autobiography by Leslie (1985) Commercial Radio.

[90] Detail on Hong Kong film in the seventies is taken from: Hill, John and Pamela Gibson, eds, *World Cinema: Critical Approaches* (New York: Oxford University Press, 2000); Hong Kong Twenty-first International Film Festival, *Hong Kong Cinema Retrospective: Fifty Years of Electric Shadows* (Hong Kong: Urban Council, 1997); Law Kar, ed., *Hong Kong Cinema in the Eighties: A Comparative Study with Western Cinema* (Hong Kong: Urban Council, 1991); Lent, John, *The Asian Film Industry* (Austin: University of Texas Press, 1990); Nowell-Smith, Geoffrey, ed., *The Oxford History of World Cinema* (Oxford: Oxford University Press, 1996); Server, Lee, *Asian Pop Cinema: Bombay to Tokyo* (San Francisco: Chronicle Books, 1999); Fu Poshek and Davis Desser, eds, *The Cinema of Hong Kong: History, Arts, Identity* (Cambridge: Cambridge University Press, 2000); Pang, Laikwan and Day Wong, eds, *Masculinities and Hong Kong Cinema* (Hong Kong: Hong Kong University Press, 2005).

[91] *Erotic Dream of Red Chamber*, Seasonal Film Corporation, Fine Arts DVD, FADS-00054. Leslie's account of this film is in Autobiography by Leslie (1985) Commercial Radio. See also: *Mingpao*, 17 July 2003 (Too Kit, 'Bo Gorgor'); *Time Asia*, 3 April 2003 (Richard Corliss, 'That Old Feeling: Days of Being Leslie'); Leslie's interview in Fredric Dannen *Hong Kong Babylon* (1997). Later reviewers have been kinder; see: 'The Shining Star – In Reminiscence of Leslie's Artistic Life', seminar, 3 April 2005, Hong Kong International Trade & Exhibition Centre, Lam Kay To, http://www.leslie-cheung.info/20050403.html.

[92] *Mingpao*, 17 July 2003 (Too Kit, 'Bo Gorgor').

[93] Autobiography by Leslie (1985) Commercial Radio; *City Magazine*, 1985 (Mak Uen Shou, 'Cheung Kwok-wing Cohabited with a Love Swindler'). *Daydreamin'*, re-issued by Polydor on CD980702-3B. Some photos of the time can be seen on Youtube at: http://www.youtube.com/watch?gl=HK&feature=relat ed&hl=zh-TW&v=GLug-yYF6yU.

[94] Autobiography by Leslie (1985) Commercial Radio; *City Magazine*, 1985 (Mak Uen Shou, 'Cheung Kwok-wing Cohabited with a Love Swindler').

[95] http://www.youtube.com/watch?v=e4YMMR2vPpl. The first of these songs was composed by Michael Lai Siu-tin.

Notes to pages 52-61

⁹⁶ Chitose Shima, *All About Leslie* (Tokyo: Sangyo Henshu Center Co., 1999).

⁹⁷ 'Legendary Years of Our Leslie: A Biography', by Eunike, http://xoomer. virgilio.it/nguidett/biography01.htm.

⁹⁸ Autobiography by Leslie (1985) Commercial Radio. A Youtube clip of the music and some of the show is at: http://www.youtube.com/watch?v=AplCUhW8 OG0&feature=PlayList&p=1ED21090ADA4AD42&playnext=1&index=92.

⁹⁹ http://blog.sina.com.cn/s/blog_60c38c6ft; http://www.lesliecheung.cc/main/library/944.

¹⁰⁰ Leslie interview with Teresa Mo, Cable TV. Leslie mentioned this cryptically in Chitose Shima, *All About Leslie* (Tokyo: Sangyo Henshu Center Co., 1999).

¹⁰¹ *Under the Same Roof: Teenagers*, in *Collective Memories of Leslie Cheung; the Works of 1970s-2000s* (Hong Kong: RTHK, DVD 010927).

¹⁰² *The Spirit of the Sword*; Asiaview Entertainment YesAsia DVD 1005053622 issued 8 October 2007.

¹⁰³ Autobiography by Leslie (1985) Commercial Radio.

¹⁰⁴ Leslie mentions them frequently in: Autobiography by Leslie (1985) Commercial Radio. Paul Chun Bo-law's real name was David Chan Chun-man.

¹⁰⁵ Leslie's friend, Jimmy Ngai Siu-yun, spoke of this time in: *City Entertainment*, 11 August 1991 (Ngai Siu-yun. 'A Living Legend from 23 to 34 Years Old').

¹⁰⁶ Autobiography by Leslie (1985) Commercial Radio.

¹⁰⁷ Autobiography by Leslie (1985) Commercial Radio.

¹⁰⁸ *South China Morning Post*, 9 November 1997.

¹⁰⁹ *South China Morning Post*, 9 November 1997.

¹¹⁰ Interview with anonymous friend of Leslie, 11 April 2011.

¹¹¹ *Ming Pao Weekly/ Ming Chow*, 30 August 1986 (Sek Kei, 'Film Teahouse'); 901, 1986 ('Leslie is afraid of getting married').

¹¹² *Dog Bites Dog Bone* has not been released on VCD or DVD.

¹¹³ Email to the author from Graham Elsom, 11 April 2011.

¹¹⁴ Autobiography by Leslie (1985) Commercial Radio.

¹¹⁵ Autobiography by Leslie (1985) Commercial Radio.

¹¹⁶ *Lover's Arrow*, re-issued by Polydor as CD 980710-9B.

¹¹⁷ Chong, Milan, *Pop Stars in Hong Kong* (Hong Kong: Sing Tao Educational Publications, 1989).

¹¹⁸ *No Big Deal (You ni mei ni)*; *Hong Kong Standard* 11 July 1981.

¹¹⁹ http://www.youtube.com/watch?v=9VqdgUuwg0w; http://www.tudou.com/programs/view/2z-bDxFk3ac/.

Notes to pages 61-65

120 For a review of *Gone with the Wind* see: http://www.spcnet.tv/ATV-TV-Series/Gone-With-the-Wind-review-r2112.html. A clip with music is on Youtube at: http://www.youtube.com/watch?v=NGVZG6SsOOc.

121 *Pairing*, Panorama Entertainment 10 VCD Boxset, PANCD304067.

122 'Legendary Years of Our Leslie: A Biography', by Eunike, http://xoomer.virgilio.it/nguidett/biography01.htm.

123 *Under the same Roof: Dead Knot*, in *Collective Memories of Leslie Cheung; the Works of 1970s-2000s* (Hong Kong: RTHK, DVD 010927).

124 *The Young Concubine*, in *Collective Memories of Leslie Cheung; the Works of 1970s-2000s* (Hong Kong: RTHK, DVD 010927). See also: *Hong Kong Standard*, 11 July 1981; *Hong Kong Twenty-third International Film Festival*, *Hong Kong New Wave: Twenty Years After* (Hong Kong: Urban Council, 1999), p.180; 'Leslie Cheung Artists Studies Website', 'Never Wanna Be Apart from Leslie: In Reminiscence of Leslie Cheung's Artistic Life' 30 April, 2003, Hong Kong Baptist University, http://www.leslie-cheung.com/leslie/2004/5-31/14148.html, http://www.leslie-cheung.com 2004-5-31 1:39:28, for discussion of the popularity of the show's theme music.

125 *Encore* has not been released on VCD or DVD. For Leslie's own comment see: Autobiography by Leslie (1985) Commercial Radio. See also: *Next Magazine*, 1997 ('Interview With Leslie', http://lesliecheung.cc/Magazine/1997/next97/next97.htm); 'The Shining Star – In Reminiscence of Leslie's Artistic Life', seminar, 3 April 2005, Hong Kong International Trade & Exhibition Centre, Lam Kay To, http://www.leslie-cheung.info/20050403.html.

126 Autobiography by Leslie (1985) Commercial Radio.

127 Evans Chan, 'Leslie Chang [sic] – Rich, Young, Famous', *Hong Kong Standard*, 4 April 1982.

128 Jean Yung Jing-Jing appeared also under the name Mary Jean Reimer Lau.

129 http://thirty-something-hk.blogspot.hk/2011/03/1980.html.

130 *Collective Memories of Leslie Cheung: the Works of 1970s-2000s*, RTHK Intercontinental Video DVD, 010927.

131 Autobiography by Leslie (1985) Commercial Radio. He told the same story to *City Magazine*, 1985 (Mak Uen Shou, 'Cheung Kwok-wing Cohabited with a Love Swindler').

132 'Legendary Years of Our Leslie: A Biography', by Eunike, http://xoomer.virgilio.it/nguidett/biography01.htm. Suet Lee is also written Suit Li and Michelle Yim was known also as Mai Suet.

133 Autobiography by Leslie (1985) Commercial Radio.

Notes to pages 66-72

[134] *Cosmopolitan Weekly* (*City Magazine*), 1985 (Zha Hsiaohsin, 'Cheung Kwok-wing Boldly Thrusts Forward to Refute Kai Yee Lin', http://lesliecheung. cc/Magazine/1985/metropolitan/text.htm); *City Magazine*, 1985 (Mak Uen Shou, 'Cheung Kwok-wing Cohabited with a Love Swindler'). See also: *City Entertainment*, 11 August 1991 (Ngai Siu-yun. 'A Living Legend from 23 to 34 Years Old').

[135] Chitose Shima, *All About Leslie* (Tokyo: Sangyo Henshu Center Co., 1999).

[136] *City Entertainment*, 11 August 1991 (Ngai Siu-yun, 'A Living Legend from 23 to 34 Years Old').

[137] *City Entertainment*, 11 August 1991 (Ngai Siu-yun, 'A Living Legend from 23 to 34 Years Old').

[138] Ngai was later to write the screenplay for the famous Chinese gay film *Lan Yu*.

[139] Suzie Wong's real name is Lau Ko-chung. In 2010, she came out as a lesbian and announced her partner was Taiwanese actress Elaine Jin.

[140] Autobiography by Leslie (1985) Commercial Radio.

[141] Autobiography by Leslie (1985) Commercial Radio.

[142] *Make a Wish*, Asia Television Ltd and Fat Kee records Ltd DVD FADVD7007 and VCD FAVCD8088.

[143] *Tai Chi Master I & II*; East Media Entertainment Inc, YesAsia DVD 1012162133 issued 15 November 2008.

[144] *Agency 24*, Asiaview Entertainment (US) YesAsia VCD 1001906026 issued 23 October 2002.

[145] *Job Hunter* has not been released on VCD or DVD. See: *Hong Kong Standard*, 11 July 1981.

[146] *On Trial*, Wing Artist Entertainment, Winson Entertainment Distribution DVD, WDV 34060. Leslie discusses this film in: Autobiography by Leslie (1985) Commercial Radio.

[147] Autobiography by Leslie (1985) Commercial Radio.

[148] Autobiography by Leslie (1985) Commercial Radio.

[149] *City Entertainment*, 11 August 1991 (Ngai Siu-yun, 'A Living Legend from 23 to 34 Years Old').

[150] *Hong Kong Standard*, 11 July 1981; Autobiography by Leslie (1985) Commercial Radio.

[151] Autobiography by Leslie (1985) Commercial Radio.

[152] Autobiography by Leslie (1985) Commercial Radio.

[153] *Hong Kong Standard*, 4 April 1982.

Notes to pages 73-77

[154] Autobiography by Leslie (1985) Commercial Radio.

[155] *Teenage Dreamers*, SB Celestial Pictures, Intercontinental Video Ltd VCD 611438. See: Hong Kong Twenty-third International Film Festival, *Hong Kong New Wave: Twenty Years After* (Hong Kong: Urban Council, 1999).

[156] Autobiography by Leslie (1985) Commercial Radio. The film soundtrack is on the VCD of *Teenage Dreamers*, SB Celestial Pictures 611438.

[157] *The Cheap Detective*, Asia Television and Fat Kee Recordings DVD FADVD7008, and VCD FAVCD8089.

[158] *Hong Kong Standard*, 4 April 1982.

[159] *Hong Kong Standard*, 4 April 1982: 'Leslie Chang [sic] – Rich, Young and Famous.'

[160] *Hong Kong Standard*, 4 April 1982 (Evans Chan, 'Leslie Chang [sic]– Rich, Young, Famous').

[161] *Energetic 21*, Fortune Star Legendary Collection, Joy Sales Films and Video Distributors VCD, JS/VCD/3050/HK.

[162] Detail of Hong Kong cinema in the early eighties is taken from: Abbas, Ackbar, *Hong Kong: Culture and the Politics of Disappearance* (Minneapolis: University of Minnesota Press, 1997); Browne, Nick, ed., *New Chinese Cinemas: Forms, Identities, Politics* (Cambridge: Cambridge University Press, 1994); Fu Poshek and Davis Desser, eds, *The Cinema of Hong Kong: History, Arts, Identity* (Cambridge: Cambridge University Press, 2000); Hill, John and Pamela Gibson, eds, *World Cinema: Critical Approaches* (New York: Oxford University Press, 2000); Hong Kong Twenty-first International Film Festival, *Hong Kong Cinema Retrospective: Fifty Years of Electric Shadows* (Hong Kong: Urban Council, 1997); Law Kar, ed., *Hong Kong Cinema in the Eighties: A Comparative Study with Western Cinema* (Hong Kong: Urban Council, 1991); Law Kar and Frank Bren, *Hong Kong Cinema: A Cross Cultural View* (Lanham, Maryland: Scarecrow Press, 2004); Lent, John, *The Asian Film Industry* (Austin: University of Texas Press, 1990).

[163] Autobiography by Leslie (1985) Commercial Radio.

Notes to pages 77-81

[164] *Nomad,* Hong Kong Movie, Mei Ah Entertainment DVD, DVD-283. See: *Asia Week,* ('In Acting He Draws from Experiences of the Pains in Real Life, http://lesliecheung.cc/memories/leepikwah_eng.htm); Morton, Lisa, *The Cinema of Tsui Hark* (Jefferson, NC: McFarland and Company, 2001); Abbas, Ackbar, *Hong Kong: Culture and the Politics of Disappearance* (Minneapolis: University of Minnesota Press, 1997); Browne, Nick, ed., *New Chinese Cinemas: Forms, Identities, Politics* (Cambridge: Cambridge University Press, 1994); Fu Poshek and Davis Desser, eds, *The Cinema of Hong Kong: History, Arts, Identity* (Cambridge: Cambridge University Press, 2000); Hong Kong Twenty-third International Film Festival, *Hong Kong New Wave: Twenty Years After* (Hong Kong: Urban Council, 1999); *Leslie Legacy: His Charm, Charisma and Craft Remembered in Celluloid* (Memorial booklet, Hong Kong film commemoration in the Hong Kong Cultural Centre and the Hong Kong City Hall, 11-12 May 2003); Stewart, Clare, and Philippa Hawker, eds, *Leslie Cheung* (Flinders Lane, Australia: Australian Centre for the Moving Image, 2003); Teo, Stephen, *Hong Kong Cinema: The Extra Dimensions* (London: British Film Institute Press, 1997); 3sat.de (German TV station), Andrea Bette. 'The Gender of the Stars: On the Actor and Pop Star Leslie Cheung.

[165] Leslie did not discuss it in Autobiography by Leslie (1985) Commercial Radio but did, peripherally, later in ATV, 25 June 1989, 'Interview with Leslie Cheung' by James Wong and two others.

[166] This is picked up in: *Leslie Legacy: His Charm, Charisma and Craft Remembered in Celluloid* (Memorial booklet, Hong Kong film commemoration in the Hong Kong Cultural Centre and the Hong Kong City Hall, 11-12 May 2003); Stewart, Clare, and Philippa Hawker, eds, *Leslie Cheung* (Flinders Lane, Australia: Australian Centre for the Moving Image, 2003).

[167] Interview with anonymous friend of Leslie, 27 October 2007.

[168] The concert is at: 'Live Performance at Academy Hall, 10 August 1982', http://www.seewise.net/CyberAudio/Live.html.. For comment on Leslie's practising, see: Chong, Milan, *Pop Stars in Hong Kong* (Hong Kong: Sing Tao Educational Publications, 1989).

[169] Florence Chan interview in *Ming Pao,* 6 April 2003.

[170] Chitose Shima, *All About Leslie* (Tokyo: Sangyo Henshu Center Co., 1999); http://e.gmw.cn/2013-03/29/content_7161.

[171] *City Magazine,* 1985 (Mak Uen Shou, 'Cheung Kwok-wing Cohabited with a Love Swindler'); ATV, 25 June 1989, 'Interview with Leslie Cheung' by James Wong and two others; Chitose Shima, *All About Leslie* (Tokyo: Sangyo Henshu Center Co., 1999).

[172] *City Entertainment,* 11 August 1991 (Ngai Siu-yun. 'A Living Legend from 23 to 34 Years Old').

[173] *Crossroads: Woman at 33,* in *Collective Memories of Leslie Cheung; the Works of 1970s-2000s* (Hong Kong: RTHK, DVD 010927).

Notes to pages 82-89

[174] Autobiography by Leslie (1985) Commercial Radio. Anita recalled the early days of their friendship in *Ming Pao*, 12 April 2003 (Anita Mui, 'No More Unjustice To Gorgor Please', http://lesliecheung.cc/memories/anitamui_eng.htm), Disc 2

[175] This meeting has passed into Leslie legend and is mentioned in passing by many. Jimmy Ngai Siu-yun recalled it in interview. Florence Chan mentioned that Leslie and Daffy had been together for 20 years to: *Ming Pao* 6 April 2003. D.J. So Si Wong mentioned it at Leslie's funeral.

[176] Interview with anonymous friend of Leslie, 27 October 2007.

[177] Welsh, Frank, *A History of Hong Kong* (London: Harper Collins, 1997), pp. 510-512.

[178] *Next Magazine*, 1997 ('Interview With Leslie', http://lesliecheung.cc/Magazine/1997/next97/next97.htm). *Once upon an Ordinary Girl*, Sensasian.com, Modern Audio VCD V0920H.

[179] *The Drummer* (Japanese version), Broadway, Yesasia DVD, 1003627638, issued 8 October 2004. An earlier Cantonese version on VCD has not been traced. Leslie discussed making this film in: Autobiography by Leslie (1985) Commercial Radio.

[180] No video recording of *First Time* has been released, though it can be found online.

[181] Chong, Milan, *Pop Stars in Hong Kong* (Hong Kong: Sing Tao Educational Publications, 1989).

[182] Autobiography by Leslie (1985) Commercial Radio; Chitose Shima, *All About Leslie* (Tokyo: Sangyo Henshu Center Co., 1999).

[183] Autobiography by Leslie (1985) Commercial Radio.

[184] Interview with anonymous friend of Leslie, 11 April 2011.

[185] *The Wind Blows On*, Capital Artists CD-03-1004.

[186] Autobiography by Leslie (1985) Commercial Radio.

[187] Chitose Shima, *All About Leslie* (Tokyo: Sangyo Henshu Center Co., 1999). See also: *Next Magazine*, 1997 ('Interview With Leslie', http://lesliecheung.cc/Magazine/1997/next97/next97.htm).

[188] Interview with anonymous friend of Leslie, 27 October 20007.

[189] 'Legendary Years of Our Leslie: A Biography', by Eunike, http://xoomer.virgilio.it/nguidett/biography01.htm.

[190] The tour is recounted by Law in: Law Kai-yui, 'The Singer's Shirt', http://lesliecheung.cc/memories/singer.htm.

[191] Law's most famous script in the West is probably that of his 1997 film, *The Soong Sisters*.

[192] *A Bit of Craziness* is currently unavailoable on CD.

Notes to pages 89-102

[193] Interview with anonymous friend of Leslie, 27 October 2007.

[194] Interviews with anonymous friends of Leslie, 27 October 2007 and 11 April 2011.

[195] *Little Dragon Maiden*, SB Celestial Pictures, Intercontinental Video VCD 100536.

[196] See Chapter 5.

[197] *The Fallen Family*, TVB VCD, 2005.

[198] *Monica* was re-issued by Universal Music in 2010.

[199] MVs of 'Thanks, Monica' are at: *History: His Story*, Capital Artists 4 disc compilation VCD CD-03-1333, 2004; Youtube: : http://www.youtube.com/watch?v=UD92ECnCrTc.

[200] Autobiography by Leslie (1985) Commercial Radio; Chong, Milan, *Pop Stars in Hong Kong* (Hong Kong: Sing Tao Educational Publications, 1989); *Next Magazine*, 1997 ('Interview With Leslie', http://lesliecheung.cc/Magazine/1997/next97/next97.htm); Eiji Ogura, *Leslie Cheung, We Will Never Forget You, Memories Of Leslie's Friends*; *Cut*, no. 172, November 2004 (Shino Kokawa, 'Leslie, It's You Who Caused the Wind to Blow in Asia').

[201] Interview with anonymous friend of Leslie, 27 October 2007.

[202] Autobiography by Leslie (1985) Commercial Radio.

[203] *Behind the Yellow Line*, SB Celestial Pictures, Intercontinental Video VCD 612459.

[204] See the YouTube clip: http://www.youtube.com/watch?v=MNTfvlFapoU.

[205] http://www.youtube.com/watch?v=a8SBF445_2s.

[206] No video recording of *Double Decker* is available. It can be seen online.

[207] *Merry Christmas*, Fortune Star, Deltamac Hong Kong VCD, 7174. Leslie mentions the movie in: Autobiography by Leslie (1985) Commercial Radio.

[208] 'Legendary Years of Our Leslie: A Biography', by Eunike, http://xoomer.virgilio.it/nguidett/biography01.htm.

[209] *For Your Love Only* is currently unavailable on CD.

[210] Chong, Milan, *Pop Stars in Hong Kong* (Hong Kong: Sing Tao Educational Publications, 1989).

[211] *The Intellectual Trio*, Fortune Star, Deltamac Hong Kong VCD 7097.

[212] *Crazy Romance*, Fortune Star, Deltamac Hong Kong DVD 78077.

[213] *Summer Best Collection* is currently unavailable on CD.

[214] *City Magazine* 1985 (Zha Hsiaohsin, 'Cheung Kwok Wing Boldly Thrusts Forward to Refute Kai Yee Lin', http://lesliecheung.cc/Magazine/1985/metropolitan/text.htm).

Notes to pages 102-108

215 The concert can occasionally be watched in part on Youtube.

216 *Ready, Steady, Go,* 2 August 1985.

217 The show is described by Jenny Leung in 'Leslie Charm Thrills fans', *Hong Kong Standard*, 7 August 1985 and Ken Martinus in 'Return of a Superstar', *Hong Kong Standard*, 12 August 1985.

218 *Ming Pao*, 12 April 2003 (Anita Mui, 'No More Unjustice To Gorgor Please', http://lesliecheung.cc/memories/anitamui_eng.htm). Leslie and Anita are in concert together on Youtbue at: http://vids.myspace.com/index.cfm?fuseaction=vids.individual&videoid=51470001. For Anita's concerts, see: Law Kar, ed., *Hong Kong Cinema in the Eighties: A Comparative Study with Western Cinema* (Hong Kong: Urban Council, 1991).

219 See the recording of this incident on Youtube: http://www.youtube.com/watch?gl=HK&feature=related&hl=zh-TW&v=1D-wP2audUU.

220 Chong, Milan, *Pop Stars in Hong Kong* (Hong Kong: Sing Tao Educational Publications, 1989). *Hong Kong Standard*, 16 December 1989. Excerpts from the concert are on Youtube at: http://www.tudou.com/programs/view/JGboQxDbGFw/.

221 There are occasional excerpts from *Mystery Love* shown on YouTube. It is also referred to as the *Leslie Cheung Special '85*.

222 *For Your Heart Only*, Deltamac, Fortune Star VCD 7186.

223 The interview is on the net at several sites, for instance translated at: http://all-about-leslie.blogspot.com/2007/12/autobiography-by-leslie-1985-commercial.html.

224 Autobiography by Leslie (1985) Commercial Radio.

225 *City Magazine*, 1985 (Mak Uen Shou, 'Cheung Kwok-wing Cohabited with a Love Swindler').

226 *City Magazine* (1985) Zha Hsiaohsin.

227 *City Entertainment*, 11 August 1991 (Ngai Siu-yun. 'A Living Legend from 23 to 34 Years Old').

228 *Mingpao*, 12 April 2003 (Anita Mui, 'No More Unjustice To Gorgor Please', http://lesliecheung.cc/memories/anitamui_eng.htm).

229 *Ming Pao Weekly/ Ming Chow*, 30 August 1986 (Sek Kei, 'Film Teahouse'); 901, 1986 ('Leslie is Afraid of Getting Married'.

230 *Cosmopolitan Weekly* (*City Entertainment*), 11 August 1991 (Ngai Siu-yun. 'A Living Legend from 23 to 34 Years Old').

231 *Hong Kong Standard*, 11 October and 23 November 1985.

Notes to pages 108-115

[232] *Cosmopolitan Weekly* (*City Entertainment*), 11 August 1991 (Ngai Siu-yun. 'A Living Legend from 23 to 34 Years Old'). Leslie sang with Elisa Chan again in 1986 in the popular song "Who Can Make Me Crazy?"; http://www.youtube.com/watch?v=dvZ1LH7ETbw.

[233] For the rivalry between the stars, see: Hammond, Stefan, 'Leslie's Demons', goldsea.com, 1997.

[234] *Stand Up*, Capital Artists CD 03-1352. See Shanghai Daily 19 November 2003 for death of its lyricist, Lam Chun-keung. A MV of 'Stand Up' is at: *History: His Story*, Capital Artists 4 disc compilation VCD CD-03-1333, 2004.

[235] *Hong Kong Standard* of 20 October 1986 covers Michael Lai's intentions and comments on Leslie's inability to read music.

[236] On the change to a rock n'roll style, see: Chong, Milan, *Pop Stars in Hong Kong* (Hong Kong: Sing Tao Educational Publications, 1989).

[237] Leslie told this story at: ATV, 25 June 1989, 'Interview with Leslie Cheung' by James Wong and two others. See discussion of Cantopop, rivalry etc in Hammond, Stefan, 'Leslie's Demons', goldsea.com, 1997. The rivalry and its effects on fans is mentioned also in the *South China Morning Post*, 14 January 1994.

[238] *Last Song in Paris* is not available on video recording.

[239] *Hong Kong Standard*, 21 April 1986.

[240] Chong, Milan, *Pop Stars in Hong Kong* (Hong Kong: Sing Tao Educational Publications, 1989). An excerpt from Leslie's performance in Canada is on Youtube at: http://www.tudou.com/programs/view/JGboQxDbGFw/.

[241] *Hong Kong Standard*, 1 August 1986.

[242] 'Brains and not Beauty is What Leslie Looks for in His Ideal Girl', *Hong Kong Standard*, 20 October 1985.

[243] 'Legendary Years of Our Leslie: A Biography', by Eunike, http://xoomer.virgilio.it/nguidett/biography01.htm.

[244] *A Better Tomorrow*, Deltamac, Fortune Star DVD78007.

[245] For discussion of *A Better Tomorrow*, see: Browne, Nick, ed., *New Chinese Cinemas: Forms, Identities, Politics* (Cambridge: Cambridge University Press, 1994); Hammond, Stefan, 'Leslie's Demons', goldsea.com, 1997; Teo, Stephen, *Hong Kong Cinema: The Extra Dimensions* (London: British Film Institute Press, 1997); Fitzgerald, Martin, and Paul Duncan, *Hong Kong's Heroic Bloodshed* (Harpenden, Herts: Pocket Essentials, 2000); Heard, Christopher, *Ten Thousand Bullets: The Cinematic Journey of John Woo* (Los Angeles: Lone Eagle, 2000); Bliss, Michael, *Between the Bullets: The Spiritual Cinema of John Woo* (Lanham, Maryland: Scarecrow Press, 2002); *Time Asia*, 3 April 2003 (Richard Corliss, 'That Old Feeling: Days of Being Leslie'); Fang, Karen, *John Woo's A Better Tomorrow* (Hong Kong: Hong Kong University Press, 2004); *Cut*, no. 172, November 2004 (Shino Kokawa, 'Leslie, It's You Who Caused the Wind to Blow in Asia').

Notes to pages 116-124

246 *Story of a Discharged Prisoner* is at http://hkmdb.com/db/movies/view.

247 He is credited in some sources with an appearance as a special guest star in a TVB serial, *The Way of the Dragon*, but there is no record of such a series; for *Turn Around and Die* see http://en.wikipedia.org/wiki/List_of_TVB_series_(1986)

248 Interview with anonymous friend of Leslie, 27 October 2007.

249 'Legendary Years of Our Leslie: A Biography', by Eunike, http://xoomer.virgilio.it/nguidett/biography01.htm.

250 'Legendary Years of Our Leslie: A Biography', by Eunike, http://xoomer.virgilio.it/nguidett/biography01.htm.

251 Discussion of his fan club and its President Lettie Lee, is in: *100 Marks' Magazine*, 1986 ('Side story of Leslie in Concert '86', http://lesliecheung.cc/Magazine/1986/sidestory/info.htm).

252 *100 Marks' Magazine*, 1986 ('Side story of Leslie in Concert '86', http://lesliecheung.cc/Magazine/1986/sidestory/info.htm).

253 Interview with Amanda Lee, 30 November 2012.

254 *Hong Kong Standard*, 18 August 1986.

255 *Hong Kong Standard*, 20 October 1986.

256 'Brains and not Beauty is What Leslie Looks for in His Ideal Girl', *Hong Kong Standard*, 20 October 1986.

257 'Brains and not Beauty is What Leslie Looks for in His Ideal Girl', *Hong Kong Standard*, 20 January 1986.

258 'Brains and not Beauty is What Leslie Looks for in His Ideal Girl', *Hong Kong Standard*, 20 October 1986.

259 *Leslie Cheung Kwok-wing (Allure Me)*, Capital Artists re-issue CD, 1 December 2005.

260 For detail of the concert, see: *Hong Kong Standard*, 8 and 29 September 1986 and 30 December 1986. Also in the *South China Morning Post*, December 1986 'A Night to Come Closer'. Also: *100 Marks' Magazine*, 1986 ('Side story of Leslie in Concert '86', http://lesliecheung.cc/Magazine/1986/sidestory/info.htm).

261 *Hong Kong Standard*, 3 September 1986.

262 Excerpts from the Concert are on Youtube at: http://www.lesliecheung-dreamworld.com/Concerts/Concert1986/Concert1986.htm. A description is in 'A Night to Come Closer', *Hong Kong Standard*, 30 December 1986.

263 Leslie's Konica advertisement, with him singing 'Thanks, Monica', is at: http://www.videomeli.com/video/XdNukN5rTUw/leslie-konica-commercial-1986.html.

264 *Love and Admiration* is not currently available.

265 For the split, see: *Hong Kong Standard*, 28 February, 9 & 29 April, 23 July, 14 November 1987.

Notes to pages 125-133

[266] 'Brains and not Beauty is What Leslie Looks for in His Ideal Girl', *Hong Kong Standard*, 20 October 1986.

[267] 'Leslie Cheung to Leave CA', *Hong Kong Standard*, 28 February 1987.

[268] 'Leslie Leaves Capital Artists', *Hong Kong Standard*, 9 April 1987.

[269] *Hong Kong Standard*, 29 April 1987.

[270] *Hong Kong Standard*, 23 July 1987.

[271] No recording is available of *Leslie Cheung Meets You at the Ocean Palace Restaurant Night Club*. *Mingpao Weekly*, June 1987.

[272] 'Legendary Years of Our Leslie: A Biography', by Eunike, http://xoomer.virgilio.it/nguidett/biography01.htm.

[273] *Hong Kong Standard*, 23 July 1987.

[274] *100 Marks' Magazine*, 1987 ('Leslie's 'Best Companion' at home', http://lesliecheung.cc/Magazine/1987/100marks6/100marks6.htm).

[275] *City Entertainment*, 11 August 1991 (Ngai Siu-yun. 'A Living Legend from 23 to 34 Years Old').

[276] *A Chinese Ghost Story*, Deltamac, Fortune Star DVD78035.

[277] For discussion of *A Chinese Ghost Story*, see: Law Kar, ed., *Hong Kong Cinema in the Eighties: A Comparative Study with Western Cinema* (Hong Kong: Urban Council, 1991); Nowell-Smith, Geoffrey, ed., *The Oxford History of World Cinema* (Oxford: Oxford University Press, 1996); Hammond, Stefan, 'Leslie's Demons', goldsea.com, 1997; S.F.L., 'Gentleman Leslie', *Orient Extrême Cinéma*, No. 1, January 1997, pp 14-19, Teo, Stephen, *Hong Kong Cinema: The Extra Dimensions* (London: British Film Institute Press, 1997); Stokes, Lisa Odham, and Michael Hoover, *City on Fire: Hong Kong Cinema* (London: Verso, 1999); *Cahiers Du Cinema*, no. 579, May 2003 ('Leslie Cheung's Days Of Being Wild'); *Positif*, June 2003 (Lorenzo Codelli and Hubert Niogret, 'Leslie Cheung 1956 - 2003', http://www.jeanmichelplace.com/fr/revues/detail.cfm?ProduitID=607&ProduitCode=1); Stewart, Clare, and Philippa Hawker, eds, *Leslie Cheung* (Flinders Lane, Australia: Australian Centre for the Moving Image, 2003); Law Kar and Frank Bren, *Hong Kong Cinema: A Cross Cultural View* (Lanham, Maryland: Scarecrow Press, 2004).

[278] *100 Marks' Magazine*, 1987 ('Leslie's 'Best Companion' at home', http://lesliecheung.cc/Magazine/1987/100marks6/100marks6.htm).

[279] *South China Morning Post*, 'Leslie Cheung Wins TV ad deal' 1988. The advertisement can be seen, with Leslie singing, on Youtube at: http://www.youtube.com/watch?v=2La-7TLhag0.

[280] *Entertainment and TV Times*, 1988.

[281] *A Summer Romance '87*, Cinepoly CD 983364-7.

[282] See *Hong Kong Standard*, 23 July and 5 October 1987.

Notes to pages 133-138

[283] 'Legendary Years of Our Leslie: A Biography', by Eunike, http://xoomer.virgilio.it/nguidett/biography01.htm.

[284] *Hong Kong Standard*, 3 September 1987.

[285] *Hong Kong Standard*, 14 November 1987.

[286] *A Better Tomorrow II*, Deltamac, Fortune Star VCD 7104.

[287] For discussion of *A Better Tomorrow II*, see: Dannen, Fredric and Barry Long, *Hong Kong Babylon: An Insider's Guide to the Hollywood of the East* (London: Faber and Faber, 1997); Stokes, Lisa Odham, and Michael Hoover, *City on Fire: Hong Kong Cinema* (London: Verso, 1999); Heard, Christopher, *Ten Thousand Bullets: The Cinematic Journey of John Woo* (Los Angeles: Lone Eagle, 2000).

[288] For Hong Kong film in the mid to late eighties, see: Lent, John, *The Asian Film Industry* (Austin: University of Texas Press, 1990); Law Kar, ed., *Hong Kong Cinema in the Eighties: A Comparative Study with Western Cinema* (Hong Kong: Urban Council, 1991); Browne, Nick, ed., *New Chinese Cinemas: Forms, Identities, Politics* (Cambridge: Cambridge University Press, 1994); Nowell-Smith, Geoffrey, ed., *The Oxford History of World Cinema* (Oxford: Oxford University Press, 1996); . Dannen, Fredric and Barry Long, *Hong Kong Babylon: An Insider's Guide to the Hollywood of the East* (London: Faber and Faber, 1997) Fitzgerald, Martin, and Paul Duncan, *Hong Kong's Heroic Bloodshed* (Harpenden, Herts: Pocket Essentials, 2000).

[289] *Rouge*, Intercontinental Video, Fortune Star DVD, digitally remastered, no serial number.

[290] For discussion of *Rouge*, see: Law Kar, ed., *Hong Kong Cinema in the Eighties: A Comparative Study with Western Cinema* (Hong Kong: Urban Council, 1991); Browne, Nick, ed., *New Chinese Cinemas: Forms, Identities, Politics* (Cambridge: Cambridge University Press, 1994); Logan, Bey, *Hong Kong Action Cinema* (London: Titan Books, 1995); Abbas, Ackbar, *Hong Kong: Culture and the Politics of Disappearance* (Minneapolis: University of Minnesota Press, 1997); Teo, Stephen, *Hong Kong Cinema: The Extra Dimensions* (London: British Film Institute Press, 1997); Hammond, Stefan, 'Leslie's Demons', goldsea.com, 1997; S.F.L., 'Gentleman Leslie', *Orient Extrême Cinéma*, No. 1, January 1997, pp 14-19; Stokes, Lisa Odham, and Michael Hoover, *City on Fire: Hong Kong Cinema* (London: Verso, 1999); Hill, John and Pamela Gibson, eds, *World Cinema: Critical Approaches* (New York: Oxford University Press, 2000).*Cahiers Du Cinema*, no. 579, May 2003 ('Leslie Cheung's Days of Being Wild'); *Leslie Legacy: His Charm, Charisma and Craft Remembered in Celluloid* (Memorial booklet, Hong Kong film commemoration in the Hong Kong Cultural Centre and the Hong Kong City Hall, 11-12 May 2003); Stewart, Clare, and Philippa Hawker, eds, *Leslie Cheung* (Flinders Lane, Australia: Australian Centre for the Moving Image, 2003); Chiu Hung Ping in *World Movies*, no. 413, (Chiu Hung Ping, 'Falling Like Cherry Blossoms').

Notes to pages 138-147

[291] Leslie mentioned this in his radio interview ATV, 25 June 1989, 'Interview with Leslie Cheung' by James Wong and two others.

[292] *Hong Kong Commercial Daily*, 23 March 2002 ('Cheung Kwok Wing - The Trend-Setting Superstar').

[293] 'Leslie Cheung Artists Studies Website', 'Never Wanna Be Apart from Leslie: In Reminiscence of Leslie Cheung's Artistic Life' 30 April 2003, Hong Kong Baptist University, http://www.leslie-cheung.com/leslie/2004/5-31/14148.html, http://www.leslie-cheung.com 2004-5-31 1:39:28.

[294] *Ming Pao* 1998 (Lam Bing, 'If Destiny Wants Them To Be Together, Leslie and Wong Kar Wai Will Meet Again', http://lesliecheung.cc/Magazine/1998/mingpao/interview/interview.htm).

[295] *Virgin Snow*, Cinepoly CD 170834-9.

[296] There is no available recording of *Concert 428*.

[297] *Backstage* is occasionally available on Youtube. See also: *South China Morning Post*. 1987, 'Leslie Cheung wins TV ad deal'; *Hong Kong Standard*, 21 May and 21 October 1988; *South China Morning Post* 'Leslie Cheung wins TV ad deal' 1987

[298] 'Leslie Launches Pepsi Campaign', *Hong Kong Standard*, 21 May 1988. Another Pepsi advertisement of that year is on Youtube at: http://www.dailymotion.com/video/xwrrm_pepsi-89_ads.

[299] *Cheung Kwok-wing*, Cinepoly CD 174352-6.

[300] *Hot Summer*, Cinepoly CD 170835-0.

[301] The concert is discussed at: 'In Concert: Leslie Cheung', *Hong Kong Standard*, 23 April 1988; Sally Ratcliffe, 'A Star in the Making', 'Leslie Lends a Helping Hand', 6 August 1988, and Shirley Chan, 'Record Maker, Record Breaker', 27 August 1988, *Hong Kong Standard*; Yim, Steven, 'Cheung Woos Fans with a Bubbling Extravaganza', ? 1988; *Hong Kong Standard* 6 and 27 August 1988.

[302] For the first time, Leslie's concert was issued as two CDs by Cinepoly, 980922-78 and 88.

[303] Excerpts from *Leslie Cheung in Concert '88* are on Youtube at: http://www.youtube.com/watch?gl=GB&hl=en-GB&v=foLXtvzIwa4 and http://www.youtube.com/watch?v=lrACl6vCJ48.

[304] *Leslie in Concert '88*, Cinepoly CDs 980922-78 and 88.

[305] 'Go West, Young Man', *Hong Kong Standard*, 3 September 1988.

[306] Chitose Shima, *All About Leslie* (Tokyo: Sangyo Henshu Center Co., 1999).

[307] 'I Want $10 Million', *Hong Kong Standard*, 20 February and 'Will Leslie Bail Out', 2 April 1988.

[308] 'Legendary Years of Our Leslie: A Biography', by Eunike, http://xoomer.virgilio.it/nguidett/biography01.htm.

Notes to pages 147-157

[309] 'Go West Young Man', *Hong Kong Standard*, 3 September 1988.

[310] 'Ma Yi Jung Regrets She is not Able to Direct Her Idol's Movie' (3 April 2003).

[311] Leslie recounted this in: Chitose Shima, *All About Leslie* (Tokyo: Sangyo Henshu Center Co., 1999).

[312] *Hong Kong Standard*, 6 August and 15 October 1988.

[313] *Hong Kong Standard*, 2 April and 6 August 1988.

[314] 'Legendary Years of Our Leslie: A Biography', by Eunike, http://xoomer.virgilio.it/nguidett/biography01.htm.

[315] Chiu Hung Ping in *World Movies*, no. 413, (Chiu Hung Ping, 'Falling Like Cherry Blossoms').

[316] Interview with anonymous friend of Leslie, 27 October 2007.

[317] *Aces Go Places V* is discussed in: Law Kar, ed., *Hong Kong Cinema in the Eighties: A Comparative Study with Western Cinema* (Hong Kong: Urban Council, 1991); Stokes, Lisa Odham, and Michael Hoover, *City on Fire: Hong Kong Cinema* (London: Verso, 1999).

[318] *Hong Kong Standard*, 25 February 1989.

[319] 'Legendary Years of Our Leslie: A Biography', by Eunike, http://xoomer.virgilio.it/nguidett/biography01.htm.

[320] *Hong Kong Standard* 25 February 1989 (Shirley Chan, 'Buzz: A Change in Cheung').

[321] There is no video recording of *Sunset in Paris*. It can be viewed on Youtube at http://www.youtube.com/watch?v=YUZLdQ19M_c..

[322] The making of *Sunset in Paris* is discussed in: *Hong Kong Standard*, 23 and 29 April 1988.

[323] Leslie's Korean chocolate advertisement is on Youtube at: http://www.lesliecheung-dreamworld.com/Video/Advertisements.htm#KoreanAdvertToYou.

[324] Leslie's performance at the Miss Asia Pageant is on Youtube at: http://www.youtube.com/watch?v=h3Nt9fnPcMQ.

[325] Issued on VCD by Universe Laser & Video, U333, VCD 2252.

[326] Leslie ATV interview, 25 June 1989, with James Wong and two others.

[327] *Leslie Cheung Kwok-wing*, Cineploy CD 173628-4.

[328] Chitose Shima, *All About Leslie* (Tokyo: Sangyo Henshu Center Co., 1999).

[329] Welsh, Frank, *A History of Hong Kong* (London: Harper Collins, 1997), pp. 482-524.

[330] Welsh, Frank, *A History of Hong Kong* (London: Harper Collins, 1997), p. 524.

Notes to pages 158-162

[331] The effect of the June the 4th incident on Hong Kong film is discussed in: Law Kar, ed., *Hong Kong Cinema in the Eighties: A Comparative Study with Western Cinema* (Hong Kong: Urban Council, 1991); Hong Kong Twenty-first International Film Festival, *Hong Kong Cinema Retrospective: Fifty Years of Electric Shadows* (Hong Kong: Urban Council, 1997).

[332] *Hong Kong Standard*, 20 January 1986.

[333] *Hong Kong Standard*, 20 February 1988.

[334] 'Legendary Years of Our Leslie: A Biography', by Eunike, http://xoomer.virgilio.it/nguidett/biography01.htm, quoting an aricle by Leslie.

[335] *Ming Pao* no. 1820, 2003, (Wong Lai Ling, interview with Florence Chan).

[336] *Ming Pao* no. 1820, 2003, (Wong Lai Ling, interview with Florence Chan).

[337] Leslie speaking at the last concert of the series.

[338] *Positif*, 1998 ('Berlin Film Festival', http://xoomer.virgilio.it/nguidett/berlin.htm); no. 455, 1999 ('Michael Ciment and Hugo Niogret interview', 21 February 1998).

[339] Chitose Shima, *All About Leslie* (Tokyo: Sangyo Henshu Center Co., 1999).

[340] Leslie speaking at the last concert of the series.

[341] Leslie speaking at the last concert of the series.

[342] Chitose Shima, *All About Leslie* (Tokyo: Sangyo Henshu Center Co., 1999).

[343] *Positif*, 1998 ('Berlin Film Festival', http://xoomer.virgilio.it/nguidett/berlin.htm); no. 455, 1999 ('Michael Ciment and Hugo Niogret interview', 21 February 1998).

[344] Leslie interview about *Love* album; 1995.

[345] *Hong Kong Standard*, 25 February 1989 (Shirley Chan, 'Buzz: A Change in Cheung').

[346] *Hong Kong Standard*, 16 December 1989.

[347] *Hong Kong Standard*, 25 February 1989 (Shirley Chan, 'Buzz: A Change in Cheung').

[348] *Hong Kong Standard*, 16 December 1989.

[349] *Hong Kong Standard*, 29 April 1989.

[350] Leslie's speech on the last day of the concert series.

[351] *Positif*, 1998 ('Berlin Film Festival', http://xoomer.virgilio.it/nguidett/berlin.htm); no. 455, 1999 ('Michael Ciment and Hugo Niogret interview', 21 February 1998); Chitose Shima, *All About Leslie* (Tokyo: Sangyo Henshu Center Co., 1999).

[352] *Next Magazine*, 1997 ('Interview with Leslie', http://lesliecheung.cc/Magazine/1997/next97/next97.htm.

Notes to pages 162-175

[353] Balke, Gerd, *Hong Kong Voices* (Hong Kong: ?, 1989); *Positif*, 1998 ('Berlin Film Festival', http://xoomer.virgilio.it/nguidett/berlin.htm); no. 455, 1999 ('Michael Ciment and Hugo Niogret interview', 21 February 1998); Chitose Shima, *All About Leslie* (Tokyo: Sangyo Henshu Center Co., 1999).

[354] Balke, Gerd, *Hong Kong Voices* (Hong Kong: ?, 1989); *Aera Magazine*, 1998 (Hiro Ugaya, 'I'm a Perfectionist Either With Movies or Songs'); *Positif*, 1998 ('Berlin Film Festival', http://xoomer.virgilio.it/nguidett/berlin.htm); no. 455, 1999 ('Michael Ciment and Hugo Niogret interview', 21 February 1998); Chitose Shima, *All About Leslie* (Tokyo: Sangyo Henshu Center Co., 1999).

[355] Balke, Gerd, *Hong Kong Voices* (Hong Kong: ?, 1989).

[356] 'Legendary Years of Our Leslie: A Biography', by Eunike, http://xoomer.virgilio.it/nguidett/biography01.htm.

[357] This account is taken from an unattributed magazine article by Leslie.

[358] *Salute*, Cinepoly CD 982410-08.

[359] *Final Encounter of the Legend*, Cinepoly CD 173591-9.

[360] Interview with Amanda Lee, 30 November 2012.

[361] *Hong Kong Standard*, 16 December 1989 and 14 January 1990.

[362] *Hong Kong Standard*, 14 January 1990 (Anita Fung, 'Bobby's Star Shines Bright').

[363] Film of the *Final Encounter of the Legend* concert is on the Karaoke DVD recording, New Century Workshop, Corrys, NC0102D.

[364] Chu Wing Lung: *Cheung Kwok Wing – A Movement Free Dance Act*, Leslie Cheung Cyberworld, The One and Only Leslie Cheung (*City Entertainment*: Hong Kong, no date, pre April 2004).

[365] *Ming Pao* no. 1820, 2003, (Wong Lai Ling, interview with Florence Chan).

[366] Interview with anonymous friend of Leslie, 27 October 2007.

[367] Interview with anonymous friend of Leslie, 27 October 2007.

[368] Interview with anonymous friend of Leslie, 27 October 2007.

[369] *TV and Entertainment Times*, 6-12 July 1992 (James Giddings, 'Leslie Cheung A Man's Woman Reversing the Roles in Chen Kaige's New Movie').

[370] *TV and Entertainment Times*, 6-12 July 1992 (James Giddings, 'Leslie Cheung, A Man's Woman Reversing the Roles in Chen Kaige's New Movie').

[371] Interview with Amanda Lee, 30 November 2012.

[372] Commercial Radio Hong Kong, 'Who Will Understand', Connie Chan Bo Chu.

[373] *A Chinese Ghost Story II*, Deltamac, Fortune Star VCD7004.

Notes to pages 175-177

[374] As was noted before the making of the film by the *Hong Kong Standard*, 6 August 1988.

[375] ATV, 25 June 1989, 'Interview with Leslie Cheung' by James Wong and two others.

[376] Un-refernced interview with Lam Gai-to, in 'What People Said About Leslie', Red Mission.

[377] *Leslie Cheung Final Encounter with the Legend*, Cinepoly CD 846 301-2.

[378] *Dreaming*, Cinepoly CD 982544-8.

[379] *Days of Being Wild*, Media Asia, Megastar Video Distribution VCD MS/VCD/663/Hong Kong.

[380] For discussion of *Days of Being Wild*, see: *South China Morning Post*, 23 December 1990 ('Wong's Wild Way'); *City Entertainment*, 11 August 1991 (Ngai Siu-yun. 'A Living Legend from 23 to 34 Years Old'); Abbas, Ackbar, Hong Kong: *Culture and the Politics of Disappearance* (Minneapolis: University of Minnesota Press, 1997); Dannen, Fredric and Barry Long, *Hong Kong Babylon: An Insider's Guide to the Hollywood of the East* (London: Faber and Faber, 1997); Hammond, Stefan, 'Leslie's Demons', goldsea.com, 1997; Teo, Stephen, *Hong Kong Cinema: The Extra Dimensions* (London: British Film Institute Press, 1997); S.F.L., 'Gentleman Leslie', *Orient Extrême Cinéma*, No. 1, January 1997, pp 14-19; Fonoroff, Paul, *At the Hong Kong Movies: 600 reviews from 1988 till the Handover* (Hong Kong: Film Biweekly, 1998; Fu Poshek and Davis Desser, eds, *The Cinema of Hong Kong: History, Arts, Identity* (Cambridge: Cambridge University Press, 2000); Hill, John and Pamela Gibson, eds, *World Cinema: Critical Approaches* (New York: Oxford University Press, 2000); Morton, Lisa, *The Cinema of Tsui Hark* (Jefferson, NC: McFarland and Company, 2001); Yau, Esther C.M., ed., *At Full Speed: Hong Kong Cinema in a Borderless World* (Minneapolis: University of Minnesota Press, 2001).Stewart, Clare, and Philippa Hawker, eds, *Leslie Cheung* (Flinders Lane, Australia: Australian Centre for the Moving Image, 2003); Dissanayake, Wimal, *Wong Kar-wai's Ashes of Time* (Hong Kong: Hong Kong University Press, 2003); *Asia Weekly*, April 2003 (Perry Lam Pui-li, 'In acting he draws from experiences of the pains in real life'); *Cahiers Du Cinema*, no. 579, May 2003 (Maggie Cheung, 'Leslie Cheung's Days Of Being Wild'); *Leslie Legacy: His Charm, Charisma and Craft Remembered in Celluloid* (Memorial booklet, Hong Kong film commemoration in the Hong Kong Cultural Centre and the Hong Kong City Hall, 11-12 May 2003); Tambling, Jeremy, *Wong Kar-wai's Happy Together* (Hong Kong: Hong Kong University Press, 2003); *Cut*, no. 172, November 2004 (Shino Kokawa, 'Leslie, It's You Who Caused the Wind to Blow in Asia'); Hawker, Philippa, Australian Centre for the Moving Image, 'Forever Cheung' (2003); 'The Shining Star – In Reminiscence of Leslie's Artistic Life', seminar, 3 April 2005, Hong Kong International Trade & Exhibition Centre, Lam Kay To, http://www.leslie-cheung.info/20050403.html; *World Movies*, no. 413, (Chiu Hung Ping, 'Falling Like Cherry Blossoms').

Notes to pages 179-188

381 *Cahiers Du Cinema*, no. 579, May 2003 (Maggie Cheung, 'Leslie Cheung's Days Of Being Wild').

382 *Once a Thief*, Deltamac, Fortune Star DVD 78118.

383 For discussion of *Once a Thief*, see: Teo, Stephen, *Hong Kong Cinema: The Extra Dimensions* (London: British Film Institute Press, 1997); Fonoroff, Paul, *At the Hong Kong Movies: 600 reviews from 1988 till the Handover* (Hong Kong: Film Biweekly, 1998); Bordwell, David, *Planet Hong Kong: Popular Cinema and the Art of Entertainment* (Cambridge, Massachusetts: Harvard University Press, 2000); Fitzgerald, Martin, and Paul Duncan, *Hong Kong's Heroic Bloodshed* (Harpenden, Herts: Pocket Essentials, 2000); Heard, Christopher, *Ten Thousand Bullets: The Cinematic Journey of John Woo* (Los Angeles: Lone Eagle, 2000).

384 'Homosexual Film Role for Leslie', *Hong Kong Standard*, 19 May 1991.

385 *South China Morning Post* 16 May 1993 (Thea Klapwald, 'Leslie Cheung Gets Real/It's the Real Me At Last').

386 Interview with anonymous friend of Leslie, 27 October 2007.

387 *The Banquet*, Pan-Asia, Inc, VHS; Mei Ah Laser Disc VCD.

388 Leslie's part can be seen on Youtube at: http://www.youtube.com/watch?v=Mw4DgFV7aMI.

389 'Exemplary Pop Singers Rewarded', *Hong Kong Standard*, 18 December 1991.

390 'Top Actor Given Police Protection', *Hong Kong Standard*, 15 January 1992; Dannen, Fredric and Barry Long, *Hong Kong Babylon: An Insider's Guide to the Hollywood of the East* (London: Faber and Faber, 1997); *New Republic*, 14 and 21 July 1997 (Fredric Dannen, 'Making all the Right Moves').

391 For triad activity in film industry, see Dannen, Fredric and Barry Long, *Hong Kong Babylon: An Insider's Guide to the Hollywood of the East* (London: Faber and Faber, 1997); Fitzgerald, Martin, and Paul Duncan, *Hong Kong's Heroic Bloodshed* (Harpenden, Herts: Pocket Essentials, 2000); *New Republic*, 14 and 21 July 1997 (Fredric Dannen, 'Making all the Right Moves').

392 'Top Actor Given Police Protection', *Hong Kong Standard*, 15 January 1992.

393 For discussion of *All's Well Ends Well*, see: Fonoroff, Paul, *At the Hong Kong Movies: 600 reviews from 1988 till the Handover* (Hong Kong: Film Biweekly, 1998).

394 *Hong Kong Standard*, 19 May 1991 ('Homosexual Film Role for Leslie').

395 *Arrest the Restless*, Deltamac, Fortune Star DVD 78089.

396 For discussion of *Arrest the Restless*, see: Dannen, Fredric and Barry Long, *Hong Kong Babylon: An Insider's Guide to the Hollywood of the East* (London: Faber and Faber, 1997); Fonoroff, Paul, *At the Hong Kong Movies: 600 reviews from 1988 till the Handover* (Hong Kong: Film Biweekly, 1998); , Clare, and Philippa Hawker, eds, *Leslie Cheung* (Flinders Lane, Australia: Australian Centre for the Moving Image, 2003).

Notes to pages 188-191

[397] *TV and Entertainment Times*, 6-12 July 1992 (James Giddings, 'Leslie Cheung, A Man's Woman Reversing the Roles in Chen Kaige's New Movie).

[398] *Men's Uno*, April 2004 (Ngan Luen, 'Remembrance of Our Beloved Idol').

[399] 'Legendary Years of Our Leslie: A Biography', by Eunike, http://xoomer.virgilio.it/nguidett/biography01.htm.

[400] *Farewell My Concubine*, Miramax Classics DVD 17368.

[401] For discussion of *Farewell My Concubine*, see: *TV and Entertainment Times*, 6-12 July 1992 (James Giddings, 'Leslie Cheung: A Man's Woman Reversing the Roles in Chen Kaige's New Movie); *South China Morning Post*, 13 December 1992, 'Cheung, the Concubine, Tiptoes Past the Censors - 1 January 'Immersed in the World of Chinese Opera' - 14 January, 16 and 23 May, 25 July, 1 and 16 August, 1, 2 and 14 September, 19 December 1993; *Dallas Morning News*, 12 November 1993 ('Top Attraction: Farewell To My Concubine'); *Hong Kong Standard*, 13 March 1994; *Vancouver Sun*, 14 March 1994 (Peter Birnie, 'Star Turn'); S.F.L., 'Gentleman Leslie', *Hong Kong - Orient Extrême Cinéma*, No. 1, January 1997, pp 14-19; Dannen, Fredric and Barry Long, *Hong Kong Babylon: An Insider's Guide to the Hollywood of the East* (London: Faber and Faber, 1997); Hong Kong Twenty-first International Film Festival, *Hong Kong Cinema Retrospective: Fifty Years of Electric Shadows* (Hong Kong: Urban Council, 1997); *Yang ± Yin: Gender In Chinese Cinema* (Interview with Stanley Kwan), 1997; Hammond, Stefan, 'Leslie's Demons', goldsea.com, 1997; *Positif*, 1998 ('Berlin Film Festival', http://xoomer.virgilio.it/nguidett/berlin.htm); no. 455, 1999 ('Michael Ciment and Hugo Niogret interview', 21 February 1998); *Aera Magazine*, 1998 (Hiro Ugaya, 'I'm a Perfectionist Either With Movies or Songs'); Chitose Shima, *All About Leslie* (Tokyo: Sangyo Henshu Center Co., 1999); Chen Kaige, 'The Eyes of Leslie Cheung', http://lesliecheung.cc/memories/eyes_of_leslie_cheung.htm, http://ent.563.net/article/2003/2003-4-30/37553.html (30 April 2003); *Time Asia*, 3 April 2003 (Richard Corliss, 'That Old Feeling: Days of Being Leslie'); 'Leslie Cheung Artists Studies Website', 'Never Wanna Be Apart from Leslie: In Reminiscence of Leslie Cheung's Artistic Life' 30 April 2003, Hong Kong Baptist University, http://www.leslie-cheung.com/leslie/2004/5-31/14148.html, http://www.leslie-cheung.com 2004-5-31 1:39:28; *Leslie Legacy: His Charm, Charisma and Craft Remembered in Celluloid* (Memorial booklet, Hong Kong film commemoration in the Hong Kong Cultural Centre and the Hong Kong City Hall, 11-12 May 2003); Stewart, Clare, and Philippa Hawker, eds, *Leslie Cheung* (Flinders Lane, Australia: Australian Centre for the Moving Image, 2003); Red Forum, Tai Sing Pao, 20 March 2004, 'Movies Which Leslie Did Not Star In Or Failed To Finish'; *Cut*, no. 172, November 2004 (Shino Kokawa, 'Leslie, It's You Who Caused the Wind to Blow in Asia'); Pang, Laikwan and Day Wong, eds, *Masculinities and Hong Kong Cinema* (Hong Kong: Hong Kong University Press, 2005); Yao, Ashley (a Chinese book about Leslie's movies); 3sat.de, Andrea Bette. 'The Gender of the Stars: On the Actor and Pop Star Leslie Cheung'.

[402] http://rthk.hk/classicschannel/.

Notes to pages 194-202

[403] Farewell *My Concubine*'s Xiao Si (apprentice of Chen Dieyi) talks about Leslie.

[404] 'Never Wanna Be Apart from Leslie: In Reminiscence of Leslie Cheung's Artistic Life' 30 April 2003, Hong Kong Baptist University, http://www.lesliecheung.com/leslie/2004/5-31/14148.html, http://www.leslie-cheung.com 2004-5-31 1:39:28.

[405] For instance, in: *Leslie Legacy: His Charm, Charisma and Craft Remembered in Celluloid* (Memorial booklet, Hong Kong film commemoration in the Hong Kong Cultural Centre and the Hong Kong City Hall, 11-12 May 2003); *Time Asia*, 3 April 2003 (Richard Corliss, 'That Old Feeling: Days of Being Leslie').

[406] S.F.L., 'Gentleman Leslie', *Hong Kong - Orient Extrême Cinéma*, No. 1, January 1997, pp 14-19.

[407] 'Gong Li and Company the Centre of Attention', *South China Morning Post*, 23 May 1993.

[408] 'Beijing Silences a Prodigal Son and his Concubine' and 'The Concubine Controversy', *South China Morning Post*, 25 July 1993; 'Hello and Farewell to Winning Movie', *South China Morning Post*, 29 July 1993.

[409] 'The Day When the Movie Industry Thumbed its Nose at China's Leaders', *South China Morning Post*, 1 August 1993.

[410] 'Controversial Film to Be Shown', *South China Morning Post*, 16 August 1993; 'Farewell to Concubine Drawing in Audiences', *South China Morning Post*, 2 September 1993.

[411] 'Taiwan Embraces Concubine', *South China Morning Post*, 19 December 1993.

[412] 'Controversial Chinese Film Nears Ultimate Movie Accolade', *Hong Kong Standard*, 13 March 1994.

[413] *All's Well Ends Well Too*, Wide Sight DVD, no number.

[414] *The Eagle Shooting Heroes*, Mei Ah Entertainment VCD035.

[415] For discussion of *The Eagle Shooting Heroes*, see: Paul Fonoroff, 'Pointed View of the Swashbuckling Sagas', *South China Morning Post* 14 February 1993); S.F.L., 'Gentleman Leslie', *Hong Kong - Orient Extrême Cinéma*, No. 1, January 1997, pp 14-19; Fonoroff, Paul, *At the Hong Kong Movies: 600 Reviews from 1988 till the Handover* (Hong Kong: Film Biweekly, 1998).

Notes to pages 203-209

[416] For discussion of the Hong Kong film industry in the early '90s, see: Nowell-Smith, Geoffrey, ed., *The Oxford History of World Cinema* (Oxford: Oxford University Press, 1996); Hong Kong Twenty-first International Film Festival, *Hong Kong Cinema Retrospective: Fifty Years of Electric Shadows* (Hong Kong: Urban Council, 1997); Hill, John and Pamela Gibson, eds, *World Cinema: Critical Approaches* (New York: Oxford University Press, 2000); Dissanayake, Wimal, *Wong Kar-wai's Ashes of Time* (Hong Kong: Hong Kong University Press, 2003); Law Kar and Frank Bren, *Hong Kong Cinema: A Cross Cultural View* (Lanham, Maryland: Scarecrow Press, 2004); Curtin, Michael, *Playing to the World's Biggest Audience: The Globalization of Chinese Film and TV* (Berkeley and Los Angeles, California: University of California Press, 2007).

[417] *The Bride with White Hair*, Universe Laser & Video Co, VCD 1215.

[418] For discussion of *The Bride with White Hair*, see: *South China Morning Post* 27 June, 27 and 29 August 1993; Logan, Bey, *Hong Kong Action Cinema* (London: Titan Books, 1995); S.F.L., 'Gentleman Leslie', *Hong Kong - Orient Extrême Cinéma*, No. 1, January 1997, pp 14-19; Hong Kong Twenty-first International Film Festival, *Hong Kong Cinema Retrospective: Fifty Years of Electric Shadows* (Hong Kong: Urban Council, 1997); Fonoroff, Paul, *At the Hong Kong Movies: 600 reviews from 1988 till the Handover* (Hong Kong: Film Biweekly, 1998); Stokes, Lisa Odham, and Michael Hoover, *City on Fire: Hong Kong Cinema* (London: Verso, 1999); *Sing Pao*, 7 April 2003, (Song Song, 'Big Brother Gor Gor', http://lesliecheung.cc/memories/singpao6.htm); Morton, Lisa, 'Leslie Cheung Tribute 2003', http://www.asianfilm.org/modules.php?name=Encyclopedia&op=content&tid=58, http://www.lisamorton.com/leslietrib.html; 'Leslie Cheung as a Star and his Art-mind', interview with Wada Emi, *Kinejun*, no. 1384; 'Leslie Cheung Artists Studies Website', 'Never Wanna Be Apart from Leslie: In Reminiscence of Leslie Cheung's Artistic Life' 30 April 2003, Hong Kong Baptist University, http://www.leslie-cheung.com/leslie/2004/5-31/14148.html, http://www.leslie-cheung.com 2004-5-31 1:39:28; 3sat.de, Andrea Bette. 'The Gender of the Stars: On the Actor and Pop Star Leslie Cheung'.

[419] 'Bombs Hurled in Movie Set "Extortion Bid"', *South China Morning Post*, 27 June 1993.

[420] 'Leslie Cheung Artists Studies Website', 'Never Wanna Be Apart from Leslie: In Reminiscence of Leslie Cheung's Artistic Life' 30 April 2003, Hong Kong Baptist University, http://www.leslie-cheung.com/leslie/2004/5-31/14148.html, http://www.leslie-cheung.com 2004-5-31 1:39:28.

[421] Interview with anonymous friend of Leslie, 27 October 2007.

[422] 'It's the Real Me at Last', *South China Morning Post*, 16 May 1993.

[423] 'Legendary Years of Our Leslie: A Biography', by Eunike, http://xoomer.virgilio.it/nguidett/biography01.htm.

[424] *The Bride with White Hair 2*, Wide Sight VCD WSVCD1217.

Notes to pages 209-213

425 For discussion of *The Bride with White Hair 2*, see: Stokes, Lisa Odham, and Michael Hoover, *City on Fire: Hong Kong Cinema* (London: Verso, 1999).

426 *Vancouver Sun*, 14 March 1994 (Peter Birnie, 'Star Turn').

427 'No More Sad Songs for Youthful Actor Cheung', *Hong Kong Standard*, 24 June 1994.

428 *Next Magazine*, 1997 ('Interview With Leslie', http://lesliecheung.cc/Magazine/1997/next97/next97.htm).

429 'Star wars Leave the Singers on Sidelines', *South China Morning Post*, 14 January 1994.

430 *It's a Wonderful Life*, Wide Sight VCD WSVCD1225.

431 *It's a Wonderful Life* is discussed at: Stokes, Lisa Odham, and Michael Hoover, *City on Fire: Hong Kong Cinema* (London: Verso, 1999).

432 *Hong Kong Standard*, 24 June 1994. See also: China Morning Post. *Hong Kong Visitor* (Hong Kong: South China Morning Post, 1994).

433 *He's a Woman, She's a Man*, Fitto Mobile Laser Disc Distribution Co, VCD FMO10 A&B.

434 *He's a Woman, She's a Man* is discussed at: Hong Kong Twenty-first International Film Festival, *Hong Kong Cinema Retrospective: Fifty Years of Electric Shadows* (Hong Kong: Urban Council, 1997); Teo, Stephen, *Hong Kong Cinema: The Extra Dimensions* (London: British Film Institute Press, 1997); Hammond, Stefan, 'Leslie's Demons', goldsea.com, 1997; S.F.L., 'Gentleman Leslie', *Hong Kong - Orient Extrême Cinéma*, No. 1, January 1997, pp 14-19; Fonoroff, Paul, *At the Hong Kong Movies: 600 reviews from 1988 till the Handover* (Hong Kong: Film Biweekly, 1998); Stokes, Lisa Odham, and Michael Hoover, *City on Fire: Hong Kong Cinema* (London: Verso, 1999); Chitose Shima, *All About Leslie* (Tokyo: Sangyo Henshu Center Co., 1999); Bordwell, David, *Planet Hong Kong: Popular Cinema and the Art of Entertainment* (Cambridge, Massachusetts: Harvard University Press, 2000); *Leslie Legacy: His Charm, Charisma and Craft Remembered in Celluloid* (Memorial booklet, Hong Kong film commemoration in the Hong Kong Cultural Centre and the Hong Kong City Hall, 11-12 May 2003); 'Leslie Cheung Artists Studies Website', 'Never Wanna Be Apart from Leslie: In Reminiscence of Leslie Cheung's Artistic Life' 30 April, 2003, Hong Kong Baptist University, http://www.leslie-cheung.com/leslie/2004/5-31/14148.html, http://www.leslie-cheung.com; Stokes, Lisa Odham, *Peter Ho-Sun Chan's 'He's a Woman, She's a Man'* (Hong Kong: Hong Kong University Press, 2009).

435 *Leslie Legacy: His Charm, Charisma and Craft Remembered in Celluloid* (Memorial booklet, Hong Kong film commemoration in the Hong Kong Cultural Centre and the Hong Kong City Hall, 11-12 May 2003).

Notes to pages 217-218

[436] 'Leslie Cheung Artists Studies Website', 'Never Wanna Be Apart from Leslie: In Reminiscence of Leslie Cheung's Artistic Life' 30 April 2003, Hong Kong Baptist University, http://www.leslie-cheung.com/leslie/2004/5-31/14148.html, http://www.leslie-cheung.com 2004-5-31 1:39:28.

[437] 'Love in the Air at Film Awards', *South China Morning Post*, 1 March 1995.

[438] *Long & Winding Road*, Mei Ah Entertainment VCD CF 40245V.

[439] *Long & Winding Road* is discussed at: Teo, Stephen, *Hong Kong Cinema: The Extra Dimensions* (London: British Film Institute Press, 1997); Fonoroff, Paul, *At the Hong Kong Movies: 600 reviews from 1988 till the Handover* (Hong Kong: Film Biweekly, 1998).

[440] *Over the Rainbow, Under the Skirt*, Fitto Entertainment (Hong Kong) VCD.

[441] *Hong Kong Standard*, 24 June 1994 ('No More Sad Songs for Youthful Actor Cheung').

[442] *South China Morning Post*. Hong Kong Visitor (Hong Kong: *South China Morning Post*, 1994).

[443] *Ashes of Time*, Mei Ah Entertainment VCD075.

[444] *Ashes of Time* is discussed at: *South China Morning Post*, 15 August 1993 (Scarlet Cheng, 'A Director's Dream, and Actor's Nightmare'); Abbas, Ackbar, *Hong Kong: Culture and the Politics of Disappearance* (Minneapolis: University of Minnesota Press, 1997); Dannen, Fredric and Barry Long, *Hong Kong Babylon: An Insider's Guide to the Hollywood of the East* (London: Faber and Faber, 1997); Hong Kong Twenty-first International Film Festival, *Hong Kong Cinema Retrospective: Fifty Years of Electric Shadows* (Hong Kong: Urban Council, 1997); Teo, Stephen, *Hong Kong Cinema: The Extra Dimensions* (London: British Film Institute Press, 1997); Fonoroff, Paul, *At the Hong Kong Movies: 600 reviews from 1988 till the Handover* (Hong Kong: Film Biweekly, 1998); Stokes, Lisa Odham, and Michael Hoover, *City on Fire: Hong Kong Cinema* (London: Verso, 1999); Fitzgerald, Martin, and Paul Duncan, *Hong Kong's Heroic Bloodshed* (Harpenden, Herts: Pocket Essentials, 2000); *Time*, 3 May 2000 (Stephen Short, 'Bedroom Pinup'); Hill, John and Pamela Gibson, eds, *World Cinema: Critical Approaches* (New York: Oxford University Press, 2000); Dissanayake, Wimal, *Wong Kar-wai's Ashes of Time* (Hong Kong: Hong Kong University Press, 2003); *Asia Week*, ('In Acting He Draws from Experiences of the Pains in Real Life, http://lesliecheung.cc/memories/leepikwah_eng.htm); *Leslie Legacy: His Charm, Charisma and Craft Remembered in Celluloid* (Memorial booklet, Hong Kong film commemoration in the Hong Kong Cultural Centre and the Hong Kong City Hall, 11-12 May 2003); Stewart, Clare, and Philippa Hawker, eds, *Leslie Cheung* (Flinders Lane, Australia: Australian Centre for the Moving Image, 2003). (HK784.5B C5 S8); Tambling, Jeremy, *Wong Kar-wai's Happy Together* (Hong Kong: Hong Kong University Press, 2003); *Hong Kong Commercial Daily*, March 23, 2002 (Economic News, 'Cheung Kwok Wing - The Trend-Setting Superstar')..

Notes to pages 220-229

445 Anonymous record of the discussion at Hong Kong University on 29 March 1999 by a fan who was present, at: http://lesliecheung.cc/Special/hku/part1_eng.htm.

446 *The Chinese Feast*, Wide Sight VCD WSVCD1242.

447 *The Chinese Feast* is discussed at: *Hong Kong Standard*, 12 January 1995; Paul Fonoroff, 'Romance Takes a Backseat as Kenny Bee Gets Cooking', *South China Morning Post*, 3 February 1995; Dannen, Fredric and Barry Long, *Hong Kong Babylon: An Insider's Guide to the Hollywood of the East* (London: Faber and Faber, 1997); S.F.L., 'Gentleman Leslie', *Hong Kong – Orient Extrême Cinéma*, No. 1, January 1997, pp 14-19; Stokes, Lisa Odham, and Michael Hoover, *City on Fire: Hong Kong Cinema* (London: Verso, 1999); Bordwell, David, *Planet Hong Kong: Popular Cinema and the Art of Entertainment* (Cambridge, Massachusetts: Harvard University Press, 2000).

448 'Legendary Years of Our Leslie: A Biography', by Eunike, http://xoomer.virgilio.it/nguidett/biography01.htm.

449 'Cheung's Point on Pressure', *Hong Kong Standard*, 19 February 1995.

450 See also: *Galaxy Production*, 7 September 2000 (Thomas Huong, 'Leslie tells Malaysia, 'They are not worth it!!', http://www.galaxy.com.my/press/musicnet.htm).

451 'Cheung's Point on Pressure', *Hong Kong Standard*, 19 February 1995; see also: Branda DJ, *Love* album interview 1995; *KPS Entertainment Express*, 1998.

452 *South China Morning Post* 16 May 1993 (Thea Klapwald, 'Leslie Cheung Gets Real/It's the Real Me At Last').

453 *Oriental Sunday*, no. 201, 2001 ('Leslie is always found guilty of unsound accusations').

454 Welsh, Frank, *A History of Hong Kong* (London: Harper Collins, 1997), pp. 482-558.

455 *Aera Magazine*, 1998 (Hiro Ugaya, 'I'm a Perfectionist Either With Movies or Songs').

456 Chitose Shima, *All About Leslie* (Tokyo: Sangyo Henshu Center Co., 1999).

457 *Positif*, 1998 ('Berlin Film Festival', http://xoomer.virgilio.it/nguidett/berlin.htm); no. 455, 1999 ('Michael Ciment and Hugo Niogret interview', 21 February 1998).

458 *Galaxy Production*, 7 September 2000 (Thomas Huong, 'Leslie tells Malaysia, 'They are not worth it!!', http://www.galaxy.com.my/press/musicnet.htm).

459 Interview with Amanda Lee, 30 November 2012.

460 *Love*, Rock Records CD RD 1319.

461 Leslie's interview for Branda DJ for the *Love* album, 1995; *South China Morning Post*, 20 December 1996 and 1 January 1997.

Notes to pages 229-233

[462] *Next Magazine*, 1997 ('Interview With Leslie', http://lesliecheung.cc/Magazine/1997/next97/next97.htm).

[463] *South China Morning Post*, 8 October 1995.

[464] *The Phantom Lover*, Wide Sight VCD WSVCD1264.

[465] *The Phantom Lover* is discussed at: *South China Morning Post*, 1 March, 'Yu Got It Made' – 16 April, 23 April, 'Resembling the Phantom' and 'Ghostly Lover Breaks Movie Sound Barrier' – 14 July, 16 July, 'Shallow Phantom Love' - 21 July and 'Phantom Role Fits Like Glove' - 27 July 1995; May Fung, 'Another Phantom Stakes His Claim', *Hong Kong Standard*, 16 July 1995; *Movie Stories*, 1995 (Chiu Wing, 'Cheung Kwok Wing: It Won't Be Long For Us To Meet Again'); *Yang ± Yin: Gender In Chinese Cinema* (interview with Stanley Kwan); S.F.L., 'Gentleman Leslie', *Hong Kong - Orient Extrême Cinéma*, No. 1, January 1997; Fonoroff, Paul, *At the Hong Kong Movies: 600 Reviews from 1988 till the Handover* (Hong Kong: Film Biweekly, 1998); Stokes, Lisa Odham, and Michael Hoover, *City on Fire: Hong Kong Cinema* (London: Verso, 1999).

[466] 'What People Have Said About Leslie'.

[467] *Hong Kong Entertainment News in Review*, 2 April 2003 ('Leslie Cheung Kwok-Wing Commits Suicide').

[468] Interview with anonymous friend of Leslie, 27 October 2007.

[469] *South China Morning Post*, 18 January 1996.

[470] *Tristar*, Wide Sight VCD WSVCD1268.

[471] 'Films Fight for New Year Success', *South China Morning Post*, 11 February 1996; Hong Kong Twenty-first International Film Festival, *Hong Kong Cinema Retrospective: Fifty Years of Electric Shadows* (Hong Kong: Urban Council, 1997); Teo, Stephen, *Hong Kong Cinema: The Extra Dimensions* (London: British Film Institute Press, 1997); Bordwell, David, *Planet Hong Kong: Popular Cinema and the Art of Entertainment* (Cambridge, Massachusetts: Harvard University Press, 2000).

[472] Hammond, Stefan, *Hollywood East: Hong Kong Movies and the People Who Make Them* (Lincolnwood, Illinois: Contemporary Books, 2000).

[473] Interview with anonymous friend of Leslie, 27 October 2007.

[474] *Temptress Moon*, Mei Ah Entertainment DVD-199.

[475] 'Storms Halt Tempest' - 30 October, 'Eclipse of the Moon' - 11 December 1994, *South China Morning Post*.

Notes to pages 234-239

[476] *Temptress Moon* is discussed at: S.F.L., 'Gentleman Leslie', *Hong Kong - Orient Extrême Cinéma*, No. 1, January 1997, pp 14-19; Hammond, Stefan, 'Leslie's Demons', goldsea.com, 1997; *Los Angeles Times*, 22 June 1997 (Kevin Thomas, 'A Career in Full Bloom'); Chitose Shima, *All About Leslie* (Tokyo: Sangyo Henshu Center Co., 1999); Bordwell, David, *Planet Hong Kong: Popular Cinema and the Art of Entertainment* (Cambridge, Massachusetts: Harvard University Press, 2000); Farewell Banquet with Crew of Temptress Moon, in *Cheung Kwok Wing: It Won't Be Long For Us To Meet Again* by Chiu Wing, 2003; Stewart, Clare, and Philippa Hawker, eds, *Leslie Cheung* (Flinders Lane, Australia: Australian Centre for the Moving Image, 2003); *Time Asia*, 3 April 2003 (Richard Corliss, 'That Old Feeling: Days of Being Leslie'); *Positif*, June 2003 (Lorenzo Codelli and Hubert Niogret, 'Leslie Cheung 1956 - 2003', http://www.jeanmichelplace.com/fr/revues/detail.cfm?ProduitID=607&ProduitCode=1); Ren-lei, 'Ren-Lei Talking About God-Father Gor-Gor', http://lesliecheung.cc/memories/yanlui_eng.htm,; National University of Defense Technology, Los Angeles, Alumni Website, Huang Lo, 1 April 2005, '2005 Sound of the Wind and Shadow of the Moon, Fondly Remembers Leslie Cheung'; 'Leslie's Legacy' http://lesliecheung.cc/memories/magazines/legacy/nomad.htm.

[477] *Shanghai Grand*, Mei Ah Laser Disc Co VCD0475.

[478] *Shanghai Grand* is discussed at: Paul Fonoroff, 'Banality by the Bag-load in Tsui's Shanghai Stinker', *South China Morning Post*, 19 July 1996; S.F.L., 'Gentleman Leslie', *Hong Kong - Orient Extrême Cinéma*, No. 1, January 1997, pp 14-19; Fonoroff, Paul, *At the Hong Kong Movies: 600 reviews from 1988 till the Handover* (Hong Kong: Film Biweekly, 1998).

[479] *Who's the Woman, Who's the Man*, Mei Ah Entertainment DVD-592.

[480] *Who's the Woman, Who's the Man* is discussed at: Hammond, Stefan, 'Leslie's Demons', goldsea.com, 1997; Fonoroff, Paul, *At the Hong Kong Movies: 600 reviews from 1988 till the Handover* (Hong Kong: Film Biweekly, 1998); Server, Lee, *Asian Pop Cinema: Bombay to Tokyo* (San Francisco: Chronicle Books, 1999); Stokes, Lisa Odham, and Michael Hoover, *City on Fire: Hong Kong Cinema* (London: Verso, 1999).

[481] *Yang Yin* is not available on video recording.

[482] *Yang Yin* is discussed at: Stewart, Clare, and Philippa Hawker, eds, *Leslie Cheung* (Flinders Lane, Australia: Australian Centre for the Moving Image, 2003); Pang, Laikwan and Day Wong, eds, *Masculinities and Hong Kong Cinema* (Hong Kong: Hong Kong University Press, 2005).

[483] *Next Magazine*, 1997 ('Interview With Leslie', http://lesliecheung.cc/Magazine/1997/next97/next97.htm).

[484] *Red*, Rock Records CD ROD 5132. 'Leslie Cheung Kwok-wing', *South China Morning Post*, 20 December 1996.

[485] Commercial Radio Hong Kong, January 2006, Lam Jik, 'Leslie's Passing and his Songs'.

Notes to pages 239-244

[486] *South China Morning Post*, 2 June 1996; *KPS Entertainment Express*, 1998.

[487] Radio Television Hong Kong, October 1996 (Chow Kwok Fung, interview with Leslie on 'Crossover 97' concert).

[488] *Next Magazine*, 1997 ('Interview with Leslie', http://lesliecheung.cc/Magazine/1997/next97/next97.htm).

[489] 'Leslie's New Year Present', *South China Morning Post*, 6 October 1996.

[490] See the DVD recording of the concert, *Leslie Cheung Live in Concert 97*, Rock (Hong Kong) Co, ROL 5150.

[491] 'Leslie proves He's Still a Showman', *South China Morning Post*, 16 December 1996; 'Cheung Flirts with New Image', *Hong Kong Standard*, 22 December 1996.

[492] Zhang man-ling, *My Heart Aches, My Heart Really Aches*.

[493] Hammond, Stefan, 'Leslie's Demons', goldsea.com, 1997.

[494] Chitose Shima, *All About Leslie* (Tokyo: Sangyo Henshu Center Co., 1999); 3sat.de, Andrea Bette. 'The Gender of the Stars: On the Actor and Pop Star Leslie Cheung'; *Ming Pao Weekly* 'Best Performing Award to Leslie' 2001; *Hong Kong Entertainment News in Review*, 2 April 2003 ('Leslie Cheung Kwok-Wing Commits Suicide'); 'Leslie Cheung Artists Studies Website', 'Never Wanna Be Apart from Leslie: In Reminiscence of Leslie Cheung's Artistic Life' 30 April 2003, Hong Kong Baptist University, http://www.leslie-cheung.com/leslie/2004/5-31/14148.html, http://www.leslie-cheung.com 2004-5-31 1:39:28; *City Entertainment*, 2004, Chu Wing Lung: 'Cheung Kwok Wing – A Movement Free Dance Act'; Friedland, Lucy, 'Journey Into the East – An Ongoing Travel Journal'.

[495] 'Leslie Proves He's Still a Showman', *South China Morning Post*, 16 December 1996.

[496] *South China Morning Post*, November 1997 ('Leslie Cheung Flirts with New Image').

[497] *Hong Kong Standard*, 22 December 1996.

[498] *Oriental Sunday*, no. 201, 2001 ('Leslie is always found guilty of unsound accusations').

[499] *Oriental Sunday*, Number 201, 2001.

[500] *Viva Erotica*, Universe DVD 5023.

[501] *Viva Erotica* is discussed at: Paul Fonoroff, 'Yee So-So on Soft Core', *South China Morning Post*, 6 December 1996; Fonoroff, Paul, *At the Hong Kong Movies: 600 Reviews from 1988 till the Handover* (Hong Kong: Film Biweekly, 1998); Stokes, Lisa Odham, and Michael Hoover, *City on Fire: Hong Kong Cinema* (London: Verso, 1999); *Hong Kong Commercial Daily*, 23 March 2002 (Economic News, 'Cheung Kwok Wing - The Trend-Setting Superstar'); *Shenzhen Daily*, 25 March 2005 (Law Chi-leung interview, http://www.sznews.com/jb/20050325/ca1507377.htm); 'The Shining Star – In Reminiscence of Leslie's Artistic Life', seminar, 3 April 2005.

Notes to pages 247-248

502 Eiji Ogura, 'Leslie Cheung, We Will Never Forget You' in *Memories Of Leslie's Friends*.

503 *Straits Times*, 25 April 1997 ('Organiser of Leslie Cheung's Concerts Sued').

504 'Cheung's Got It, but He Won't Be Flaunting It', *Hong Kong Standard*, 13 March 1997.

505 *Time Asia*, 3 April 2003 (Richard Corliss, 'That Old Feeling: Days of Being Leslie').

506 *All's Well End's Well '97*, Garry's Trading Co DVD GAD200465. The film is discussed at: Fonoroff, Paul, *At the Hong Kong Movies: 600 Reviews from 1988 till the Handover* (Hong Kong: Film Biweekly, 1998).

507 *Happy Together*, Mei Ah Laser Disc Co VCD795.

508 *Happy Together* is discussed at: 'Pushing the Gay Envelope' - 29 December 1996, 'Not a Gay Day' - 5 January 1997, *South China Morning Post*; *Next Magazine*, 1997 ('Interview With Leslie', http://lesliecheung.cc/Magazine/1997/Next97/Next97.htm); Doyle, Christopher, *Don't Try for Me Argentina: Photographic Journal of 'Happy Together'*, a Wong Kar-Wai Film (Hong Kong: City Entertainment, 1997); Hammond, Stefan, 'Leslie's Demons', goldsea.com, 1997; Fonoroff, Paul, *At the Hong Kong Movies: 600 Reviews from 1988 till the Handover* (Hong Kong: Film Biweekly, 1998); Channel V, 1998 ('*Printemps* Album Launch, Kyoto'); *Ming Pao* 1998 (Lam Bing, 'If Destiny Wants Them To Be Together, Leslie and Wong Kar Wai Will Meet Again', http://lesliecheung.cc/Magazine/1998/mingpao/interview/interview.htm); Stokes, Lisa Odham, and Michael Hoover, *City on Fire: Hong Kong Cinema* (London: Verso, 1999); *Film-Dienst*, 52, 1999, no. 21, pp. 16 – 17 (Andrea Bette, 'Masculine-feminine: Hong Kong's Androgynous Superstar Leslie Cheung'); Chitose Shima, *All About Leslie* (Tokyo: Sangyo Henshu Center Co., 1999); Hammond, Stefan, *Hollywood East: Hong Kong Movies and the People Who Make Them* (Lincolnwood, Illinois: Contemporary Books, 2000); Yau, Esther C.M., ed., *At Full Speed: Hong Kong Cinema in a Borderless World* (Minneapolis: University of Minnesota Press, 2001); *Leslie Legacy: His Charm, Charisma and Craft Remembered in Celluloid* (Memorial Booklet, Hong Kong film commemoration in the Hong Kong Cultural Centre and the Hong Kong City Hall, 11-12 May 2003); . Stewart, Clare, and Philippa Hawker, eds, *Leslie Cheung* (Flinders Lane, Australia: Australian Centre for the Moving Image, 2003); *Time Asia*, 3 April 2003 (Richard Corliss, 'That Old Feeling: Days of Being Leslie'); 'Leslie's Legacy' http://lesliecheung.cc/memories/magazines/legacy/nomad.htm; Tambling, Jeremy, *Wong Kar-wai's Happy Together* (Hong Kong: Hong Kong University Press, 2003); *Cut*, no. 172, November 2004 (Shino Kokawa, 'Leslie, It's You Who Caused the Wind to Blow in Asia'); 3sat. de, Andrea Bette. 'The Gender of the Stars: On the Actor and Pop Star Leslie Cheung'.

Notes to pages 249-256

[509] Hong Kong Film Archive, *Fifty Years of the Hong Kong Film Production and Distribution Industries: An Exhibition* (Hong Kong: Urban Council, 1997); Abbas, Ackbar, *Hong Kong: Culture and the Politics of Disappearance* (Minneapolis: University of Minnesota Press, 1997); *New Republic*, 14 and 21 July 1997 (Fredric Dannen, 'Making all the Right Moves'); Bordwell, David, *Planet Hong Kong: Popular Cinema and the Art of Entertainment* (Cambridge, Massachusetts: Harvard University Press, 2000); Dissanayake, Wimal, *Wong Kar-wai's Ashes of Time* (Hong Kong: Hong Kong University Press, 2003).

[510] Doyle, Christopher, *Don't Try for Me Argentina: Photographic Journal of 'Happy Together', a Wong Kar-Wai Film* (Hong Kong: City Entertainment, 1997).

[511] Pushing the Gay Envelope' - 29 December 1996, 'Not a Gay Day' - 5 January 1997, *South China Morning Post*.

[512] 'Not a Gay day', *South China Morning Post*, 5 January 1997; 'Views of Gay Theatre', *South China Morning Post*, 30 May 1997; 'A Gay Old Time', *South China Morning Post*, 9 November 1997.

[513] *Time Asia*, 3 April 2003 (Richard Corliss, 'That Old Feeling: Days of Being Leslie'); *Next Magazine*, 1997 ('Interview With Leslie', http://lesliecheung.cc/Magazine/1997/next97/next97.htm).

[514] Stewart, Clare, and Philippa Hawker, eds, *Leslie Cheung* (Flinders Lane, Australia: Australian Centre for the Moving Image, 2003).

[515] *Leslie Cheung Live in Concert 97*, Rock Records CD ROD 515.

[516] This MV appears occasionally on Youtube.

[517] *Next Magazine*, 1997 ('Interview With Leslie', http://lesliecheung.cc/Magazine/1997/next97/next97.htm).

[518] Hammond, Stefan, 'Leslie's Demons', goldsea.com, 1997.

[519] 'Pressure on Stars to Sing in China', *South China Morning Post*, 14 June 1997.

[520] *Los Angeles Times*, 22 June 1997 (Kevin Thomas, 'A Career in Full Plume').

[521] *South China Morning Post*, 2 September 1997.

[522] *Next Magazine*, 1997 ('Interview With Leslie', http://lesliecheung.cc/Magazine/1997/next97/next97.htm).

[523] 'Legendary Years of Our Leslie: A Biography', by Eunike, http://xoomer.virgilio.it/nguidett/biography01.htm.

[524] *South China Morning Post*, 1 January 1997.

[525] 'Legendary Years of Our Leslie: A Biography', by Eunike, http://xoomer.virgilio.it/nguidett/biography01.htm.

Notes to pages 257-262

526 *Ming Pao* 1998 (Lam Bing, 'If Destiny Wants Them To Be Together, Leslie and Wong Kar Wai Will Meet Again', http://lesliecheung.cc/Magazine/1998/mingpao/interview/interview.htm); *Positif!* ('Berlin Film Festival', http://xoomer.virgilio.it/nguidett/berlin.htm); no. 455, 1999 ('Michael Ciment and Hugo Niogret interview', 21 February 1998); Channel V, 1998 ('*Printemps* Album Launch, Kyoto'); Nakagawa Yosuke, November 20, 2005, httpp://blog.livedoor.jp/yoyogi2222/archives/50151785.html, http://bbs.ent.163.com/board/rep.jsp?b=zhangguorong&i=147380.

527 *Positif*, 1998 ('Berlin Film Festival', http://xoomer.virgilio.it/nguidett/berlin.htm); no. 455, 1999 ('Michael Ciment and Hugo Niogret interview', 21 February 1998).

528 Zhong Lu-ming http://all-about-leslie.blogspot.com/2007/04/leslies-charm-cannot-be-resisted.html.

529 *Ninth Happiness*, Mei Ah Entertainment VCD1050.

530 *Ninth Happiness* is discussed at: *Ming Pao* 1998 (Lam Bing, 'If Destiny Wants Them To Be Together, Leslie and Wong Kar Wai Will Meet Again', http://lesliecheung.cc/Magazine/1998/mingpao/interview/interview.htm); Stokes, Lisa Odham, and Michael Hoover, *City on Fire: Hong Kong Cinema* (London: Verso, 1999).

531 *Aera Magazine*, 1998 (Hiro Ugaya, 'I'm a Perfectionist Either with Movies or Songs'); Leslie interview for *A Time to Remember*, 1998.

532 Zhong Lu-ming http://all-about-leslie.blogspot.com/2007/04/leslies-charm-cannot-be-resisted.html.

533 *KPS Entertainment Express*, 1998.

534 Channel V, 1998 ('Printemps Album Launch, Kyoto').

535 *Printemps*, Rock Records CD RD 1468.

536 'Ma Yi Jung Regrets She is not Able to Direct Her Idol's Movie', 3 April 2003.

537 See Chapter 22.

538 *City Entertainment*, 5-13 February 1998.

539 'Legendary Years of Our Leslie: A Biography', by Eunike, http://xoomer.virgilio.it/nguidett/biography01.htm.

540 *Ming Pao* 1998 (Lam Bing, 'If Destiny Wants Them To Be Together, Leslie and Wong Kar Wai Will Meet Again', *http://lesliecheung.cc/Magazine/1998/mingpao/interview/interview.htm).

541 *Hong Kong Standard*, 14 September 1998.

542 *Anna Magdalena* can be watched in part on Youtube at: http://www.iidrama.com/Chinese_movie/Anna_Magdalena-994-1.html.

543 Chitose Shima, *All About Leslie* (Tokyo: Sangyo Henshu Center Co., 1999).

Notes to pages 263-271

544 Chitose Shima, *All About Leslie* (Tokyo: Sangyo Henshu Center Co., 1999).

545 Chitose Shima, *All About Leslie* (Tokyo: Sangyo Henshu Center Co., 1999).

546 Chitose Shima, *The Time of Leslie* (Tokyo: Sangyo Henshu Center Co., 2004).

547 Chitose Shima, *All About Leslie* (Tokyo: Sangyo Henshu Center Co., 1999.

548 Chitose Shima, *The Time of Leslie* (Tokyo: Sangyo Henshu Center Co., 2004).

549 *A Time to Remember*, City Connection DVD, CL-DVD 379.

550 *A Time to Remember* is discussed at: Babcock, Todd, letter, 'Time to Remember', 30 November 1998, and his interview in 1999; *Ming Pao* 1998 (Lam Bing, 'If Destiny Wants Them To Be Together, Leslie and Wong Kar Wai Will Meet Again', http://lesliecheung.cc/Magazine/1998/mingpao/interview/interview.htm); *Hong Kong Standard*, 20 July 1998.

551 *Hong Kong Standard*, 20 July 1998.

552 Babcock, Todd, letter, 'Time to Remember', 30 November 1998; 'What People Have Said About Leslie'.

553 Talk in Hong Kong University, 29 March 1999, record by an anonymous fan.

554 http://www.complit.hku.hk/faculty/faculty.html.

555 *Moonlight Express*, Mei Ah Entertainment DVD-579 with CD MMCD87003.

556 *Moonlight Express* is discussed at: *Hong Kong Standard*, 9 August 1998 and 1 and 18 June 1999; Chitose Shima, *All About Leslie* (Tokyo: Sangyo Henshu Center Co., 1999); *City Entertainment*, no. 520 ('A Story behind the Legend'); Takako Tokiwa, website, 7 April 2003.

557 Chitose Shima, *All About Leslie* (Tokyo: Sangyo Henshu Center Co., 1999).

558 Takako Tokiwa, website, 7 April 2003.

559 These MTVs are occasionally viewable on Youtube.

560 *Hong Kong Standard*, 22 October 1999.

561 *Hong Kong Standard*, 22 October 1999.

562 *Hong Kong Standard*, 10 March 1999.

563 Chitose Shima, *All About Leslie* (Tokyo: Sangyo Henshu Center Co., 1999); Chitose Shima, *The Time of Leslie* (Tokyo: Sangyo Henshu Center Co., 2004).

564 Chitose Shima, *All About Leslie* (Tokyo: Sangyo Henshu Center Co., 1999).

565 Red Mission, Julie Ng, 'Achievements and Awards of Leslie'.

Notes to pages 271-277

566 Leslie's concert in Singapore is on Youtube at: http://www.youtube.com/watch?v=7FMcFPjVilk&feature=related; http://www.youtube.com/watch?v=UB30-3E0vqg&feature=related; http://www.youtube.com/watch?v=DMMl7LFQTwk&feature=related; http://www.youtube.com/watch?v=radMRmHNvDM&feature=related; http://www.youtube.com/watch?v=uXtuZO9OdQU&feature=related and http://www.youtube.com/watch?v=5P0Ll8efTdg&feature=related.

567 *Countdown with You* is currently unavailable on CD.

568 Commercial Radio Hong Kong, Lam Jik, 'Leslie's Passing and his Songs'.

569 'All about Leslie' (*Celebrity Talk Show 30*, Asia Television Ltd, Universe Laser & Video).

570 No video recording of *Left Right Love Destiny* is available.

571 'Legendary Years of Our Leslie; A Biography', Eunike, 18 February 2006, http://xoomer.virgilio.it/nguidett/biography01.htm.

572 *The Kid*, Mei Ah Laser Disc Co, DVD-246.

573 *The Kid* is discussed at: Chitose Shima, *All About Leslie* (Tokyo: Sangyo Henshu Center Co., 1999); *City Entertainment*, no. 520 ('A Story behind the Legend'); *South China Morning Post*, 10 April 2002 (Winnie Chung, 'Inner Secrets'); 'Leslie Cheung Artists Studies Website', 'Never Wanna Be Apart from Leslie: In Reminiscence of Leslie Cheung's Artistic Life' 30 April 2003, Hong Kong Baptist University, http://www.leslie-cheung.com/leslie/2004/5-31/14148.html, http://www.leslie-cheung.com 2004-5-31 1:39:28.

574 Chitose Shima, *All About Leslie* (Tokyo: Sangyo Henshu Center Co., 1999).

575 *City Entertainment*, no. 520 ('A Story behind the Legend').

576 *Hong Kong Standard*, 11 December 1999.

577 'Legendary Years of Our Leslie: A Biography', by Eunike, http://xoomer.virgilio.it/nguidett/biography01.htm.

578 *Hong Kong Standard*, 11 February 2000.

579 Translation of an interview Leslie gave Vanni, DJ of Commercial Radio, just before the concert is at: http://xoomer.virgilio.it/nguidett/radiochat.htm.

580 *Untitled* is not currently available on CD.

581 Leslie singing 'Pillow' is on Youtube at: http://www.youtube.com/watch?v=qg-3ymesKTY.

582 Leslie singing 'I Honestly Love You' is on Youtube at: http://www.youtube.com/watch?v=NuFUAJnUAYc.

583 *Hong Kong Standard*, 28 January 2000.

584 'Legendary Years of Our Leslie: A Biography', by Eunike, http://xoomer.virgilio.it/nguidett/biography01.htm.

Notes to pages 278-283

585 *Time*, 3 May 2000 (Stephen Short, 'Bedroom Pinup').

586 *Double Tap*, Universe Laser & Video Co VCD 2497.

587 *Double Tap* is discussed at: Man Hong interview in China, 2000, http://www.lesliesky.com/cgi-bin/topic.cgi?forum=35&topic=379&show=0; *Hong Kong Commercial Daily*, March 23, 2002 (Economic News, 'Cheung Kwok Wing - The Trend-Setting Superstar'); 'The Shining Star – In Reminiscence of Leslie's Artistic Life', seminar, 3 April 2005; *Shenzhen Daily*, 25 March 2005 (Law Chi-leung interview, http://www.sznews.com/jb/20050325/ca1507377.htm).

588 Man Hong interview in China, 2000, http://www.lesliesky.com/cgi-bin/topic.cgi?forum=35&topic=379&show=0; *Hong Kong Commercial Daily*, March 23, 2002 (Economic News, 'Cheung Kwok Wing - The Trend-Setting Superstar').

589 *Shenzhen Daily*, 25 March 2005 (Law Chi-leung interview, http://www.sznews.com/jb/20050325/ca1507377.htm).

590 *Okinawa Rendez-vous*, Mei Ah Entertainment VCD 1956.

591 *Okinawa Rendez-vous* is discussed at: Chow Shui Yum, 'Okinawa Rendez-vous' (May 2004).

592 'What People Have Said About Leslie.'

593 *Big Heat* is not currently available on CD.

594 Commercial Radio Hong Kong, 2003, Lam Jik, 'Leslie's Passing and his Songs'.

595 Reported in *Oriental Sunday*, no. 201, 2001 ('Leslie is always found guilty of unsound accusations').

596 'Leslie Cheung Artists Studies Website', 'Never Wanna Be Apart from Leslie: In Reminiscence of Leslie Cheung's Artistic Life' 30 April, 2003, Hong Kong Baptist University, http://www.leslie-cheung.com/leslie/2004/5-31/14148.html, http://www.leslie-cheung.com 2004-5-31 1:39:28.

597 Irasia.com, 4 April 2001.

598 *Ming Pao Weekly*, 1 April 2004, ('VCD in Remembrance of Cheung Kwok Wing', track 2, part 2).

Notes to pages 283-298

[599] *Star*, 13 September 2000; Reports in the press on *Ming Pao Weekly* Best Performing Award to Leslie (2001); *Hong Kong Commercial Daily*, March 23, 2002 (Economic News, 'Cheung Kwok Wing - The Trend-Setting Superstar'); *Time Asia*, 3 April 2003 (Richard Corliss, 'That Old Feeling: Days of Being Leslie'); *Ming Pao Weekly*, 1 April 2004, ('VCD in Remembrance of Cheung Kwok Wing', track 2, part 2); 'Leslie Cheung Artists Studies Website', 'Never Wanna Be Apart from Leslie: In Reminiscence of Leslie Cheung's Artistic Life' 30 April 2003, Hong Kong Baptist University, http://www.leslie-cheung.com/leslie/2004/5-31/14148.html, http://www.leslie-cheung.com 2004-5-31 1:39:28; 'Feeling as if Stabbed by a Knife', 15 January 2005,

http://ashesoftime.tianyablog.com/blogger/view_blog.asp?blogID=16419&CategoryID=0&idWriter=0&Key=0&NextPostID=1068651&PageNo=2; *Kuai Bao*, 28 February 2006 (Xun Yi, 'Florence Chan Reveals The Cause Of Leslie Cheung's Death – He Was Killed By The Paparazzi'),

http://www.kuaibao.net/cdsb/GB/2006/02/28/73261.html,

http://www.leslietong.com/lovehouse/dispbbs.asp?boardID=331&ID=29821&page=1)..

[600] Leslie told this story himself in his speech at the ceremony for the award of the Ming Pao Outstanding Award for Performing Arts in 2000.

[601] *Passion Tour*, Universal DVD 060-839-9.

[602] *Ashes to Ashes*, in RTHK, Intercontinental Video DVD 010927.

[603] *Ashes to Ashes* is discussed at: *Hong Kong iMail*, 28 September 2000; Wang Lee Hom, 'Uncle Leslie Has Taught Me The Important Thing As An Artist' in *Never Forget Leslie*, p.20, http://lesliecheungforever.net/Leehom-e.html.

[604] *Ashes to Ashes*, in RTHK, Intercontinental Video DVD 010927.

[605] Interview with an anonymous friend, 2006.

[606] *Ashes to Ashes*, in RTHK, Intercontinental Video DVD 010927.

[607] *Galaxy Production*, 7 September 2000 (Thomas Huong, 'Leslie tells Malaysia, 'They are not worth it!!'); *Music Net*, 7 September 2000 (Thomas Huang, 'The Legend Arrives'); *The Star*, Brian Cheong, 'Leslie's Last Fling (Passion Tour in Malaysia)'.

[608] *Music Net*, 7 September 2000 (Thomas Huang, 'The Legend Arrives').

[609] *The Star*, Brian Cheong, 'Leslie's Last Fling (Passion Tour in Malaysia)'.

[610] Man Hong interview in China, 2000, http://www.lesliesky.com/cgi-bin/topic.cgi?forum=35&topic=379&show=0.

[611] *The Sun*, 19 October 1999.

[612] IS Department Hong Kong, 31 October 2000.

[613] See Chapter 23.

[614] Chitose Shima, *The Time of Leslie* (Tokyo: Sangyo Henshu Center Co., 2004).

Notes to pages 293-303

[615] *Time Asia*, 3 April 2003 (Richard Corliss, 'That Old Feeling: Days of Being Leslie').

[616] *HKiMail*, 22 January 2001.

[617] *Leslie Cheung Passion Tour* Universal Cd 548 591-2.

[618] See Youtbue of the interview at: http://www.youtube.com/watch?v=SXcchpp DujM&feature=related;

http://www.youtube.com/watch?v=UsNQwV6vogU&feature=related;

http://www.youtube.com/watch?v=0Di6BfOigMI&feature=related; and translation online at: http://www.lesliecheung.cc/Special/translation/teresamo.htm; also mentioned at: *Time Asia*, 7 May 2001 (Richard Corliss/Stephen Short, 'Forever Leslie').

[619] *South China Morning Post*, 3 March 2001.

[620] Leslie and Kazuhiro Nishijima's MV of 'Bewildered' is on Youtube at; http://www.youtube.com/watch?v=Tt0iAHS8pe8.

[621] *Advocate*, 13 May 2003 (Lawrence Ferber, 'Leslie Cheung – Actor Singer'); Commercial Radio Hong Kong, 2003, Lam Jik, 'Leslie's Passing and his Songs'.

[622] See also: *Pop Asia*, 'Interview', April 2002.

[623] *Cashflow*, no. 41, June 2003 (James Wong, 'In Fond Memory of Leslie Cheung').

[624] *Cashflow*, no. 41, June 2003 (James Wong, 'In Fond Memory of Leslie Cheung').

[625] *Leslie Forever* is not currently available on CD.

[626] Leslie at the CASH ceremony is on Youtube at: http://www.youtube.com/watch?v=BdMlTSPTMvA&feature=related.

[627] See Chapter 24.

[628] Chitose Shima, *The Time of Leslie* (Tokyo: Sangyo Henshu Center Co., 2004).

[629] 'Feeling as if Stabbed by a Knife', 15 January 2005. http://ashesoftime.tianyablog.com/blogger/view_blog.asp?blogID=16419&CategoryID=0&idWriter=0&Key=0&NextPostID=1068651&PageNo=2, D.

[630] *Oriental Sunday*, no. 201, 2001 ('Leslie is always found guilty of unsound accusations').

[631] Leslie and Anita's MV is on Youtube at: http://www.youtube.com/watch?v=XIiWR8E1SZs&p=33DE254C60D185C4&playnext=1&index=18.

[632] 'Legendary Years of Our Leslie: A Biography', by Eunike, http://xoomer.virgilio.it/nguidett/biography01.htm.

[633] 'Legendary Years of Our Leslie: A Biography', by Eunike, http://xoomer.virgilio.it/nguidett/biography01.htm.

Notes to pages 304-308

[634] *South China Morning Post*, 10 April 2002.

[635] *Kinejun*, no. 1384, 2003, interview with Wada Emi, Kinejun, no. 1384, 2003.

[636] 'Leslie Cheung Artists Studies Website', 'Never Wanna Be Apart from Leslie: In Reminiscence of Leslie Cheung's Artistic Life' 30 April 2003, Hong Kong Baptist University, http://www.leslie-cheung.com/leslie/2004/5-31/14148.html, http://www.leslie-cheung.com 2004-5-31 1:39:28.

[637] Lee Pik-wah, http://lesliecheung.cc/memories/leepikwah_eng.htm.

[638] *Kinejun*, no. 1384, 2003 (interview with Wada Emi).

[639] 'Leslie Cheung Artists Studies Website', 'Never Wanna Be Apart from Leslie: In Reminiscence of Leslie Cheung's Artistic Life' 30 April 2003, Hong Kong Baptist University, http://www.leslie-cheung.com/leslie/2004/5-31/14148.html, http://www.leslie-cheung.com 2004-5-31 1:39:28.

[640] *Pop Asia*, 'Interview', April 2002; Red Forum, Tai Sing Pao, 20 March 2004, 'Movies Which Leslie Did Not Star In Or Failed To Finish'.

[641] Red Forum, Tai Sing Pao, 20 March 2004, 'Movies Which Leslie Did Not Star In Or Failed To Finish'.

[642] Lee Pik-wah, http://lesliecheung.cc/memories/leepikwah_eng.htm; Yu Siu Wah in 'Leslie Cheung Artists Studies Website', 'Never Wanna Be Apart from Leslie: In Reminiscence of Leslie Cheung's Artistic Life' 30 April, 2003, Hong Kong Baptist University, http://www.leslie-cheung.com/leslie/2004/5-31/14148. html, http://www.leslie-cheung.com 2004-5-31 1:39:28.

[643] *Next* no. 795, 2005 (Lilian Lee Pik Wah, 'It Came Too Late').

[644] *Kinejun*, no. 1384, 2003, interview with Wada Emi.

[645] Ren-lei, 'Ren-Lei Talking About God-Father Gor-Gor', http://lesliecheung.cc/memories/yanlui_eng.htm.

[646] Press summary in 'Leslie Cheung Internet Fan Club', www.lesliecheung.com; http://forum.lesliecheung.com/Forum62/HTML/000054.html.

[647] *Pop Asia*, 'Interview', February 2002.

[648] *Kinejun*, no. 1384, Emi Wada interview, 2003.

[649] *Hong Kong Commercial Daily*, 23 March 2002 (Economic News, 'Cheung Kwok Wing - The Trend-Setting Superstar').

[650] *Inner Senses*, Universe Laser & Video Co, VCD 3611.

Notes to pages 308-314

[651] *Inner Senses* is discussed at: *Hong Kong Commercial Daily*, 23 March 2002 (Economic News, 'Cheung Kwok Wing - The Trend-Setting Superstar'); *Pop Asia*, 'Interview', April 2002; *Asia Week*, ('In Acting He Draws from Experiences of the Pains in Real Life, http://lesliecheung.cc/memories/leepikwah_eng.htm); Winnie Chung, 'Inner Secrets', *South China Morning Post*, 10 April 2002; *Hong Kong Entertainment News in Review*, 2 April 2003 ('Leslie Cheung Kwok-Wing Commits Suicide'); *Time Asia*, 3 April 2003 (Richard Corliss, 'That Old Feeling: Days of Being Leslie'); Kelly, Stephen, 'Why Does It Have to Be Like This?': Leslie Cheung, 1956-2003', 2003; 'Leslie Cheung Artists Studies Website', 'Never Wanna Be Apart from Leslie: In Reminiscence of Leslie Cheung's Artistic Life' 30 April 2003, Hong Kong Baptist University, http://www.leslie-cheung.com/leslie/2004/5-31/14148. html, http://www.leslie-cheung.com 2004-5-31 1:39:28; *Shenzhen Daily*, 25 March 2005 (Law Chi-leung interview, *http://www.sznews.com/jb/20050325/ca1507377.htm); 'The Shining Star – In Reminiscence of Leslie's Artistic Life', Seminar, 3 April 2005.

[652] *Hong Kong Commercial Daily*, 23 March 2002 (Economic News, 'Cheung Kwok Wing - The Trend-Setting Superstar'); *Pop Asia*, 'Interview', April 2002; *Asia Week*, ('In Acting He Draws from Experiences of the Pains in Real Life, http://lesliecheung.cc/memories/leepikwah_eng.htm); Winnie Chung, 'Inner Secrets', *South China Morning Post*, 10 April 2002.

[653] Red Forum, Tai Sing Pao, 20 March 2004, 'Movies Which Leslie Did Not Star in Or Failed To Finish'.

[654] 'Legendary Years of Our Leslie: A Biography', by Eunike, http://xoomer.virgilio.it/nguidett/biography01.htm.

[655] Legendary Years of Our Leslie: A Biography', by Eunike, http://xoomer.virgilio.it/nguidett/biography01.htm.

[656] Legendary Years of Our Leslie: A Biography', by Eunike, http://xoomer.virgilio.it/nguidett/biography01.htm.

[657] *Ming Xin Za Zhi*, 1 April 2004 (Florence Chan interview).

[658] Maggie Cheung interview, *Cahiers du Cinema*, no. 579, May 2003.

[659] 12 April 2003 (Anita Mui, 'No More Unjustice To Gorgor Please', http://lesliecheung.cc/memories/anitamui_eng.htm).

[660] *Ming Pao*, 12 April 2003 (Anita Mui, 'No More Unjustice To Gorgor Please', http://lesliecheung.cc/memories/anitamui_eng.htm).

[661] Winnie Chung, 'Inner Secrets', *South China Morning Post*, 10 April 2002.

[662] Red Forum, Tai Sing Pao, 20 March 2004, 'Movies Which Leslie Did Not Star in Or Failed To Finish'.

[663] *Ming Pao* April 2003 (Law Kai Yu, 'Songs Behind the Door', http://lesliecheung.cc/memories/lawkaiyui2.htm).

Notes to pages 314-321

[664] A video of an interview with Leslie and Stephen Chow is at: http://www.youtube.com/watch?v=WK7RSmR_WAU&feature=related.; see also *All Music Shop Newsletter* May 2003, 'Forever Leslie (1956-2003)'.

[665] *Kinejun*, no. 1384, 2003, interview with Wada Emi.

[666] Lee Pik-wah, http://lesliecheung.cc/memories/leepikwah_eng.htm; Red Forum, Tai Sing Pao, 20 March 2004, 'Movies Which Leslie Did Not Star in Or Failed To Finish'.

[667] Lee Pik-wah, http://lesliecheung.cc/memories/leepikwah_eng.htm.

[668] Lee Pik-wah, http://lesliecheung.cc/memories/leepikwah_eng.htm.

[669] Red Forum, Tai Sing Pao, 20 March 2004, 'Movies Which Leslie Did Not Star In Or Failed To Finish'.

[670] Kelly, Stephen, 'Why Does It Have to Be Like This?': Leslie Cheung, 1956-2003', 2003.

[671] Press summary in 'Leslie Cheung Internet Fan Club', www.lesliecheung.com; http://forum.lesliecheung.com/Forum62/HTML/000054.html.

[672] *Hong Kong Entertainment News in Review*, 2 April 2003 ('Leslie Cheung Kwok-Wing Commits Suicide'); *Ming Pao*, 6 April 2003 (interview with Florence Chan); Lee Pik-wah, http://lesliecheung.cc/memories/leepikwah_eng.htm.

[673] *Ming Xin Za Zhi*, 1 April 2004 (Florence Chan interview).

[674] Press summary in 'Leslie Cheung Internet Fan Club', www.lesliecheung.com; http://forum.lesliecheung.com/Forum62/HTML/000054.html.

[675] *Ming Xin Za Zhi*, 1 April 2004 (Florence Chan interview).

[676] 'Legendary Years of Our Leslie: A Biography', by Eunike, http://xoomer.virgilio.it/nguidett/biography01.htm.

[677] *Ming Xin Za Zhi*, 1 April 2004 (Florence Chan interview).

[678] 'Legendary Years of Our Leslie: A Biography', by Eunike, http://xoomer.virgilio.it/nguidett/biography01.htm.

[679] *Crossover* is not available on CD.

[680] . 'Love Gorgor', Interview with Lam Jik.

[681] *Ming Xin Za Zhi*, 1 April 2004 (Florence Chan interview).

[682] Hardin, Kimeron and Marny Hall, *Queer Blues* (Oakland: New Harbinger, 2001).

[683] Hardin, Kimeron and Marny Hall, *Queer Blues* (Oakland: New Harbinger, 2001).

Notes to pages 321-327

[684] *Ming Pao*, 12 April 2003 (Anita Mui, 'No More Unjustice To Gorgor Please', http://lesliecheung.cc/memories/anitamui_eng.htm); Teresa Mo commented on Leslie's rejection of her offers to help in her Commercial Radio programme; *Hong Kong Entertainment News in Review*, 2 April 2003 ('Leslie Cheung Kwok-Wing Commits Suicide').

[685] *Ming Pao*, April 2003 (Law Kai Yu, 'Songs Behind the Door', http://lesliecheung.cc/memories/lawkaiyui2.htm).

[686] The reports of trouble within their relationship is mentioned in *Hong Kong Entertainment News in Review*, 2 April 2003 ('Leslie Cheung Kwok-Wing Commits Suicide').

[687] *Ming Pao*, 6 April 2003 (interview with Florence Chan).

[688] *Kinejun*, no. 1384, 2003, interview with Wada Emi.

[689] *Ming Xin Za Zhi*, 1 April 2004 (Florence Chan interview).

[690] Morton, Lisa, *The Cinema of Tsui Hark* (Jefferson, NC: McFarland and Company, 2001).

[691] 'Legendary Years of Our Leslie: A Biography', by Eunike, http://xoomer.virgilio.it/nguidett/biography01.htm.

[692] 12 April 2003 (Anita Mui, 'No More Unjustice To Gorgor Please', http://lesliecheung.cc/memories/anitamui_eng.htm).

[693] *Hong Kong Entertainment News in Review*, 2 April 2003 ('Leslie Cheung Kwok-Wing Commits Suicide').

[694] 'Legendary Years of Our Leslie: A Biography', by Eunike, http://xoomer.virgilio.it/nguidett/biography01.htm.

[695] 'Legendary Years of Our Leslie: A Biography', by Eunike, http://xoomer.virgilio.it/nguidett/biography01.htm.

[696] 'Legendary Years of Our Leslie: A Biography', by Eunike, http://xoomer.virgilio.it/nguidett/biography01.htm.

[697] *South China Morning Post*, 1 August 2002.

[698] 'Legendary Years of Our Leslie: A Biography', by Eunike, http://xoomer.virgilio.it/nguidett/biography01.htm.

[699] *Ming Pao* no. 1820, 2003, (Wong Lai Ling, interview with Florence Chan).

[700] Kelly, Stephen, 'Why Does It Have to Be Like This?': Leslie Cheung, 1956-2003', 2003.

[701] 'Legendary Years of Our Leslie: A Biography', by Eunike, http://xoomer.virgilio.it/nguidett/biography01.htm.

[702] Maggie Cheung interview, *Cahiers du Cinema*, no. 579, May 2003.

[703] 'Leslie's Footprints in Oriental Bangkok'.

Notes to pages 328-333

704 The MV of his appearance is at: http://www.youtube.com/watch?v=TjVnQzkcqGo.

705 Red Forum, Tai Sing Pao, 20 March 2004, 'Movies Which Leslie Did Not Star in Or Failed To Finish'.

706 *Shenzhen Daily*, 25 March 2005 (Law Chi-leung interview, http://www.sznews.com/jb/20050325/ca1507377.htm).

707 'Legendary Years of Our Leslie: A Biography', by Eunike, http://xoomer.virgilio.it/nguidett/biography01.htm.

708 Commercial Radio Hong Kong, 2003, Lam Jik, 'Leslie's Passing and his Songs'.

709 'Legendary Years of Our Leslie: A Biography', by Eunike, http://xoomer.virgilio.it/nguidett/biography01.htm.

710 'Legendary Years of Our Leslie: A Biography', by Eunike, http://xoomer.virgilio.it/nguidett/biography01.htm.

711 Stewart, Clare, and Philippa Hawker, eds, *Leslie Cheung* (Flinders Lane, Australia: Australian Centre for the Moving Image, 2003); Red Forum, Tai Sing Pao, 20 March 2004, 'Movies Which Leslie Did Not Star In Or Failed To Finish'..

712 Email to the author from Father Lionel Xavier to the author, 13 June 2006.

713 Press summary in 'Leslie Cheung Internet Fan Club', www.lesliecheung.com; http://forum.lesliecheung.com/Forum62/HTML/000054.html.

714 ' Press summary in 'Leslie Cheung Internet Fan Club', www.lesliecheung.com; http://forum.lesliecheung.com/Forum62/HTML/000054.html; *All Music Shop Newsletter* May 2003, 'Forever Leslie (1956-2003) – The Legend Lives On'; Kelly, Stephen, 'Why Does It Have to Be Like This?': Leslie Cheung, 1956-2003', 2003.

715 *South China Morning Post*, 31 March 2004 (Vivienne Cow, 'Mainland Glamour for Hong Kong's Oscars'; Matthew Scott, 'If We Knew More').

716 'Six Hours before the Death of Leslie Cheung – Last Lunch with Best Friend', *Ming Pao Weekly*, 26 March 2011.

717 'Six Hours before the Death of Leslie Cheung – Last Lunch with Best Friend', *Ming Pao Weekly*, 26 March 2011. Wada Emi made an interesting remark which may bear on this story in an interview she gave to the magazine *Kinejun* in 2003: 'I do not want to ask why he went to Mandarin Hotel, why the window in that hotel could be opened [sic]. When we met in Central, we used to meet at the Conrad Hotel... The window of that hotel could not be opened.'

718 Press summary in 'Leslie Cheung Internet Fan Club', www.lesliecheung.com; http://forum.lesliecheung.com/Forum62/HTML/000054.html.

719 Press summary in 'Leslie Cheung Internet Fan Club', www.lesliecheung.com; http://forum.lesliecheung.com/Forum62/HTML/000054.html.

Notes to pages 334-338

[720] *Xinmin Za Zhi*, 1 April 2004 (Florence Chan interview).

[721] Press summary in 'Leslie Cheung Internet Fan Club', www.lesliecheung.com; http://forum.lesliecheung.com/Forum62/HTML/000054.html.

[722] *Xinmin Za Zhi*, 1 April 2004 (Florence Chan interview).

[723] *Xinmin Za Zhi*, 1 April 2004 (Florence Chan interview).

[724] Copy of an entry in the register of deaths, number 9208AY, H620249, registered on 7 July 2003 after direction by Coroner Michael Chan. 'Certified dead on 1 April 2003, Queen Mary Hospital'.

[725] Press summary in 'Leslie Cheung Internet Fan Club', www.lesliecheung.com; http://forum.lesliecheung.com/Forum62/HTML/000054.html.

[726] Press summary in 'Leslie Cheung Internet Fan Club', www.lesliecheung.com; http://forum.lesliecheung.com/Forum62/HTML/000054.html.

[727] *Apple Daily*, 2 April 2003; *Xinmin Za Zhi*, 1 April 2004 (Florence Chan interview).

[728] *All Music Shop Newsletter*, May 2003, 'Forever Leslie (1956-2003) – The Legend Lives On; Press summary in 'Leslie Cheung Internet Fan Club', www.lesliecheung.com; http://forum.lesliecheung.com/Forum62/HTML/000054.html.

[729] 'Leslie Cheung Commits Suicide', *Hong Kong Entertainment News*, 2 April 2003; *Apple Daily*, 2 April 2003. .

[730] *Apple Daily*, 2 April 2003; Press summary in 'Leslie Cheung Internet Fan Club', www.lesliecheung.com; http://forum.lesliecheung.com/Forum62/HTML/000054.html.

[731] Leslie Cheung Commits Suicide', *Hong Kong Entertainment News* ,2 April 2003. Florence Chan dealt with these scurrilous rumours robustly in: *Ming Xin Za Zhi*, 1 April 2004 (Florence Chan interview).

[732] *Xin Min Za Zhi*, 1 April 2004 (Florence Chan interview). See also: *Kuai Bao*, 28 February 2006 (Xun Yi, 'Florence Chan Reveals The Cause Of Leslie Cheung's Death – He Was Killed By The Paparazzi',

http://www.kuaibao.net/cdsb/GB/2006/02/28/73261.html, http://www.leslietong.com/lovehouse/dispbbs.asp?boardID=331&ID=29821&page=1). In this she says: 'GorGor chose death because he didn't want the outside world to know about his sickness. He was losing control of himself more and more. In the end he was afraid of appearing in public in case some problems might occur and this would give an opportunity for others to write something about him. He really didn't wish to have such incidents happening to him so he made that decision.'

[733] Copy of an entry in the register of deaths, number 9208AY, H620249, registered on 7 July 2003 after direction by Coroner Michael Chan. 'Certified dead on 1 April 2003, Queen Mary Hospital'.

Index

100 Years of Chinese Film History, 118
2000 Most Successful Person in China award, 294
Abbas, Ackbar, 26, 267
Abbas, Alisha, 53, 311, 321
Abbas, Ayesha, 53, 232, 311, 321
Admiralty, 330
Africa, 119
Alan (friend), 36
All's Well series, 205
Ambassador Hotel, 56
Ambient Bistro, 286
"Amore", 216
Amsterdam, 248
Anzenchitai, 127
Apple Daily, 255, 262
Arabia, 78
Argentina, 240, 250, 251
Arsenal Street Police Headquarters, 186
Asia Pacific Film Festival, 184-185
Asia Week, 309
Asian Broadcasting Union's
Asian Amateur Singing Contest '77, 45
Aska (Asuka) – see Chage and Aska
"Are You Ready for Love", 155
Atlantic City, 88-89, 248, 291-292
ATV, 70, 75, 80, 81, 155, 232, 272
Australia, 94, 120, 165, 253, 282, 290
Babida, Chris, 95, 143, 227
Bad, 132
BAFTA, 200
Balke, Gerd, 162-163

Banana Club – see Club Banana
Bancroft, Todd, 265, 267
Bang Bang Restaurant, 55
Bangkok, 88, 288, 327
Baptist College, 31
BBDO, 132
Beatles, the, 216
Bedtime Stories, 251
Bee Kenny – see Chung Chun-to
Beijing, 157, 163, 188, 193, 197, 199, 227, 230, 241, 254, 262, 266, 314, 320
TV, 267
Beijing Workers' Sports Stadium, 254
Berger, Santa, 257
Berlin, 257
Berlin Film Festival, 131, 245, 257
Best TV Serial Soundtrack, 277
Bexley, 37
Big Parade, The, 192
Bird, Kathryn, 253
bird flu, 256
"Blue Balloon", 35
Bowie, David, 35, 242
Boy George, 251
Brando, Marlon, 22
Bride, 205
"Bridge over Troubled Waters", 184
Bridgewater, Ann, 143, 146, 156
  music;
  "A Rainy Day without an Umbrella", 143
Bright, 277
British Columbia, 173, 228
British Film Institute, 100 Years of Cinema, 237

Broadcast Drive, 47, 48
Broadway, 281
Brown, Father Lionel Xavier, 30, 330
Bucheon, 310
Buddhist Wong Fung Ling College, 32-33
Buenos Aires, 251, 252
Bund, The, 235
Bund, The, Part II, 235
Cable TV, 53
Caesar's Palace, 293
Café de Coral, 94
California, 200
Campion, Jane, 198
Canada, 27, 94, 111, 113, 120, 121, 127, 134, 147, 149, 158, 161, 162, 165, 173-175, 183-184, 185, 188, 208, 209, 211, 218, 226-228, 231, 238, 292
Cannes, 188, 234
Cannes Film Festival, 192
Cantopop, 48, 51, 55, 86, 102, 109-110, 164, 242, 256, 275, 283
Cape Collinson crematorium, 13
Capital Artists, 79-80, 82, 85, 86, 87-88, 89, 92, 94, 99, 101, 103, 110, 111, 120, 122, 124, 125-126, 132, 133, 150, 225, 241, 261
Capra, Frank, 212
Cartier, 55, 66, 100
Cat Street Café, 189
Cathay Pacific Airways, 273
Cats, 146
Causeway Bay, 232, 277, 289, 295, 299, 332
CCTV
    CCTV-MTV (Beijing) Music Award Outstanding Artist in Asia, 290
    News, 14
Centennial of Chinese Film History, Most Favourite Film, 181
Central, 21, 26, 56, 112, 188, 251, 324, 325, 333, 334
Central do Brasil, 257
Cha Leung-yung, Louis – see Jin Yong
Chage and Aska (Asuka), 260
Chan Chuen, 76
Chan, Evans, 75-76
Chan Fang On-sang, Anson, 269, 275, 290
Chan Ho-sun, Peter, 213, 237
Chan, Justin, 141
Chan, Jackie, 50, 94, 118, 144, 149, 150, 186, 192, 194, 259, 262, 275, 325, 326, 328
Chan Kar-Seung, Gordon, 280
Chan Kit-ling, Elisa, 81, 108, 123, 331, 336
Chan, Nat, 101
Chan Pak-keung, Danny, 55-56, 57, 58, 63, 64, 65, 67, 68, 69, 70, 71, 73, 74, 86, 93, 95, 103, 104, 108, 109, 122-123, 133, 157, 188, 198, 208
TV:
    Enjoy Yourselves Tonight, 59
music:
    "Encore", 64
    Encore, 68
    "Encourage", 103
    First Love, 58
    No More Tears, 68
    "Shedding My Tears for You," 59

Sunflower, 68
Chan Po-chu, Connie, 175
Chan, Shirley, 153
Chan Siu-kei, 323
Chan Siu-po, 134, 271
Chan Suk-fun, Florence, 46, 79, 80, 86, 88, 100, 101, 110, 113, 125, 126, 127, 134, 149, 156, 159, 168, 173, 282, 284, 311, 316, 317, 319, 322, 324, 333-335, 336, 337
Chan, Willie, 144
Chang Ai Chi, Sylvia, 310-311, 315, 325
Chang, Chen, 288
Chang Suk-ping, William, 219
Chelmsford, 38, 39, 392 note 64
Chen, Alan, 141, 142
Chen, Diane, 277
Chen Guoxing, 328
Chen Koon-hei, Edison, 310
Chen Kaige, 182, 188, 191, 192, 194, 195, 196, 197, 198, 200, 201, 232, 233, 234, 235
Chen Xiu Xia, 259
Cheng Pei-pei, 81
Cheng Sau-Man, Sammi, 275
Cheng Siu-chow, Adam, 138
Cheng Yu-ling, Carol "Do Do", 174, 182
Chengdu, 266
Cheong, Brian, 288
Cheung, Aileen, 24
Cheung Chi-Leung, Jacob, 274, 285
Cheung Dai-wing, Didi, 24, 183
Cheung family, Essex, 33, 35, 37
Cheung Fat-wing, Eddie, 24, 295
Cheung Hok-yau, Jacky, 12, 13, 179, 184, 202, 211, 219, 232, 244, 269, 293, 328
Cheung Kin-Ting, Alfred, 184
Cheung Kwok-wing, Leslie:
  birth, 21
  Bright ambassador, 277
  Canada, reasons for emigrating to, 158, 159-164
  Canada, reasons for return from, 226-228
  career and contracts:
    APEX Music Production, 271
    Asian Broadcasting Union's Asian Amateur Singing Contest '77, 45-47, 80
    Capital Artists contract, 79, 125-126
    Cinema City contract, 95, 125, 135, 138
    Cinepoly contract, 124-125
    Dream League, 304, 312
    Polydor contract, 47, 65
    Rock records contract, 225, 270, 329
    RTV/ATV contract, 47, 80
    TVB contract, 80
    Universal Music Group (UMG), 270-271, 329
  Chan, Danny, friendship with - see Chan Pak-keung, Danny
  charity work, 119, 148-149, 165, 166, 184, 231, 261, 269, 271, 276, 277, 289, 290, 297, 316, 324, 329, 330
  childhood, 24-25
  China, views on, 162, 227, 255, 258-259, 265
  Commercial Radio autobiography

(1985), 40, 65, 70-71, 72, 73, 77, 79, 105-107

coffee shop, 153, 218, 232, 273, 295

Wei Nin Zhong Qin (For Your Heart Only), 232

court case, 79

death, 11, 334-335

funeral, 13

viewing at funeral home 12

wake, 13

decorator, 128

depression, 263, 284, 309, 310, 311-312, 313-317, 318-322, 323-324-326, 327-334, 336-337, 432 note 731

DD Crowd, 56, 81, 107, 149

director, desire to be, work as, 174, 213, 244, 257, 273, 285-287, 295, 303, 307, 311, 313, 314, 325

education:

    kindergarten, 26

    St. Luke's Primary School, 26-28

    Rosaryhill School, 28, 29-32

    Buddhist Wong Fung Ling College, 32-33

    Eccles Hall, 33, 34-38

    Wellington College, 40-42, 392 note 67

    Simon Fraser University, 174

English ability and voice, 30, 36, 51-52, 265

fans, 119-120, 134, 165, 166, 174, 218, 226, 233, 261, 263, 267, 269, 270, 291, 293, 295, 303, 310

German shepherd dog, Bingo, 262

girl friends & studio romances, 31, 40-41, 53, 57-58, 65-67, 69, 85, 94, 96, 105-106, 107, 108, 112, 113, 148, 149, 156, 182

Hollywood, views on, 201, 212, 258, 267, 308

Hong Kong culture, place in, 14-15, 299, 303, 308

interviews, 41, 72, 73, 75-76, 78, 102, 106, 111, 121, 122, 124, 134, 148, 153, 154, 155-156, 158, 161, 175, 208, 212, 218, 222, 225-226, 227, 228, 230, 237-238, 242, 244, 249-250, 251, 255, 257, 258, 260, 261, 262, 263-264, 266, 267, 275, 278, 287, 288, 290, 294, 296, 298, 307-308, 309, 311, 313, 324, 329

juries:

    Berlin Film Festival, 257

    Tokyo International Film Festival - Young Cinema Competition, 203

Lai, Michael, musical godfather, relationship with– see Lai Siu-tin, Michael

Luk Che, love for, 23, 106, 174

Mandarin proficiency, 193, 230

marriage proposals, 53, 66-67, 71, 294

media relations, 75-76, 101, 108, 113, 131, 152, 225-226, 231, 236, 243-244, 247, 255, 262, 263, 268-269, 270, 276, 278, 283-284, 288, 290, 296, 298-299, 307, 312, 316, 320, 322, 337

Mui Yim-fong, Anita, friendship with, 81-82 and see - Mui Yim-fong, Anita

Music Ambassador of the

Composers and Authors Society of Hong Kong (CASH), 291, 297

music, interest in, 30, 35, 41

names:

    Fat-chung, 21

    Billy, 29

    Bobby, 32, 33, 34, 40, 48, 88, 120, 168

    Frankie, 34, 38, 40

    "Three Lights", 41

    Leslie, 35, 48

    Gor Gor, 83, 120, 131, 206, 312

professionalism in acting, 54, 140, 179, 193, 194, 195, 207, 234, 267, 268, 274, 278, 279, 280, 309, 310

Ren Lei, Godfather to, 235, 307

residences:

    Broadcast Drive, 47

    Eyremont Drive, West Vancouver, 173

    Fairview Park (Gam Sau Fa Yuen), 72, 78

    Federal Gardens, Conduit Road, 106

    Kadoorie Hill, 261, 306, 307, 319, 324, 331, 332, 336

    Lai Wan, 48, 68

    Peak, the, 208

    Repulse Bay, 128, 146, 173

    Robinson Road, 78

    Taikoo Shing, 89

    Turtle Cove Bay (Kwai Pui Wan), Number 2, 231, 244, 261, 262, 293

sexual orientation, 15, 31-32, 36-39, 67, 68, 71, 76, 78, 82-84, 90, 100, 101, 105-106, 109, 111, 121, 149, 187, 196-197, 202, 206, 208, 213-216, 231, 236, 237-238, 240, 242-244, 249-250, 253, 255, 261, 253-264, 268, 272, 275, 277, 278, 281, 282, 283, 284, 294, 295, 307, 313

talent competitions, 30, 41, 45-47

Tam, Alan, rivalry with, 108-109, 111, 133, 144-145, 158, 161, 211, 254, 258, 303

Three Musketeers, the, 64, 65, 67

Tong Hok-tak, Daffy, relationship with, 82-84, 89-90, 107, 145, 146, 147, 148, 149, 158, 164, 169, 185, 194, 208, 222, 231, 237, 240, 243-244, 255, 263, 264, 270, 276, 291, 294, 298, 299, 303, 307, 316, 321, 323, 336-337

Works:

albums:

    '90 New Mix Plus Hits Collection, 176

    All These Years, 259

    Always in My Heart, 229

    Best of Leslie Cheung, The, 272

    Big Heat, 280, 281, 290

    Cheung Kwok Wing, 142

    Cheung Kwok-wing (Allure Me) (Fire of Love; The Past Love), 122

    Countdown with You, 271

    Craziness (A Bit of Craziness), 89

    Crossover, 317-318, 320, 323

    Crossover '97, 253

    Dance Remix 87, 126

Daydreamin', 51, 52
Dear Leslie, 297
Double Fantasy, 253
Dreaming, 176
Everybody, 260
Everything Follows the Wind, 329
Final Collection, 177
Final Encounter, 166, 176
For Your Love Only (Falling in Love with You; Love for You Only; Honestly Loving You; Loving You), 99, 100, 110
Gift, 260
Hot Summer, 142, 143
Legend, 253
Leslie (Leslie '89; Side Face), 152-153
Leslie Best of Music Videos, 290
Leslie Cheung Kwok-wing (Monica, Leslie–Monica), 92, 110
Leslie Cheung Passion Tour, 294
Leslie Forever, 295, 296, 317
Leslie in Concert 88, 145
Listening, 239
Love (Beloved; Fondness; Love Leslie; Strong Love), 228
Love and Admiration (Admiration; Admire; Admirer), 124
Love Songs Collection – Greatest Hits, 126

Love with All My Heart, 239
Lover's Arrow, 59
Miss You Mix, 177
Music Box, 297
Printemps, 259-260, 261
Red, 239
Salute, 165-166, 167,
Salute - 24k Gold Collection, 209
Stand Up, 110, 113
Summer Best Collection – All Because of You, 101, 108
Summer Romance '87, 132, 133, 134
Ultimate Leslie, 189
Untitled, 276, 277, 290
Virgin Snow, 140-141, 156
Wind Blows On, The (The Wind Continues to Blow), 87, 88, 233

Awards, nominations and presentations:
2000 Most Successful Person in China award, 294
Asia Top 20 list, 260
BAFTA, 200
Best TV Serial Soundtrack, 277
Cannes Film Festival Palme d'Or, 198
CASH Golden Sail Awards, 297, 324
Cashbox KTV, 260
CCTV-MTV (Beijing) Music Award

Outstanding Artist in Asia, 290
Centennial of Chinese Film History, Most Favourite Film, 181, 201
China MTV Awards, 272
China Music Awards, Millennium Best Award, 297
China Society for Performing Arts - Award for High Achievement, 200
China's Original Music Outstanding Achievement Award, 294
Commercial Radio's Chinese Pop Songs Award, 92, 100, 122, 133
Commercial Radio Channel II and Green Power, ten stars with the healthiest looks and lifestyle, 185
Commercial Radio Hong Kong Top Ten Most Beautiful People, 59
Commercial Radio Ultimate Song Chart Male Gold Award, 143, 159, 276
CSMTV's Best MTVs, 260
Golden Disc Award, 88
Golden Globe - Best Foreign Language Film, 200
Golden Horse Awards, 140, 184, 310, 325
Best Original Song, 208
Golden Melody awards, 277
Golden Rooster Awards, 324
Hong Kong film awards, 140, 212, 221, 297, 314
Best Actor, 181, 182, 217, 245, 252, 310, 328
Best Original Film Song, 208, 230
Hong Kong Film Critics Society, 275, 310
Hong Kong Film Festival, Special Award of Best Hong Kong Film of the Past 10 Years, 181
IFPI Award, 143
IFPI's Best Album of the Year, 153, 272
Japanese Film Critics Society - Best Actor Award (Foreign Movie), 200
Metro Radio's Song Chart of the Year and Gold Song of the Year, 276
Ming Pao Grand Salute Award, 296
Ming Pao Weekly, Most Outstanding Actor 2002, 310, 325
Movie Express Japan film awards, 245
Nokia star, 317

Oscars - Best Foreign Language Film, 200
Pop Music Media Association of China, Music Salute Award, 296
RTHK's Best Selling Artist, 232
RTHK, Commercial Radio, Metro Radio and TVB Best Album of the Year, 277
RTHK's Gold Song of the illennium Award, 272
RTHK Golden Needle Award, 275, 293
RTHK Silver Jubilee Award, 327
RTHK's Top Best Selling Album of the Year, 272
RTHK's Top Pick Award, 296
RTHK's Top Ten Chinese Gold Songs Awards, 100, 122, 133,143, 211, 231-232, 271, 276, 293-294, 327
RTHK's Top Ten Popular Artist, 122, 133, 290
South Korean award for best film couple, 329
Time Asia, 201
Top Ten Asian Singers for Asian Pops, 253
Toyota Weekly Top Ten Segment, 260
TVB Jade's Top Ten Chinese Solid Gold Songs Award, 92, 100, 111, 122, 124, 126, 133, 153, 158, 290, 296, 303
TVB Jade's Gold Song of the Year, 133
TVB Most Popular Male Singer, 143, 158
Universal Records Number One Artist of the Year, 319
Wah Kiu Daily News Most Promising Newcomer, 52
Wah Kiu Daily News Top Ten Popular Artist, 92
Zhi Jiang Media Eternal Charisma Award, 289

books:
All about Leslie, 263, 270
Passion in China, 297
Stark Impressions, 147

commercials:
Backstage, 142
Café de Coral, 94
Konica, 123
Pepsi, 132, 142, 329
Taiwan motorcycle, 156
To You Chocolates, 155

concerts & shows:
'86 Expo, 113
Academy Hall, Baptist College, 78
Anita Mui at the Coliseum, 269
Fantasy Gig 200, 312
August 1982, 75
Beijing Workers' Sports Stadium, 254

City Hall, 68
Concert 428, 141
Crossover 97, 239, 240-243, 247, 250, 255, 283, 285, 298, 317
Final Encounter of the Legend, 158, 166, 173, 176, 233
FM 903 Live Concert (the Pillow Concert), 276, 277
Forum de Macau Stadium, 108
Hong Kong Tri-star in Concert, 120
hotel gigs, 88
Jade Ballroom, the Furama Hotel, 112
Japan charity concert, 118
Joseph Koo & James Wong True Friendship Concert, 261
Karen Mok's first concert, 294
Ko Shan theatre, 134
Kung Hau theatre, Macau, 58, 59
Leslie Cheung in Concert '85, 102
Leslie Cheung in Concert '86, 122-124, 147
Leslie Cheung in Concert '88, 143, 147
Leslie Cheung Meets You at the Ocean Palace Restaurant
Night Club, 126-127
Malaysian National Day Ball, 58

Mandarin Films' annual spring dinner, 258
Michael Lai and Friends, 150
Millennium Gold Songs Concert, 275
Passion Tour, 282-284, 288-296, 298, 311, 337
Paul Chung benefit, 69
Peace Concert in Hiroshima, 271
Pepsico concert, 329
Pop Folk, 52, 59, 108
Queen Elizabeth II, 121
Sam Hui's farewell concert, 189
Sha Tin, 80, 102, 108
Tokyo Music Festival, 127, 166
TVB Top 10 Gold Song Awards, 111

film:
 Aces Go Places V: The Terracotta Hit, 151-152, 189
 All's Well Ends Well (Family Has Happy Affairs), 184, 185, 186, 187, 242
 All's Well, Ends Well '97, 248
 All's Well Ends Well Too, 188, 201, 230
 Anna Magdalena, 262
 Arrest the Restless, 187-188
 Ashes of Time, 218-221, 267
 Ashes to Ashes, 285-288
 Banquet, The, 184, 201
 Behind the Yellow Line (Destiny), 93, 154, 324
 Better Tomorrow, A (True

Colours of Valour; the Essence of Heroes), 115-118, 129, 131, 134, 144

Better Tomorrow II, A, 134-135, 141

Bride with White Hair, The, 205-208, 230, 305

Bride with White Hair 2, 209, 230

Chinese Feast, The (*Gold Jade Full Hall*), 221-222, 229

Chinese Ghost Story, A, 129-131, 132, 144, 166, 206, 255-256, 262

Chinese Ghost Story 2, A, 175, 179, 207, 305

Crazy Romance, 101

Days of Being Wild (*The Story of "A Fei"*), 177-181, 182, 185, 188, 325

Dog Bites Dog Bone (*Cat and Dogs*), 58

Double Decker, 95

Double Tap, 278-279, 287, 308, 309

Drummer, The, 79, 85, 103

Eagle Shooting Heroes (*Success Here and There*), 188, 202, 205, 218, 220

Encore, 59, 63, 67, 70, 85, 188

Energetic 21, 76

Erotic Dream of Red Chamber, 50, 90

Farewell My Concubine, 15, 182, 187, 188, 191-201, 227, 234, 238, 241, 242, 259, 261, 266, 315

Fatal Love, 143, 145-146, 154

First Time, 85

For Your Heart Only, 104, 232

Happy Together, 238, 240, 248-251, 261, 275, 318

He's a Woman, She's a Man (*Golden Branch, Jade Leaf*), 212-217, 236, 242, 292

Inner Senses, 297, 308-310, 325, 328

Intellectual Trio, The, 100

It's a Wonderful Life (*Big Rich Family*), 212

Kid, The, 273-275, 285, 287

Last Song in Paris, 112, 130, 154

Little Dragon Maiden, 90, 96

Long & Winding Road, 217

Merry Christmas, 95, 104, 187

Moonlight Express, 267-269

Ninth Happiness, 258, 259

Nomad, 77-78, 90, 202

Okinawa Rendez-vous, 279-280, 297

On Trial (*Job Hunter*), 67, 70, 71, 76

Once a Thief (*Criss Cross over Four Seas; Vertical and Horizontal World*), 181-182, 218

Over the Rainbow under the Skirt, 217

Phantom Lover, The, 229-231, 273

Rouge, 138-140, 144, 145, 149, 181

Shanghai Grand, 235-236, 304

Teenage Dreamers (*Lemon Cola*), 73-74, 75-76

Temptress Moon (*Shadow*

of a Flower), 201, 222, 233-235, 287, 315

Time to Remember, A (The Red Lover), 257, 258, 260, 265

Tri-star (Big Three Round), 232

Viva Erotica, 241, 244-245, 257, 278

Who's the Woman, Who's the Man (Golden Branch, Jade Leaf 2), 236

film parts:
A Fei (Teddy), 188
Ben, the "Red Devil", 72
Cheng Dieyi, 191
Chi Ken-wing, 145
Cho Yi-hang, 205
David Copper Feel, 201
Gigo, 63-64
Ho Po-wing, 249, 252, 264
Jia Bao Yu (Precious Jade), 50
Jim Law, 308
Jin, 265
Kit, 116, 131
Louis, 77, 78, 90
Ning, 130, 175, 255
Ouyang Feng (Malicious West), 219, 221
Rick Pang, 278
Sam Koo Kah-ming, 214, 237
Shang So, 187
Sing, 244
Twelfth Master, Chen Chen-pang, 138-140
Wing, 101, 217, 274
Yang Guo, 90

Yuddi, 178-180
music videos, 269
Bewildered, 295
Big Heat, 282
"Keeping Company", 260
Legend, 253
songs:
"Afraid We May Never Meet Again", 108
"American Pie", 46, 51, 80, 103, 294
"Are You Lonesome Tonight", 126
"Big Heat", 281, 294
"Bit of Craziness, A", 89
"Chase", 214, 229
"Close to You" ("Close to the Body"), 142, 145
"Crazy for You", 167
"Crazy Rock", 122
"Cruise Mood", 156
"Cupid's Arrow", 60
"Deep Affection for You", 89
"Deep Love", 146
"Do You Wanna Make Love", 60
"Don't Ask Me about Today", 135
"Dream in the Night", 317
"Dreaming of the Inner River", 295, 317
"Even Now", 51
"Everybody", 260
"Falling in Love with You" ("Loving You"), 99, 103
"Fate", 93, 299
"Fever", 294

"Fickle Love", 99
"First Time", 103
"For Your Heart Only", 276
"Forever Love You", 166
"Forward to the Days in the Future", 135, 141
"Future, The", 259
"Glass Love", 323
"Going through Winter Together", 289, 303
"H2O", 92, 101, 102, 127, 142, 276
"Happy Together", 318
"Hot Summer", 142, 145
"Hot, Hot, Hot" ("Hot, Spicy, Spicy'), 141, 145
"I", 281, 284, 285, 290, 291m 296
"I'm of Strong Sentiment", 85
"I Can't Break Away", 153, 167, 177
"I Can't Control Myself", 132
"I Do", 99, 126
"I Honestly Love You", 276, 277
"I Like Dreamin'", 51
"I Know You Are Good", 323
"If You Knew My Hidden Reason", 318
"In My Life", 216
"Just the Way You Are", 51
"Keeping Company", 260
"Killer of Love" ("Love Murderer"), 141
"Left/Right Hand" ("Left and Right Hands"), 271, 276, 277
"Let Me Disappear", 124

"Little Star", 272
"Living Like a Dream", 91
"Loneliness Is Harmful", 272
"Love and Admiration" ("Admiration"), 124, 126, 127, 145
"Love in the Snow", 141
"Love Like Magic", 259
"Love Once More", 142
"Madly in Love", 167
"Man with Intentions", 237
"Marshmallow", 260
"Midnight Black", 127
"Midnight Song", 228, 230
"Miracle", 101, 122
"Miss You Much", 166, 167, 177
"Most Beloved, The", 141
"Moon Represents My Heart, The", 298
"No Need for Too Much", 142
"Noah's Ark", 297-298
"Passing Dragonfly", 277
"Past Love" ("That Year's Love"), 118, 122, 126
"Pillow", 277
"Red", 239, 241, 283, 292
"Red Butterfly", 323
"Red Face White Hair", 207
"Restless Wind" ("Uninhibited Wind;" "Cool Wind"; "Unruly Wind"; "Wild Wind"), 99, 111, 113
"Rockin' the Pepsi Way", 132
"Side Face", 153, 167, 177

"Silence Is Golden", 142, 144, 189

"Sleepless Night" ("Don't Wanna Sleep", "I Don't Wanna Sleep"; "No Mood to Sleep"), 127, 133, 144, 167

"So Far, So Close", 318

"Stand Up", 110, 113, 124, 144, 145, 276

"Starting from Zero" ("Start from Zero"), 153, 155, 167

"Swimming Up Slowly", 85, 103

"Thanks, Monica", 92, 93, 99, 103, 110, 144, 241

"There Always Will Be Luck", 94

"There Is Love in This City", 271

"Thinking of You", 155, 167

"Thorn of Love", 155

"Thousand Dreams of You, A", 228, 235

"Thousand Tenderness, Hundred Beauty", 323

"Truth, The", 260

"Typhoon No 10", 318

"Who Can Be with Me" ("Who Will Echo with Me"; "Who Can Resonate with Me", "Who Can Share My Mind"), 122, 144

"Wind Blows Again, The", 168

"Wind Blows On, The" ("The Wind Continues to Blow"; "The Wind Still Blows"), 14, 87, 92, 103, 144, 145, 167, 168, 182, 184

"Without Love", 280

"You Hate Me Like That", 277

"Young Girl's Dream" ("Young Girl's Concern"), 99, 100

soundtrack and theme songs:

Behind the Yellow Line, 93

Better Tomorrow, A, 118, 122

Better Tomorrow II, A, 135

Bride with White Hair, The, 207, 229

Chasing Dynasties, 52

Chinese Ghost Story, A, 129, 144, 145, 167

Chinese Ghost Story 2, A, 176

Crossroads: Woman at 33, 81

Days of Being Wild, 228

Drummer, The, 85

Duke of Mount Deer, The, 94

Fallen Family, The, 91

Farewell My Concubine, 228

Fatal Love, 146

For Your Heart Only, 104, 276

He's a Woman, She's a Man, 214, 216, 218, 229

Intellectual Trio, The, 101, 177

Kid, The, 272

Last Song in Paris, 112

Leslie Cheung Special '89, Sunset in Paris, 155

Nomad, 78

Okinawa Rendez-vous, 280

Once a Thief, 182

Once upon an Ordinary Girl, 85, 103
Phantom Lover, The, 228, 230
Rouge, 145, 150
Roving Swordsman, The, 52
Spirit of the Sword, The, 54
Teenage Dreamers, 73
Temptress Moon, 228, 235
Turn around and Die, 118
Viva Erotica, 239
Who's the Woman, Who's the Man (Golden Branch, Jade Leaf 2), 237

tours:
  Australia, 120, 165, 253
  Canada, 111, 127, 165, 248, 292
  China, 165, 247-248, 253, 289-291
  Europe, 165
  Japan, 247, 253, 292, 292
  Malaysia, 93, 164-165, 288
  Netherlands, 248
  Singapore, 72, 73, 88, 93, 165, 247
  South Korea, 165
  Southeast Asia, 78
  Taiwan, 165, 248
  Thailand, 72, 73, 88, 108, 165
  United Kingdom, 248
  United States of America, 88, 111, 127, 165, 248, 291, 293

TV programmes:
  100,000 Hours, 104
  Agency 24, 69, 201
  Bandits from Canton, 61

Celebrity Talk Show 30 – "All about Leslie", 272-272
Cheap Detective, The, 75
Crocodile Tears, 53
Crossroads: Woman at 33, 81
Dynasty II, 61
Fallen Family, The, 91, 93
Gone with the Wind, 61
Heritage: the Young Concubine, 62, 64, 315
Hong Kong '81, 69
Island Stories Series: Castle of Sand, 64-65
Love Stories, 53
"Leslie Cheung Night", 259
Leslie Cheung Special '89, Sunset in Paris, 154, 179
Leslie Cheung Special '99, Left Right Love Destiny, 273
Make a Wish, 69
Miss Asia Pageant 1989, 155
Mystery Love, 104
No Big Deal, 61
Once upon an Ordinary Girl, 85, 103
Pairing, 61, 69
South Korean TV, 58
Spirit of the Sword, The, 54, 58, 72, 104
Sunset in Paris, 154, 179
Tai Chi Master II, 69, 80
Tribute to Yam Kim-fai, 273
Under the Same Roof: Teenagers, 54, 61, 62
Under the Same Roof: Dead Knot, 62
variety shows, 49, 58

TV parts:
    Johnny, 53
    Mike, 69
Unfulfilled projects:
    20-30-40, 311, 315m 325
    Cats, 146
    Chen Guoxing romance, 328
    Crouching Tiger Hidden Dragon, 287-288
    Duel to the Death (*The Sword of Master Three*), 306
    Hero, 306
    Jacky Cheung stage opera, 328
    Japanese concert series, 308
    M Butterfly, 201, 261
    Nansun Shi and Tsui Hark script, 328
    New Police Story, 328
    romance of three couples, 273
    Shanghai Family (*Shanghai Story*), 315
    Stealing Heart (*Stolen Heart*; L Production), 297, 304-305, 307, 308, 313, 314-315
    Story of Gangsters, The, 161
    thriller with John Woo and David Wong Kit, 161
    Xu Zhimo and Lu Xiaoman, 314
Cheung, Louisa, 24
Cheung Luk-ping, Ophelia, 24, 26, 30, 33, 53, 67, 163, 232, 238, 243, 267, 295, 319, 332
Cheung, Madam – see Poon Yuk-yiu
Cheung Man-yuk, Maggie, 91, 93, 154, 179, 184, 187, 202, 219, 257, 271, 312, 321, 326
Cheung, Serena, 24, 26
Cheung Tung Cho, Joe, 184
Cheung Wut-hoi (Wood-hoi), 21-23, 27, 30, 33, 37-38, 39, 42, 106, 146, 157, 243
Cheung Yiu Wing, 127, 240
Cheung Y.W., Eva, 37
Chiang Kai Shek, 265
Chiang Suk-ping, William, 241
Chiang, Sylvia, 161
Chicago International Film and Television Festival, 62
Children's Cancer Foundation, 276
China, 21, 25, 121, 142, 157, 159, 163, 165, 196, 198, 205, 227, 229, 235, 247-248, 252, 253, 255, 258, 259, 265, 266, 267, 289, 290, 304, 305, 307, 314, 324, 330, 331
    Communist Party, 157, 162, 193, 255, 265, 266
    Fifth Wave, 234
    Great Leap Forward of 1958, 25-26
    Great Proletarian Cultural Revolution, 27, 192, 195-196, 199
    June 4th Incident, 157, 162
    Politburo, 199
China MTV Awards, 272
China Music Awards, Millennium Best Award, 297
China Society for Performing Arts - Award for High

Achievement, 200
China Star Entertainment Group, 279, 333
China Television Company, 94
China's Original Music Outstanding Achievement Award, 294
Chinese University of Hong Kong, 306, 315
Ching Che, 284
Ching Siu-tung, Tony, 129, 175
Chitose Shima, 40, 263, 270
Chiu Hung-ping, Betty, 149
Choi Cheuk-lin, Charlene, 328
Choi Kai-kwong, Clifford, 63, 73
Chopard, 66
Chor Yuen (Zhang Baojian), 112
Chow Hua-jian, Emil, 227
Chow Shuk-yee, Selina, 61
Chow Sing-Chi, Stephen, 184, 186, 187, 244, 314
Chow, Tommy, 34
Chow Wai-man, Vivian, 187-188, 318
  music:
    "My Hidden Reason" ("If You Knew My Hidden Reason"), 188
Chow Yun-fat, 12, 13, 94, 115-118, 135, 168, 235, 259, 323
Chu Wing-lung, Stanley, 167, 282
Chua Lam, 155
Chung Bo-law, Paul, 55, 63, 64, 65, 68, 69, 70, 76, 103, 105, 107, 157, 208
Chung Chor-hung, Cherie, 12, 146, 154, 155
Chung Chun-to, Kenny Bee, 52, 108, 202
Chung Jan-tung, Gillian, 328
Chung King-fai (King Sir), 47

Chung, Winnie 313
Chungking Express, 179
Cinema City, 95, 100, 104, 105, 115, 125, 129, 133, 135, 137, 138, 145, 146, 151
Cinepoly Records, 125, 132, 133, 134, 140, 143, 145, 152, 156, 158, 165, 166, 176, 271
City Entertainment, 32, 261, 275, 308
City Hall, 68, 251
City Magazine, 106
Club Banana (Banana Club), 314, 321
Cocteau, Jean, 100
Coliseum – see Hong Kong Coliseum
Colombo, 75
Commercial Radio, 55, 68, 72, 105, 175
  Commercial Radio's Chinese Pop Songs Award, 92, 100, 122, 133
  Commercial Radio Ultimate Song Chart Male Gold Award, 143, 159, 276
  Commercial Radio Hong Kong Top Ten Most Beautiful People, 159, 185
  RTHK, Commercial Radio, Metro Radio and TVB Best Album of the Year, 277
Commercial TV (CTV), 49
Commonwealth Film and Television Festival, 62
Composers and Authors Society of Hong Kong (CASH), 291, 297
  CASH Golden Sail Awards, 297, 324
Confessions of a Dangerous Mind, 330
Connaught Road Central, 335
Conrad Hotel, Hong Kong, 13, 278

Contacts Magazine, 189, 251
Coolidge, Rita, 78
Corliss, Richard, 234, 278
Council on Smoking and Health (COSH), 285
"Country Road", 276.
Creedence Clearwater Revival, 30
Cronenberg, David, 201
Dance of a Dream, 298
Dannen, Frederic, 50
Dassin, Jules, 181
Dateline Bar & Restaurant, 56
Dean, James, 160, 178
Deep Purple, 30
Delon, Alain, 116, 181
Deng Ling, 199
Deng Xiaoping, 163, 199
Dion, Celine, 256
Dior, 310
Disco Disco, 56, 81, 93, 107, 188, 251
"Don't Let the Sun Go Down on Me", 286
dot.com bubble, 330
Doyle, Christopher, 219, 250
Dream of the Red Chamber, The, 50
Dunhill, 324
East Palace West Palace, 307
East Week, 325
Eccles Hall, 33, 34-38, 67
EMI, 68
Enchanting Shadow, The, 130
End Child Sexual Abuse Foundation, 269, 316, 324, 329
England, 33, 147, 256
Essex, 33, 38
Europe, 142, 144, 147, 165

Fairview Park (Gam Sau Fa Yuen), 72, 78
Falk, Peter, 75
Film Bi-weekly, 183
Film Workshop, 115
FM 903:
    Live Concert, 276
    chart, 318
Fok Yiu-leung, Clarence (Clarence Ford), 70, 71
Fong Chung-sun, Alex, 279
Forbidden City, 157
Forum de Macau Stadium, 108
Foshan, 248
France, 131, 154, 181, 229, 305
Frey, Glenn, 143
Friends, 61
Fringe Club, 250
Fry, Stephen, 320
Fukuoka, 293
Fung Sai-hung, Raymond, 104
Fung Tim-chi, 65
Furama Hotel, 112
Fusion, 332
Gable, Clark, 35
Gangs, 187
Gangs of New York, 329
Garden of Eden, 282
Gaultier, Jean-Paul, 283, 288
Gay Teddy Night, 257
Georgina, 149
Golden Bear awards, 245, 257
Golden Globe awards - Best Foreign Language Film, 200
Golden Harvest, 137, 138, 192, 237

Golden Horse Awards, 109, 140, 184, 208, 310, 325
Golden Melody awards, 277
Golden Princess, 175
Golden Rooster Awards, 324
Gone with the Wind, 35
Gong Li, 194, 198, 234, 305
Grant, Cary, 22
Grasshopper, 120, 277, 286
Green Power, 185
Green Spot, 120
Green Spot Nightclub, 286
Guangdong, 21, 22, 62
Guangzhou, 253, 289, 294
Hai Chung-man, 262
Hangzhou, 289
Happy Valley, 32, 296
    Happy Valley Race Course, 275
Harbour Hotel, 56
Hawaii, 46
Health Express, 277
Herman, Jerry, 281
Hershey Centre, 292
Heung Wah-Keung, Charles, 187, 279, 280
Hilton Hotel, 188-189
Hitchcock, Alfred, 22, 181
Ho Chiu-king, Pansy Catalina, 156
Ho Hung Sun, Stanley, 156
Ho, Tommy, 318
Hold You Tight, 257
Holden, William, 22
Hollywood, 195, 201, 203, 212, 258, 267, 308
Hong Kong:
    Administrative Service, 26
    Certificate of Education, 32
    Chief Executive, 275, 330
    Chief Secretary for Administration, 269, 275
    Consumer Council, 26
    film industry, 77, 203-205, 232, 233, 237, 244, 248-249, 256, 258, 262, 267, 273-274, 279, 280, 297, 304, 312
    financial crisis, 330-331
    Government Secretariat building, 325
    handover to China, 84, 203, 227, 240, 249, 251, 254-255, 256
    HMV Megastore, 256, 272
    Japanese occupation, 22, 25, 85
    New Wave, 76-77, 78, 90
    rioting, (1958) 25, (1965) 27
Hong Kong Academy for Performing Arts, 166
Hong Kong Association for Mentally Handicapped Children, 148
Hong Kong Coliseum, 102, 103, 104, 108, 111, 122, 123, 124, 128, 141, 143, 145, 150, 166, 167, 185, 196, 211, 239, 241, 245, 254, 294, 295, 312
Hong Kong Commercial Daily, 308, 309
Hong Kong Convention and Exhibition Centre, 184, 254, 276, 277, 297
Hong Kong Cultural Centre, 146
Hong Kong Directors' Guild Association, 186
Hong Kong Film Awards, 70, 73, 118, 131, 140, 181, 182-183, 208, 212, 214, 221, 230, 245, 252, 297, 310, 314, 328
Hong Kong Film Critics Society, 275, 310

Hong Kong Film Festival, Special Award of Best Hong Kong Film of the Past 10 Years, 181

Hong Kong International Film Festival, 308

Hong Kong Island, 53, 68, 78, 84, 106, 335

Hong Kong Jockey Club, 296

Hong Kong Performing Artistes' Guild, 324-325

Hong Kong Pop Song Composition Competition, 55

Hong Kong Standard, 72, 73, 75, 122, 134, 148, 242, 243

"Buzz" Column, 153

Hong Kong Tourist Association, 269

Hong Kong University, 26, 220, 267, 319

Hong Kong Voices, 163

Howard, Leslie, 35

Hsu Feng, 188, 192, 198, 315

Hu Jun, 307, 315

Huen Ga-ling, 257

Hui On-Wah, Ann, 138, 146, 192

Hui Koon-kit, Sam, 52, 142, 144, 151, 189

Hun Ga Jan, Catherine, 269

Hundred Flowers Film Festival, 324

Hung Hom, 240

Huthart, Gordon, 56

"I Am What I Am", 281

"I Don't Want to Think about It", 132

Iglesias, Julio, 121

Imperial Manchu Han Feast, 222

"In this Lifetime", 216

International Federation of the Phonographic Industry (IFPI), 133, 229

IFPI Award, 143

IFPI's Best Album of the Year, 153, 172

Internet, 232

Ipoh, 164

Jackson, Michael, 113, 132, 155, 248

Japan, 55, 77, 85, 86, 87, 92, 100, 117, 118, 119, 127, 129, 131, 141, 142, 144, 147, 153, 163, 166, 203, 204, 205, 206, 219, 227, 233, 239, 259, 260, 263, 265, 267-268, 269, 270, 284, 292, 293, 295, 297, 298, 305, 308, 310, 316, 318, 328

Hong Kong Film Festival, 290

Japanese Film Critics Society, 200

Jeremy, 35

Jet Tone Productions, 218, 220

Jiang Wen, 305

Jiang Zemin, 254

Jin Yong (Louis Cha Leung-yung), 90, 202, 218

Jirettai, 127

Joel, Billy, 51

John, Elton, 286

Jones, Grace, 251

Justin (Ah Jen), 256

Ka Ling, 73, 288

Kai Yee-lin, 66

Kai Tak Airport, 34

Kanagawa Kenmin Hall, 292

Kang, Ah, 307, 336

Kaohsiung, 248

Kazuhiro Nishijima (Kazu), 295

Kelly, Mrs, 36-37

Kelly, Raymond, 36-37

Kikikawa Koji, 92

King, Carol, 69

King of the Children, 192
King Sir, 47
Kingsley, Ben, 257
Knutsford Terrace, 40
Ko Chi-sum, Clifton, 95, 184, 187, 201, 205, 212, 221-222, 258
Ko Shan theatre, 134
Kong, C.Y., 272, 323
Konica, 123
Koo Ka-fai, Joseph, 141, 261
Korea, 25, 156, 233, 261
Korea, South, 58, 77, 117, 119, 131, 155, 165, 201, 229, 252, 268, 305, 310, 329
Kota Kinabalu, 164
Kowloon, 22, 48, 55, 56, 68, 82, 84, 134, 186
Kuala Lumpur, 164, 288
Kunming, 289
Kuomintang, 200, 265
Kuwait, 184
Kwan Chi-lam, Rosamund, 201
Kwan Ching-kit, Michael, 141
Kwan Kam-pang, Stanley, 13, 138, 139, 140, 230, 237, 257, 298, 328
Kwan Kuk-ying, Susanna, 91
Kwan Suk Yee, Shirley, 251
Kwok Fu-shing, Aaron, 184, 211, 275
Kwong Mun-yin, 27
Kyoto, 259
La Cage aux Folles, 281
Lai Chi Kok, 68
Lai Chi-ying, 262
Lai Ming, Leon, 184, 211, 275
Lai Siu-tin, Michael, 46, 49, 54, 58, 79, 80, 82, 85, 86, 87, 89, 91, 92, 93, 99-100, 102, 103, 110, 111-112,

120, 121, 122, 123, 124, 125-126, 127, 143, 144, 150, 164, 167-168, 258
music: "Chasing", 150
Lai Wan, 48, 68
Laker Air, 34
Lam Bing, June, 261
Lam Chi Cheung, George, 144, 147, 184, 251
Lam Chun-keung, Richard, 110
Lam Gai-to, 176, 305
Lam Gayan, Karena, 308, 310, 325
Lam Jik (Albert Leung), 13, 142, 239, 259, 272, 277, 281, 282, 296, 317, 320, 323, 329
Lam Ka-tung, 274-275
Lam Yick-wah, Edward, 251
Lam Yik Lin, Sandy, 276
Lan Kwai Fong, 56
Lan Yu, 298, 307
Las Vegas, 293
Last Emperor, The, 192
"Last Song for You", 87
Lau Chun-wai, Jeffrey, 202
Law Kai-yui, Alex, 314
Lau Kar-ling, Carina, 180, 186, 202, 219, 325
Lau Kwok-cheung, Lawrence, 187
Lau Pui-kei, Eddie, 13
Lau Tak-wah, Andy, 99, 179, 184, 186, 211, 235, 236, 275, 298
Lau Tin-lan, Tina, 163
Law Chi-leung, Bruce, 278, 308, 309, 325, 328
Law, Jude, 145
Law Ming-chu, Bonnie, 120
Law Kai-yui, Alex, 64, 88

Law Mei-mei, May, 12
Lawrence, D.H., 31
Laszlo, Victor, 144
Lee, Amanda, 120
Lee, Ang, 287
Lee, Bruce, 13, 50
Lee Dik-man, Dick, 216
Lee Lai-chan, Loretta, 96
Lee, Lettie, 119
Lee, Lilian – see Li Pik-wah
Lee Tsung-chen, Jonathan, 141
Lee Yan-Kong, Daniel, 268, 269
Leeds, 36, 39
Leeds University, 38, 39, 392 note 65
Legend of the Condor Heroes, The, 218
Lei Han, 194, 266
Leigh, Vivien, 35
Leih-Mak, Professor Felice (Dr Mak Lit Fei-fei), 319, 323, 334, 336
Leong, Alvin, "The Ace Producer", 271
Leong Po-chih, 145
Leroux, Gaston, 229
Leslie Inn, 291
Leung, Albert – see Lam Jik
Leung, Alvin, 143
Leung Chiu-wai, Tony, 13, 179, 184, 202, 219, 249, 250, 329
Leung Ka-fai, Tony, 184, 202, 212, 219, 271
Leung Yu-sang, 205
Levi's jeans, 42
Li Hanxiang, 130
Li, Jet, 186, 306
Li Kit-ming, Deborah, 332

Li Pik-wah, Lilian (Lilian Lee), 62, 138, 182, 191, 306, 315
Li Yi-mei, 333
Life on a String, 192, 198
Lin Ching-hsia, Brigitte, 185, 202, 205, 209, 219, 220, 267, 326, 329
Liu Chi Hung, 259
Liu Ye, 298
Lloyd Webber, Andrew, 146, 230
Lo Wai-yuen, Professor, 306, 315
London, 37, 38, 147, 248, 255
Lone, John, 186, 192, 201
Los Angeles, 127, 248, 255
Louis Vuitton, 55
Lui Fong, David, 120, 150
Luk Che, 23, 25, 30, 45, 68, 104, 106, 128, 146, 164, 174, 178, 183-184
Lung Kung-cheong, 296
M Butterfly, 201
Ma, Janet, 253
Ma Yi Jung, 147, 260
Ma-xu Weibang, 229
McLean, Don, 46
Macpherson, Ian, 53, 336
Macau, 40-41, 58, 73, 108, 156
MacLennan, John, 68-69
Madonna, 82, 200, 288
Maggie, 128, 268
Mahoney, Dino, 251
Mak Don-hung, Johnny, 53
Mak Kit-man, Connie, 101, 123, 144, 164
Maka, Karl, 95, 115, 151, 184
Malaysia, 93, 119, 205, 247, 265, 269
Manchester, 248

Mandarin Films, 186, 201, 205, 207, 212, 221, 229, 258
Mandarin Oriental Hotel, Bangkok, 288, 327
    Mandarin Oriental Hotel, Hong Kong, 11, 12, 14, 15, 306, 307, 333, 334, 335, 336
    Coffee Shop, 278
    health club, 333
Mandopop, 239, 256
Manilow, Barry, 51
Mao Tse Tung, 25, 27, 162, 251
Marco Polo Prince Hotel, 297
Martin, Dean, 216
Mass Transit Railway (MTR), 93
May Tower, 231
Mei Ting, 267
Melbourne, 253
Mercado, Ding, 46
Mercedes-Benz, 332
Merdeka Stadium, 288
Metro Radio's Song Chart of the Year and Gold Song of the Year, 276
    RTHK, Commercial Radio, Metro Radio and TVB Best Album of the Year, 277
Metro Showbiz chart, 318
Mid-Levels, 106, 231
Midas Films, 273
Millennium Gold Songs Concert, 275
Ming Pao, 107, 112, 202, 258, 262, 296, 311, 314, 329
    Grand Salute Award, 296
    Ming Pao Weekly, Most Outstanding Actor 2002, 310, 325
Miss Hong Kong pageant, 91, 113
Mo Sun-kwan, Teresa, 53, 106, 187, 202, 222, 286, 294, 307, 308, 310, 321, 323
Mok Ho Mun-yee, Mrs, 46, 294
Mok, Leslie, 228
Mok Man-wai, Karen, 46, 241, 245, 247, 253, 257, 262, 286, 294, 328
Mok Wa Ping, Alfred, 332-333
Mongkok, 56
Monro, Matt, 45
Monroe, Marilyn, 146
Montenegro, Fernanda, 257
Movie Express Japan film awards, 245
Mui Yim-fong, Anita, 12, 81-82, 88, 93, 103, 105, 107, 110, 111, 112, 118, 120, 123, 127, 128, 138, 140, 144, 149, 150, 154, 165, 184, 186, 237, 262, 277, 286-287, 298, 299, 304, 306-307, 310, 312, 321, 323, 325
    music:
        "Flowing like Water", 165
        "Love Is Over", 103
My Visitor, 218
Nagoya, 293
Nanjing, 291
Nanying Cantonese song, 138, 140
Nelson, Ralph, 181
New Talent Singing Awards, 80, 82, 113
New Territories, 54, 72, 80, 84, 207
New York, 88, 107, 200, 233
Newton-John, Olivia, 277
Next Magazine, 238, 255, 306
Next Media, 262
Ng, Debbie, 123
Ng Mang-tat, 182
Ng, May, 113, 134

Ng, Sandra, 222
Ng See-yuen, 50
Ngai Siu-yun, Jimmy, 56, 67, 68, 71, 81, 107-108, 180
Ngai Sze-pui, Annie, 54, 61, 69, 106
Ngan, Gary, 188
Ni Kuan, 155
Ning Jing (Ling Jing), 235-236, 304
Ningbo, 291
Niro, Robert de, 233
Nobu, 233
Nokia, 317
Norfolk, 33
Norwich, 34
Nouvelle Vague, 131
Ocean Palace nightclub, 126
Off-Guard Tonight, 41, 155-156
Once a Thief, 116
One Country Two Systems, 255
"One You Love, The", 143
"Only You in the Heart", 91
Onyx, 41
Oriental Sunday, 244, 298
Osaka, 247, 253, 293
    Osaka Festival Hall, 292
Oscars - Best Foreign Language Film, 200
Paitoon, 327
Pak Suet-sin, 25, 183, 306
Palme d'Or, 198, 199, 200
Pantene Pro-V, 185
Paris, 154, 273
Patten, Christopher, 227
Peking opera, 129, 182, 191, 193, 195-196, 241, 262
Penang, 164

Peninsula Hotel, Hong Kong, 22
People's Liberation Army, 254-255, 265
Pepsi, Pepsico, 132, 141, 155, 329
Perth, 253
Peter Stuyvesant, 288
Phantom of the Opera, 229-230
Philippines, 178, 180
Piaf, Edith, 82
Piano, The, 198
Planet Hong Kong, 275
Pok Fu Lam, 335
Polydor Hong Kong, 47, 52, 58, 59, 60, 65
Polygram Records, 125, 271
Pony Canyon Inc, 219
Poon Man-kit, 236
Poon Yuk-yiu (Madam Cheung), 22, 27, 33, 38, 47, 106, 146, 164, 231, 232, 243, 262, 298, 322
Pop Asia, 307
Pop Music Media Association of China, Music Salute Award, 296
Porsche, 231, 332
Positif, 257
Precious Stone Film Company, 305, 314
President Sauna, 56
Presley, Elvis, 126
Prince's Building, 324
Princess D, 310
Propaganda, 278
Pu Songling (Master Liaozhai), 129
Puchon International Fantastic Film Festival, 310
puppy squads, 255
Putra World Trade Centre, 164

qigong, 254
Qingdao, 305
Quarry Bay, 68
Queen Elizabeth II, 121, 122
Queen Elizabeth Stadium, 141
Queen Mary Hospital, 335
Queen's Café, 232
Queer Story, A, 251
Quidenham, 34
Radio Television Hong Kong (RTHK), 49, 54, 61, 64, 81, 191, 251, 285, 287
RTHK's Best Selling Artist, 232
RTHK, Commercial Radio, Metro Radio and TVB Best Album of the Year, 277
RTHK's Gold Song of the Millennium Award, 272
RTHK Golden Needle Award, 275, 293
RTHK Silver Jubilee Award, 327
RTHK's Top Best Selling Album of the Year, 272
RTHK's Top Pick Award, 296
RTHK's Top Ten Chinese Gold Songs Award, 100, 122, 133, 143, 211, 231-232, 271, 276, 293-294, 327
RTHK's Top Ten Popular Artist, 122, 133, 290
Raise the Red Lantern, 194-195, 306
Rebel without a Cause, 178
Red Cherry, 265
Red Sorghum, 194, 305
Rediffusion Television (RTV), 45-46, 47, 49, 50, 52, 53, 55, 58, 59, 70, 120
Reeves, Keanu, 201

Regal Films, 183, 186
Regent Hotel, 82, 108
Ren Lei, 235, 307
Repulse Bay, 128, 173
Return of the Condor Heroes, 90
Richie, Lionel, 132
Ring, The, 284
Rock Records, 88, 124, 225-226, 228, 239, 240, 253, 260, 261, 270, 329
Romeo and Juliet, 30
Rosaryhill School, 28, 29-32
Royal Hong Kong Police, 68
Sabah, 165
St. Luke's Primary School, 26-28
Saitama, 292
Salles, Walter, 257
San Francisco, 152, 248
SARS, 11, 13, 15, 330, 331, 332
Scholar Films, 219
Seagal, Stephen, 145
Second Wave, 137, 138
Seoul, 155, 261
Sha Tin, 80, 102, 157, 306
Shaanxi, 220
Shakespeare, William, 31
Shanghai, 199, 229, 233, 236, 257, 265, 266, 267, 289, 333
Shangri-la Hotel, 194
Shantou, 248
Shaw Brothers Studios, 50, 73, 79, 90, 93, 112, 116
Shek Suk, 314
Shek Tien, Dean, 135
Shenyang (Mukden), 330
Shenzhen, 266, 291
Sheraton Hotel, 58

Shi, Nansun (Shi Na-Sun), 328, 331, 336
Shi Yansheng, 193, 241, 262
Shinjuku Mirano-za theatre, 260
Short, Stephen, 295, 322
Shu Qui, 241, 244, 253, 257
Shuen Po-yuen, 32
Shum Din-ha, Lydia (Fei-Fei), 12, 138, 334
Si Hua Hotel, 225
Siao Fong-Fong, Josephine, 269, 324
Silver Bear, 257
Simington, Mortimer B., 33, 37, 38, 39
Simon Fraser University, 174
Singapore, 72, 73, 88, 93, 147, 165, 205, 216, 247, 270, 283
Media Corporation's All Star Charity Show, 271
Sino-British Joint Declaration on the Future of Hong Kong, 94
Sipadan Island, 165
Siu Mei, 132
Sixth Sense, The, 308
Snipes, Wesley, 145
Sonic City, 292
Song at Midnight, 229
Song Seung-heon, 305
South America, 318
South China Morning Post, 199, 208, 218, 242, 312
South Korea – see Korea, South
Southeast Asia, 72, 77, 78, 93, 252
Southend-on-Sea, 33, 35, 38, 41
Springfield, Rick, 110
Springsteen, Bruce, 166
"Stand Up for Love", 110
Star, The, 288

Star Ferry, 333
Starry Is the Night, 146
Stewart, James, 212
Stewart, Rod, 132
"Stories", 144
Story of a Discharged Prisoner, 116
Straits Times, 247
Strange Stories from a Chinese Studio, 129
Sudden Weekly, 298
Sun, the, 270, 290
Sung Lan Mansion, 232
Sweet Babe, 55
Switzerland, 147
Sydney, 253
Sydney Entertainment Centre, 120
Taichung, 248
Taipei, 88, 184, 225, 248, 256, 325
Taiwan, 49, 77, 88, 94, 109, 115, 124, 137, 141, 142, 147, 156, 163, 165, 192, 198, 200, 202, 204-205, 207, 208, 219, 226, 229, 233, 248, 253, 256, 259m 260, 261, 262, 265, 270, 277, 283, 305, 310
Asia Top 20 list, 260
Cashbox KTV, 260
CSMTV, 260
earthquake, 271
TVBS-G, 260
Taiyo Music Hong Kong, 92, 99
Takako Takiwa, 267, 268, 278
Tam Fu-Wing, Tommy (Ti Lung), 115-118, 134, 135, 274
Tam K.K., 71-72, 79
Tam Kar Ming, Patrick, 77, 78, 138
Tam Pak-Sin, Roman (Lo Man), 55, 56, 118, 324

music;
"Toiling Life in Wind and Rain", 118
Tam Wing-lun, Alan ("the Principal"; "the Most Favoured One"), 52, 108-109, 111, 121, 122, 132, 133, 143, 144, 149, 158, 161, 211, 233, 254, 258, 271, 272, 273, 275, 303, 324, 327
films:
If I Were For Real, 109
Tang King-sung, Edward, 126
Tang Kwong-wing, Alan, 13, 182
Tang Yat-kwan, John, 217
Teresa, 326
Thailand, 72, 73, 108, 147, 165, 205, 233, 311
Thatcher, Margaret, 84
Thunderbird, 88
Ti Lung – see Tam Fu-Wing, Tommy
Tiananmen Square, 157, 162
Tianhe Sports Stadium, 289
Tiger Kids, the, 86
Times Square, 299
Till the End of Time, 212
Time Asia, 201
Time Magazine, 235, 295, 313
Titanic, 266
To Catch a Thief, 181
To You Chocolates, 155
Tokyo, 92, 118, 247, 253, 260, 292, 293
　Film Festival, 324
　Hong Kong Movie Festival, 229
　Tokyo International Forum Hall, 292
Tokyo FM, "Toyota Weekly Album Top 10"; "Ashahi Wonda

Golden Hits", 259
Tokyo International Film Festival - Young Cinema Competition, 203
Tokyo Music Festival, 86, 127, 166
Tom.com, 282
Tomson Films, 182, 192, 198, 233
Tong Chun-yip, Kent, 58
Tong Hok-tak, Daffy, 11, 13, 27, 82-84, 96, 100, 104, 107, 108, 121, 123, 128, 131, 145, 147, 148, 149, 152, 158, 159, 164, 169, 173, 183, 185, 194, 206, 208, 222, 231, 237, 240, 243-244, 250, 255, 260, 261, 262-264, 270, 276, 288, 291, 294, 298, 299, 303, 307, 311, 312, 316, 317, 319, 321, 322, 323, 325, 327, 328, 330, 331, 332, 333, 334, 335, 336-337
Too Kit, 51
Top Ten Asian Singers for Asian Pops, 253
Topkapi, 181
Toronto, 200, 248, 292
Toyota Weekly Top Ten Segment, 260
Trewick, Michele, 134
triads, 50, 66, 117, 185-187, 203, 207
Trump Taj Mahal Casino Resort, 248, 291
Tsang Chi-wai, Eric, 213, 217, 233
Tsim Sha Tsui, 56, 82, 127, 146
Tsuen Wan, 231
Tsui Hark, 115, 129, 133, 135, 175, 176, 184, 221, 222, 255, 328, 330
Tsui Siu-fung, Paula, 82, 123, 143
music:
　"Affinity", 123
　"Windy Season, The", 82
Tung Chee-hwa, 275, 330
Tung Wah Group of Hospitals, 297

TVB, 48, 49, 55, 59, 70, 80, 81, 82, 85, 86, 91, 94, 104, 118, 125,132, 138, 154, 155, 235, 273, 287, 293, 328
Children's Charity Drive, 277
RTHK, Commercial Radio, Metro Radio and TVB Best Album of the Year, 277
TVB Jade channel, 155
TVB Jade's Top Ten Chinese Solid Gold Songs Award, 92, 100, 111, 122, 124, 126, 133, 143, 153, 158, 290, 296, 303
TVB Jade's Gold Song of the Year, 133, 158
TVB Most Popular Male Singer, 143
Twins, The, 328
"Twist and Shout", 216
United Artists (UA) Cinema, 330
United Film Organisation (UFO), 212-213, 217, 237
Universal Music Group (UMG), 270-271, 272, 273, 277, 323, 329
Number One Artist of the Year, 319
United Nations Life International, 269
United Nations' Love Forever concert, 330
United States of America, 88, 111, 127, 152, 161, 165, 201, 248, 259, 291, 293
Unity, 250
Vancouver, 111, 113, 153, 158, 162, 164, 173, 174, 175, 177, 182, 183, 218, 222, 226-227, 231, 248, 269
Hong Kong Film Week, 269
Victoria Harbour, 333
Victoria Peak, 330
Vienna, 147

Vietnamese boat people, 119
"*Voulez Vous Couchez Avec Moi*", 141
Wada Emi, 206, 305, 307, 308, 314
Wah Kiu Daily News, 52
Wah Kiu Daily News Most Promising Newcomer, 52
Wah Kiu Daily News Top Ten Popular Artist, 92
Wales, Prince of, 254
Wan Chai, 22, 23, 28, 39, 56, 141, 254, 297, 330
Wang Lee-hom, 286
Warner Brothers, 68
"We're All Alone" ("Close the window, calm the light"), 78
Wellington College, 40-42, 45
Wembley Arena, 248
Western District, 336
"When the Fringe Goes Mainstream: Gay Theatre in the Nineties", 251
Williams, Tennessee, 320
Willis, Bruce, 308
Win's Movie, 187
Wing Shya, 297
Wong (girlfriend), 31, 40-41
Wong Cheuk-ling, Ruby, 278
Wong Chin-man, Kenneth, 268, 307, 317, 336, 337
Wong Ching-ying, Jean, 234
Wong Cho-Yee, Joey, 112, 130, 154, 175, 202, 206
Wong Fei, Faye, 179, 275, 323
Wong Jim, James, 13, 41, 154, 155-156, 175, 186, 261, 296
Wong Ka-lok, Jimmy, 253

Wong Kar-wai, 100, 177, 178, 179, 218, 219, 220, 249, 250, 251, 308
Wong Kit, Dave, 161
Wong Pak-ming, Raymond, 183, 184, 186, 205, 212, 222, 248, 258
Wong Sak-chiu, Steve, 46, 47
Wong Shu-kei, Jimmy, 54, 104
Wong, Suzie, 68, 331
Wong Yiu-ming, Anthony, 303, 317, 318
Woo, John, 115, 116, 117, 135, 154, 161, 181, 183, 226
Woolf, Virginia, 320
World of Suzie Wong, The, 22
Wu Dai-wai, David, 209
Wynners, The, 52, 108
Xinmin Weekly, 333
Yam Kim-fai, 25, 183, 273
Yamaguchi Momoe, 87, 159
Yamaha's Hong Kong Festival, 55
Yan Chai Hospital, 231
Yang-Yin; Gender in Chinese Cinema, 237-238
Ye Da Ying, 265
Yee Tung-sing, Derek, 212, 306
Yeh, Sally (Yip Sin-Man), 144
Yellow Earth, 182
Yeoh Chooh-Kheng, Michelle, 269
Yeung, Albert, 58, 148
Yeung Doi-si, 107
Yeung Kuen, Richard, 79
Yeung Lok-si, Cindy, 58, 94, 107, 112, 148
Yeung Si-si, 107
Yim Suet Lee, Shirley, 65
Yim Wai-ling, Michelle, 65
Yin Yang, 188

Yip Lai-yee, Frances, 58
Yip Yuk Hing, Veronica, 202
Yiu So-yung, 30
Yokohama, 292
"You've Got a Friend", 69
Yu, Mr, 232
Yu Yan-tai, Ronny, 205, 207, 209, 230
Yuen Long, 72
Yuen Wing-yi, Anita, 12, 202, 212, 214-215, 325
Yulin, 220
Yung Jing-Jing, Jean (Mary Jean Reimer), 64, 85
Yuk Tak Che sauna, 56
Zeffirelli, Franco, 30
Zhang Fengyi, 194, 198
Zhang Manling, 193, 241
Zhang Xin, 314
Zhang Yimou, 306
Zhanjiang, 248
Zhi Jiang Media Eternal Charisma Award, 289
Zhi Jiang stadium, 289
Zongshan, 248